CARING FOR GOD'S PEOPLE

Counseling and Christian Wholeness

Philip Culbertson

FORTRESS PRESS

Minneapolis

CARING FOR GOD'S PEOPLE
Counseling and Christian Wholeness

Cover art: "All Creation praises the Lord," Nine Choirs of Angels, from the Liber Scivias (Know the Ways of the Lord) by German mystic St. Hildegaard of Bingen. © Erich Lessing/Art Resource, N.Y Used with permission.
Cover design: Marti Naughton
Book design: Beth Wright

Scripture quotations from the New Revised Standard Version of the Bible are copyright © 1989 by the Division of Christian Education of the National Council of Churches of Christ in the United States of America and are used by permission.

The publisher gratefully acknowledges the following sources for permission to reprint material in this book:
The "Wholeness Wheel" on page 5 is reprinted from Sharon Wegscheider, *Another Chance: Hope and Health for the Alcoholic Family* (Palo Alto, Calif.: Science and Behavior Books, 1981), 33.
Chart on page 38–39 is reprinted from Virginia Ramey Mollenkott, *Sensuous Spirituality: Out from Fundamentalism,* copyright © 1992 Crossroad Publishing Company.
Figures and text on pages 42–43 are reprinted from *You Can Go Home Again: Reconnecting with Your Family by Monica McGoldrick,* copyright © 1995 by Monica McGoldrick. Reprinted by permission of W. W. Norton and Company, Inc.
Diagrams and text on page 308 are reprinted from Emily S. Haight, "Paravision: A Model for Pastoral Supervision," *Journal of Supervision and Training in Ministry* 15 (1994): 87.

Library of Congress Cataloging-in-Publication Data

Culbertson, Philip Leroy, 1944–
    Caring for God's people : counseling and Christian wholeness / Philip L. Culbertson.
        p.   cm.
    Includes bibliographical references and indexes.
    ISBN 0-8006-3187-0 (alk. paper)
        1. Pastoral counseling.   I. Title
    BV4012.2 .C83 1999
    253.5—dc21
                                                            99-045725

Manufactured in the U.S.A.   AF-3187
08   07   06   05   2   3   4   5   6   7   8   9   10

Contents

Part Two: The Application

Acknowledgments

~

Surely no book is ever written alone. Though long hours must be spent in front of a computer to produce a manuscript, every writer is surrounded by those who have influenced him or her. These influences from the past are part of the community whose voices speak through the text, though they are not always responsible for what is being said. Australian therapist Michael White speaks of how we "re-member" our present, that is, the way we summon into the foreground of consciousness those whose influence is always lurking in our consciousness. And so I must begin these acknowledgments by calling upon my ancestors: those therapists and clinical supervisors who gave me the gift of psychological insight, thereby teaching me how important people-skills are in ministry. They are Dr. Jule P. Miller, Dr. Janet Hall, Dr. Stephen Gerson, Ms. Margot Woods, and Mr. Tom Davey.

I am also fortunate to be surrounded by a lively academic community of gifted teachers. Mary Caygill is my colleague and my friend. I laughingly call her my "alter ego," for that is as close as I can come to describing how important our professional relationship is to me. Four years ago we began to co-teach the whole curriculum in pastoral theology at St. John's College, and as our professional interface grew, I learned how wonderful it is to work as a team with someone of the opposite gender. Mary has helped me realize that working as a "lone ranger" in the classroom is just as dysfunctional as working as a "lone ranger" in parish ministry. Everything we do together is richer because of the depth of our colleagueship, formed in part because we are both convinced that ministry is about "being" rather than "doing," and that the future of ministry in the church demands the development of a professionally trained laity. I am also the richer for working with the other three members of our pastoral theology team at St. John's—Winston Halapua, Jenny Te Paa, and Hone Kaa. These two women and these two men—a Pakeha (white New Zealander) woman, a Tongan man, a Maori woman, and a Maori man, the four of them a complex mixture of Anglican and Methodist clergy and laity, and each with a unique life experience and presence—are so often with me in the classroom and have been with me, figuratively at least, as I have produced this manuscript.

Particular thanks go to the staff of Kinder Library at St. John's Theological College in Auckland for their support in procuring research materials and tracking down bibliographic information. I am also indebted to my close friends the Reverend James Hill Pritchett and the Reverend Lee Kiefer for their ideas that are incorporated into the chapter on Premarital Counseling, and for personal support to Jim, Jimmy, and James.

Teaching in a theological college or seminary must be one of the most wonderful jobs in the world, because one has the opportunity to learn so much from one's students. Many of the insights about how culture informs ministry and psychology have been learned from our students, particularly those in my "Understanding Oneself and Others" and "Human Relationships" classes. We have regularly sitting in front of us men and women, gay people and straight people, the young and fresh and the older and wiser, from city, town, and rural backgrounds. They come from Aotearoa New Zealand, Samoa, Tonga, Niue, Rarotonga, Fiji,

Papua New Guinea, Vanuatu, the Solomon Islands, Australia, England, Korea, China, Malaysia, Sri Lanka, India, and the Philippines. To that mix I add my own personal experience of living extensively among Israelis, Palestinians, and the French Swiss.

I myself am a middle-aged, middle-class white American male, Disciples of Christ by birth, Episcopalian by choice, and currently serving in a joint Anglican-Methodist faculty appointment. But I carry the memories, the traditions, and the voices of those many communities of men and women named above as a critical part of my identity. In this manuscript, I have tried to be both fair and sensitive to those who "member" my intellectual and faith community.

And finally, to my children who are never away from my heart. As they have grown older, we have all grown closer. Jake lived with me in Auckland while I wrote most of this book, beginning his own journeys into the traditions and values of other cultures. Katie is older and has been "gone" longer, though we are constantly on the phone with each other, wondering whether either one of us can figure out what it means to be an adult. While both my children are still trying out various styles of ministry in life, somehow this book is still a gift to them. No matter where they might be in this big fascinating world, I am blessed by their presence in my life.

Introduction

"A sophisticated pastoral care must become more globally aware than was the case in previous generations." (Charles Gerkin, 75)

One of the remarks I have heard most frequently from bishops and other church authorities during my fourteen years as a professor of pastoral theology is, "Why should people study pastoral care? Just tell them to go out there and do it!" But in contrast, one of the most frequent pleas I have heard from seminary graduates who are now in ministry is, "Help! Pastoral care is a huge responsibility and I don't feel like I know what I'm doing or that I've been adequately trained."

Ministry at this turn of the millennium is difficult, and few people feel that they are trained as adequately as they would like to be. Part of the problem is that structured theological education is still too often based on a pedagogical design that fits neither the sorts of candidates who now present for ministry education nor the needs of modern and postmodern cultures. Another part of the problem is that the church's commitment to adult education has eroded to the extent that few laity find appropriate ministry training available to them. All of us in ministry, whether lay or ordained, need to keep learning, for we never have enough theory base or up-to-date skills. Yet, where can we go to find the training that we desire and that meets the needs of the contemporary church in a pluralistic and increasingly secular society?

The Changing Face of Ministry
The other day a colleague told me that of the twenty-three people who graduated from theological training with him, only eight are now left in active ministry some twenty years later. Similar statistics seem to describe the situation in many other places. Many of those who have left active ordained ministry may have burned out, but those in lay ministry burn out as well. Ministry burnout can be attributed to several factors: the present cantankerous mood within many denominations, shifting understandings of the nature of ministry, high performance expectations, a poor sense of self-care, and unwise placement decisions by ecclesiastical superiors. Dual-role relationships (relating to others in multiple contexts in which acceptable boundaries can easily be blurred) and over- and underfunctioning (exercising too much responsibility unnecessarily, or failing to take responsibility for one's ministry obligations) are problems that afflict almost everyone in ministry at some time or another. But those in ministry also burn out because they don't know enough about human nature and human psychology—their own and others'— to work effectively with people. The demands of ministry in the increasingly complex societies of the twenty-first century mean that those in ministry must become increasingly sophisticated about "who people are" if ministry is not ultimately to lose its usefulness to society altogether. This situation is going to get worse, and in many ways, it *should* get worse. The church is marginalized in so many cultures today because a perpetuation of the "way we've always done things" renders us useless. Perhaps it needs to get worse in order to sound a wake-up call.

Ministry and Community
One of our biggest obstacles in redefining ministry to meet the needs of a rapidly

changing world is that we have so often understood ministry as occurring one-to-one. The biblical models of ministry we so often think of are the Good Samaritan or Jesus' healing of various individuals. We often overlook other metaphors of ministry such as John 10, in which a shepherd is pictured as guarding and caring for a whole flock of sheep and not simply the one lost among the ninety-nine. As the resources of ordained ministry dwindle, group models of pastoral care facilitated by teams of lay and ordained ministers become more important. Charles Gerkin outlines the task that lies ahead: "Pastoral care in its larger meaning . . . involves the pastor in giving caring attention to concerns that reach beyond the individual to the community of Christians and to the larger society" (37). So the communities that we now address pastorally must include not only whole congregations, but whole groups outside the church. Pastoral ministry in the new millennium will mean working among many types of people to whom we have not traditionally offered one-to-one care and yet who need the sort of healing that God calls us to offer.

This new challenge will mean that ministry must become an embracing and including vocation, one that is not too quick to draw lines around itself by excluding others. Again we have a biblical model, this time in the story usually referred to as the Prodigal Son. Judith Gundry-Volf and Miroslov Volf use that parable to explain how setting rigid boundaries around communities can lead us far from God: "*the real sinner is not the outcast but the one who casts the other out.* . . . In the story of the prodigal son, the sinner was the elder brother—the one who withheld an embrace and expected exclusion" (59). Pastoral ministry can no more confine itself to "good Christians" than can God's love. Pastoral ministry must be both generous and extraterritorial, working where it is needed, regardless of where faith communities and social institutions draw lines. Gundry-Volf and Volf continue: "The Spirit of embrace creates communities of embrace—places where the power of the Exclusion System has been broken and from where the divine energies of embrace can flow, forging rich identities that include the other" (60).

To be so generous, to be so faithful to that love of God which works outside of human boundaries and definitions, requires a strong sense of ministry character, which in turn is built upon a prior sense of radical self-knowledge. If ministry occurs primarily through our being, rather than through some kit-bag of pastoral tricks, then self-knowledge can never be termed selfish but must be recognized as our primary tool for effective ministry. Psychology claims that to know oneself leads to cure. The same claim is made in the Gospel of John 8:32, "The truth shall make you free." Meister Eckhart, the thirteenth-century German Dominican mystic and scholar, stated this principle even more baldly: "The only way of knowing God is to know oneself" (Fromm 1950, 45). Similarly, as Teresa of Avila wanders from room to room within the Interior Castle, she discovers that there is only one room where a soul might benefit from lingering: the room of self-knowledge (Hughes, 378). And again, from Thomas Merton: "In order to find God whom we can only find in and through the depths of our own soul, we must first find ourselves" (1961, 44). Pastoral ministry in the new millennium, when we are faced with groups and individuals to whom the church has not traditionally felt responsibility, means that we must know ourselves well and be able to articulate what our ministries are and why we are offering them.

Identity and Liminality

Edward Wimberly lists some of the many factors that shape our identity as persons and therefore as ministers (15). He calls the sum of these influences our "personal mythology," made up of the convictions and beliefs that we hold about ourselves. It is comprised of specific themes, including:

• early memories
• whether or not we feel welcomed and wanted
• our birth order in relationship to other siblings
• gender
• name and nickname
• peer and sibling relationships
• roles we played (or still play) in our family of origin
• parental discipline in our family of origin and in school
• how our parents relate(d) to each other
• the stories with which we identify.

This is, of course, only a partial list, for there are many factors, explicable and inexplicable, that shape our character. The sum of all these influences makes each one of us who we are, and because the constituent parts vary so significantly, each of us is unique. As soon as we recognize our individual uniqueness, we immediately recognize the radical otherness of others and then can move from recognition to affirmation. Here we can find our ability to love and affirm those who are so different from ourselves, by gender, culture, ethnicity, sexual orientation, life experience, expectation, or need. Those who do not know

themselves find these others threatening; those who know themselves can see the image of God in the differentness of others, not their sameness, and can marvel at the variety of God's good creation.

Gundry-Volf and Volf challenge our tendency to seek ministry only among those who are most like our own selves:

> To be a Christian does not mean to close oneself off in one's own identity and advance oneself in an exemplary way toward what one is not. It means rather to be centered on this God—the God of the other—and participate in *God's* advance toward where God and God's reign is not yet. Without such centeredness, it would be impossible either to denounce the practice of exclusion or demand the practice of embrace. (47)

Only as we know ourselves can we recognize God and find our centeredness there. Knowing ourselves means letting go of all that makes us small, including our belief that only we in ministry can mediate where God is found and where God is at work. An early missionary philosophy believed that Christians brought God to the godless, as if God were not already there. Rather, we need to comprehend the disturbing nature of prevenient grace in order to articulate the nature of our ministries. The Latin *prevenient* means "having come before." Ministry, once we have recognized God through self-knowledge, means simply being among others to point where God is already present and at work. As Henri Nouwen says, a minister is one who "can direct the eyes of those who want to look beyond their impulses and steer their erratic energy into creative channels" (44).

The ministry of recognizing and naming prevenience may well lead us into unfamiliar places. A *limen,* in Greek, is a seaport or threshold, that which stands at the boundary between the known and the unknown, the familiar and the unfamiliar. Wimberly explains: "The term *liminality* suggests a threshold of perception" (13). Thomas Merton said, "The monk is someone who takes a critical attitude towards the contemporary world and all its structure" (1974, 329). I am immediately reminded of the words of Urban T. Holmes, "To be a priest is by necessity to share deeply the anti-structural dimensions of people's lives" (222). Continuing with Merton: "the monk is able to deepen fundamental human experience only from the margins of society." What are these margins? Margins are the wilderness. The dark and scary places are like the wilderness. And yet here too we have the witness of Scripture, that God is very powerfully heard and felt in the wilderness, in intensity, and even in powerful and overwhelming intimacy which addresses but never wipes out otherness. A minister is one who works at the edges, the margins, of the known, carrying light into the darkness of the unknown. Ministry is *always* a risk-taking vocation, never one of safety and security. When we have become comfortable in a parish or community and have learned to fear the smell of risk, we can be assured that we are no longer doing ministry, no longer serving God, but ourselves.

The Shalom of God

It is often the case that health does not come without some sort of risk. A blocked artery requires the risk of open-heart surgery. Cancer treatment may require the risk of radiation or chemotherapy. Even the simplest medicines often have side effects, thus suggesting some risk in taking them.

The ultimate purpose of this risk-taking is to restore greater health in what has been broken or wounded. The biblical root Sh-L-M carries the dual meaning of both health and wholeness, and thus we can equate them—*shalem* (wholeness) and *shalom* (health/peace). Peter Steinke explains what he calls "the relational reality of life": "Shalom is a condition of well-being. It is a balance among God, human beings, and all created things. All parts are interrelated. Each part participates in the whole. Thus, if one part is denied wholeness (shalom), every other part is diminished as well" (84). Steinke's definition suggests that it is very difficult to be healthy outside of some relational context. As we shall see, a concept of human wholeness always includes a measure of relationality.

Defining shalem/shalom as relational suggests that not only does health need to be offered to individuals, but it needs to be offered to whole communities, within the church and outside of it. Again, Steinke:

> Health means all the parts are working together to maintain balance. Health means all the parts are interacting to function as a whole. Health is a continuous process, the ongoing interplay of multiple forces and conditions. . . . The various members and subsystems of a congregation interweave, much as do the organs of the human body with the ongoing interaction of cells, blood flow, nerve endings, energy sources, and waste products. (vii–viii)

Health, as defined both here and in the church, has nothing to do with getting big, getting strong, or winning. These are Western assumptions that equate health with size. Rather, health must be equated with maintenance. Maintenance comes from the

Latin words *manus* (hand) and *teneo* (keep). It is caring for something by hand. It is managing. A large part of health is maintenance (brushing teeth, washing hands, taking vitamins, exercising). In this sense, the equation between routine pastoral care and health maintenance, either of an individual or of a group, is obvious.

Of course, health and wholeness are goals. Few individuals, and virtually no communities, are 100 percent healthy. Steinke points out that a healthy congregation is one that actively and responsibly addresses or heals its disturbances, not one with an absence of troubles (10).

> Wholeness is not to be confused with oneness. Wholeness is not about seamlessness; wholeness is not sameness. Wholeness means two or more parts are interconnected. No single element of the whole is thought of as functioning independently of the other components. Wholeness is relational. In wholeness differences are not eliminated; rather, they become alive. The different parts interact and cooperate. Wholeness involves various parts coming together and interacting. (Steinke, 6)

Again, we in ministry see how dependent health and wholeness are upon the effective functioning on our own parts and on the appropriate relationality of ourselves as ministers and the radical otherness of others.

The Wholeness Wheel

When I teach I often try to show my students the interconnectedness of the parts of ourselves or of parts of groups by using a visual image called a "Wholeness Wheel." The diagram is an attempt to contradict any tendency we might have to split off parts of

our self and treat them as though they are not part of an integrated "community." The wheel teaches us that all our parts are related to each other and that health must be understood as both inclusive and comprehensive. It is very difficult to diagram wholeness. The diagram itself looks as if people are compartmentalized, but what I'm trying to convey—a three-dimensional idea in a two-dimensional drawing—is that the many identities that a human being bears affect one another. It is very hard to be relationally unhealthy and spiritually healthy, for example, for the unhealthy aspects of ourselves tend to infect the healthy just as often as the healthy affect the unhealthy. Similarly, one cannot be physically healthy if one is not volitionally healthy; and so on.

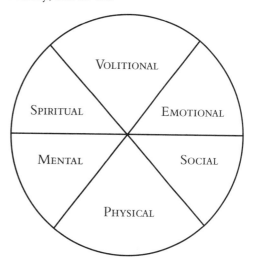

THE WHOLENESS WHEEL

Each segment of the wheel must be defined carefully, for the outplaying of a definition is necessarily shaped by issues such as gender, culture, and life experience. For example, physical health may be defined differently for those who are physically disabled from the way it is defined for those who are physically able; volitional health may be defined differently for those who come from communal cultures compared to those who come from individualistic cultures; social or relational health may defined differently for men compared to women. However, some general statements can also be made about each category.

A healthy mind is one that is active, alert, aware, and open to change. The mind is kept healthy through stimulation, creativity, active memory, and vision. Mental wholeness means holding a healthy balance among the various joys and sorrows that life throws at one, living in the present, and keeping things in perspective through constant adjustment to both internal and external changes. The healthy mind has the ability to resource all other segments of the wheel through reflection, recall, and reason.

Paul Giblin defines spirituality as "the experience of consciously striving to integrate one's life in terms not of isolation and self-absorption but of self-transcendence toward the ultimate values one perceives. Spirituality is how I cope with life. . . . the attitudes and behaviors towards self, others, God, and the world" (314). Spiritual wholeness usually includes many aspects other than the systematic faith of an institutionalized religion, for religion is but one way of being spiritual (Culbertson). Human spirituality may also encompass gatherings of family or friends, a good physical workout, meditation upon a fine piece of art, the transformative experience of music, or the beauty of nature. Spiritual wholeness requires repeated awakening and deliberate nurturing of the spirit, for as any other part of the wholeness wheel can atrophy, so can one's spirituality.

Social wholeness is achieved by finding a creative balance between respecting individuals for who they are and for the role they play. One who is socially healthy relates to a few others deeply and yet is part of an identifiable larger community, and strikes a balance therein between personal freedom and communal responsibility. Social or relational health may look very different from one culture to the next. For example, in some cultures children are expected to relate primarily to the grandparents; in other cultures to their parents. In some cultures a husband and wife may be said to turn inward, facing each other; in other cultures they are expected to turn outward, facing away from each other. In some cultures women's relationships with men are severely curtailed; in other cultures women's relationships with women are severely curtailed.

Physical wholeness rejects the body/soul split that is so typical of some forms of Christianity. As we accept that the primary tool of ministry is our own sense of being, so we cherish the physical frame that carries that being from one situation to the next. Physical health means finding an appropriate rhythm between activity and rest, stewarding our resources so that our bodies and souls are nurtured in the present, with an eye to the future. Physical wholeness encompasses both our sexuality and our spirituality.

Emotional wholeness implies being emotionally literate—that is, being able to find, name, and use our emotions appropriately. When we understand that our emotions are rooted deeply within ourselves, we realize how important it is to be able to read them, to analyze our responses, to be emotionally mature enough to balance our instincts and our intellect. Emotional wholeness requires us to be aware of a whole range of emotions, not just the "big four" of sad, happy, angry, and guilty. Emotional expression is highly regulated by culture, though human emotions remain the same across cultures. Emotional literacy means knowing our own cultural rules well enough that we can choose wisely when to break them.

Volition comes from the Latin meaning to wish or to choose. Volition has to do with things of the personal will. Since we are all individuals in relationship, volitional wholeness means having a balance between one's own freedom and others' freedom. Volitional health means that our choices are not imposed upon us by the group, nor do we impose our choices upon others. As we value our own dignity and that of others, so we value the right of each person, no matter what age or condition, to think through what is the best choice in any context and then to pursue that. Sometimes that freedom of choice will mean choosing to conform to the desires of others; at other times it will mean marching to a different drummer.

All parts of the wholeness wheel are woven together in interdependence. All must be nurtured intentionally, and all are part of the gifts that each of us brings to ministry. The neglect of one part of our interdependent self leads to ill health in other parts. No part is beyond the reach of healing, for no part is beyond the love of God.

The Role of Psychology in Ministry

From the days of the earliest church, those who train others for ministry have looked to psychology or its antecedents for clues as to how to understand people. In the fourth century, John Chrysostom drew heavily on the psychology of Greek Stoicism in his written formulations of the ideal Christian character and the problems getting there (Gerkin, 50). In the seventh century Gregory the Great included a whole series of what we would today call counseling case studies in his training manual for pastors, *The Book of Pastoral Rule* (see Culbertson and Shippee, 197–209, and Oden). So psychology and Christianity have always been in dialogue, though Christianity has been more ready to learn from psychology than psychology from Christianity.

In our own time this traditional openness of the church to influences from outside its own language and traditions clearly legitimates the adaptation within pastoral practice of secular, scientific modes of thought that have emerged from the human sciences of psychology, sociology, anthropology, and psychotherapy (Gerkin, 32). The countless psychological casualties of World War II, the rise of the CPE movement, and the influence in pastoral counseling training through the 1950s and 1960s of the theories of Carl Rogers accentuated how much the various Christian understandings of human nature relied upon psychological theory. In the 1960s and 1970s, family therapy, transactional analysis, reality therapy, cognitive therapy, the logotherapy of Victor Frankl, the gestalt therapy of Fritz Perls, and numerous other therapeutic modalities came into being and were presented as modes of therapeutic response to human relational difficulties. Not surprisingly, this was also the time in which pastoral counseling as a specialized form of ministry apart from parish pastoral care took shape and was organized as a professional guild (Gerkin, 70). Today the primary influences in pastoral counseling training tend to be Family Systems Theory, Object Relations Theory, and Narrative Counseling Theory, the three schools of thought upon which this book is based.

Understandably, my students from time to time ask me if I am training them to be counselors or pastors. I define my task as a professor of pastoral theology to be threefold: (a) to influence the personal formation of ministry character by presenting my students with the most challenging material possible; (b) to provide pastors-in-training with the most sophisticated theoretical tools possible to understand the human beings among whom they work; and (c) to affirm a sort of incarnational uniqueness in each individual by insisting that students be deeply aware of the particularities of their own culture and how different other cultures are from what we already know. This includes the cultures of ethnicity, gender, age, sexuality, spirituality, families of origin, and life experience.

To work in this way, I must explore the limens, or thresholds, at which Christian traditions and psychological traditions meet each other. I ask my students to do the same: to work in that dangerous, liminal area in which Christian faith, psychotherapeutic theory, ecclesiology, missiology, and issues of justice all intersect. I do this that they might enter ministry with the finest people-skills, those ways of being that make ministers effective and that keep those among whom we minister safe.

Much of the material I use in the classroom, and much of the material in this book, is drawn from the "secular" world of counseling and psychotherapy. The reader will notice that the terms *pastor, minister,* and *caregiver* are used interchangeably in this book, and all are intended to pertain to those who exercise ministry in the church, whether lay or ordained. Some quotations make reference to "counselor" or "therapist." These should be read as pertaining to those in ministry as well, for the wisdom behind these quotations is applicable to ministry skills.

The bottom line of ministry is relationships—with God and with other people. To know how to foster relationships of healing and wholeness with God, ourselves, and others, those in ministry need a sophisticated understanding of who people are and how they work. Of course these understandings are useful in routine pastoral counseling. But pastoral counseling is only one aspect of ministry, and in fact in many parts of the world ministers do not ordinarily offer pastoral counseling at all. Such guidance is more usually the domain of tribal elders or cultural shamans. Yet even those who come from cultures where a minister is not presumed to be a counselor still need people-skills for effective ministry.

Ministers need people-skills in every meeting they attend, in the soup kitchen, in the day-care center. They need people-skills in the aisles of the supermarket, over a hot cup of tea, at the side of the hospital bed. They need people-skills when writing a letter or answering the phone; when appointing committee members or picking new leadership to train; when leading worship, offering a meditation, or speaking at the Rotary Club. In the many opportunities for lay or ordained ministry, pastors are expected to be able to listen, assess, perceive, evaluate, and respond appropriately. In their classic work *Pastoral Care in Historical Perspective,* William Clebsch and Charles Jaekle trace the history of pastoral care through the twenty centuries of church life, dividing it into four types: healing, sustaining, guiding, and reconciling. Good ministry in all these areas is ultimately dependent upon the pastor's people-skills: the knowledge of who people are, how they work, and what wholeness looks like. To that end, this book is offered to both those already in ministry and those in ministry training.

"I Speak in a Human Way" (Romans 3:5)

In his recent text on pastoral care, Charles Gerkin wrote:

> No longer can it be assumed that the white, middle-class cultural standards of the West are the measure by which all other societies are to be judged. Both greater knowledge of and critical capacity for evaluating differing modes of living are needed by pastors, who now often encounter in their own congregations persons from widely varying cultural backgrounds. Thus a sophisticated pastoral care must become more globally aware than was the case in previous generations. (75)

Gerkin is right; no longer can those in ministry afford simply to be literate in their own native culture. The world is too small. Anyway, we no longer live in isolation from each other, and there are simply too many people in this world who need ministry for us to be monocultural any longer. It is even harder to write a book on pastoral care that addresses fairly and equally the many cultures among which we live. I'm sure a better book than this will be written soon, one that succeeds even better at speaking to issues of ministry in a voice that makes sense to even more of humanity. But I have tried to show that even after two thousand years of pastoral theology and practice, the church has yet to learn how to live out its mission without hurting or marginalizing

others or diminishing their pride in their own cultural heritage. If Gerkin defines correctly that "Pastoral care needs to have as its primary focus the care of all God's people through the ups and downs of everyday life, the engendering of caring environments within which all people can grow and develop to their fullest potential" (88), then we in ministry must become aware that human environments need to be protected, defended, and sometimes challenged, as vigorously as we protect and defend the ecological environments of this world. Each and every creature, from kiwi to human, is unique. When their worth is erased, they are destroyed, and God's creation is that much more impoverished.

The Structure of This Book

Chapters 1, 2, and 3 of this book are devoted to an explanation and application of the three schools of psychotherapeutic theory that I believe are most useful for those in ministry: Family Systems Theory, Narrative Counseling Theory, and Object Relations Theory. *Family Systems Theory* springs originally from cybernetics, the science of understanding how responsive living beings are to the context within which they live. Family Systems Theory looks at the intergenerational heritage out of which one has sprung—our parents, grandparents, and great-grandparents—and how each of us continues to carry the effects of everything that happened to them and how they coped with life. *Narrative Counseling Theory* analyzes the way we construct and utilize stories about ourselves and others in order to form and maintain a sense of identity. *Object Relations Theory* is built upon assumptions: how we assume we are cared for, whom we belong to, who others are in relationship to ourselves, and what signals us that we are safe. All three of these theories interweave in intriguing ways, and all tell us much about how we know ourselves and God.

Chapters 4 through 8 undertake an application of these three theories to some of the specific situations we encounter in ministry. In particular, these chapters concentrate on situations of transition and potential crisis in the human life span: preparation for marriage, being married, getting divorced, establishing a sexual identity, and facing loss. In these critical moments in life, those in ministry as well as those seeking ministry ask, "What do I do now?" "Why me?" "How do I understand what's happening?" "Where is God?"

The final two chapters of this book address the praxis of pastoral ministry. Chapter 9 explores some of the factors that make pastoral counseling work and keep it safe for both counselor and counselee. Chapter 10 tackles the biggest deficiency in most people's ministry: a sense of a healthy self and the access to supportive professional supervision. Both of these issues need to be moved into a position of more open conversation in the church. If ministry is all about "being" rather than "doing," then we are obliged to offer to God's ministry the finest "being" that we can muster.

BIBLIOGRAPHY

Clebsch, William, and Charles Jaekle. *Pastoral Care in Historical Perspective*. New York: Prentice-Hall, 1964.

Culbertson, Philip. "The Shadow of the Transcendent: Valuing Spirituality in Psychotherapy." *Forum: The Journal of the New Zealand Association of Psychotherapists* 4 (June 1998): 14–37.

Culbertson, Philip, and Arthur Bradford Shippee, eds. *The Pastor: Readings from the Patristic Period*. Minneapolis: Fortress, 1990.

Fromm, Erich. *Psychoanalysis and Religion*. New Haven: Yale University Press, 1950.

Gerkin, Charles. *An Introduction to Pastoral Care*. Nashville: Abingdon, 1997.

Giblin, Paul. "Marital Conflict and Marital Spirituality." In *Clinical Handbook of Pastoral Counseling,* vol. 2. Robert Wicks and Richard Parsons, eds. 313–28. New York: Paulist, 1993.

Gundry-Volf, Judith, and Miroslav Volf. *A Spacious Heart: Essays on Identity and Belonging*. Harrisburg: Trinity Press International, 1997.

Holmes, Urban T. *Ministry and Imagination*. New York: Seabury, 1976.

Hughes, Sheila Hassel. "A Woman's Soul Is Her Castle: Place and Space in St. Theresa's Interior Castle." *Literature and Theology* 11:4 (December 1997): 376–84.

Merton, Thomas. *The Asian Journal of Thomas Merton*. London: Sheldon, 1974.

———. *The New Man*. New York: Farrar, Straus and Giroux, 1961.

Nouwen, Henri J. M. *The Wounded Healer*. Garden City, N.Y.: Image, 1979.

Oden, Thomas. *Care of Souls in the Classic Tradition*. Philadelphia: Fortress, 1984.

Steinke, Peter. *Healthy Congregations: A Systems Approach*. Washington, D.C.: Alban Institute, 1996.

White, Michael. *Narratives of Therapists' Lives*. Adelaide: The Dulwich Centre, 1997.

Wimberly, Edward. *Recalling Our Own Stories: Spiritual Renewal for Religious Caregivers*. San Francisco: Jossey-Bass, 1997.

Part One

~

The Theory

I. Family Systems Theory

"The majority of problems presented to [pastoral counselors] will be marital and family difficulties." (Bascue and Lewis, 268)

~

Caregivers become a part of every family they counsel and of many families in their congregations. Caregivers have their own families and have access to many others. We know all sorts and descriptions of families: married couples with young children, married couples who can't have children, married couples who choose not to have children; married couples with one parent in residence, single people with one parent in residence; solo parents with a child or children living with them, single parents whose children live elsewhere; stepfamilies and blended families and divorced couples who share the custody of children; grandparents raising their grandchildren; adult brothers and/or sisters living together; gay and lesbian couples without children; gay and lesbian couples with children. The range of family configuration in any society is much wider than the public media suggest, and we must be careful not to limit our ministry to a particular type of family, for all families are deserving of equal access to a loving and supportive ministry of the church.

The word *family* is also used in even broader senses. In more communal societies such as the Polynesian, African, or Asian, a family is generally defined as a larger social unit. White cultures often call this "the extended family" to distinguish it from "the nuclear family," though in communal cultures such families are not really "extended"

because there is no "nuclear" form to measure it against. Families in communal cultures almost always include at least three generations of direct blood relationship, and often include aunts, uncles, cousins, and even more distant relatives, all counted as a part of the family unit. This would have been a much more typical arrangement in biblical times, and when we find family mentioned in either the Hebrew Bible or the New Testament, we must consider the configuration carefully. For example, the House (family) of Abraham included his blood relatives as well as his slaves, especially his mistress Hagar. We know as well that Jesus spent a great deal of time with one family that consisted simply of two sisters and a brother: Mary, Martha, and Lazarus, with Martha as the head of the household (see Luke 10:38). Scriptures are not especially supportive of the nuclear family, nor is such a family as we now define it even mentioned there, as can be seen from Appendix A attached to this chapter. If anything, the teachings of Jesus cast a skeptical eye on the family, no matter what its configuration, for it is seen as a potential form of idolatry (Hay, 85; see Matthew 3 and 10). Today we also speak of the household or family of faith, our "brother and sister" Christians (the family as a community of love or a voluntary mutual commitment of unrelated people), and even the Family of Humankind.

Anne Borrowdale identifies three particular uses of the family concept within Christian tradition (40). The first we have identified as the blood or affectional kith and kin; and the second as a form of social organization larger than the nuclear. The third type identified by Borrowdale is "The Family," a symbolic, idealized fiction. She writes:

Families continue to manage as best they can, family form is changing, but it is "The Family" as an ideological and theological construct which is at the centre of the moral crisis. What happens to that construct has some effect on the other two understandings of family as kith and kin, and of family as household; but it gets in the way of reaching a proper understanding of what is going on in family life today. This is partly because the idea of "The Family" has been misused for ideological and political ends, but also because it has become a symbol for many other values. (55)

When addressing pastoral care and counseling theory, this is the least useful form of the word.

Ministry is done within the bounds of very flesh–and–blood families, with all their joys and problems. James Framo portrays the complexity of family life:

> Families can provide the deepest satisfactions of living: unreserved and unconditional love; gratifying bonding; measureless sacrifice; enduring dependability; compassionate belonging; the joys and warmth of family holidays, dinners, and vacations; the fun and play; the give and take; and knowing your family is always *there* when needed. Still, the hurts and damage that family members can inflict upon one another are infinite: scapegoating; humiliation and shaming; parentification; crazy-making; physical, sexual, and psychological abuse; cruel rejections; lies and deceit; and the manifold outrages against the human spirit. (7)

Family Systems Theory is designed to address the effects of living in such complex social units, by focusing on the heritage we each receive as a result of all these "passions, hates, loves, mysteries, paradoxes, measureless sac-

rifices, joys, injustices, jealousies, storms, comforts, bonds, and patterns" (Framo, 208).

The family, then, and particularly the nuclear family, can be seen as just one very specific means of organizing the relationships between parents and children. It is not, as has sometimes been claimed within the church, some sort of "natural," instinctive, and "sacred" unit. Family Systems Theory generally focuses on the nuclear family and the generation just above it, however, for while it is the minority configuration in first-world societies today, it is the "symbol system" within which we are most often trained to think.

The Family as System

The word *system* is rooted in Latin and Greek words that mean "to place together," so a system can be thought of as a corporate entity that is the sum of individual entities placed together (Rosenblatt, 49). The system unites and organizes its separate entities into a whole. A family is a system that has an integrity all its own and that operates in a consistent and only slowly changing, sometimes inefficient manner (Allen, 54). The manner in which the system operates is determined by a set of unspoken rules and roles that specify how individual parts of the system contribute to the functioning of the whole. These rules and roles are designed to keep the system in a state of balance or, as it is called in Family Systems Theory, "homeostasis." Friedman defines homeostasis as "the tendency of any set of relationships to strive perpetually, in self-corrective ways, to preserve the organizing principles of its existence" (1985, 24). For most families, homeostasis signals predictability, control, and "normalcy," no matter how dysfunctional the homeostatic system might be.

What distinguishes systems thinking from the view of families taken in individual psychology is the emphasis on the interactive dynamics among the people in the system. In systems thinking, a person is not a freestanding, constant entity but achieves her or his nature of the moment through interaction. In different relationships the individual is different and is defined by others—and defines himself or herself—differently (Rosenblatt, 59–60). There is no clearly delineated canon of texts on Family Systems Theory, no single set of readings that defines the field, although for some who work with Family Systems Theory there may be a kind of personal canon (Framo, 88). However, two implications of family theory for pastoral practice should be mentioned by way of introduction to the exploration that follows:

> The first is that family therapy is not to be distinguished from individual-model counseling by how many come to the session. It is possible to do family therapy while seeing only one member. The differentiating characteristic of the family approach is the focus on the system rather than the person, not the quantity of counselees seen simultaneously.
>
> Second, the criterion for which family members should be seen is who is most motivated rather than who has the symptom. That may or may not be the same person. (Friedman 1984, 280–81)

Most of the material in this chapter is based on a certain approach to Family Systems Theory as shaped by Murray Bowen over the past two decades. Bowen's material has been made more accessible for both Christian and Jewish pastoral caregivers through the writings of Rabbi Edwin Friedman. Bowen died in 1990, Friedman in 1996.

The Nuclear Family

The nuclear family is generally defined as two adult parents of opposite sexes, married legally, with two nonadult children at home. Though it is simply a stereotype popularized in the 1950s, the nuclear family, both as a romantic fiction and as a symbol, continues to be the norm against which the many other possible family configurations are measured. The term usually has a number of other agglutinate associations, such as middle-class, stable, happy, and secure. These too are often fictions.

A number of other assumptions are made about the nuclear family that are also incorrect. It is not the basic unit of society (Dicks, 107). In first-world countries the individual is the basic unit; in communal societies the extended family or tribe is the basic unit. The nuclear family is not a guarantee of safety, emotional stability, or social health; it may be "a haven in a heartless world" (Rudy), but just as often it is not. Nor is it the preferred Christian way of living. Christians are called to live in communities of love (Borrowdale, 74), however they may be configured, and there is little in Christian tradition that would give pride of place to the nuclear family over other configurations.

While the Christian Right sometimes speaks of "family values," these values are often not clearly described or agreed upon. At times family values can be defined in a way that demands a crippling obedience, a paralyzing personal sacrifice, or a debasement of the power and humanity of various family members, women and children in particular. James Nelson offers a different sense of family values:

> Each of us needs a place where the gifts of life make us more human, where we are

linked with ongoing covenants to others, where we can return to lick our wounds, where we can take our shoes off, and where we know that—within the bounds of human capacity—we are loved simply because we are. (130)

These are family values as Christian as any other, for they are about unconditional love and acceptance, modeling God's love for us. What determines whether something is Christian is not its structure, but the values that are lived out by people who call themselves Christian. "Family values" also point us in the direction of family dysfunction, however, for in the linking, returning, and loving that Nelson refers to, we find that families repeat patterns that are sometimes generations old.

In the end, the nuclear family, like all other family configurations, is an unconscious cybernetic system, governed by unconscious stimuli and responses that are simultaneously predictable and chaotic and as capable of giving dis-health as they are of giving health. A family is a living organism—even the most rigidly structured one. Influences leave (die) and enter (are born), parts act in unison and react in opposition, and a carefully structured balance is always sought by the family members for their own good, however they may individually understand that. A family has a developmental cycle as well, both within a generation and across several (Combrinck-Graham). Family Systems Theory seeks to understand why one family will absorb a tragedy in a relatively healthy manner, while another family will disintegrate in the face of an identical tragedy. It seeks this understanding by treating the family as an organic system, an ecological environment in which each component is responsive both to identifiable laws and influences and to the actions of other components within the same system.

In Family Systems Theory, the family is usually spoken of as an "emotional system." The dynamics of systemic stimulus and response are set in place beginning early in a couple's courtship and then follow through their marriage, various relationships with families of origin, the adjustment of the spouses to each other before children, the addition of the first child, their adjustment as a three-person relationship system, and then the addition of each subsequent child. Life crises, such as the death of a grandparent, the debilitating illness of one member of the system, or loss of employment, negatively influence the family's emotional functioning, often making overt the reactive system that has covertly governed the health of the whole family unit.

There are a number of other lenses through which we can examine the family dynamics as a system. Some of these lenses are metaphors, such as the word *house*, one of the most common biblical words connoting "family." Yet another metaphor is the family as a battlefield, replete with generals (the parents), privates (the children), heroes, enemies, strategies of attack and defense, classified information (family secrets), truce negotiations, and conflicting loyalties (in today's blended families, both children and adults may well be directly related to nuclear family units living elsewhere; Rosenblatt, 38–39). The meaning and interpretation of metaphors within family systems will be explored later in this chapter.

Another lens depicts the family as a collection of subunits. Love and attention are rarely distributed evenly throughout a family system. Children may be united against parents; a child may be emotionally closer to one parent than to another; parents may be so narcissistic that ordinary family dynamics get reversed, with the children taking care of the needs of the parents. Another lens would be the family as a fragile ecosystem, which responds to intrusion, manipulation, or trauma from external sources, just as the surface of a lake responds to a storm (Bowen, 507). Yet another lens would be the family as an accident of nature, in which people are related by blood ties but have no sense of affection or attachment to each other. In fact, what holds any family together is not blood ties, but a set of shared experiences and various unspoken agreements about how the members are going to "be" together (Laing).

A final lens should be mentioned, again a metaphor. A family is like a vast stage upon which characters appear to act out their parts and then disappear. The plot would not be the same without each character, and the stage space is always changed by the entrance and exit of each new actor. A family is like a stage play whose characters are in roles. They are expected to remain in that role, and only if they do will other members of the "cast" know their lines. If a character acts in an arbitrary and unexpected manner, or recites lines that are not part of the expected script, the rest of the characters will attempt to force the play to go on as rehearsed, by responding to the surprise in a variety of ways. Only by understanding what has been rehearsed can we as caregivers help get the play back on track toward an ending that satisfies the majority of the characters.

Culture and Intergenerational Roles
Roles within a family system are determined by the family's needs and internal dynamics. Everyone has a role in a family, but if the family is small, one may carry more than one role, simultaneously or sequentially. We have roles because we volunteer for them, but we are also drafted for them, quite covertly. Typical family roles have many names, depending in part upon the theoretician who analyzes them. Among the better known roles are:

- the Good Child: the child who accepts the responsibility for decreasing tension in the family by excelling in activities that seem to focus the family's attention on the positive.
- the Standard-Bearer: the child who is catapulted up and out of the family in order to achieve (Friedman, 1984, 287–88). The family will tolerate a great deal of tension and make many sacrifices for a child who will assume this role. Conversely, the standard-bearer who fails will receive a disproportionate amount of family disappointment.
- the Mascot: the child who is a pleasure to have around because he or she is genial, companionable, and entertaining, creating the illusion of family peace and warmth.
- the Clown: the child who can make the family laugh, particularly in order to distract the family from its internal tensions.
- the Avenger: the child who acts out the parental or intergenerational rage (Allen, 147–48).
- the Savior: the child who acts out the parents' unfulfilled ambitions.
- the Enabler: the child or parent who always covers for everyone, often meeting their needs without being asked, including the self-destructive needs of other members of the family. An illustration frequently given is the wife who keeps the refrigerator full of beer for her alcoholic husband.

- the Switchboard: the child or adult through whom all family communication goes. In such families, no one speaks directly to the others, particularly about painful or controversial subjects, and no one dares to point out that the emperor wears no clothes.
- the Lost Child: the one no one can remember, the one who is always inadvertently left out, the one whose complaints are not heard and whose needs take little priority.

Adopting a role teaches us a certain way of being in the world. A role is constantly reinforced within a family system, and we suppress any feelings contradictory to our role in order to meet the needs of our larger family environment. Once we have adopted a role, we carry it for the rest of our lives, recreating it over and over again in a variety of situations, at times whether that is appropriate or not. In the end, we don't *have* a role; we *become* a role. In the case of the more negative roles such as the scapegoat, we don't *have* a problem, we *become* a problem.

Roles are also influenced by culture. More traditional cultures make a sharp distinction between the rights and obligations of the oldest son and the youngest son. Completely unrelated words may be used to describe these two sibling positions; for example, in Maori the eldest son is the *matamua* and the youngest son is the *potiki*. Biblical culture gave great precedence, or primogeniture, to the eldest son in a patriarchal system. The eldest son inherited the greater share of the father's estate as well as the authority within the family to direct its future. One of the intrigues in the book of Genesis is the repeated intergenerational pattern of "the disinherited firstborn," in which primogeniture is repeatedly over-turned in spite of cultural expectations (see Culbertson, 1993).

Roles and expectations are shaped by a culture's gender constructions as well. In patriarchal cultures, including the biblical, daughters can only be the family's "standard-bearer" if there are no sons; even then a male relative such as a nephew may assume the mantle of authority rather than a female in direct biological descent. Because gender is a social construction specific to a particular culture, roles and expectations are easily attached to gender identity. For example, in most cultures of the world today, men are expected to adopt the role of decision-maker in the public sphere, while women play a secondary role in all spheres except the domestic.

The role of "self-sacrificer," the expectation that one's personal needs will take second place to the needs of others, is a role that women bear disproportionately in patriarchal cultures. Self-sacrifice, however, in spite of its canonization as a Christian virtue, is often destructive of the self, of the identity of the one who is expected to make the sacrifice on behalf of others, particularly when that sacrifice is not voluntary. David Allen calls this "the altruistic paradox" (67–68): in sacrificing self for the sake of another's good, we may destroy our self to the degree that we eventually become destructive of the other. He continues:

> What I mean by self-sacrifice corresponds to the first type of Jung's "alienations" of the self. It is the *consistent* camouflaging of characteristics of one's own basic nature in order to fill a role in one's family or culture that seems to make the rest of the family or cultural system more comfortable. Self-sacrifice is the attempt to change oneself like a chameleon, so that

one appears to be what significant others seem to require in order to maintain their own equilibria. It is the process of developing a pseudo, false, or pretend self. (68–69)

Self-sacrifice is not synonymous with the temporary suppression of the self. We all have certain collective obligations and considerations with which to concern ourselves that are entirely right and valid, and for which we must let go of needs that feed only our own egos. Patterns of involuntary self-sacrifice, however, disempower and ultimately lead to destructive distortions in social interactions. Self-sacrificers ultimately become manipulators of other people. Despite their apparent "selfishness," they have sacrificed their true selves, along with their need for potency. What on the surface appears to be a contradiction—a "selfish" self-sacrificer—is really no contradiction at all. Anything gained through phony selfishness is ruined or devalued (Allen, 191).

Self-sacrifice is one of many roles and expectations that a family system will struggle to keep in place in order to maintain the power balance and predictability of interaction that the family has come to identify as both normal and safe. When someone decides to make new choices around his or her designated role, the entire system may experience it as a major threat to the family's survival. Hence, roles are set firmly in place and family members will usually resist vigorously anyone's attempt to redefine the role or to leave the system altogether.

Women's self-sacrifice is one example of how roles and expectations may extend across several successive generations. In Family Systems Theory this is called "the multigenerational transmission process" (Bowen, 477). In fact, systems theory analy-sis requires that fairly complete information be available for at least three, and preferably four or more generations, in order to identify the intergenerational patterns at work. Access to generational statistics and, more importantly, biographical information can produce great knowledge quickly. For example, in six generations one is the product of sixty-four families of origin. We are the product not only of the biogenetic heritage of all these people, but also of their patterns of behavior, adaptability, compensation, projection, avoidance, and resolution.

When doing generational research and systems analysis, it is tempting to concentrate only on what has gone wrong over the course of successive generations. But the generations before us have also migrated and adapted, solved problems, overcome obstacles, and survived in the face of great odds. There is as much strength to be found in the intergenerational process as there is dysfunction. Novelist Madeleine L'Engle speaks of the value of mutability in our heritage:

> Tradition is important to me. But in my own life, traditions have had to change, to be renewed, rediscovered. New traditions have had to replace old ones. When our children left the nest, the tradition of the family around the table, together, for dinner, had to change. The dinner table is important, and the tradition of lighted candles, a well-set table, food prepared with love has remained, but the people around the table vary with what is going on in my life. (23)

The most common use of Family Systems Theory is the analysis of patterns in previous generations to understand why things are working as they are in this generation. And of the three counseling approaches upon which this book is based, Family Systems is the most likely to generate blaming of families or individuals in our past. Such blaming should be avoided where possible, for much of what has gone wrong in the past was itself an attempt by someone to gain control over a threatening situation. Other dysfunctional inheritances of the past are unintended. Their result was not thought through carefully; the future could not, of course, be foreseen. Nonetheless, even "unintentional abuse" can produce anger in future generations. James Framo explains:

> I view anger as an almost inescapable ingredient in the intergenerational encounter, stemming from the fact that all human beings require socialization in order to survive—a process bound to create some resentment toward parent figures, who, of necessity, must frustrate. As someone once put it, "No one has ever been loved the way everyone wants to be loved." The sense of outrage that we all feel about injustices done to us as children seems to be a deep and abiding one. Freud is presumed to have said (and if he didn't say it he should have) that what we love above all else is ourselves as children. Therefore, "How *could* they have done those awful things to that sweet, innocent child that was me?" (60)

Once those seeking care have understood the irrationality of their desire to blame, using Framo's argument, they should be ready to move on to establishing greater containment of the spillover from their past. Though we are molded by our family of origin, we do not need to be defined by them for the rest of our lives.

Families or individuals may research the past to understand the present; however, families or individuals who continue looking backwards, whether out of nostalgia or out of blame, are described by Sherman and Fredman as "Lot's wife" (33). Most Western-oriented theories of family therapy note the importance of maintaining generational boundaries between grandparents, parents, and children. They believe that a family functions most effectively if there are appropriate, distinct boundaries regarding rules, roles, responsibilities, and interactions for the parents and children (Sherman and Fredman, 123). For example, a grandparent may undercut the disciplinary behavior of the parent with a child or may treat the parent as another child in the family on the same level as the grandchildren. In such cases the family structure is regarded as misaligned. While Family Systems Theory assumes there is always leakage through the process of multigenerational transmission, healing may begin with the reestablishment of appropriate boundaries that protect generations from some of each other's dysfunction.

While it is true that the family of origin is the most powerful force in organizing and framing later life experiences and choices, there are many other influences that have an impact on the human being and that may even counteract the negative effects of one's family as well. Among such factors are the following: positive experiences with someone outside the immediate family, such as a grandparent, aunt or uncle, a teacher, minister, or mentor, or good friends; special skills or high intelligence that the individual has, such as artistic talents, skills in sports, or school successes that create opportunities outside the family; inherent personality traits or temperament that enable the individual to handle malevolent family processes better; developmental, life-cycle, or serendipitous events that moderate pathological family forces, economic, social, ethnic, or spiritual influences; or for some, the fortuitous selection of a spouse who fits one's needs (Framo, 128).

Sociometrics and Systems Theory

The basic tools for Family Systems work are the analysis of present reactive behavior by the careseeker and other members of the nuclear family, explorations into one's past family of origin, particularly through the use of a type of family tree called a "genogram," and narrative. The pastoral counselor will often have to direct the counselee to family-of-origin members and their close friends to uncover specific information. Data is then analyzed, and hypotheses formulated and tested. It must be remembered that all conclusions drawn are simply hypothetical; the nature of family analysis is such that it cannot be stated as scientifically provable data. We are dealing with the human psyche in such work, a complex system embedded within a complex system and ultimately beyond factual human knowing.

The role of narrative in pastoral care will be explored in depth in the subsequent chapter, but here we must note that narrative is important in Family Systems work. We shape our perceptions of reality by turning them into stories, and every family is full of stories of many kinds. The stories contain what we presume are the "facts" about what happened in our families of origin, how people responded, who did what to whom, and what the effect was of various decisions to act or not act. The caregiver serves as both teacher and interpreter. Because we are never "done" with our explorations of how our family of origin

worked and how we presently work, Murray Bowen believes that Family Systems work must include the caregiver teaching the careseeker the basic analytical principles of the method so that the careseeker may continue explorations on his or her own once any formal counseling process has terminated. As well, the caregiver serves as interpreter, for the careseeker will often lack the objectivity to make the connections between past and present, or to see the influence of intergenerational patterns, until a great deal of personal interpretive experience has been acquired.

Triangulation

The easiest analytic tool to learn in Family Systems Theory is the theory of triangles. This theory is based on the assumption that any relationship between two people is subject to an inherent instability when threatened. Once tension is felt, the two people in a relationship dyad have three options: they can move toward the other person, they can move away, or they can stand still (fight, flight, or freeze; see Guerin et al., 8). This is called "emotional reactivity," and is easily observable by the pastor. The choice among the three options is fueled by patterns formed during infancy and reinforced through life experience. Emotional pursuers will move closer to their dyad partner when tension is perceived (abandonment anxiety); emotional distancers will move away (incorporation anxiety). Neither move stabilizes the relationship, but may actually increase the sense of danger. What may stabilize the rocky dyadic relationship is the focus on or addition of a third party, just as adding a third leg to a two-legged stool makes it stable enough to sit on. Focusing on a third person allows the two partners in the dyad to avoid facing what is wrong between them. The more intense the anxiety on either part, the more likely are the efforts to stabilize the dyad by activation of a triangle. Triangulation will appear to temporarily reduce the dyad's stress, but will not address its source.

Some examples will illustrate: (1) If a husband and wife have marital problems, they will usually focus on one of their children as a problem or source of pride. Looking away from each other toward the third party allows them not to face what is wrong in their marriage. In this sense they have moved closer to each other, though the new intimacy is based only on the presence of a third person and thus is not true intimacy. (2) A pastor and his congregation may be at a point of deep mistrust. Rather than facing the problem between them, both may turn on the pastor's wife, blaming her for their problems. In that case, the pastor and the congregation may actually move further away from each other (incorporation anxiety), while avoiding the true source of tension. (3) Guerin et al. describe what they call "The Wedding Gift Triangle":

> A culturally acceptable way for a man to avoid the pressure of a relationship with his mother without cutting her off is to hand her over to his wife. He gives her the responsibility of keeping in touch with his mother, seeing to it that his children have a relationship with her, buying gifts and birthday cards for her. In other words, a husband turns over to his wife the emotional or actual responsibility for his parents. After the wedding his mother becomes the wife's ally, or the wife's problem, or both, while the husband avoids real contact with his mother.
>
> In this triangle, the husband's primacy of attachment is blurred and difficult to assess. Most often he assumes a distant position in relation to both his mother and his wife. The mother and wife have several ways they can deal with this dynamic. They may both like the idea and join together. They might form an alliance to shape up their distant son and husband, or they might simply bypass him, allowing him his distance and focus their energies on bringing up the children or even a joint business venture. In such cases, the wife is usually in flight from her family of origin, looking for membership and a sense of belonging in a new and different clan. (173–74)

People live in webs of triangles. A person-to-person relationship is conceived as an ideal within which two people can communicate freely about the full range of personal issues between them. Most people cannot tolerate more than a few minutes on a personal level. When either party becomes anxious, he or she begins talking about a third person (triangles in other people), or the communication becomes impersonal and they talk about things (Bowen, 499). Thus even our common human tendency to gossip with someone about someone else is usually a form of triangulation.

If we imagine a husband and a wife with one child, we can see that a triangle is normally the most stable relationship unit. Yet, even within a stable triangle, there is a great deal of movement. The husband and wife may focus on the child, the child and the father may focus on the mother, the mother and child may focus on the husband. Again, danger may explain this shifting character. When the triangle is in a state of tension, the outside position is the preferred position, in a posture that says, "You two fight and leave me out of it." The person perceiving the danger can then attempt to withdraw further, or can attempt to form a more intimate alliance with one or the other member of the dyad.

Not every group of people automatically forms a triangle. It is characteristic of a threesome that each person in a threesome has a sense of freedom and an ability to focus on self rather than looking to see where the others stand before taking his or her own stand—in other words, being determined by them. Guerin et al. chart the distinction between a threesome and a triangle (47):

THREESOMES	TRIANGLES
Each twosome can interact one-on-one.	Each twosome's interaction is tied to the behavior of the third person.
Each person has options for his or her behavior.	Each person is tied to reactive forms of behavior.
Each person can take "I" positions without trying to change the other two.	No one can take an "I" position without needing to change the others.
Each person can allow the other two to have their own relationship without interference.	Each person gets involved in the relationship between the other two.
Self-focus is possible and the usual situation [*sic*].	No self-focus in anyone, and everyone is constantly focused on the other two.

In healthy triangles, focus and tension move constantly among the several points, resulting in an even distribution of stress throughout the nuclear system. In unhealthy triangles, the stress becomes stuck repeatedly in one leg of the triangle. A common unhealthy pattern is one in which the mother and child form the close twosome and the father is the outsider. In this triangle, the minute-to-minute process of emotional forces shifts around the triangle, but when forces come to rest, it is always with each in the same position. Another common triangle is expressed in sibling conflict. Bowen claims that this conflict is due almost universally to a triangulated relationship between mother and two children in which the mother has a positive relationship to each child, so that the conflict is fought out between the children (479). Conflict becomes "stuck" on one leg of the triangle because people relate to each other by way of patterns repeated endlessly.

Over time, people believe that they know each other well. They make assumptions about each other, and they stop listening because they "know" what the other will say and do. Such assumptions become self-fulfilling prophecies, fixing beliefs and behavior rigidly. By contrast, if a person realizes that he or she can never really know another person, he listens to that person to get to know him or her as best he can. Faulty assumptions are corrected, and one-on-one relationships are more possible. Triangles become less fixed, and it takes higher levels of stress to push potential triangles to activation (Guerin et al., 65).

Once a triangle has become established, it may go dormant in a system, but will always be waiting to be reactivated should the situation warrant, or even in another generation. Sometimes triangles become so energized, however, that they spill over outside the family. When the nuclear system can no longer contain the discomfort and tension of the family, outside systems are triangulated in, such as a school, the police, or the medical community. Thus we understand that the three points of a triangulated relationship need not necessarily be three persons. A powerful family member may die, yet retain a strong influence in the family system. This would produce a triangle comprised of, for example, a mother, a son, and the memory of the deceased father. One triangle point may be an institution, as in a vicar, her husband, and the congregation. A triangle point may be an influential social construction, such as a mother, a daughter, and the cultural expectations of feminine behavior. Donaldson-Pressman and Pressman report the case of a client whose unhappily married parents had for years communicated through the dog: "Buffy, tell your Daddy that Mommy wants to go out Saturday night" (33)!

A minister is constantly being triangulated into situations, particularly when counseling more than one person. An engaged couple will attempt to triangle in the person doing their premarital counseling, thereby reducing the pastor's effectiveness. A married couple in distress will act out their triangulation patterns in the presence of their caregiver. A team of two counselors will become triangulated with a family unit. Guerin et al. put it succinctly: "Remember, without becoming paranoid, that every individual or couple you deal with is a problem in search of a triangle" (12). With experience, a caregiver can learn to use, but not be used by, this dynamic.

Differentiation and Individuation

In Family Systems Theory, two terms must be carefully distinguished from each other: *differentiation and individuation*. Bowen is himself not systematically clear about this distinction, sometimes separating the two terms (471–75) and at other times confusing them (539). The two are closely related but address different aspects of the self.

Bowen begins his discussion of differentiation by citing a scientific instrument he has created called "The Differentiation of Self Scale." He explains:

> This is a scale for evaluating the level of "differentiation of self" from the lowest possible level of "undifferentiation," which is at 0 on the scale, to the highest theoretical level of "differentiation," which is at 100 on the scale. The greater the degree of undifferentiation (no-self), the greater the emotional fusion into a common self with others (undifferentiated ego mass). . . . The differentiation of self scale is an effort to assess the basic level of self in a person. The basic self is a definite quality illustrated by such "I position" stances as: "These are my beliefs and convictions. This is what I am, and who I am, and what I will do, or not do." The basic self may be changed from *within* self on the basis of new knowledge and experience. The basic self *is not negotiable in the relationship system* in that it is not changed

by coercion or pressure, or to gain approval, or enhance one's stand with others. (472–75)

Bowen goes on to characterize those at the lower end of the scale as living in a "feeling controlled world." They do not distinguish feeling from fact, and major life decisions are based on what "feels" right. Primary life goals are oriented around love, happiness, comfort, and security; these goals come closest to fulfillment when relationships with others are in equilibrium. So much life energy goes into seeking love and approval, or attacking the other for not providing it, that there is little energy left for self-determined, goal-directed activity. They do not distinguish between "truth" and "fact," and the inner feeling state is the most accurate possible expression of truth. On the other hand, those on the higher end of the scale "are operationally clear about the difference between feeling and thinking, and it is as routine for them to make decisions on the basis of thinking as it is for low-level people to operate on feelings. . . . Moving into the upper half of the scale one finds people who have an increasing capacity to differentiate between feelings and objective reality."

So differentiation begins with knowing the difference between one's feelings and one's thinking, and this in turn leads to individuation. Bowen appears to believe that if we act on feelings only, we are incapable of taking "I" stands that are clear, constructive, and minimally influenced by the needs of others for fusion. The actual taking of an "I" stand is, however, not differentiation, but individuation.

Fusion is the inability in relationships to know the difference between "mine" and "yours": my boundaries and yours, my feelings and yours, my needs and yours. Fusion

is bliss for many people, for they no longer have to take care of their own needs, shoulder their own burdens, or solve their own problems: they can foist all these off on their partner. A family does all this handing off to each other via what Bowen calls "the family projection process." Some people insist they cannot be happy without being married, but this usually means they are looking for someone else to do their emotional work for them. Because individuation is difficult, most people prefer to perpetuate some degree of fusion, and the primary tool in a family's fight against individuation is guilt. Bowen writes:

> Each small step toward the "differentiation" of a self is opposed by emotional forces for "togetherness," which keeps the emotional system in check. The togetherness forces define the family members as alike in terms of important beliefs, philosophies, life principles, and feelings. . . . The togetherness amalgam is bound together by assigning positive value on thinking about the other before self [self-sacrifice], living for others, and feeling responsible for the comfort and well-being of others. If the other is unhappy or uncomfortable, the togetherness force feels guilty and asks, "What have I done to cause this?" and it blames the other for lack of happiness or failure in self. (494–95)

This guilt is produced by what David Allen calls "disqualifications," the negative mirroring that members of a fused family can give to anyone who attempts to individuate. Disqualifications can take the form of "a wide range of communicational phenomena, such as self-contradictions, inconsistencies, subject switches, tangentializations, incomplete sentences, misunderstandings, obscure style or mannerisms of speech, the literal interpretation of metaphor and the metaphorical interpretation of literal remarks, etc." (Allen, 62). The end result is to apply great pressure on the one individuating to return to the prior position of fusion, to adopt again the pseudoself which the family found comfortable and predictable, rather than threaten the family system further. One who persists in individuation in spite of systemic opposition will feel unsupported, groundless, and anxious. Allen notes that such family dynamics are even more evident in cultures that are evolving or are in chaotic periods of history (112).

The three areas in which lack of differentiation is most frequently manifest in a nuclear family are marital conflict, sickness or dysfunction in a spouse, and projection onto one or more children (Bowen, 503). Ministers will recognize these as frequent reasons for which married parishioners present for counseling. Those who are "victimized" by family fusion have three choices: to perpetuate the fusion through cooperation, joining forces with "the enemy"; to flee into denial or emotional and geographical isolation; or to "defect in place," to remain in contact with the family but to push the issue of their own mature individuation through what Bowen calls "an open relationship."

Bowen defines cut off as "emotional distancing, whether the cut-off is achieved by internal mechanisms or physical distance" (535). The principal manifestation of emotional cut off is denial of the intensity of the unresolved emotional attachments to parents, acting and pretending to be more independent than one is. The giveaway for emotional cut off is that the more intense the cut off with one's parents, the more vul-

nerable one is to repeat the same pattern in future relationships, perhaps by marrying someone with the same personality structure as the person to whom one is most fused. For a high percentage, the adolescent period is one in which there is denial of the attachment to the parents and the assumption of some rather extreme postures in order to claim being grown up. The intensity of the denial and the pretending in adolescence is a remarkably accurate index of the degree of unresolved emotional attachment to the parents. Adolescent "rebellion," then, is a sign of how closely connected a teenager is to his or her parents. Allen believes that individuals under the age of twenty-one or twenty-two have not developed a self powerful enough to challenge and change the family homeostasis in a mature and successful manner (217).

The more obvious forms of cut off include family members who will not speak to one another, or those who flee to a different geographical location without reaching proper closure with their families of origin. In both cases, the individual is highly likely to create a "substitute" family from new social relationships. In neither case can the family-of-origin dysfunction be considered as resolved.

The opposite of cut off is what Bowen calls "an open relationship," or, more graphically, "defecting in place" (537). An open relationship is one in which people remain in touch with each other, and yet are comfortable claiming an "I position," expressing and negotiating difference of opinion and lifestyle and living into their increasing individuation. Guerin et al. explain further:

> Part of being a grown-up entails developing ease at stepping up and assuming responsibility for one's own emotions and

the relationship behavior that these emotions drive. If any of us fails at this key developmental task, that person is doomed to a life of angry, resentful victimhood.... An important antidote to this therapeutic trap is to emphasize the importance of being able to self-focus—that is, to work at seeing the parts of ourselves that contribute significantly to our own pain and our relationship discomfort. (43)

The road to individuation, then, is through self-focus, the ability to see that a relationship problem is the result not only of another person's limitations but also of one's own. In this way, a break is made from the deterministic nature of family systems. By identifying a problem, finding a solution, and accepting responsibility for one's own contribution to that problem, its hold over us is broken and we can move further into maturity. Individuation, then, is the process of coming into our own, of freeing ourselves from the prison of destructive thought patterns and role functioning inherited from our own intergenerational background (Allen, 24).

Sibling Position

Research in Sibling Position Theory was begun early in this century by psychotherapist Alfred Adler. The firstborn child, Adler argued, is "dethroned" by the birth of the next sibling. Firstborns who manage to overcome this trauma try to emulate parents. In their role as surrogate parents, firstborns may overemphasize the importance of law and order and become "power-hungry conservatives." As Adler reasoned, "Sometimes a child who has lost his power, the small kingdom he ruled, understands better than others the importance of power and authority." Secondborns try harder than their older siblings, he maintained, because

they are always playing catch-up. The secondborn "behaves as if he were in a race, is under full steam all the time, and trains continually to surpass his older brother and conquer him." As a result, secondborns are "rarely able to endure the strict leadership of others." Youngest children are not subject to dethronement and are said to become lazy and spoiled. "A spoiled child can never be independent," Adler insisted. Those lastborns who feel particularly overshadowed by their older siblings may experience a sense of inferiority. When lastborns do decide to compete with older siblings, Adler argued, they are often successful in later life (Sulloway, 55–56).

Today the two most influential names in Sibling Position Theory are Walter Toman and, more recently, Frank Sulloway. Sibling Position Theory is a subset of Family Systems Theory, seeking to examine the way that we are affected by family birth order. Speaking simplistically, eldest children are expected to carry the greatest responsibility, particularly if they are sons. Youngest children are given the most room to be themselves; children in between must compete for the limited resources that the family has to offer. Natural birth order is not an adequate explanation, however, for we must also look at "functional" birth order—the way that culture, family tradition, and intergenerational life experience and expectations cause one child to be treated one way and another child another. If an older child has mental retardation, the next oldest child may be treated as a firstborn. If a youngest child dies, a middle child may suddenly be treated as a youngest child. A secondborn boy may have place of preference in the family over a firstborn girl. These are all examples of what is called "functional" birth order.

What psychologists once thought to be the "shared family environment" is not really shared. Many environmental factors that are extremely important—age, size, and power, as well as status and privilege within the family—are dissimilar for siblings. For siblings growing up within the same family, nonshared experiences have two general sources. The first source is *chance experiences,* many of which occur outside the family—at school, for example. The second source is *systematic influences,* most of which occur within the family. The concept of "niches" is useful in this regard and describes how individuals develop differing roles within the family system. The concept of niches derives from the field of ecology, where it exemplifies how different species use available resources within their environments. Family niches may be conceptualized in a similar manner. Siblings compete with one another in an effort to secure physical, emotional, and intellectual resources from parents.

Families, then, are best seen as containing an array of diverse niches, each occupied by a different individual and each presenting differing vantage points on life. From these differing perspectives, family members experience the same events differently. Families do share some interests and social values. But siblings differ even in their interests and values, and these differences are caused, in substantial part, by differences in niches within the family (Sulloway, 352). The effect of sibling position, then, is traceable to both nature and nurture.

Applying Family Systems Theory

Family Systems work can be done with one counselee, two counselees, or a whole family. In the published literature, its most frequent application is by one counselor working with more than one counselee, such as two adults in a committed relationship, or a parent and a young adult child. The first task is to establish a therapeutic alliance with *each* member of the couple, called "joining" by Murray Bowen (Framo, 49). Bowen used a specific methodology to secure such an alliance, always beginning his work with the most motivated person in the room (Bowen, 481; Guerin et al., 11).

For example, when working with a husband and wife, Bowen would first converse with the husband and instruct the wife not to interrupt. Once the husband had finished speaking, Bowen would ask the wife to say what she was *thinking* while she was listening, and the husband is instructed not to interrupt. Bowen's request was clearly for the wife's thoughts, rather than her feelings. Bowen believed that a husband and wife already know quite well what each other is feeling; sensitivity to feelings is a basic survival skill in married relationships. But what Bowen was trying to get at is what he called "the person's secret thinking life," believing that while listening, people are remembering issues, responses, entitlements, and behaviors that originated in the family-of-origin era of their life. Sequential, one-on-one listening, then, serves two purposes: for the counselor it reinforces the alliance, and for the listening partner it allows the other person to connect a partner's behavior with the listener's memories and reactions in a way that their source can be explored.

In working with a couple, Bowen was aware that he could easily be co-opted as the third point in a triangle within the counseling room. To offer himself as that third point was an intentional move in the therapeutic process, yet it was equally important that he not get sucked in emotionally to the couple's system. The counselor thus remains "in touch but de-triangled" (Bowen, 481). The counselor can remain detriangled through a variety of techniques, including claiming a firmly observing "I position," and through the use of paradox. Sherman and Fredman explain:

> Paradox is a contradiction that follows correct deduction from consistent premises. The most famous and the most frequently studied and reported is that class known as the "Be Spontaneous Paradox." A command to be spontaneous creates a no-win situation. The person who refuses to act spontaneously remains unspontaneous. Anything that is initiated is only a reaction to the command and hence not spontaneous. (189)

Adler was the first to recognize the importance of using paradox in counseling, calling it the "anti-negative, or spitting in the client's soup." He defined paradox as recognizing the client's strongly held belief or behavior, accepting it, and exaggerating it. For example, Adler might advise the mother of a child who refused to perform to become more inadequate and helpless than the child, thus stimulating the oppositional child to mobilize himself into greater activity. In this way, clients who take a negative position are forced to become more positive in order to remain negative. By joining with the client's negative position, Adler in effect co-opted it. When ministers consider using paradox, they must do so carefully, for used incorrectly it can create more damage than good. When used correctly, however, it is a powerful tool for getting people who are stuck moving again.

The ability of the Family Systems counselor to help is based on three factors: (1) as complete knowledge as possible of the family-of-origin structure out of which the counselee proceeds; (2) the ability to identify and apply relationship patterns in the counselee's background and their effect on the counselee's present function; and (3) the ability of the counselor to involve the counselee in the background investigation and the current analysis. Careseekers must understand that the responsibility to change lies with them alone; they are not responsible for change by anyone else in the past or present system. David Allen remarks: "What they can do is to stop protecting the others in a self-destructive manner" (229). To this end, a Family Systems counselor often assumes an educational role, teaching counselees the basics of Family Systems analysis, how to do research in their multigenerational background, and how to see patterns and develop hypotheses for testing. Murray Bowen actually preferred the term *teacher* rather than *counselor* or *therapist;* Guerin et al. suggest *coach* as an appropriate alternative (129). To reframe the pastor's role automatically reframes the mood and goals of the pastoral relationship, and perhaps the term *guide* is more empowering of counselees than the term *counselor.*

One of the most important sources of information about a counselee is "family stories." The principles of Narrative Counseling Theory will be explored in the next chapter, but here it is important to point out that the two schools of counseling theory do overlap in using the same method of information gathering. As the minister listens attentively to the counselee's stories, a great deal of information can be gleaned; Bowen comments, "One always has an adequate supply of appropriate stories to be used for particular situations" (509).

Related to the use of stories is the use of photographs.

Specific examination of family photographs can yield a wealth of data about the family's developmental history and the relationships of its members to each other. Family cutoffs can be both identified and ameliorated.

The therapist can observe many important behaviors: which pictures were shown first and last; who in the family was left out; how quickly or slowly each picture is presented; how much interest or anxiety is aroused; and how much joking and laughing accompanies the presentation. Pictures can be examined to determine closeness and distance of each family member to others and the general atmosphere of the photographs. Usually, alignments, splits, role behaviors, boundaries, communication processes, and family structures are thrown into sharp relief in this process. Customs, traditions, and special times together often are revealed. (Sherman and Fredman, 20)

The universal appeal of nostalgia and reminiscence makes the family photograph album a helpful instrument for studying the impact of the past on the present.

Systems Theory presumes that many people are present with each of us at all times. Just as Selma Fraiberg spoke of "ghosts in the nursery" (see chapter 3), systems theorist James Framo speaks of the "ghosts" that haunt even the counselor: "Every therapist has personal associations to transactions that occur in family sessions. Along these lines I once wrote a paper on how the ghosts of the therapist's family enter treatment sessions" (56). But while we may be surrounded by an "invisible cloud of witnesses," in the minister's study there may be only one caregiver and one careseeker visible. This does not stop the application of Family Systems Theory, for the name

describes a counseling approach rather than the number of people present. Sherman and Fredman point out that one counselee can form a "strategic alliance" with a counselor, creating a special relationship that can help the counselee redefine his or her place in a larger family system (131–32). Once the counselee has decided to individuate within the system (staying in touch by defecting in place), the counselee's change necessarily causes a reaction in the homeostatic system, which in turn brings other changes.

Other theorists advocate working with whole families at a time, often with three generations present in the counseling room. Framo suggests that sessions with a large number of family members be held over successive weekends, with a two-hour session on Friday night and another on Saturday morning (39). These sessions would include the client him- or herself, carefully prepared and debriefed. When one works with this sort of large-group intensity, one can see what Framo calls the "gut issues" of family life: "profound caring, rejection, dehumanization, shaming, hypocrisy, futility, compassionate sacrifice, disqualification, paralysis of feeling, devotion, disappointment, conspiracies of silence, deep satisfaction, persecution, safety, and the joy of belonging" (69).

Systems work is not a magic cure-all. As in all counseling situations, there are many variables at work over which neither counselor nor counselee/s have control. The homeostatic forces of a system are so great, and a system may be so resistant to change, that sometimes healing can be brought only to one or two people within the system, while the rest remain unrepentant. Eventually both counselor and counselee may come to realize that some parents are emotionally bankrupt and are beyond efforts at reconciliation with the counselee. In such situations, theorist Donald Williamson suggests that "parental rights" be terminated. He states:

> This means that the older parent no longer has any special position or privilege simply because of his historical role as biological and psychological source. Neither duty or obligation is intrinsically required or owed....The adult generation can offer support without assuming emotional responsibility or burden for the welfare, the happiness, or the survival of the aging parents. And this support may be offered "spontaneously" rather than "indebtedly." (Framo, 153–54)

In Systems Theory, parental intimidation of adult children is the ultimate intimidation. When this behavior will not cease, when authority will not be shared in a way that empowers each of the family's generations, a careseeker must be encouraged to get on with life.

Genograms

As mentioned earlier in the chapter, Systems Theory depends on a number of sociometric techniques. Because sociometric instruments involve transferring mental and emotional material onto paper, they offer many advantages, as listed by Sherman and Fredman (71):

1. They move the therapy from an intellectual or emotional discussion to experimental enactment.
2. They place past, present, and anticipated future into a here-and-now operational framework.
3. They contain an important element of personal identification and projection.
4. They expose and dramatize roles and role perceptions.

5. They are surprisingly different from what clients expect in therapy.
6. They are interesting.
7. They constitute a form of metacommunication.
8. They focus attention on the social unit and social interaction process.

Of the several instruments, the genogram is the most commonly used in Family Systems work.

A genogram looks much like a traditional family tree but serves a very different purpose. While the idea of genogram was developed by Murray Bowen, its form was not standardized until relatively recently through the work of Monica McGoldrick and Randy Gerson. A genogram is a visual diagram of family structure that may be used to elicit and identify family patterns. Traditionally, medicine has relied heavily on history-taking as providing 60 to 80 percent of the necessary information for the diagnosis of dysfunctions (Lieberman, 63).

There is no reason to suppose that the genogram contributes any less to the understanding of family pathology. In addition to the information usually plotted on a family tree (names, dates of births, marriage, divorces, and deaths), a genogram also plots the multigenerational history of addictions, affairs, stillbirths and abortions, mental illness or overemotionality, patterns of intimate fusion and distancing, frequent or catastrophic tragedy, family secrets, suicides, cut offs, repeated occupations, abuse, migrations, sexual attitudes and experience, unusual life experience or achievements, the naming of members of one generation after a previous one, intergenerational expectations and disappointments, communication patterns, strategic alliances, the influence of gender roles and stereotypes, the impact of particularly close family friends, and the effect of local and world events such as natural disasters, a stock market crash, and so forth. This material must be available in detail for at least three, and preferably four, successive generations for a genogram to yield patterns. It is not difficult to learn to construct genograms using McGoldrick and Gerson's book, and ministers often learn to use genograms with others by doing their own genogram first, for the analysis of a genogram takes some experience. As Bowen comments: "I believe and teach that the family therapist usually has the very same problems in his own family that are present in families he sees professionally, and that he has a responsibility to define himself in his own family if he is to function adequately in his professional work" (468). Computer programs are now available to help with this analysis, and two sample genograms are attached to the end of this chapter (Appendix B).

Gathering the genogram information is the task of the careseeker and may involve specific research directed by the caregiver. Here is another place at which Family Systems Theory and Narrative Counseling Theory intersect, for in a sense a genogram is a map of family stories. The counselee may have to undertake a "voyage home," as Bowen called it, to do research in areas in which the counselee does not know the family history adequately. In fact, in using genograms in my own counseling practice, I am constantly surprised at how little people know of their own pasts. Once sufficient information has been gathered, the counselor and the counselee sit together to do the analysis. The search for patterns may necessitate further phone calls or visits home by the counselee. A number of people report running into resistance from their families, often because the family is

protecting a secret or hiding its pain or shame.

David Allen's book, *A Family Systems Approach to Individual Psychotherapy* (259–306), provides a great deal of advice about how genogram research can be conducted in an empathic manner that generates support from other family members rather than eliciting anger and disruption.

Understanding Metaphors

Another sociometric technique sometimes used in Family Systems work is called "The Family Floor Plan," a method to chart the relationships among space, place, and emotions. The counselee is asked to draw a floor plan of the house in which he or she spent most of childhood. The counselee then adds the specific family members connected with each room, the emotions that characterized various rooms, which spaces were public and which private, whether there were spaces where the client was never allowed, specific memories connected with each room, and some suggestion of the counselee's relation to the environment outside the house. Counselor and counselee then discuss what has been learned by the drawing.

The most common biblical metaphor for a family is "house." But as the floor-plan exercise would reveal, houses also have internal walls, private spaces, secret spaces, and ghosts. A house may also have a leaky roof, water in the basement, and rot in the flooring. Although the structure of most family houses contains bedrooms, a kitchen, a bathroom, and perhaps recreational rooms, houses have diverse structural designs and very different interior designs. Some houses do not have any closed doors, other have areas that are off limits to the different generations. Some fit the children's activities while others meet the needs of the grandparents. Some have at least one parent home most of the day, whereas others have parents who are barely home at all (Haber, 30). Some rooms are safe, and some are not.

A metaphor is a figure of speech in which a word or phrase that ordinarily applies to one kind of object or idea is applied to another, thus suggesting a likeness or analogy between them. Rosenblatt explains:

> The word "metaphor" originates in Latin and Greek roots that refer to a transfer. Saying "My love is a red, red rose" transfers the meanings of a red rose (beauty, freshness, striking color, delicacy, life, impermanence) to the loved one, thus communicating a richer sense of why the person is loved. To say "My family is a military unit" transfers the meanings associated with military units (rigid hierarchy, strict rules, disciplined activity, inattention to feelings, acting in accordance with roles and statuses rather than individual preferences and desires, arming against enemies) to a family, thus communicating a richer sense of how the speaker's family is experienced. (12)

One problem with metaphors is that while highlighting similarities by analogy, attention is drawn away from uniqueness and from any evidence that contradicts the similarity. Thus describing a family as a "house" draws attention away from the ways family members are dissimilar, the large amount of time in which they do not interact together or are physically distant from each other, the difficulty of meeting individual needs within the family, and the vital importance to each member of connection with people and stimulation outside the family.

Our positive association with houses can also prevent us from seeing that some families, like houses, are places of confinement,

as in the term *house arrest*. Rosenblatt cautions further:

> The metaphor of family as entity obscures the extent to which family members may compete intensely for resources, may have extremely different values and needs, and may experience the family (and much else) differently. . . . To the extent that treating the family as an entity gives greater voice to the family member with the most power, the voices of women and children in a society in which many factors operate to give men more power are muffled or silenced. Moreover, treating the family as an entity creates the illusion of equal participation in family life by women and men, an illusion that hides the extent to which childrearing and other family responsibilities have been much more the work of women than of men.

Thus Rosenblatt, Haber, and others suggest that we should speak of families by using a variety of metaphors, just as in the church we increasingly use a variety of metaphors to describe God, not limiting ourselves any longer only to the metaphor "Father."

Rosenblatt suggests alternative metaphors for family, including "the family as a river" and "the family as an aquarium." Thinking of the family as a river gives one a sense of something that reaches back and extends forward in time, just as the multigenerational transmission system does. But a family that is a river also loses substance as it flows; family members move away, die, or are lost in other ways, and family energy and enthusiasm are dissipated (Rosenblatt, 44). For the family to continue, new members must come into the flow, through birth, adoption, marriage, or some other way, and the family's energy, enthusiasm, time, and resources must be replenished. Like an aquarium, a family contains its members and separates them from the out-side. Like an aquarium, family boundaries contain not only the creatures who belong but also the sustaining medium necessary for life. Some families, however, have boundaries like glass: you can see in and out, but little of worth can actually transpire across the boundary. Rosenblatt extends the metaphor:

> It is not stretching the aquarium metaphor too far to say that a family, like an aquarium, can lose the capacity to sustain its members. . . . Moreover, once family, like an aquarium, becomes hazardous, members may be irreversibly damaged if they are not quickly removed. For example, alcohol addiction, incest, and physical violence may be permanently damaging to family members. (92)

The counselor may wish to combine genograms, narratives, and metaphors, for all fit nicely together. Sherman and Fredman emphasize the richness to be gained through extended exploration of metaphor (14–15):

1. Imagery and metaphor are not bound by the ordinary rules of space, time, and movement.
2. Imagery and metaphor are not bound by the rules of linear logic.
3. Imagery and metaphor are suggestive [of new ideas and solutions].
4. Imagery and metaphor are safe experiences.
5. Imagery and metaphor are empowering and lead to greater self-control.
6. Imagery and metaphor are surprising.

Family Boundaries

Genograms will reveal how much families and family members are affected by internal and external boundaries. Boundaries define psychological space but can be deceptive. As Anderson and Mitchell observe, "In the family with a thick and impenetrable outer boundary, there are usually some very flimsy boundaries between individuals inside" (102). In other words, families that appear from the outside to be unusually close may in fact be the least respectful, or even most abusive, of each other when viewed from inside.

All boundaries are sociocultural constructions (Rosenblatt, 77). One way to think about the metaphor of family boundary is that a family boundary, like a border between two countries, has two sides. Either side could make it difficult for anything or anyone to cross the boundary. The things that establish and maintain family boundaries are called "rules," rules that say who can and should do what, where, how, and with whom. The rules for a family are generally unwritten and derive from both the culture and the family's cumulative experience. R. D. Laing points out that there are even "rules against seeing the rules, and hence against seeing all the issues that arise from complying with, or breaking, them" (106). He illustrates this principle with the equation: "Rule A: Don't. Rule A1: Rule A does not exist. Rule A2: Rule A1 does not exist" (113). Yet a family's rules are constantly challenged and modified through interaction with the outside, through the members' interaction with each other, and through attempts to adapt the rules to new contingencies.

Moreover, the boundary metaphor highlights margins and edges. This will lead the pastor to look away from the scapegoat and toward those who are at the edge of the family, for there one will most likely find, for example, the lost child. The boundary metaphor also highlights interpersonal interactions at the edges of the family, such as the way the family interfaces with neighbors, governments, the schools, the medical system, and so on, for no family exists independent of influences from the environment, social system, and culture that surround it.

Donaldson-Pressman and Pressman have written effectively on "the narcissistic family," that is, the family in which the narcissism of one or both parents overwhelms and distorts the family system. Many cultures of the world are increasingly narcissistic, and the pastor can therefore expect to see more and more narcissistic families within the church.

> In the overtly narcissistic family, there may be no rules at all governing boundary issues such as privacy. Privacy may be a totally unfamiliar concept. People's possessions, time, and very bodies may be the property of a parent, caretaker, or stronger, more powerful sibling. . . . In the covertly narcissistic family, there may be clear rules governing all manner of boundary issues, including physical privacy. The problem, however, is twofold. First, the rules may be broken by the parents as their needs dictate, and second, there are no boundaries in terms of emotional expectations for the child. The children are always expected to meet the parents' needs, but the needs of the children usually are met only by happy coincidence. . . . Children in narcissistic families do not learn how to set boundaries, because it is not in the parents' best interests to teach them. (Donaldson-Pressman and Pressman, 36)

Narcissistic families may have an exaggerated scapegoat who bears the parental frustration at all that life denies them.

Because of the sociocultural construction of gender, men and women may differ in boundary permeability. Such differences can account for tensions between women and men in a family about such things as the appropriate level of self-disclosure of feelings within the family or in relationships with outsiders. Rosenblatt argues that differing gender perceptions of appropriate boundaries prove the impact of the social environment on families:

> Comparisons of boundary permeability between women and men, to the extent that they focus us on gender and not on the context of gender . . . obscure how sexism in the family, community and society may force women to have more permeable boundaries, for example, by allowing them less privacy in the home so that they have no choice about boundary permeability or by more often causing them to feel intense sorrow, frustration and anger, which must be processed in a friendship relationship. (90–91)

A floor plan of a typical American house may prove Rosenblatt's point. Each member of the family has a room of his or her own, but whereas the father will have a basement workshop or a study, the mother will have only the kitchen, which is public, not private, space.

Feminism and Family Systems Theory

Feminist therapists Marianne Walters, Betty Carter, Peggy Papp, and Olga Silverstein understand that "the present paradigms of family therapy are based on the value system of the American family of the forties and fifties and lag sadly behind the social changes already in full swing" (15). It is certainly true that a focus on one family, even a multigenerational one, tends to discourage sensitivity to the issues and impact of heterosexism and classism in patriarchal societies, as in most Western societies, and privileges the advantaged at the expense of the disadvantaged. We now know that in a patriarchal society the traditional family structure significantly disempowers women. The above feminist writers cite the research of Jessie Bernard in her 1972 book, *The Future of Marriage*:

> Bernard documents a considerable body of research that reveals that men gain physically, socially, and psychologically from being married; but this is not true for women, for whom marriage poses a mental health hazard. Married women, as compared with married men or single women, tended to suffer more from inertia, insomnia, nightmares, headaches, dizziness, heart palpitations, and various other pains and ailments. Married men, on the other hand, showed fewer signs of psychological distress than either single men or married women. Despite the fact that men traditionally refer to marriage as "a trap," statistics show that it is twice as advantageous to men as to women in terms of survival. Women start out with developmental advantages that marriage then reverses. (202)

Edwin Friedman helps us remember that every statement also implies its opposite: "blaming cultural factors for the emotional process is one of the most common ways in which family members avoid responsibility for their own contributions and dupe therapists into thinking they are hearing important causal information" (1984, 282).

The pastor who is adopting a Family Systems approach must be careful that sexist values and roles are not simply reversed. For instance, *role complementarity* consigns women to the domestic sphere, a sphere that is always less advantaged than the public sphere, ordinarily dominated by men. Role complementarity positions instru-mental tasks such as earning money through work as the province of males, and expressive or emotional tasks such as nurturing, building and maintaining relationships, and child rearing as the province of females. Counseling work that addresses family roles as revealed in genograms must instead aim for *role symmetry*, in which each gender engages in both instrumental and expressive tasks, in both work and nurturing. This model reflects an egalitarian approach to power between male and female and a more democratic and consensual approach to parental management of children. This is the emerging model of marriage; companionate marriage will be addressed in chapter 4. Family Systems Theory has the capacity to work cooperatively with Feminist Theory (Libow, Raskin, and Caust). In order for this to happen, ministers must be particularly careful to avoid claiming any specific family structure as "normal" or any specific gender role as "natural." The necessary correctives are to understand that cultures and societies affect family roles in powerful and heinous ways, and to address every family as a unique structure whose preferred homeostasis is its own inbuilt definition of normalcy. In this way we can see that traditional family structures and traditional gender roles have as much capacity to be dysfunctional as functional, and that pastoral concerns must always be focused as much on justice as they are on compassion.

Conclusion

Working with multiple individuals is perhaps the most difficult of all pastoral tasks, but systems theory is the easiest and quickest way to understand the dynamics of complex and fused relationships. As cultures and societies change, "the family" becomes increasingly slippery to identify and respond to, yet Family Systems Theory seems to go far in explaining the processes at work in any group of emotionally invested people—whether a nuclear family, an extended family, a blended family, a parish "family," a circle of friends, a congregation, a community, or a corporate institutional "family" such as the church. Triangulation, intergenerational transmission, emotional shock waves, secrets, fusion, differentiation, the way a group "stories" itself, roles, rules, and boundaries—all apply to any group situation in which a sense of belonging is at stake. All these help us understand why a group of people behaves the way it does and how its members respond, and how we as pastoral caregivers are called to live out our ministry responsibly.

When a system is confronted with threat, it will usually defend itself by shutting others out. The system will hide its defenses and dysfunctions, so that pastoral ministry becomes an exercise in futility. But used wisely, Family Systems Theory generates a sense of curiosity and excitement among those involved, causing them to open up so that the pastor may offer new avenues of differentiation, individuation, and Christian wholeness.

BIBLIOGRAPHY

Allen, David. *A Family Systems Approach to Individual Psychotherapy*. Northvale: Jason Aronson, 1988.

Anderson, Herbert, and Kenneth Mitchell. *Leaving Home*. Louisville: Westminster/John Knox, 1993.

Bascue, Loy, and Roy Lewis. "Marital and Family Therapy Skills for Pastoral Therapists." In *Clinical Handbook of Pastoral Counseling,* vol. 1. Robert Wicks, Richard Parsons, and Donald Capps, eds. 267–78. New York: Paulist, 1985.

Borrowdale, Anne. *Reconstructing Family Values*. London: SPCK, 1994.

Bowen, Murray. *Family Therapy in Clinical Practice*. Northvale, N.J.: Jason Aronson, 1985.

Combrinck-Graham, Lee. "A Developmental Model for Family Systems." *Family Process* 24:2 (June 1985): 139–50.

Culbertson, Philip. "Blessing Jacob's Sons, Inheriting Family Myths." *Sewanee Theological Review* 37:1 (Christmas 1993): 52–76.

Dammann, Carrell. "Private Practice." In *Practicing Family Therapy in Diverse Settings*. Michael Berger, Gregory Jurkovic and Associates, eds. 17–44. San Francisco: Jossey-Bass, 1984.

Dicks, Russell L. *Premarital Guidance*. Englewood Cliffs, N.J.: Prentice-Hall, 1963.

Donaldson-Pressman, Stephanie, and Robert M. Pressman. *The Narcissistic Family: Diagnosis and Treatment*. San Francisco: Jossey-Bass, 1994.

"Family Values, Christian Values: A Roundtable Discussion." *The Christian Century* (January 31, 1996): 104–8.

Framo, James. *Family-of-Origin Therapy: An Intergenerational Approach*. New York: Brunner/Mazel, 1992.

Frazier, Shervert. "Psychotrends." *Psychology Today* 27 (January 1, 1994): 32–37, 64, 66.

Friedman, Edwin. "Churches and Synagogues." In *Practicing Family Therapy in Diverse Settings*. Michael Berger, Gregory Jurkovic and Associates, eds. 271–300. San Francisco: Jossey-Bass, 1984.

———. *Generation to Generation: Family Process in Church and Synagogue*. New York: Guilford, 1985.

Furstenberg, Frank, Jr. "The Future of Marriage." *American Demographics* 18 (June 1, 1996): 34–40.

Guerin, Philip, Thomas Fogarty, Leo Fay, and Judith Gilbert Kautto. *Working with Relationship Triangles: The One-Two-Three of Psychotherapy*. New York: Guilford, 1996.

Haber, Russell. *Dimensions of Psychotherapy Supervision: Maps and Means*. New York: W. W. Norton, 1996.

Hay, David. "Mark 3:20–35 from the Perspective of Shame/Honor." *Biblical Theology Bulletin* 17 (1987): 83–87.

L'Engle, Madeleine. "Bones." In *Rattling Those Dry Bones: Women Changing the Church*. June Steffensen Hagen, ed. 16–25. San Diego: LuraMedia, 1995.

Laing, R. D. *The Politics of the Family and Other Essays*. New York: Vintage, 1971.

Laird, Joan. "Women and Ritual in Family Therapy." In *Rituals in Families and Family Therapy*. Evan Imber-Black, Janine Roberts, and Richard Whiting, eds. 331–62. New York: W. W. Norton, 1988.

Libow, Judith, Pamela Raskin, and Barbara Caust. "Feminist and Family Systems Therapy: Are They Irreconcilable?" *American Journal of Family Therapy* 10 (1982): 3–12.

Lieberman, Stuart. "Transgenerational Analysis: The Genogram as a Technique in Family Therapy." *Journal of Family Therapy* 1 (1979): 51–64.

McGoldrick, Monica. *You Can Go Home Again: Reconnecting with Your Family*. New York: W. W. Norton, 1995.

McGoldrick, Monica, and Randy Gerson. *Genograms in Family Assessment*. New York: W. W. Norton, 1985.

Mollenkott, Virginia Ramey. *Sensuous Spirituality: Out from Fundamentalism*. New York: Crossroad, 1992.

Nelson, James B. *Between Two Gardens: Reflections on Sexuality and Religious Experience*. New York: Pilgrim, 1983.

Neufeld, Dietmar. "Eating, Ecstasy, and Exorcism (Mark 3:21)." *Biblical Theology Bulletin* 26:4 (winter 1996): 152–62.

Rosenblatt, Paul. *Metaphors of Family Systems Theory: Toward New Constructions*. New York: Guilford, 1994.

Rudy, Kathy. *Sex and the Church: Gender, Homosexuality, and the Transformation of Christian Ethics*. Boston: Beacon, 1997.

Sherman, Robert, and Norman Fredman. *Handbook of Structured Techniques in Marriage and Family Therapy*. New York: Brunner/Mazel, 1986.

Sulloway, Frank. *Born to Rebel: Birth Order, Family Dynamics, and Creative Lives*. New York: Pantheon, 1996.

Toman, Walter. *Family Therapy and Sibling Position*. Northvale: Jason Aronson, 1993.

Walters, Marianne, Betty Carter, Peggy Papp, and Olga Silverstein. *The Invisible Web: Gender Patterns in Family Relationships*. New York: Guilford, 1988.

Appendix A to Chapter I

"Diverse Forms of Family Mentioned or Implied in the Hebrew and Christian Scriptures," from Virginia Ramey Mollenkott, *Sensuous Spirituality: Out from Fundamentalism* (New York: Crossroad, 1992), 194–97.

1. **Patriarchal** (father-ruled) **extended families** including grandparents, servants, etc.: Abraham's household numbered 318 men, not counting women and children.

Genesis 14:14

2. **Polygamous marriage**: one man with several or many wives and/or concubines and their children.

Deuteronomy 21:15

3. **Monogamous husband and promiscuous wife**: Hosea and Gomer.

Hosea 1–3

4. **Female-headed extended family**: Rahab and her household.

Joshua 6:17, 25

5. **Matrilocal families**: Jacob and Moses lived for long periods with the birth-families of their wives.

Genesis 29–31
Exodus 2:21-22

6. **Single parents** and their children:
a widow and her two sons;
a widow and her resurrected son.

2 Kings 4:1-7
Luke 7:11-12

7. **Levirate marriages**: a man marrying the widow of his deceased brother.

Deuteronomy 25:5-10
Matthew 22:23-27

8. **Families in which the wife clearly held prestige**:
Lappidoth and Deborah, judge of Israel;
Nabal and Abigail, who saved the family by placating King David after Nabal's rudeness;
Shallum and Huldah, a prophet consulted by the King of Judah.

Judges 4:4
1 Samuel 25:2-35

2 Kings 22:14ff.

9. **Monogamous marriage** and the ideal of "one-fleshedness."

Genesis 2:24
Matthew 19:5

10. **Same-sex partnerships**:
Naomi and Ruth, later modified to an extended   Ruth 1:16-17
family in which Naomi was declared the mother
of Ruth's son;

the two disciples on the road to Emmaus, who   Luke 24:29
invited Jesus to "stay with us."

11. **"Trial marriages"**: among the Hebrews,   Exodus 21:8
sex was not prohibited during the betrothal
period, and even at weddings, the major ceremony was the sexual intimacy itself—cf. the
Song of Solomon and the "premarital sex" of
Ruth and Boaz, Ruth 3:7.

12. **Unrelated adults sharing a home**: the   Acts 9:36-39
widows who mourned Dorcas apparently lived
in community.

13. **Related single adults sharing a home**:   Luke 10:38-40
Martha, Mary, and Lazarus: Luke 10:38 indicates
that Martha headed the household.

14. **Celibate singles**: Jesus, John the Baptist,
Paul (?).

15. **Spiritual marriages**: a Christian man and   1 Corinthians 7:36-38
"his virgin" cohabiting except for sexual inti-
macy—an approved practice until the end of
the fourth century.

16. **A "homeless household"**: Jesus.   Matthew 8:20

17. **A Christian commune**: all property was   Acts 4:32
held in common.

18. **An equal-partner, dual-career marriage**:   Acts 18:2-3, 19, 26
Priscilla and Aquila both traveled with Paul, team-
taught the Bible, and were tentmakers by trade.

Additional Forms of Family Mentioned or Implied in the Hebrew and Christian Scriptures, suggested by participants at Families 2000, a conference sponsored by the National Council of Churches of Christ
(Chicago, April 1991).

19. **Immigrant families**:
Joseph to Egypt; family followed. Elimelech,   Genesis 42–46
Naomi, and their sons to Moab.   Ruth 1:1-2

20. **Adoption within the extended family**:
Hadassah (Esther) was adopted by her cousin   Esther 2:15, 20
Mordecai;
Ephraim and Manasseh were adopted by their   Genesis 48:6
grandfather Jacob.

21. **Cross-cultural adoptive family**:
Moses was adopted by Pharaoh's daughter;   Exodus 2:10
believers are adopted into God's family.   Romans 8:14

22. **Cross-class adoptive family**: Eliezer, a   Genesis 15:2-3
slave born in Abraham's household, was adopt-
ed by Abraham.

23. **Women living together in a harem**   Esther 2:3
under the custody of a eunuch.

24. **Cohabitation without marriage**: Sam-   Judges 16:4ff.
son and Delilah.

25. **Marriage in which sexual intimacy   2 Samuel 6:16-23
ceases** because of alienation: King David and
Michal.

26. **Nomad families living in tents** in the
desert:
Jacob's family;   Genesis 25:27 etc.
Israel's forty years of wandering.   Numbers 14:33 etc.

27. **Widow living with her parents**: Orpah   Ruth 1:8, 14-15

28. **Divorced man in second marriage**:   Esther 2:17
King Ahasuerus and Queen Esther, after Vashti
was rejected.

29. **Women married by force**: the daughters   Judges 21
of Shiloh abducted by the Benjamites; and
women taken as the spoils of war.

30. **Surrogate motherhood**:
Hagar bore Ishmael for Abraham and Sarah;   Genesis 16:1-15
Bilhah bore Dan and Naphtali for Jacob and   Genesis 30:1-7
Rachel;
Zilpah bore Gad and Asher for Jacob and Leah.   Genesis 30:9-13

31. **Families established through incest**:   Genesis 19:31-38
Lot's children conceived by his daughters.

32. **Interracial/intercultural marriages**:
Moses married Zipporah of Midian;   Exodus 2:15-21
Esau married two Canaanite wives;   Genesis 27:46
Ruth of Moab married Boaz of Israel;   Ruth 4:9-10
Ahasuerus, King of Medes and Persians, mar-   Esther 2:17
ried Esther, a Jew;
Timothy had a Jewish mother and a Greek   Acts 16:1-3
father.

33. **Childless marriages**: Tamar's to Er and   Genesis 38:6-10
Onan.

34. **Blended families**:
Jepthah was Gilead's son by a harlot; Gilead's   Judges 11:1-3
sons by his wife rejected Jepthah.
Herod Antipas and Herodias (with Salome,   Luke 3:19
Herodias's daughter by her previous marriage).

35. **"Commuter marriages"**:
Peter, traveling with Jesus; his wife and her   Matthew 8:14
mother living at home.
Joanna, wife of Chuza (Herod's steward), travel- Luke 8:3
ing with Jesus.

36. **People with physical or mental disabil-**   Luke 17:12
ities living together.

37. **Younger people caring for elderly**
people:
John and Mary, Jesus' mother;   John 18:15-16
Rufus and his mother.   Romans 16:13

38. **Religiously mixed marriages**.   1 Corinthians 7:12-16

39. **Unrelated people living in an ascetic**   Matthew 19:11-12
religious community, adopting children to
perpetuate community: the Essenes.

40. **Unrelated people traveling with Jesus**,   Luke 8:1-3
supported by several of the women.

Appendix B to Chapter I

"Reading a Genogram" from Monica McGoldrick, *You Can Go Home Again: Reconnecting with Your Family* (New York: W. W. Norton, 1995), 37–38.

Males are drawn as squares, females as circles: male = □   females = ○

Dates of birth and death are written above the person's symbol. Age is shown within the square or circle. Death is indicated by an X through the symbol. Approximate dates are shown with a ? or a ~ (~1898 or ? 1989).

Couples are shown by a line connecting their symbols as follows, with the relevant dates written on the line.

Children are shown left to right, oldest to youngest.

Here is an example of some of the things you can show:

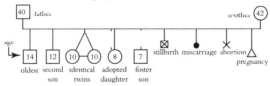

In addition to lines showing kinship, a second set of lines can show emotional relationships between people.

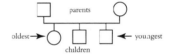

On an actual genogram the relationship lines might look like this:

A serious mental or physical problem is shown by filling in left side of square or circle.   ◧ ◑

Drug or alcohol problems are shown by filling in the bottom half of the square or circle.   ⬒ ◓

Sample Genogram: The Freud Family (from McGoldrick, *You Can Go Home Again*, 164–65)

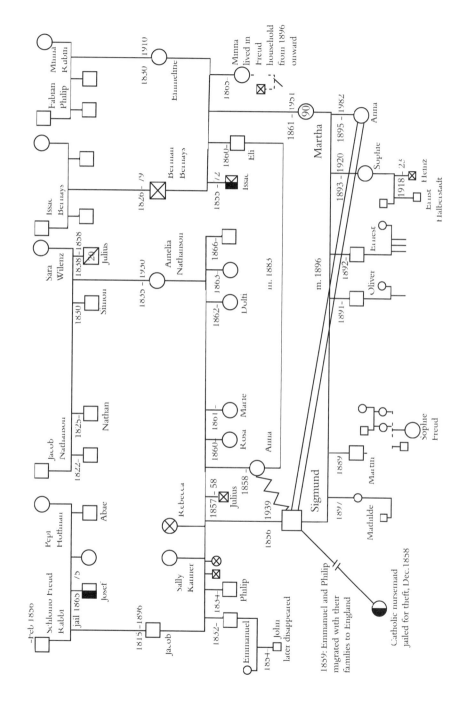

2. Narrative Counseling Theory

"All psychology is either biography or autobiography." (Thomas Szasz)

~

The use of stories in Christian counseling and spiritual direction has become quite popular in the last decade. A host of books have been issued, drawing primarily on the mystical aspects of various religions, which offer readers a series of delightful tales purported to open up the mysteries of faith and the universe. These stories are often unexegeted, as if their meaning were obvious to the reader.

This chapter is not about such stories, not about Sufi tales or rabbinic midrashim or the collected teachings of the Baal Shem Tov, the desert fathers, or Anthony de Mello. These all have their place in tradition and, used carefully, within spiritual direction as well. Their place within serious pastoral counseling is dubious, and hence they must be distinguished from the types of narrative discussed here. This chapter is about the many kinds of narrative which surround our ordinary, everyday life—the stories our families tell us, the stories by which we describe ourselves and what has happened to us in the world, and the complicated but silent scripts we rehearse over and over again inside our heads.

Narrative is not a difficult concept for people today. Prehistoric cave paintings are stories, as are Egyptian hieroglyphics. The alphabets we use began as pictographs, pictures that combined to tell a story. Much interpersonal dialogue is the exchange of stories, and such conversations in extended form are the building blocks for the great works of fictional literature. We are familiar with cinema and television scripts, with characters and unfolding plots, with sitcoms, docudramas, and made-for-TV movies based on "real-life dramas." Nor should narrative be a difficult concept for any Christian, for our faith is built on stories.

The earliest Christian kerygma was shared through storytelling—at first the resurrection story, gradually embellished over time until even the miraculous birth narratives were added. Storytelling remains the primary vehicle for Christian *anamnesis*, that refusal to forget which we celebrate through eucharistic liturgies. Since it was early church custom for elders in the community to preside at the Eucharist, we may presume that Christian tradition conveys a special reverence for the ability of stories told by elders to shape and reaffirm our faith identities. The Christian story is a way in which the faithful are taught who they are supposed to be and how they should live. Story, in the form of witness and proclamation, has been an evangelistic tool to invite those outside to join our family and become renewed by sharing our memories. These are the stories that Tradition and Community tell us, and out of this mix of gospel, kerygma, anamnesis, creedal statements (the Nicene Creed actually has a plot that unfolds), church history, evangelistic narrative, and parish lore, our identity as Christians is formed.

To understand how impossible it is to separate identity from narrative, we need first to analyze and understand the value and classical structure of a story.

The Historical Value of Stories

It might be claimed that human history is simply a collection of stories about what happened to groups of people. Certainly most historians argue that there is no such thing as objective or factual history, but only a variety of interpretations by those present and those who follow. Interpretation allows for subsequent revision as new material comes to light, as is, of course, the case with scientific theory as well. But it is interesting that while even the great minds of human history have appreciated the central role of story in human history, they have not been able to agree on what value stories have or how significant is their impact.

The question "What do stories do?" is one of the great puzzles of our time. Narratologist Dan McAdams offers five different historical answers to that question: stories provide (a) mundane pleasure, (b) sublime pleasure, (c) moral instruction, (d) psychological instruction, or (e) integration (1988, 50–52). In his famous Parable of the Cave (*The Republic*, Book VII), Plato dismissed most stories as mundane pleasure. They are as incapable of carrying important truths as are shadows cast on the wall of a cave. In the nineteenth century, poet Percy Bysshe Shelley understood stories to be a record of the best and happiest moments of the best and happiest minds. Sir Philip Sydney, writing in the last century, emphasized the pedagogical value of stories, which he believed were designed to teach moral truths to the readers. As early as the seventeenth century, John Dryden set forth the claim that in addition to moral truths, stories convey psychological truths. In our own time, such thinkers as Bruno Bettelheim and Claude Lévi-Strauss have argued that stories provide us with an emotional catharsis which in turn leads to personal integration. Their argument is reminiscent of Aristotle (*de Poetica* 1448b): the pleasure of tragedy is

that it teaches us to imitate the ultimate good and then to experience the reward of self-respect when we recognize the results of that good within ourselves. This imitation becomes possible only through the clear depiction of the tragedy that has befallen another, such as "the forms of the lowest animals, and dead bodies." To the insightful, such depictions yield catharsis as opposed to pride, that is, a firmer resolve to rededicate oneself to higher values. All of these answers are contained within the current work on the role of narrative in psychological development, but even these do not exhaust the possibilities we will consider in this chapter.

The Many Types of Stories

The corpus of story literature through the centuries and across many human cultures has yielded an extraordinary range of tales, but some would claim that there are common themes that appear repeatedly and thus function as a means of classifying the variety into more narrow channels. The foundational classification comes from Kluckholn and Murray: every story is (a) like all other stories, (b) like some other story, and (c) like no other story. Yale literary critic Northrop Frye reduced all stories to four archetypal forms: comedy, romance, tragedy, and irony. Lawrence Elsbree provides a different taxonomy of five forms: stories about establishing or consecrating a home, stories about engaging in a contest or fighting a battle, stories about taking a journey, stories about enduring suffering, and stories about pursuing personal fulfillment, or consummation. Of course some stories combine various themes, and in general, the more sophisticated a story, the more themes it will weave together.

The Structure of a Simple Story

Even the simplest story has an identifiable set of basic characteristics, often referred to as its "narrative grammar." These characteristics include the setting, the characters, the initiating event, the attempt, the consequence, the reaction, the catharsis, and the denouement (McAdams 1993, 25–28). To illustrate how these characteristics function in a familiar story, we can apply them to the children's story usually known in German as "Little Red Cap" and in English as "Little Red Riding Hood." The story appears here in its first published English translation, of 1845, from the tales of the Brothers Grimm (Sutton, 83-101).

1. Setting

2. Characters (Red Cap, Grandmother, Mother, Wolf, Huntsman)

There was once upon a time a sweet little maid who was beloved by every one who saw her; but she was loved most of all by her grandmother, who knew not what to give her, she was so fond of her. Once she presented her with a cap of red velvet, and, as it became her so well, and she hardly ever wore any other afterwards, she was called by everybody, *Little Red Cap*.

3. Initiating Event (mother's request: "take this cake")

Her mother said to her one day, "Come, Red Cap, here are a piece of cake and a flask of wine, carry them to your grandmother; she is ill and weak, and they will help to make her strong; and be sure you behave yourself prettily and civilly, and salute her kindly from me; take care too that you walk on in an orderly way, and run not off the road, else you will fall and break the glass, and then your grandmother will get nothing."

4. Response / Attempt (she obeys)

Red Cap said, "All that I will do quite right," and she kissed her mother and set off on her journey.

5. Consequence (meets wolf on the way)

Now her grandmother's house was in the middle of a wood, some miles distant from the village where Red Cap's mother lived; and just when Red Cap had got to the wood the wolf came up to her: but Red Cap did not know what a wicked animal he was, so she was not at all afraid of him.

"Good day to you, Little Red Cap," said he.

"Many thanks to you, Mr. Wolf," answered the little maid.

"And where are you going so early in the morning, Red Cap?"

"To my grandmother."

"What are you carrying under your apron, Red Cap?"

"Wine and cake, for my sick grandmother; we baked the cakes yesterday, that they might be nice and firm."

6. Reaction (reveals to wolf where grandma lives)

"But, Red Cap, where does your grandmother live?"

"A good way farther on, in the wood," answered the little maid. "There you will see the house, and you may know it by the tall tree which grows up to the chimney-top."

7. Conflict of Intention (Red wants to carry cakes; wolf wants to eat her)

When he heard this, the wolf said to himself, "This nice young maid will be a sweet morsel for me, if I can only catch her." But he was afraid to touch her just then, lest the woodcutters or the hunters should see him;

so he thought of a scheme. He went on a little way by Red Cap's side, and talked to her again. "Red Cap, only look at these beautiful flowers which grow all about in the wood. Why don't you look round you? I believe, too, you are not listening to the birds as they sing so sweetly. You walk along just as if you were going to school; and yet it is pleasant out here, in the wood!"

Red Cap raised her eyes, and when she saw how the bright sun darted his rays here and there through the trees, and how beautifully the flowers bloomed all around her, she thought to herself, "Ah! if I could bring a nosegay to my grandmother—this would indeed please her much; it is still early, and I shall be sure to get there by the right time." So she set down her cakes and wine, sprang into the wood, and sought all about for the prettiest flowers. And when she had pulled one, it seemed as if there was a still prettier one beyond it; so she ran and ran, first after one and then after another, farther and deeper into the wood.

But the wolf went as straight as his legs would carry him to the grandmother's house, and tapped at the door.

"Who is there?" said she.

"Little Red Cap," answered he. "I have brought you some cakes and a flask of wine. Open the door to me."

"Pull the latch," cried the grandmother. "I am ill, and cannot get up." The wolf pulled the latch, and without speaking a word, went straight to the bed, and swallowed the poor grandmother up. Then he took her clothes and put them on, placed her great cap on his head, and lay down in the bed and drew the curtains before it.

Red Cap all this time was running about gathering flowers in the wood, and looking at the little birds which were perched upon the bushes around her; and when she had got as many in her lap as she could carry, she remembered her grandmother, and hastened back to the road.

8. Crisis/Catharsis (recognizes the trick)
When she got to the house she could not help wondering that the door stood open, and when she came into the room, everything seemed so strange that she said to herself, "Oh dear, how dull I feel to-day, when before I used to be so glad with my grandmother!" Then she went to the bed and drew back the curtains, and there was her grandmother (as she thought), with her cap pulled deep over her face and looking so strange. "Ah, grandmother, what great ears you have!"

"That is that I may hear you better, child."

"Ah, grandmother, what large eyes you have!"

"That is to see you the better."

"Ah, grandmother, what great hands you have!"

"That is that I may lay hold of you the better."

"Ah, grandmother, what a dreadfully large mouth you have!"

"That is that I may the better eat you."

9. Denouement (solves the problem)
And as the wolf said these words he sprang out of the bed upon poor little Red Cap, and was opening his mouth to eat her up, when, behold, an arrow shot him through the body, and he fell dead at her feet.

A huntsman had been going by; and when he saw the door of the old grandmother's cottage standing open, he thought he would look in and see what was the matter. So he slipped in quietly behind the door, and heard all that the wolf said to Red Cap; and just when he saw that he was about to devour her, he aimed an arrow at the wicked animal and killed him; so little Red Cap was saved.

10. Moral/Lesson/Interpretation

The good huntsman then led her home to her mother, and she told him all the story by the way; and as he left her at the door, he said to her, "See that you never run away from the road again, all your life, nor do what your mother has forbidden you."

Multiple Endings, Multiple Meanings

The reader may be uncomfortable with the moralistic ending here of "Little Red Riding Hood." That reader would be in good company, for by tracking the story's ending, we see the ways in which it has been adapted to meet both cultural and personal needs down through history. The next English translation, in 1853, has no parental moral attached, but simply leaves grandma, Red Cap, and the wolf all dead from the hunter's gun (in the original German version, Red Cap and her grandmother are rescued from the wolf's stomach). In the Brothers Grimm version, Red Cap finds her own way home and voluntarily decides to be more heedful of her mother's suggestions in the future; in the first English version, she seems too thick to find her way home, so that the woodsman has to lead her and then leave her with a strict warning about defying authority. Sutton comments:

> The English version would thus seem to adopt a different approach to the learning processes of children. It suggests that children are not able to draw their own conclusions from their experiences . . . but need to have the correct attitudes incul-

cated into them by adult authority figures. Only when children have been repeatedly subjected to the rational and moral admonitions of grown-ups, only then are they deemed capable of learning and internalizing the important lessons in life. (101)

In James Finn Garner's *Politically Correct Bedtime Stories,* grandma cuts off the woodsman's head and sets up an "alternative household based on mutual respect and cooperation" with her granddaughter and the wolf (4).

By way of this simple exercise, we can see that even the most traditional stories, even from the most traditional societies, are malleable and may be employed by the narrator or storyteller to convey a widely divergent set of messages.

We might understand that the ending of a story is malleable because the body of the story itself is open to being interpreted in a variety of ways. I first learned this while tucking my son into bed one night. He asked for a bedtime story, and since I had been doing academic research on the literary structure of parables from classical Hellenism, the Bible, and rabbinic literature, I began by telling him a classic fable from Aesop. But instead of adding the usual "moral" of the story—the pithy little attachment by which Aesop cued his listeners to draw a particular lesson from the tale—I asked Jacob to tell me what lesson the story was meant to teach. As I'd anticipated, he came up with a completely different lesson from what Aesop had pointed to and could even justify his conclusion from clues inside the story.

In general, that multiple and even conflicting meanings can be drawn from a single story is known as "reader" or "listener response theory." Bandler and Grinder use the illustration of a simple sentence, "My father scares me" (1979, 68). For one listener, this may mean that his father put a loaded .38 to his head. For someone else it may simply mean that his father walked through the living room and didn't say anything! This same principle should be familiar to students of the Bible. For example, one of the great works of St. Augustine is his commentary on Genesis 1, in which he identifies nine different meanings to each verse of that chapter and explains why each possible interpretation is equally valid. We come, then, to one of the most basic theories of narrative psychology: that the meaning of any utterance is in what is heard—or in the response that the utterance generates—and not within the intentions of the author or storyteller from whom the utterance originates. No matter how clear or well-intentioned, neither the storyteller nor the preacher has any control over what is heard, and what is heard is, bottom line, the truest meaning.

Metaphors, Axioms, and Nuclear Stories

Stories exist within cultures in other, less recognizable forms than the classic one just described. A metaphor may establish a storyline, and what is called "unpacking a metaphor" is in certain respects much like laying out the kinds of story that are entailed by the metaphor (Schafer 1992, 32). An axiom functions in the same way. For example, the caution "There's no use crying over spilled milk" implies a setting (perhaps a kitchen or a breakfast table), a cast of characters (one who spills and cries and one who observes), an initiating event (the need to assuage thirst), an attempt (to pour the milk or to pick up the glass), a

consequence (the milk is spilled), a reaction (someone bursts into tears), and perhaps a catharsis and a denouement. So even such short sayings can be unpacked to produce a simple but satisfying narrative, but as well, they often imply moral judgments, values, warnings, and behavioral expectations.

These truncated stories also produce varying reactions in their listeners. "There's no use crying over spilled milk" will have agglutinated memories attached to it for many people. Perhaps we heard our mother say that at breakfast, and we can suddenly remember the setting or hear her voice. Perhaps someone said it in another context to absolve us for an accident we were feeling guilty about, and so we hear in it a note of forgiveness. The same sentence can mean caution or comfort, depending on a complex set of variables. We must then approach stories we hear in counseling not by asking "What does this story mean?" but "What does this story do?"

The theory set forth thus far is necessary background to understanding the three different classes of stories that shape human identity. The three are Family Narratives (the stories all families tell about their past, themselves, and us as we are born into them); Self-Identifying Narratives (the stories we tell out loud about who we understand ourselves to be and what has happened to us during the course of our lifetime); and Intersubjective Narratives (the stories and scripts we silently construct and rehearse in our heads all day long). Each of the three will be explained in detail.

FAMILY NARRATIVES

The three classes of narrative comprise a relatively new counseling field sometimes known as "personology," a holistic term emphasizing coherence of the many narrative selves of one individual. Dan McAdams explains:

> Historically grounded in the writings of Henry A. Murray, personology has traditionally emphasized the study of the *whole person* in his or her sociohistorical context. In addition, personologists have traditionally adopted *biographical* approaches to the study of human lives and have often focused their inquiries upon fundamental human *motives*. (1988, 20)

Every family is littered with interesting stories about its past. We both grow up with family stories and are shaped by family stories. Some stories are told and retold; other stories exert their power inside the family by never being told. We are still products of the effect these stories produce, even when we have little recollection of them. Elizabeth Stone observes: "All of us, long after we've left our original families, keep at least some of these stories with us, and they continue to matter, but sometimes in new ways. . . . We are always in conversation with them, one way or another. . . . They can, along with other powerful cultural archetypes, maybe from fiction or film, serve as our role models and guides" (8).

Why Families Tell Stories

Family stories are always a mix of healthy stories and unhealthy stories, the latter usually referred to as "family myths." Healthy narratives, even when they involve an element of fantasy, encourage a sense of belonging through common ownership of the stories. By providing this matrix of shared meaning, they define family boundaries, making clear who belongs to "us" and to whom we belong. They create a sense of homeostasis, or equilibrium, for they artic-ulate our family's values and beliefs and our sense of connectedness with our familial and cultural past history. They also make life easier, alleviating us of some of the many decisions which we must make in the course of a day. As John Byng-Hall points out, "The family script can provide routines for family life which can be followed almost automatically. Imagine having to negotiate every action without familiar pathways—we would never get beyond breakfast!" (1995, 3). In general, healthy family narratives are rooted in a traceable historical accuracy. They should never be rigid or imprisoning. They are gentle and humorous, thus allowing for human frailty by not demanding that people live up to unrealistic expectations.

Among the first psychotheorists to identify the negative power of stories within family systems was Antonio Ferreira. In his seminal 1963 article, Ferreira defined "family myths" as

> beliefs shared by all family members, concerning each other and their mutual position in the family life. . . . In terms of the family inner image, the family myth refers to the identified roles of its members. . . . The individual family member may know, and often does, that much of that image is false and represents no more than a sort of official party line. But such knowledge, when [and if] it exists, is kept so private and concealed that the individual will actually fight against its public revelation. . . . For the family myth "explains" the behavior of the individuals in the family while it hides its motives. (457–58)

Why should a family hold on to a myth regardless of its truth? First, for most family members, these are not myths but reality. We become convinced that this is the way things are supposed to be within any family unit. Second, these myths are useful to the individual members of the family. They define each person's role, the family expectations for success or failure (relieving individual members from having to take responsibility for their own fate), avoid conflict by establishing clear lines of authority and nonnegotiable rules, and even predict the future!

Ferreira and Stone refer to family stories as "family myths because, like classical myths, they are meant to explain *why*—why the flood covered the earth, why the desert is parched, why my Aunt Naomi wound up spending half of her life locked up with only half a brain in her head, why my father annually tried to drink and drug himself into oblivion" (Stone, 98–99). In folklore terms, these are etiological tales. Like both myth and epic, the concern of family stories is not factual truth, though most members of the family believe them to be true at least on a grand scale.

Helm Stierlin defines the two functions that family myths fulfill as being "defensive functions" and "protective functions."

> *Defensive functions* come into play when the family members collusively distort their shared family reality—i.e., when they, in their attempt to ward off pain and conflict, obscure, deny, or rationalize what they do or do not do, and did or did not do, to each other. . . . *Protective functions* of myths, in contrast, operate on the level of the family's relations with outsiders. . . . In order that they may serve family members to defend themselves successfully against an awareness of what they do and did to each other, myths often need to be sold to, and accepted by, the outside world. (118)

Family myths are a form of authoritative discourse, a narrative style that holds so much power over the family that we might say it creates the family rather than the family creating it. Family myths tend to close off present possibilities; as Heilbrun, describing how literary biographies actually dictate the way we think of their subjects, says: "biography has made certain facts unthinkable" (29). As well, family myths close off future possibilities, for they are always a rehearsal for the beliefs and values of generations to come.

The Family as an Interpretive Community

Every family has a major stake in perpetuating itself, and in order to do so, it must unrelentingly push the institutions that preserve it—the institution of marriage especially, but also the institution of heterosexual romantic love, which, if all goes the way the family would have it go, culminates in marriage, children, and enhanced family stability. "Behavior that threatens family stability or continuity—sexuality that gets out of hand or illegitimacy that brings an unknown bloodline into the family—has to be censured" (Stone, 150). In this way, a family becomes a social unit that shares interpretive strategies, in other words, an interpretive community. A commonality of interpretation creates the sense of belonging or family loyalty. As Stanley Fish explains:

> How can any one of us know whether or not he is a member of the same interpretive community as any other of us? . . . The only 'proof' of membership is fellowship, the nod of recognition from someone in the same community, someone who says to you what neither of us could ever prove to a third party: "we know." (173)

The nature of an interpretive community is to encourage conformity to the community's particular hermeneutic. Members will necessarily agree with each other in the long run in order to maintain the community's purposes and goals, even if they are unstated. Interpretive communities can tolerate some difference of opinion, as long as the community's unity is not threatened. According to Michael White and David Epston, approaching a family hermeneutic as a systemic interpretive method,

> rather than proposing that some underlying structure or dysfunction in the family determines the behavior and interactions of family members, would propose that it is the meaning that members attribute to events that determines their behavior. (3)

In other words, the family's unstated but identifiable hermeneutic strategy, determined by its values and sense of purpose, precedes, and thus determines, individual behavior within the family.

The family interpretive community constantly monitors new developments to determine whether they are a threat to the accepted family narrative. Cross-referencing between the family script and what is currently happening enables any significant divergence from the norm to be spotted. Family scripts can then operate automatically with a minimum of fuss (Byng-Hall 1995, 68). Elizabeth Stone suggests that many families have a resident "switchboard and arbitrator," someone who delivers messages within the family and shapes communication in order to defuse family tensions or remind the family of its narrative resources (165–66). When the family is presented with some stimulus or crisis with which it has no prior experience, however, the family is likely to go on "high alert" and will search through its narrative to discover whether there are any forgotten tools to help it defend the challenge to its homeostasis. Sometimes the adequate tools cannot be found within the accepted narrative. This is particularly likely to happen in situations where some past experience was so painful that conscious access to it as a potential solution is blocked. In such cases, a family is likely to retreat deeply into a deceptive fantasy, or to dissolve.

Types of Family Narrative

Ferreira, Stierlin, and Byng-Hall each offer different taxonomies to explain the several types of family narrative. For Ferreira, family myths reflect either a theme of unhappiness ("someone needs to rescue one or more of our members because we do not have the internal resources to solve family problems on our own"), or a theme of happiness ("we must cling to the belief that all is well, no matter the evidence to the contrary") (57). In either case, the myth inhibits creative solutions or the reestablishment of a more healthy family myth. Stierlin divides defensive family myths into three categories (119–21). *Myths of Family Harmony* maintain a public front of togetherness, family harmony, and happiness. These myths can be maintained only by throwing contrary perceptions into what George Orwell, in *1984*, called "memory holes." *Myths of Exculpation and Redemption* are constructed around the joint memory of what a certain person, inside or outside the family, living or dead, did or did not do to the family. Inside a family, such a person may be termed "the black sheep" or "the skeleton in the closet." Accounts are drawn up, blame and fault are assigned, and the possibility of reconciliation is prematurely foreclosed.

Myths of Salvation claim that a family can be rescued from pain, conflict, injustice, and suffering by some omnipotent figure or agency. In such a family one might hear the plaintive cry, "If your father were alive, he'd know what to do," or "Our problems will disappear just as soon as we win the lottery."

John Byng-Hall organizes family narratives, both positive and negative, into five categories (1995, 144–46):

1. *Family yarns or tales.* They are told for fun, often by a particular member of the family, such as the grandfather. These yarns give permission to fantasize—to play with a variety of potential images. Heroes are often preposterously larger than life and as a result are always just about to step on a banana skin, which may indeed provide the punch line to the stories.

2. *Fables or cover stories.* Occasionally whole episodes are fabricated and presented as truth. Most commonly this is done quite consciously, for example, to explain away a father's absence in prison. A psychotic or demented member of the family may also start up a story that joins the mythology.

3. *Family secrets.* An important way of ensuring that a story is told and retold, this time in private, is to make it a secret. The secret ultimately may become that the secret is no longer a secret. Even "real" secrets, because they cannot be openly explored, become bathed in fantasy or become reenacted unwittingly.

4. *Recalled events.* Some events are recounted, often in response to an inquiry, in a way that shows that a real struggle for accuracy is going on. Supporting evidence is sought. Other people are asked for their recollections; photos and old letters are brought out. This represents the family's attempt to discover what historians call historical actuality. Although the final account will inevitably still be colored, the aim is to inform not to indoctrinate, and so these should not be included in family mythology (insofar as that term is understood negatively). They provide the building blocks of a healthy family history.

5. *Family legends.* These stories, again often based on some event, are deliberately and openly told and retold down the generations because they contain important messages about how the family should or should not behave and how it should see itself. These are presented as true, but are nevertheless edited and reedited by each generation.

Many of the above categories become more attractive to a family as they devolve, through repetition, from complex phenomena into simple cause-and-effect tales. Family stories do not easily encompass intricate analyses or explanations of the many causes for an event. But at least they offer possible, if not always plausible, explanations that can be adroit solutions to our anxieties. Family stories offer simple, one-dimensional causes, and in so doing, allow us to put a fence around the event, releasing us from our preoccupation with it so we can move on with the business of living (Stone, 98–99).

Rituals are another important part of the family's inherited narrative. Family rites of passage such as baptisms, marriages, and funerals are not only the common occasion for sharing and reclaiming the family's narratives, but often create new narratives to complement what has already become tradition. As well, birthdays and holidays have particular foods, rules, sequences, and gender roles attached to them that are as firmly implanted as are family myths.

Secrets and Cognitive Dissonance

In 1988, John Bowlby published a classic essay entitled "On Knowing What You Are Not Supposed to Know and Feeling What You Are Not Supposed to Feel" (1988, 99–118). Bowlby described children who have witnessed a suicide of a parent, but are then told by the surviving parent that he or she died of some other cause. The example is given of a girl who found her father hanging, but was told he was killed in a car accident. In the case of children of alcoholics, the explanation "Daddy just has a touch of the flu today" creates a discrepancy between what the children know and what they are told to "know." Similarly, abused children are often told that the abuse did not happen. Bowlby describes how this process of imposed denial leads to two contradictory models of the same event. He argues that the child involved is likely to identify with the actions held in the memory, even if he or she has been taught an overlaying set of beliefs. When the child becomes a parent there is a possibility of reenacting something from a past episode while believing or doing and saying something quite different. For example, a sexually abused child may grow up to be an abuser of children and yet remain in deep denial.

The incongruency between what one experiences sensorily and what one is told or taught to believe is called "cognitive dissonance." Family rules, family myths, and secrets often inhibit the confronting of the mismatch between belief and action. Michael Goldberg, citing Herbert Fingarette's study *Self-Deception*, points out that "the person engaged in self-deceptive practices will try to develop an elaborate 'cover-story' to protect him from having to 'spell out' what he has in fact been doing, of hav-ing to face up to life" (103–4). The same principle holds true for family units. Self-deception is a form of anesthetic for families in trouble, but the long-term consequences for its individual members are extremely serious, as Bowlby's essay shows.

A family will attempt to render its self-deceptive myth in a manner as internally consistent and natural as possible. Whenever inconsistencies between belief and action or event and explanation occur, the family will draw upon its wells of ingenuity to elaborate its myth and to protect its plausibility. The tactic is transparent in the counseling process: there will also be some feature of family life that is persistently avoided or kept secret. Self-deception becomes a policy, even more than a strategy, in such families. What is missing within the familial unit is the courage to address the dissonance and the creativity to discover how to approach the family's dilemma without at the same time destroying it.

Characteristics of Family Scripts

A narrative gets played out in a family because a "script" has developed around it. A plot sequence, a cast of characters, and an anticipated end to the drama all create a script that a family can then play out over and over again, even when it knows that the end of the drama is disastrous and emotionally abusive. The propensity to run the same script repeatedly is a form of Freudian repetition compulsion. Marital scripts and couple scripts are subsets of family scripts, but they function in the same manner.

John Byng-Hall identifies seven types of family scripts (1995).

1. *The Intergenerational Script:* A script that operates vertically between more than two generations.

2. *The Transgenerational Script:* A script that operates horizontally, either between a couple or a couple and their children. The elements are usually inherited from grandparents, but the grandparents are no longer present as players in the script, as they would be in an Intergenerational Script.

3. *The Replicative Script:* A scenario learned in childhood by someone who is now adult, but continues to be played out. The pastor should label these positively, as demonstrating loyalty to the family of origin.

4. *The Corrective Script:* A reaction script, attempting to behave in a manner opposite from childhood patterns. It can be given a positive frame by pointing out to parents, for example, that they are struggling to provide a better experience for their children than their parents provided for them.

5. *The Improvisational Script:* A scriptless script, played out by a family faced with events or crisis it does not have the repertoire to deal with.

6. *The Innovative Script:* An intentional attempt to try new things. Sometimes the innovative script is the result of new approaches discovered during an improvisational script. It can be reframed through compliments about the couple's courage in exploring the unknown.

7. *The Problem-Solving Script:* Of particular interest to the minister, for problem-solving scripts often reveal the basic dysfunction of the couple. Many such scripts are the result of a family's being caught between two choices (a dilemma) instead of seeing three alternatives (a choice).

Individual scripts are usually generated from childhood experience, and then within marriage, interwoven or merged with the scripts of the other partner. Because they are formed in childhood, scripts contain values, beliefs, and behavior patterns from generations past. A mature adult learns to process these scripts in "the theater of the mind," but not to play them out within relationships. This makes them more problematic, for mental scripts are not visible; they can be detected only by the results they create.

A script demands that its cast of characters play roles, and here Narrative may overlap with Family Systems Theory. Roles denote typecasting, and family members both volunteer unconsciously for these roles and are drafted into them. Will Campbell describes roles in his family of origin, and how "normal" they come to appear for the various cast members who play out the narratives:

> By role, designation, category and assignment Joe was the worker. I was the sickly one and therefore something of a drone. Sister was just that—Sister. Daughter with three brothers and thus special. Paul was the baby. We lived that way and if those categories and designations and roles seemed unfair to any of us we never discussed it. That's who each one was. One did not ponder identity. Everyone knew and understood, without being told. Without asking questions. *This* is who I am. *That* is who you are. The question, "Who am I?" need not, and did not, come up. That's the way we lived. (11)

Byng-Hall offers a taxonomy of family roles (1995, 138). "Ideal images" are the behaviors toward which each person strives or is pressured by other family members to adopt. "Disowned or repudiated images" are those behaviors and attitudes which are prohibited and disapproved of in others or denied in oneself, even if they can be observed by others. Often the one playing this role is called "the scapegoat." "Consensus role images" are those about which there is unchallenged agreement, as in Will Campbell's description. The family myth represents the final compromise between each individual's need to be seen in a particular light and the evidence that it is not the whole story. The bargain is often, "I won't point out your bad points so long as you leave me in peace." As a general rule, children who are heavily scripted when young carry those scripts into adulthood and continue to play them out unless there has been some sort of therapeutic intervention.

How We Learn to Share Scripts

Katherine Nelson studied children in order to learn how scripts get interwoven, merged, and renegotiated verbally. In her study, a group of children between ages three and eight who did not know one another were given a shared task to accomplish and their behavior was observed and analyzed. For example, two girls were given the task of buying a snack together. They spent a considerable amount of time finding out what each other's scripts for snacks were. They shared stories about meals and snacks, reminiscing about past outings and what they had had to eat. Once each knew what the other meant by the word *snack,* they ran out to buy one together.

The same sorts of negotiation occur regularly in the early years of marriage and family-building, and they occur when people are conversing cross-culturally. Those who do not develop shared scripts are usually isolated socially. Obviously, it is beneficial to all members of a family to find ways to share scripts with the others, in order to avoid isolation and to assure themselves of their membership within the familial interpretive community.

Reshaping Family Scripts in Counseling

In attempting to bring health to family narratives, a two-pronged counseling approach is recommended: identifying and analyzing family myths, and assisting the family to reedit scripts and narratives through improvisation.

Family myths and scripts can be identified and analyzed only if they are broken down into the smallest possible component parts. Byng-Hall suggests that the family be encouraged to identify a typically dysfunctional narrative or paradigmatic family script (1995, 5). This he terms a "scenario." Since scenarios often begin as attempts at a solution, they should be talked through sufficiently to discover what problem they were designed to address and how they have now outlived their usefulness. Often "problem-solving" scenarios, when repeated over and over in a destructive manner, come to feed upon the predictable disastrous outcome. Unraveling them should help release the hold they have on people.

The genogram is of particular assistance in identifying family myths. (On how to construct and analyze genograms for use in pastoral counseling, see the previous chapter; see also McGoldrick and Gerson, and Scarf, chaps. 2–4.) The genogram should be drawn on a large enough piece of paper that intergenerational narratives can be added to it. Such a genogram is usually begun by the third or fourth counseling session, and often grandparents are invited to join in its construction. Stories added to the genogram can be traced from generation to generation in order to see how they have functioned over time, and how they have been edited to meet changing circumstances. The grandparents may take particular care to ensure that the grandchildren are imbued with the "correct" version of the family narratives; this in turn will often reveal how values and rules have become rigid across generations.

The second therapeutic approach involves the reediting process, perhaps with a particular emphasis on improvisation. Improvisation should not be confused with reframing, which is more appropriate in treating self-defining narratives than family narratives.

Family narratives are by definition flexible, because they must be adapted slightly from generation to generation to retain their holding power as circumstances, contexts, and relationships change. The mutability of a myth can sometimes be tested by observing the way children in the family use it. "The reaction of the children usually gives the game away. A particular look comes over their eyes as they hear a story for the umpteenth time. . . . It can be interesting to ask one of the children to finish the story. This will frequently reveal some differences, showing already how reediting can occur between each generation" (Byng-Hall 1979, 115). This reediting involves some degree of improvisation and innovation by family members, laying the ground for the sort of work the pastor needs to do to help break the myth's hold on the family. The extent of reediting and adaptation will always be naturally limited, however, by the family unit's drive toward homeostasis and continuity. Many narrative theorists believe that the course of human development should be traced not via the standard Eriksonian stages of development, but by following the manner in which a narrative changes over the course of time. For example, the way I tell the story of my relationship with my father will be different at age five, age fifteen, age thirty, and age

fifty. This mutation is the true measure of my personal human development. The human developmental course can be traced by alternating periods of stability and instability in the way any myth is kept alive.

A further influence on the life history of a narrative is the reaction it generates. Narratives used confidently inside the family may produce a quite different reaction outside the family, such as when one gets married. The new spouse's response to a familiar family narrative will influence the way it is told in the future. Affirmation by the new spouse will cause the narrative to become more retrenched. Disinterest, dismay, or disgust by the new spouse may cause the myth to be altered or, more dangerously, to go underground where it still exerts influence on the new relationship but is less easy to identify. Reactions may be delivered verbally and consciously, or nonverbally and unconsciously.

The counselor's task in working with the family is to encourage sufficient fluidity in the family narrative that humor is restored and individual uniqueness given room. Primary clinical questions might be, "Of which narrative is this scenario a part?" "What purpose does this narrative serve in the family?" "How much editing can the narrative stand without destroying the family's sense of continuity with the past?" "Who is the person in the system with the greatest investment in retaining the rigidity of the narrative?" "Who is the person in the system with the greatest investment in exploring the improvisational possibilities within the narrative?"

Once a family has begun to identify its historic pattern of editing the narrative, the counselor can encourage improvisation with the narrative. New narrative strategies can then be incorporated, with therapeutic assistance, into the family narrative by repeating them often enough that they gain power to compete with the old narratives or myths. Again, the use of a story genogram and the involvement of grandparents would seem to be indispensable tools in the shift toward healthier family narratives.

SELF-DEFINING NARRATIVES

Some narrative therapists take the approach, as described above, that human identity is molded by the stories we inherit that create us and that we tend to repeat compulsively throughout our adult lives. Our narrative selves are the product, not the source, of the story we live out. Alternatively, other narrative therapists take a more constructionist approach, that while we are born into a family narrative, adolescent individuation means taking responsibility for constructing narratives by which we choose to identify ourselves. Roy Schafer explains:

> Although the person may be a repetitive and largely preprogrammed author, he or she cannot be that entirely, for there is no one program to be applied to everything identically. The person must select and organize in order to construe reality in one adaptive way or another or one maladaptive way or another. . . . An author of existence is someone who constructs experience. (1992, 23)

The individual thus becomes an agent or an actor in his or her own right within the larger family narrative.

The Product of Others' Words

We are born as storytellers who as yet have no stories. When we are born, we enter stories that began without us—the story of our parents' own childhood and adolescence in their families of origin, the story of our parents' marriage, the story of their anticipation over our arrival, and, for many, the story of our parents' adjustment to the children who preceded us. In other words, we are born into the midst of ongoing intergenerational and transgenerational stories that are a part of a family system—a new actor in an old family script.

At first we learn to tell imitative stories; as the audience for our family's stories, we listen and soon begin to mimic as best we can. In the meantime, we are learning other names and stories. Our parents are like casting directors, and may even go so far as to suggest that we imitate some person from generations before or embody our parents' dreams. Our parents teach us to name external objects, relationships, emotions, and moral values; if we did not have parents, we would not easily learn to name any of those things. Our parents give us their own stories and the stories of others: the books they read to us at night, the television shows they watch with us. We learn that there is a right way to tell a story and a wrong way: the right way is that which gives us a sense of belonging to the family and which generates responses of approval and security. We begin the extended process of merging our version of the stories we have inherited with the family, the community, and the culture around us, until we get the results we want. All these stories develop in tandem with the unfolding family narratives, for, in Erikson's terms, we are psychosocial—both psychologically and socially alive.

Gradually, as our senses of individuation and subjectivity mature, we begin to learn to tell our own stories, putting family stories to our personal uses, including rewriting the endings. Ralph Waldo Emerson put it hauntingly: ". . . History is an impertinence and an injury, if it be anything more than a cheerful apologue or parable of my being and becoming" (40). We tire of being only the product of the stories we are told and seek to "individuate," to establish our own identity, all the while cherishing a certain continuity with our past. Some part of our identity will remain irrevocably the product of the stories told us in our childhood about who we have been and who we are destined (or expected) to become. Russian literary theorist M. M. Bakhtin has pointed out how extensively every human being is the product of others' words: "I live in a world of others' words. And my entire life is an orientation in this world, a reaction to others' words, beginning with my assimilation of them (in the process of initial mastery of speech) and ending with assimilation of the wealth of human culture" (1986, 143). The words of others tell us whether we are good or bad, welcome or unwelcome in the world, the careers we may choose, the family's expectations about the way we should relate to other men and other women.

Eventually we come of age and tell the story of our own lives, making the past our prologue. We become our own person and, in so doing, make choices about rearranging and reediting, rejecting and reincorporating the stories we have inherited. We *will* ourselves to become our own person. We learn to say to our families, usually beginning in adolescence, "I am a part of you and/but I am my own person." To make our own meaning out of our myriad stories is to achieve balance—at once a way to be part of and apart from our families, a way of both holding on and letting go. We begin to

ask, "Why am I telling this story *this* way right now? What would it mean if I told it differently? Am I telling this story in a way that will lead me to greater integration and self-health, or in a way leading away from greater integration and self-health?" The will to individuation marks the transition from the absolute determinism of the self as the product of others' words to assuming mastery over one's own destiny. Bakhtin calls it "life as authoring" (Kozulin, 338). As Brett Webb-Mitchell points out, "*Who* we are will help decide *what* we will do, and *how* we do what we do in this world" (221).

Limitations on the Self-Defining Narrative

Even as we move into a more structured self-defining narrative, we are still working within restrictions. In his book *The Doors of Perception*, Aldous Huxley observes that as we learn a language, we become the heirs of the wisdom of people who have gone before us. At the same time, we also become victims. Of that infinite set of experiences we might have had, certain ones are given names, labeled with words, and thereby incorporated into our identity. Unlabeled experiences and perceptions intrude less often into our consciousness. The restrictions are not only the result of the particular family we are born into, or the language we are taught to speak, but also of the particular culture whose definitions and expectations we bear.

Teaching cross-culturally for the last several years, I have learned how deeply affected each person is by the culture in which he or she is raised. Many indigenous South Pacific cultures do not allow one to have sexual dreams. In Tongan culture, one is allowed only to dream dreams that can be interpreted as prophecy. In Santa Yisabel culture, only the wisest woman in the village is allowed to dream at all. Similarly, cultures teach us what we can wish for and which emotions one is allowed to feel. John Byng-Hall suggests that no matter how powerful our particular family myths and narratives may be, the cultural mythology is even stronger (1995, 58). Because of a society's drive to maintain a workable harmony, meanings at all levels of narrative must be congruent and so support and maintain each other. Culture and society mediate our choice of symbolization and limit our arbitrariness, all in turn restricting the possibilities in constructing a self-identifying narrative.

Self-narratives are also limited by what is termed "narrative bias." Ross and Conway list three major problems within people's remembering their own past: (1) selective recall, that is, the censoring of the stories or details we choose to remember (a logical extension of the Freudian concepts of suppression and repression); (2) reinterpretation and reexplanation of the past, or the tailoring of stories in order to fit the needs of the present moment or to incorporate new information and even wishful thinking; and (3) the filling of gaps in the memory by inferring what probably happened ("truth as the way it ought to have been"). In such a view, every author of a self-defining narrative may be regarded as a "personal historian." Greenwald even pictured the self as a "totalitarian" historian who—as occurs with recorded history in Orwell's *1984*—constantly "refabricates" the story of his or her personal past. In addition to the narrative biases already mentioned, memory problems are in turn shaped by the three types of "cognitive biases" that make people revise their own history, "thereby engaging in practices *not* ordinarily admired by historians": (1) egocentricity (the self perceived

as more central to events than it is), (2) benefitance (the self perceived as selectively responsible for desired, but not for undesired, outcomes), and (3) conservatism (the self resistant to change) (Greenwald, 604).

As we construct our identities through narrative, we confer upon certain experiences in our lives a salience or centrality that denotes that they are very, very special. These incidents may be highly positive or negative. They may mark perceived transformations of self—identity turning points—or they may affirm perceived continuity and sameness. They may involve things we did or things that were done to us. They may entail private moments or shared experience with an entire community. But not everything is selected for retention in our memories. The structuring of a narrative requires recourse to a selective process in which we prune, from our experience, those events that do not fit with the dominant evolving stories that we and others have about us. Thus, over time and of necessity, much of our stock of lived experience goes unstoried and is never "told" or expressed. It remains amorphous, without organization and without shape (White and Epston, 11–12). Those things which lie unstoried are the raw materials by way of which reframing becomes possible. When persons experience problems for which they seek pastoral support, these vital aspects of their lived experience that contradict the dominant narrative may be restoried to provide new insight and opportunity.

Framing

To frame, in technical terminology, means to construct a sustaining personal narrative. Like family narratives, self-defining narratives are structured around a story line tracing heroic successes, failures succumbed to or averted, archetypes and icons, rules, assumptions and introjects, stereotypes and iconoclasms, and an extremely individualized cause-and-effect chain. Not only do we, as humans, give meaning to our experience by "storying" our lives, but we are also empowered to "perform" our stories through our knowledge of them. Stories can, of course, be liabilities as well as assets. For instance, most of us have a multiplicity of stories available to us about ourselves, others, and our relationships. Some of these stories promote competence and wellness. Others serve to constrain, trivialize, disqualify, or otherwise pathologize ourselves, others, and our relationships. Since we live so much of our self-identifying narrative unconsciously, the caregiver's first task is to make the unconscious conscious. This process demands a certain element of reflective praxis and seasoned maturity. The framing process therefore seems best suited for use with men and women in their late thirties to late forties or beyond, when they are at the stage of life that Daniel Levinson calls "Becoming One's Own Man" (60).

In his book *The Stories We Live By*, psychologist Dan McAdams suggests a seven-step process by which a careseeker may be assisted in denominating the component parts of his or her self-defining narrative (1993, 256–64). McAdams believes that this process can be used effectively by any caring listener, not simply by those trained in psychotherapy:

STEP ONE: The interview begins with a general question about *life chapters*:

> I would like you to begin by thinking about your life as if it were a book. Each part of your life composes a chapter in the book. Certainly, the book is unfinished at this point; still, it probably already con-

tains a few interesting and well-defined chapters. Please divide your life into its major chapters and briefly describe each chapter. You may have as many or as few chapters as you like, but I would suggest dividing it into at least two or three chapters and at most about seven or eight. Think of this as a general table of contents for your book. Give each chapter a name and describe the overall contents of each chapter. Discuss briefly what makes for a transition from one chapter to the next. This first part of the interview can expand forever, but I would urge you to keep it relatively brief, say, within thirty to forty-five minutes. Therefore, you don't want to tell me "the whole story" here. Just give me a sense of the story's outline—the major chapters in your life.

The life-chapters question enables the storyteller, the careseeker, to provide his or her life with an organizing narrative framework. Most people organize their life chapters in a quasi-chronological manner, with earliest chapters linked to childhood. For others, a thematic organization seems to work better. They may have a chapter on relationships, another on school and work, and so on. Both the listening caregiver and the storyteller should pay careful attention to the kind of language employed in this opening exercise, as a clue to personally meaningful images, symbols, and metaphors.

STEP TWO: The second section of the interview moves from the general to the specific by asking the storyteller to describe in great details eight *key events* in his or her story:

> I am going to ask you about eight key events. A key event should be a specific happening, a critical incident, a significant episode in your past set in a particular time and place. It is helpful to think of

such an event as constituting a specific moment in your life that stands out for some reason. . . . These are particular moments in a particular time and place, complete with particular characters, actions, thoughts, and feelings [a happy summer or a tough year in high school would not qualify, for they take place over an extended period of time]. . . . For each event, describe in detail what happened, where you were, who was involved, what you did, and what you were thinking and feeling in the event. Also, try to convey the impact this key event has had in your life story and what this event says about who you are or were as a person. Did this event change you in any way? If so, in what way? Please be very specific here.

The eight key events are

1. *Peak experience*: A high point in the life story; the most wonderful moment of your life.

2. *Nadir experience*: A low point in the life story; the worst moment in your life.

3. *Turning point*: An episode wherein you underwent a significant change in your understanding of yourself. It is not necessary that you comprehended the turning point as a turning point when it in fact happened. What is important is that now, in retrospect, you see the event as a turning point, or at minimum as symbolizing a significant change in your life.

4. *Earliest memory*: One of the earliest memories you have of an event that is complete with setting, scene, characters, feelings, and thoughts. This does not have to seem like an especially important memory. Its one virtue is that it is early.

5. *An important childhood memory*: Any memory from your childhood, positive or negative, that stands out today.

6. *An important adolescent memory*: Any memory from your teenage years that stands out today. Again, it can be either positive or negative.

7. *An important adult memory*: A memory, positive or negative, that stands out from age twenty-one onward.

8. *Other important memory*: One other particular event from your past that stands out. It may be from long ago or recent times. It may be positive or negative.

This second exercise is explicitly directive on purpose. People are most articulate and insightful when talking about particular, concrete episodes in their lives. By contrast, discussions of general trends and abstract formulations are rarely as vivid or revealing of personality or identity. In doing this step, one must struggle to comprehend the significance of the particular movement in the encompassing pattern of one's overall life narrative. At the same time, one must be ready to entertain different and conflicting meanings of the same episode. One should also pay attention to the absence of the obvious, with the caregiver asking, for example, "Why does the death of your father *not* stand out as the worst thing that ever happened in your life?"

STEP THREE: The interview moves from key events to *significant people*:

> Every person's life story is populated by a few significant people who have a major impact on the narrative. These may include, but not be limited to, parents, children, siblings, spouses, lovers, friends, teachers, coworkers, and mentors. I want you to describe *four* of the most important people in your life story. At least one of these should be a person to whom you are not related. Please specify the kind of relationship you had or have with each person and the specific way he or she has had an impact on your life story. After describing each of these, tell me about any particular heroes or heroines you have in your life.

STEP FOUR: After spending a considerable amount of time on the past and the present, the interview now moves to the *future script:*

> As your life story extends into the future, what might be the script or plan for what is to happen next in your life? I would like you to describe your overall plan, outline, or dream for your own future. Most of us have plans or dreams that concern what we would like to get out of life and what we would like to put into the future. These dreams or plans provide our lives with goals, interests, hopes, aspirations, and wishes. . . . Describe your present dream, plan, or outline for the future. Also, tell me how, if at all, your dream, plan, or outline enables you (1) to be creative in the future and (2) to make a contribution to others.

It will be noted that step four pays particular attention to transitions, just as Daniel Levinson's schema of the development stages of a male's life also places great emphasis on transition. The storyteller should be encouraged to identify where the story is going, and how it will get there from here.

STEP FIVE: The fifth section pertains to *stresses and problems:*

> All life stories include significant conflicts, unresolved issues, problems to be solved, and periods of great stress. . . . Please describe *two* areas in your life where at present you are experiencing at least one of the following: significant stress, a major conflict, or a difficult problem or challenge that must be addressed. For each of the two, describe the nature of the stress, problem, or conflict in some detail, outlining the source of the concern, a brief history of its development, and your plan, if you have one, for dealing with the future.

STEP SIX: Moving now toward the conclusion of the framing exercise, it is important to consider *personal ideology:*

> Now I will ask you a few questions about your fundamental beliefs and values. Please give some thought to each of these questions and answer each with as much detail as you can. (1) Do you believe in the existence of some kind of God, deity, or force that reigns over or in some way influences or organizes the universe? Explain. (2) Please describe in a nutshell your religious beliefs. (3) In what ways, if any, are your beliefs different from those held by most of the people you know? (4) Please describe how your religious beliefs have changed over time. Have you experienced any periods of rapid change in your religious beliefs? Explain. (5) Do you have a particular political orientation? Explain. (6) What is the most important value in human living? Explain. (7) What else can you tell me that would help me understand your most fundamental beliefs and values about life and the world?

The framing process concludes with STEP SEVEN: The last section of the process asks you to take stock of what you have said by entertaining an overall *life theme:*

> Looking back over your entire life story as a book with chapters, episodes, and characters, can you discern a central theme, message, or idea that runs throughout the text? What is the major theme of your life? Explain.

The framing of the details of one's self-defining personal myth, or coherent life narrative, is a search for "narrative intelligibility" (Cohler, 557) and is a necessary process prior to "reframing," the next process of changing one's personal myth as an option for greater health and personal integration.

Reframing the Self-Defining Narrative

The counseling literature offers at least three different therapeutic techniques for reframing. Robert Brizee gives this basic definition of reframing:

> We are constantly revising our interpretations of our past events. The event cannot change, but the interpretations can—and do. Often far beyond our own awareness, we are modifying, reshaping, reframing, and reunderstanding our past. We put new frames and matting around old pictures and they look different. . . . It might be likened to a series of pictures sent back to earth from an ascending rocket, each one giving us a new perspective on that increasingly tiny point where a person stands. The point remains the same, but the context is constantly changing. (79–80)

Possibly the two most famous methods of reframing are suggested by Richard Bandler and John Grinder. The first method is outlined in chapter 3 of their book *Frogs into Princes*, and while too technical to detail here, is certainly worth the reader's exploring independently. Bandler and Grinder's second method of reframing is described in the book *ReFraming: Neuro-Linguistic Programming and the Transformation of Meaning*. They distinguish between a "meaning change" and a "context change." In the meaning change, a client's behavior is not inherently bad, but the meaning she attaches to that behavior needs to be changed to the positive. Beginning with the question "What else could this behavior mean?" they provide the following example of a meaning change:

> One day in a workshop, Leslie Cameron-Bandler was working with a woman who had a compulsive behavior—she was a clean-freak. She was a person who even dusted light bulbs! The rest of her family could function pretty well with everything the mother did except for her attempts to care for the carpet. She spent a lot of her time trying to get people not to walk on it, because they left footprints—not mud and dirt, just dents in the pile of the rug. . . . When this particular woman looked down at the carpet and saw a footprint on it, . . . she would rush off to get the vacuum cleaner and vacuum the carpet immediately.
>
> What Leslie did with this woman is this: she said "I want you to close your eyes and see your carpet, and see that there is not a single footprint on it anywhere. It's clean and fluffy—not a mark anywhere." . . . Then Leslie said *"And realize fully that it means you are totally alone, and that the people you care for and love are nowhere around."* The woman's expression shifted radically, and she felt terrible! Then Leslie said, "Now, put a few footprints there and look at those footprints and know that the people you care most about in the world are nearby." And then, of course, [the woman] felt good again. (1982, 5–6)

A context change is necessary to put narratives or behavior into a more positive context. Byng-Hall does that when he relabels a replicative script from "repetition compulsion" to "loyalty to the family of origin." Every experience in the world and every behavior is appropriate, given some particular context, some particular frame. In one context, repeated behavior is compulsively inappropriate; in another context, it may comfort parents that their children have not lost touch with the value system within which they were raised. Beginning with the question "In what context would this particular behavior that the person is complaining about have value?" Bandler and Grinder offer the following example of a context change:

> Virginia [Satir] was working with a family. The father was a banker who was professionally stuffy. . . . The wife was an extreme placater, in Virginia's terminology. . . . The daughter was an interesting combination of the parents. She thought her father was the bad person and her mother was the groovy person, so she always sided with her mother. However, she *acted* like her father.
>
> The father's complaint in the session was that the mother hadn't done a very good job of raising the daughter, because the daughter was so stubborn. At one time when he made this complaint, Virginia interrupted what was going on. She turned around and looked at the father and said, "You're a man who has gotten ahead in your life. Is this true? . . . So you have some tenacity, don't you?"
>
> "Yes."
>
> "Well, there is a part of you that has allowed you to be able to get where you are, and to be a good banker. And sometimes you have to refuse people things that you would like to be able to give them, because you know if you did, something bad would happen later on."
>
> "Yes."
>
> "Well, there's a part of you that's been stubborn enough to really protect yourself in very important ways."
>
> "Well, yes. But, you know, you can't let this kind of thing get out of control."
>
> "Now I want you to turn and look at your daughter, and to realize beyond a doubt that you've taught her how to be stubborn and how to stand up for herself, and that is something priceless. This gift that you've given to her is something that can't be bought, and it's something that may save her life. Imagine how valuable that will be when your daughter goes out

on a date with a man who has bad intentions." (1982, 8–9)

Yet a different approach to reframing is suggested by Michael White and David Epston. They seek for what they call "unique outcomes," aspects of lived experience that have not already been incorporated into the client's self-defining narrative. They "include the whole gamut of events, feelings, intentions, thoughts, actions, etc., that have a historical, present, or future location and that cannot be accommodated by the dominant story" (16). Once these unique outcomes have been identified, counselees can be invited to ascribe meaning to them. Success in this ascription of meaning requires that the unique outcomes be plotted into a reshaped self-defining narrative.

A third but closely related approach to reframing is suggested by John Byng-Hall (1995, 77). When a typical family scenario has occurred between counseling sessions, he begins the next session by asking each person present to identify anything "new" in the way they acted out the familiar script. Once one of those present has discovered some new behavior or response, even if it only be the slightest departure from the well-worn script, Byng-Hall then builds on that new response to bring about a change in the old script and to offer a renewed sense of hope.

Those counselees who can grasp that there is some sort of connection between their problem and the past, and although unclear as to its nature are intrigued by it, are likely to be able to reframe their self-defining narrative much more easily. With them the minister can then choose, when working short-term, to ignore the history or, if her skill is in using history, she can choose to use the careseeker's insight into his or her past to help change the present. In this way reframing becomes an effective tool for both pastors and families.

INTERSUBJECTIVE NARRATIVES

The first class of narrative psychology or "personology" that we examined is the family narrative. The second class of personology is the self-defining narrative. There is a third class that can be termed "intersubjective narratives." It is not significantly different from Object Relations Theory as explained in the following chapter, but in order to complete the whole picture of personology in this chapter, a few remarks are necessary.

In the family narrative, past and present generations are the storytellers. In the self-defining narrative, the individual as a whole person is understood to be the storyteller, attempting to construct a sustaining and integrated narrative about him- or herself. In the intersubjective narrative, the analytic task is more complex. Roy Schafer asks this riddle:

> How many selves and how many types of self are stated or implied in the following account?
>
> A male analysand says to his analyst: "I told my friend that whenever I catch myself exaggerating, I bombard myself with reproaches that I never tell the truth about myself, so that I end up feeling rotten inside, and even though I tell myself to cut it out, that there is more to me than that, that it is important for me to be truthful, I keep dumping on myself."
> (1992, 25)

Carl Jung and many others have described human beings as "a collection of selves." If our internal or intersubjective dialogue is capable of keeping track of so many different selves, how are they all generated and why are there so many? And *who* is the storyteller from which each self originates as a distinct unit with its own script and plot?

The idea of an intersubjective model of external reality, by which we rehearse various alternative behaviors and reactions before they arise, was first proposed in 1943 by Craik in his book *The Nature of Explanation*. Craik hypothesized that an individual is likely to deal with the present and the future in a much "fuller, safer, and more competent manner" if possible actions have been tested out in his or her own head before responding. One bridge between Craik's theories and classical Object Relations Theory is John Bowlby's study *Attachment and Loss*. Bowlby described mental representations of relationships that enable a child to make predictions about the parent's (or attachment figure's) likely behavior so that he or she can feel secure in the knowledge that the parent will be available when needed. The child would also rehearse his or her own repertoire of actions that would "hook" the parent into providing the attention the child desired. In later life, patterns of rehearsal are transferred from attachment figures to the many other relationships that make up our adult network.

The protagonist in these various internal dramas is one of the several selves constructed by "the narrative person," the internal storyteller who generates the many selves inside each of us. To rehearse reactions is to construct a plot, consistent with the components of the classical story line, such as setting, characters, plot, initiating event, and so on. These intersubjective narratives can be played with, improvised within, and rewritten before they are acted out, or even before they become part of one's self-defining narrative.

The Development of the Intersubjective Narrative

"In identity, life gives birth to art and then imitates it. We create stories, and we live according to narrative assumptions." (McAdams, 1988, ix)

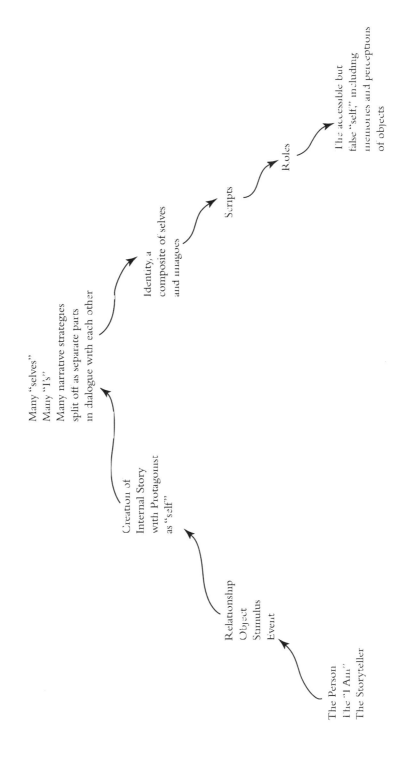

The Person
The "I Am"
The Storyteller

Relationship
Object
Stimulus
Event

Creation of
Internal Story
with Protagonist
as "self"

Many "selves"
Many "I's"
Many narrative strategies
split off as separate parts
in dialogue with each other

Identity, a
composite of selves
and images

Scripts

Roles

The accessible but
false "self," including
memories and perceptions
of objects

As John Byng-Hall explains:

> One of the advantages of the concept of a working model is that it takes into account the various active experimental maneuvers that the mind takes in planning some future event based on knowledge of what has happened in the past. It is not just a preset program—like computer software. The idea of a "working" model also implies something that can be built up and experimented with in the mind by imagining the possible effect of trying different ways of relating to people, and then putting some of the more promising ideas into practice; it is a tool for finding a way that works. (1995, 64–65)

ADDRESSING NARRATIVES IN COUNSELING

Coherence is not the usual characteristic of family narratives, self-defining narratives, or intersubjective narratives, yet without some degree of coherence, a family or individual often becomes paralyzed by conflicting narratives and self-contradictory scripts. As Roy Schafer puts it, "People entering psychoanalysis do not tell the kind of life-historical stories that would be desirable either for purposes of maximum intelligibility or followability or for purposes of facilitating change. For one thing, their spontaneous or rehearsed initial accounts prove, on close inspection, to include gaps, contradictions, ambiguities, fragments of heterogeneous psychological theories, and bewildering actions and reactions" (1981, 37). The development of a coherent life story then becomes a major goal in narrative counseling.

Both narratives and identity serve multiple functions, but their primary function has been identified by Bruno Bettelheim and Claude Lévi-Strauss as "integration," or the putting together of disparate parts into a cohesive and sustaining whole. From the point of view of narrative psychology, we might then say that those who present for counseling do so because their narratives do not match either their affective or their lived experience, or because there are significant aspects of their emotional or behavioral history that contradict the dominant narrative they are attempting to maintain. The diagnosis, therefore, might be termed "narrative dissonance," a condition parallel to cognitive dissonance. Sir Laurens van der Post states the problem plainly: "Human beings can live without food, more than without meaning. . . . When a man possesses his story, he has all he needs for survival; but if he loses his story, he's in peril" (Simpkinson, 34).

Developmental theorist Erik Erikson describes the final task of the human life cycle to be the achievement of "ego integrity" as opposed to despair. Erikson, like Carl Jung and any number of other psychotheorists, believed that without a sense of integration beginning in midlife, one could not survive later life with any sense of self-worth, dignity, and satisfaction. In other words, creating a healthy, sustaining, integrated personal narrative is what adulthood is about. In his classic study *Young Man Luther,* Erikson writes:

> To be adult means among other things to see one's own life in continuous perspective, both in retrospect and prospect. By accepting some definition as to who he is, usually on the basis of a function in an economy, a place in the sequence of generations, and a status in the structure of society, the adult is able to selectively reconstruct his past in such a way that, step for step, it seems to have planned him, or better, he seems to have planned

it. In this sense, psychologically we do choose our parents, our family history, and the history of our kings, heroes, and gods. By making them our own, we maneuver ourselves into the inner position of proprietors, of creators. (111–12)

Making a narrative consciously one's own is the process of integration. Integration will necessitate being aware of the Wholeness Wheel (chapter 1), so that all aspects of the human personality are incorporated into an integrated personology.

Because each of us lives in the midst of three different types of narrative—family, self-defining, and intersubjective—the construction of an integrated narrative necessitates a three-pronged approach by caregivers, as follows:

Family Narratives	History of the narratives via a genogram; emphasis on improvisation and innovation.
Self-Defining Narratives	Narratives need to be first framed, and then reframed.
Intersubjective Narratives	Externalization and personification.

Of course, most pastoral counselors will not have the opportunity to work therapeutically with counselees long enough to unpack all three types of narrative. But because integration is not only the goal but also a natural human drive, it can be expected that change in one type of narrative will normally produce changes for the better in the other two types of personal narrative. Narrative or personological treatment may be considered to have been effective as the storyteller constructs a narrative that is coherent, empathic, generative, and secure.

Conclusion

The personological approach is relatively easily mastered by pastoral counselors and works well across cultures and between genders. Cross-culturally, many nonwhite cultures are storytelling cultures, so that the basic materials will feel familiar to the counselee, even though the analytic tools may be unfamiliar. Dan McAdams provides an important caution, however:

Concepts such as "maturity" and "healthy development" are shaped by cultural assumptions that we rarely call into question. Most of us, as middle- or upper-middle-class citizens of a Western democracy, tend to believe that mature adults should shoulder some responsibility for their own lives, work as well as play, assume productive roles in society, strive for psychological autonomy and financial independence, prepare their children for the challenges of modern life, and so on. As a society, we tend to value freedom, autonomy, mastery, and responsible commitment among adults. Our beliefs concerning how people should and do shape their lives in their twenties and thirties are guided by these values. Views of adult development are likely to be very different in other societies, however. (1993, 96–97)

Counselors using this approach need to make every effort to comprehend the basic values of the counselee's culture before undertaking any sort of pastoral intervention.

Elizabeth Stone claims that women are the storytellers in any culture (19–20). Mothers and daughters tell stories as they are making the bed or folding the laundry together. Women tell each other stories over coffee or, in other societies, while preparing food or hauling water. But as Carolyn Heilbrun points out, women's stories are almost always told in private, and rarely in public (46–47). Therefore a pastor should be aware that a woman's telling her story publicly in the effort to achieve coherence may be a somewhat uncomfortable activity and perhaps produce highly emotional responses. Men's strength may be telling their story publicly; certainly we are aware of a whole raft of short-story literature by men such as O. Henry, Joel Chandler Harris, and Edgar Allan Poe. Perhaps it is true that both men and women are skilled storytellers, though in the manner of telling and the accompanying affective response, the minister needs to be aware of significant gender differences.

The Christian and Jewish traditions are almost impossible to imagine without the powerful influence of narrative. Indeed, a very early rabbinic commentary on the book of Deuteronomy (*Sifre Devarim* 49 to Deut. 11:22) connects God's acts of creation with the art of storytelling: "If you wish to recognize The-One-Who-Spoke-and-the-World-Came-Into-Being, study the literature of stories, for there you will recognize Him . . . and cleave to His ways." Constructing a coherent and integrated personal narrative is not an act of narcissism, but an *imitatio dei*. By "selectively reconstructing our past," as Erikson puts it, we attain the status of "creator." We "create" a self that is whole and purposeful because it is embedded in a coherent and meaningful story. As adults, we impose an integrated narrative structure on our lives where no narrative existed before. We create a coherent narrative so that our lives, and the lives of others, will make sense. Through story we determine who we were, who we are, and who we may become in the future.

BIBLIOGRAPHY

Bakhtin, Mikhail Mikhailovich. *The Dialogic Imagination: Four Essays.* Michael Holquist, ed. Caryl Emerson and Michael Holquist, trans. Austin: University of Texas Press, 1981.

———. *Speech Genres and Other Late Essays.* Caryl Emerson and Michael Holquist, eds. Austin: University of Texas Press, 1986.

Bandler, Richard, and John Grinder. *Frogs into Princes: Neuro-Linguistic Programming.* Moab, Utah: Real People, 1979.

———. *ReFraming: Neuro-Linguistic Programming and the Transformation of Meaning.* Moab, Utah: Real People, 1982.

Bowlby, John. *Attachment and Loss.* Vol. 1: *Attachment.* London: Hogarth, 1969, 2d ed., 1982.

———. *A Secure Base: Clinical Applications of Attachment Theory.* London: Routledge, 1988.

Brizee, Robert. *The Gift of Listening.* St. Louis: Chalice, 1993.

Byng-Hall, John. "Re-editing Family Mythology during Family Therapy." *Journal of Family Therapy* 1 (1979): 103–16.

———. *Rewriting Family Scripts: Improvisation and Systems Change.* New York: Guilford, 1995.

Campbell, Will. *Brother to a Dragonfly*. New York: Seabury, 1977.

Cohler, Bertram. "The Human Studies and the Life History: The *Social Science Review* Lecture." *Social Service Review* 62 (1988): 552–75.

Craik, K. J. W. *The Nature of Explanation*. Cambridge: Cambridge University Press, 1943.

Elsbree, Lawrence. *The Rituals of Life: Patterns in Narratives*. Port Washington, N.Y.: Kennikat, 1982.

Emerson, Ralph Waldo. "Self-Reliance." In *Essays: First and Second Series*. New York: First Vintage, 1990.

Erikson, Erik. *Young Man Luther: A Study in Psychoanalysis and History*. New York: W. W. Norton, 1958.

Ferreira, Antonio J. "Family Myth and Homeostasis." *Archives of General Psychiatry* 9 (November 1963): l, 55–61 [457–63].

Fish, Stanley. *Is There a Text in This Class? The Authority of Interpretive Communities*. Cambridge: Harvard University Press, 1980.

Frye, Northrop. *Anatomy of Criticism*. Princeton: Princeton University Press, 1957.

Garner, James Finn. *Politically Correct Bedtime Stories*. New York: Macmillan, 1994.

Goldberg, Michael. *Theology and Narrative: A Critical Introduction*. Philadelphia: Trinity Press International, 1991.

Greenwald, Anthony G. "The Totalitarian Ego: Fabrication and Revision of Personal History." *American Psychologist* 35 (1980): 603–18.

Heilbrun, Carolyn. *Writing a Woman's Life*. New York: Ballantine, 1988.

Huxley, Aldous. *The Doors of Perception*. New York: Harper and Row, 1963.

Kluckholn, Clyde, and Henry Alexander Murray. *Personality in Nature, Society, and Culture*. New York: Alfred Knopf, 1953.

Kozulin, Alex. "Life as Authoring: The Humanistic Tradition in Russian Psychology." *New Ideas in Psychology* 9:3 (1991): 335–51.

Levinson, Daniel. *The Seasons of a Man's Life*. New York: Ballantine, 1978.

McAdams, Dan P. *Power, Intimacy and the Life Story: Personologial Inquiries into Identity*. New York: Guilford, 1988.

———. *The Stories We Live By: Personal Myths and the Making of the Self*. New York: William Morrow, 1993.

McAdams, Dan, and Richard Ochberg, eds. *Psychobiography and Life Narratives*. Durham: Duke University Press, 1988.

McGoldrick, Monica, and Randy Gerson. *Genograms in Family Assessment*. New York: W. W. Norton, 1985.

Nelson, Katherine. "The Ontogeny of Memory for Real Events." In *Remembering Reconsidered*. U. Neisser and E. Winograd, eds. 244–76. Cambridge: Cambridge Univer-sity Press, 1988.

Ross, Michael, and Michael Conway. "Remembering One's Own Past: The Construction of Personal Histories." In *Handbook of Motivation and Cognition*. R. M. Sorrentino and E. T. Higgins, eds. 122–44. Chichester: John Wiley, 1986.

Scarf, Maggie. *Intimate Partners: Patterns in Love and Marriage*. New York: Ballantine, 1987.

Schafer, Roy. *Narrative Actions in Psycho-analysis*. Worcester, Mass.: Clark University Press, 1981.

———. *Retelling a Life: Narration and Dialogue in Psychoanalysis*. New York: Basic, 1992.

Simpkinson, Anne. "The Instinctive Life: An Interview with Sir Laurens van der Post." *Common Boundary* (November/December 1993): 32–37.

Stierlin, Helm. "Group Fantasies and Family Myths—Some Theoretical and Practical Aspects." *Family Process* 12:2 (1973): 111–25.

Stone, Elizabeth. *Black Sheep and Kissing Cousins: How Our Family Stories Shape Us.* New York: Times Books, 1988.

Sutton, Martin. "'Little Red Riding-Hood' Revised and Rationalized: The First English Translation of the Grimms' 'Rotkäppchen' (*KHM* 26)." *Bulletin of the John Rylands University Library of Manchester* 76:3 (1994): 83–101.

Webb-Mitchell, Brett. "The Importance of Stories in the Act of Caring." *Pastoral Psychology* 43:3 (January 1995): 215–25.

White, Michael, and David Epston. *Narrative Means to Therapeutic Ends.* New York: W. W. Norton, 1990.

3. Object Relations Theory and Intersubjective Narratives

"We cannot understand fully what compels human beings to seek after that which they name 'God' until and unless we understand something about our relationship to our teddy bears." (John McDargh, xiii)

In the previous chapter I identified three types of narrative psychology, or "personology," and discussed two of them: Family Narratives and Self-Defining Narratives. A third type of narrative approach, which I have called the Intersubjective Narrative, is so closely related to Object Relations that the two need to be explored simultaneously. As I stated earlier, Carl Jung and many others have described human beings as a "collection of selves." If our internal or intersubjective dialogue is capable of keeping track of so many different selves, how are they all generated and why are there so many? *Who* is the storyteller from which each self originates as a distinct unit with its own script and plot, and who is the audience? The answers to these questions may be found in the school of psychotherapy called Object Relations Theory.

Assumptions and Adaptability of Object Relations Theory

All psychological theories have underlying assumptions, without the critique of which we cannot assess their applicability in a multicultural church. The primary set of assumptions behind Object Relations Theory concerns what is to be expected in the relationship between infant and parents.

These parent-infant expectations differ from culture to culture, even within the United States. Naming those expectations is part of discerning the applicability of Object Relations Theory in cross-cultural ministry. Daniel Stern lists the following traditional assumptions about infant-parent relations in first-world cultures.

- The society places a great value on babies—on their survival, well-being, and optimal development.
- The baby is supposed to be desired.
- The culture places a high value on the maternal role, and a mother is, in part, evaluated as a person by her participation and success in the maternal role.
- The ultimate responsibility for care of the baby is placed with the mother, even if she delegates much of the task to others.
- It is expected that the mother will love the baby.
- It is expected that the father and others will provide a supporting context in which the mother can fulfill her maternal role for an initial period.
- The family, society, and culture do not provide the new mother with the experience, training, or adequate support for her to execute her maternal role easily or well. (174)

In the instance of any culture in which one or more of Stern's seven points does not apply, some of the insights of Object Relations Theory will need to be adjusted.

In most instances, the primary parent in any society is the infant's mother. The infant's earliest memories and impressions are formed while nursing at the breast. Because breast-feeding is the norm in almost every culture, even if only for a short while, most Object Relations theorists speak of the mother-infant dyad as the primal matrix within which a child's identity is formed for the rest of its life. Here is laid down the basis for an affectional relationship and for what Erik Erikson calls "basic trust" (Horner, 17).

Within the past two decades, the traditional roles of white Western mothers and fathers in infant care have begun to change significantly. Research in infant-parent psychology has not kept up with these rapid changes. We simply do not have enough information to know what will happen to infants as men move into the role of primary parent (Stern, 190). But the language of Object Relations theorists has begun to change in order to reflect new parenting roles. For example, British psychologist Andrew Samuels recently suggested a solution for the sexism inherent in D. W. Winnicott's terminology by coining the term *the good-enough mother of either sex*. In order both to avoid sexist assumptions and to challenge the prevalence of the "blame-the-mother syndrome," I will use the term *primary parent* throughout the rest of this chapter wherever possible.

Object Relations Theory is considered by many to be particularly suited to communal cultures, as well as to Western individualistic cultures, because of its strong emphasis on human relationships, as opposed to the more Freudian emphasis on internal drives, repression, and neurosis. Object Relations does not focus on isolated individuals but on what happens when people come into contact with other people. In other words, Object Relations puts the nature of personal relationships in the very center of human inquiry about the meaning of existence. As well, Object Relations Theory seems less "gendered" than most traditional psychotherapeutic theory.

Jill Savege Scharff and David Scharff describe Object Relations as "the psychoanalytic method closest to sharing feminist values, because our approach is nonauthoritarian and because we care about women's experience" (65). Because of this inherent inclusivity, Object Relations Theory is a rich mine for understanding pastoral work in a variety of ministry situations.

The Formation of Object Representations

An "object" is a mental representation of, most commonly, a person, though it may also represent a place, thing, idea, fantasy, or memory. An object is the product of some sort of relationship, thus being created through some event or interaction, and is invested with a particular emotional energy such as love, hate, or fear.

Christians might grasp this concept of "object" by comparing it to an icon. An icon is a picture or representation, most commonly of a person (for example, Christ, St. Peter), though it may also represent an event (the ascension, the annunciation), a thing (Sophia, the four Gospels), or an abstract concept (the relationship between the members of the Godhead, a city descending from heaven). An icon is the material product of the perceived relationship between the artist of the icon and a particular aspect of the Divine, but is created only within the limits of the artist's imagination; it cannot transcend the artist's tools or cultural conditioning. The purpose of the icon is to capture some moment in the artist's relationship with the Divine, and the subject matter of an icon usually suggests some sort of action (for example, dining at the heavenly banquet, Joseph hugging the Christ child, sitting in ecumenical council). Icons are invested with emotional energy, intimated through the expression on a face (astonishment), a hand gesture (a blessing), the juxtaposition of characters ("mother-love"), or physical posture (gazing up in wonderment). But there are at least two significant differences between an "object" and an icon. An icon is tangible: it is painted on a hard surface in an identifiable style according to the dictates of tradition and can be held in one's hands. An object exists only inside one's mind. An icon traditionally is never a self-portrait of the artist. An object can be a representation of another person, thing, idea, and so on, or a representation of one's own self.

"Object relations" are the interactions among one's mental representation of one's self (the object-self, self-representation, or self-object), one's mental representations of another person, thing, idea, and so on (the object-other, the internal object representation, or illusory other), and the "factual" reality of persons, things, ideas, and so forth external to oneself (the external object). Object Relations Theory thus speaks of "the interpersonal that becomes the intrapsychic," that is, the events and characteristics of the "factual" relationship between two people that, once internalized, become the templates through which relationships are conducted, and through which one comes to perceive one's own identity and what to expect out of life. Althea Horner explains, "What is at first *interpersonal* becomes structured as enduring organizations of the mind—that is, it becomes *intrapsychic*—and then what has become intrapsychic once again becomes expressed in the interpersonal situation" (7). These object relations are not static images but are intricate, powerful influences on how we feel about ourselves and relate to other people. They are fluid templates that both predetermine our response to others and are shaped by the way others respond to us. In this sense, the object representations take on a life of their own as independent agencies capable of generating their own internal dialogic narrative in a subjective terrain. Templates are unique to the individual who carries them in his or her mind, for they are the direct result of that person's unique subjectively interpreted experiences within particular systems of relationship.

Object representations are formed first and most significantly within the relationship between a newborn or a very young infant and its primary parent. Since infants cannot talk, the obvious question is how we can know what is going on in their heads. C. Ellis Nelson identifies the two sources of data for understanding the development of infants: the "observed" infant and the "clinical" infant (23–24). Data from the observed infant comes from researchers in human development who up until a few decades ago were mainly interested in the delineation of physical achievements, such as the infant's ability to sit up or the capacity for perceiving and thinking about objects. Some of these researchers are now concerned about how infants feel about themselves and other persons. The second source of data—the clinical infant—comes from psychoanalysts who are in a therapeutic relationship with adults. Using transference, countertransference, and projective identification, psychoanalysts create a life story with their patients, including events that took place during the first few years of life. Though data from both sources remains necessarily hypothetical, the conclusions are widely accepted today in a variety of fields in addition to counseling.

An infant initially relates to a body part of the primary parent (in the case of a nursing mother, to the breast) or "partial objects," and later to the primary parent as a whole ("whole object"), and eventually to other people and things outside of itself. But an infant's cognitive abilities and mental mechanisms are extremely limited, to the extent that it can process informational input, such as sensations, experience, satisfaction, and frustration, only in partial and highly subjective ways. The infant's inner world is thus a rich amalgam of actual experiences as filtered through limited perceptions, which in turn evolves over the early years in accordance with the child's maturing cognitive capacities and actual experience. These foundational constructions, or prototypes, determine the shape and nature of all subsequent representations that build upon them. "In other words," writes Michael St. Clair, "current relationships tend to be a new edition of some previous important relationship, a kind of repetition of a relationship from the past" (1994, 8).

A number of writers employ an exegesis of the classical fairy tale "Cinderella" to explain the basic principles of Object Relations Theory. St. Clair writes:

> An observer might wonder how a young woman like Cinderella could make the decision to marry the prince after only one wonderful evening with the young man. The object relations theorist seeks to understand her "internal world," and that inner world in this instance might be flooded with feelings of painful emotional deprivation. Cinderella had lost her mother and was perhaps neglected by an inattentive father. Her attempts to protect herself against that pain might have meant that she uses psychological defenses of

splitting, whereby she tends to see females as either all good (her fairy godmother) or as all bad (her stepmother and stepsisters). If she felt poorly about herself, it makes sense that she might be attracted to a perceived magical and idealized male, the prince, who showed interest in her and who would whisk her away from her drab world. Obviously a relationship built more on fantasy than realistic knowledge is going to have problems although we never hear the rest of the story, whether the prince and Cinderella get a divorce. (1994, 8–9)

The simple polarity of "good" and "bad" females reveals obviously projected qualities, constructed out of an infantile mind which must "split" in order to digest, since no one is completely good or completely bad. We note further that the "good" female is also omnipotent (revealing that the classification is projected rather than actual): she waves her wand and wishes come true. Notice also the "dark and repressed" side of the story: the only good mother in the story is the dead one. The live (step)mother is a monster who has given birth to beasts. Cinderella's father is absent, apparently preferring the stepmother. The fairy godmother, like the coach and horses and perhaps even the happy ending, exists only for Cinderella herself, with no real existence outside of the escapist dreams of the young woman.

C. Ellis Nelson points out how rarely a constructed representation corresponds to its subject's reality:

> This situation is caused in part because we know a person only in the relationship we have had with the person and what that person has selected to reveal; it is caused in part because we form our image of a person out of our special psychological needs which may not be based on what

the person really is. Thus, the image we have of other people is real in our minds and may endure despite evidence to the contrary. (32)

Healthy adults move from part objects and split or dichotomous object representations to integration. From an Object Relations point of view, mature mental health is measured by one's ability to readjust one's extant object representations to external reality. Leroy Howe describes the move from personality disorder to mental health as follows:

> In the "construction" of our object relations, our internalized representations can become congruent with the "real" world to the extent that we become less dependent on others and thus better able to tolerate their being persons in their own right. The more self-sufficient we are, the more open we can become to refashioning our images of others and seeing those others as centers of independent feeling, thinking, and acting; persons of dignity, worth, and need in their own right; creatures bearing the image and love of their Creator. Only when we are willing to affirm the "reality" of the objects external to us on their own terms do genuine *relationships* become possible, in which there is respect, sharing, and mutual self-giving on the basis of what is and can be rather than of what each participant wishes things to be. (95)

The first phase in achieving integration is called "object constancy." Most individuals enter the early stages of object constancy around age four, though it remains a challenge to be met again and again in life. The most succinct definition of early object constancy is "the capacity to recall good *feelings* about a parent while seriously disappointed in him or her" (Hamilton, 55). The

advanced stages of emotional object constancy are called "object permanency."

The Historical Development of Object Relations Theory

Having laid out a minimal explanation of basic Object Relations Theory, an in-depth discussion of the more advanced parts of the theory, such as projection and introjection, splitting, projective identification, transitional object formation, and psychological maturity, will be postponed temporarily while we first place the development of these theories in historical perspective.

Sigmund Freud introduced the idea of "object" in his 1905 "Three Essays on the Theory of Sexuality." Freud argued that people can relate to an "object," a thing such as a shoe or a stocking, as though it were a sexual partner or a loved one. An object, then, is the target of a drive, as indeed all of Freud's thinking is ordered on the assumption that there are innate biological drives. Freud did not develop the concept of object to any further extent. In England in the 1930s, W. R. D. Fairbairn rejected Freud's drive-based biologism, proposing that people do not seek drive satisfaction so much as they seek relationships. As Nancy McWilliams illustrates, "a baby is not so much focused on *getting mother's milk* as it is on having the experience of *being nursed*, with the sense of warmth and attachment that is part of that experience" (29–30). The less emphasis a theorist ascribes to innate biological factors, the more weight will be given to how an individual develops a self through relationship within a family and how this self in turn relates in a characteristic way toward others.

Object Relations Theory evolved slowly and untidily out of Freud's original work.

Melanie Klein, a student of Freud's, was born in Vienna but moved to London. Her theoretical framework is still Freud's: the infant is first of all narcissistic—relating only to itself, its own ego; its first relationship to other people (objects) is a result of the narcissistic pleasure it derives from them. Contradicting Freud, who set the Oedipus complex at about age five or six, Klein believed it began much earlier (around age two), as the infant engaged the father to defend it against the mother's potential to consume it. Klein thus explained the *pavor nocturnus*, the night terrors so typical to two-year-olds, as an externalization of the infant's internal guilt at turning away from the mother, the fear of being abandoned, and the anxiety that the father might prove an inadequate attachment object to defend it (1926, 60). Night terrors, then, are already an expression of the oedipal struggle. Klein also emphasized the infant's active contribution to the formation of its own object identity and its inner world of object relations. The internal life of objects could be either conscious or unconscious. As well, she pioneered the concepts of "splitting" and "projective identification," both of which will be discussed later, and then perhaps acted them out through her bitter rivalry with Freud's own daughter and disciple, Anna.

During the 1930s and 1940s, Klein and W. R. D. Fairbairn of Edinburgh, Scotland, influenced each other's ideas in published works that began the divergent streams of Object Relations Theories. Fairbairn considered internal objects to be not mental representations but agencies capable of generating their own psychological activity, as I have already suggested, in that they become characters in their own internally generated scripts. Fairbairn used Object Relations Theory to explain the internal mental structure of schizoids, as those who were unable to integrate the many split constructions within their own self.

Donald W. Winnicott, a London pediatrician who did psychiatric work with children, produced works that are singular, original, and not as systematized as the writings of other theorists in the field. Yet his essays and case studies are quite readable. Winnicott put forward the concept of True Self and False Self, both developing from the child's interaction with the environment but with the latter being an adaptive mechanism designed to filter or deflect the parts of external objects that the child is incapable of dealing with. One of his most significant contributions to the development of the field was the idea of the "transitional object," including the ways that a child's "blankie" enables it eventually to symbolize. Winnicott also coined the terms *holding environment, mirroring,* and *the good-enough mother,* all of which will be explained later in this chapter.

Responding to evolutionary theory, John Bowlby (1907–90) argued that attachment behavior is instinctual. Attachment behavior is defined as "seeking and maintaining proximity to another individual" (Bowlby 1988). In the context of a relationship, attachment behavior is the way in which an individual maintains proximity to another specific individual for the purposes of safety. Bowlby used the concept of an internal working model to describe the mental representation of relationships that enable a child to make predictions about his parent's (or attachment figure's) likely behavior so that he or she can feel secure in the knowledge that the parent will be available when needed. More specifically, the child needs images of a repertoire of actions that can be tried in order to reach the parent, such as calling or crying or running toward the parent. The child also needs another set of images about the parent's predictable responses.

Fear is at the heart of the need to attach, if protection from predation is the function of attachment behavior. Bowlby notes how a high susceptibility to fear leads to anxious attachment. It is often the case, though, that there is no danger in what is feared. This has been termed an irrational fear or phobia. Bowlby argues that phobias are often the remains of threats or perceptions of danger that a young child absorbed. The susceptibility to fear in adulthood is lessened when a person has become confident, through continued experience in childhood, that an attachment figure will be available and responsive when he or she is afraid. The expectations built up are usually quite an accurate reflection of the lived experience of the person. A certain level of anxiety is innate or "ontological," however, and this animates continuing forms of attachment behavior, even in adults.

Bowlby (1988) identified three main patterns of attachment, and subsequently two others have been identified. Adult attachment is the developmental successor of the patterns established in childhood.

> *Secure Attachment.* Secure attachment exists when children, through experience, come to trust that their attachment figure will be available and will act appropriately when they are frightened. This enables them to explore their world with confidence. Subsequently, adults who have secure attachment patterns will be able to maintain healthy functional relationships

of intimacy, and maintain appropriate relational boundaries.

> *Anxious/ambivalent Attachment.* This arises when the attachment behavior of the child is responded to inadequately by the primary parent or the child had been subject to separations or controlled by threats of abandonment. This child is clingy and lacks confidence to explore the world, though it is the ambivalence, rather than the clinginess, which identifies those with this style.

> *Anxious/avoidant Attachment.* This is where the child has been constantly deprived of love and security and becomes increasingly emotionally self-sufficient. The child may increase physical distance, ignore parental behavior and initiations, or fail to engage in conversation. In general the child maintains a neutral affect.

> *Anxious/controlling Attachment.* The child takes direct control of the interaction upon reunion, assuming roles which may be more appropriate to the parent. These may include *controlling-punitive behavior*, ordering the parent around or rejecting and humiliating the parent, and *controlling-caregiving behavior*, exhibiting overly solicitous behavior as the child attempts to infantilize the parent.

> *Chaotic/disorganized Attachment.* This category is utilized to describe the behavior of children who are clearly insecure but do not fit the above categories. This may be because the child shows unusual behaviors (for example, extreme fearfulness, depression, or sexualized behavior) or due to a combination of the other anxiety patterns.

Margaret Mahler, born in Hungary and trained in Vienna, immigrated to New York City where her work with children resulted in influential articles and books from the 1950s through the 1970s. Employing a careful method of clinical observation,

Mahler identified the phases and subphases of the "psychological birth" of the human infant in a manner that has become foundational in the field, including the concepts of "normal autism," "mother-infant symbiosis," "hatching," "rapprochement," and "object constancy."

Otto Kernberg, another Viennese, took medical and psychiatric training in Chile and continued further psychiatric work at the Menninger Clinic in Kansas. His books and articles, which built on the ideas of those already mentioned, began to appear in the 1970s. Kernberg used a feeding metaphor to describe how a child normally "metabolizes" or psychologically digests early relational units of feelings and images. Frustration in the parent-child relationship keeps the child from integrating these psychological building blocks, so that these units (of self images and object images) remain "undigested." Kernberg's work was particularly influential in identifying the characteristics of borderline personality disorder.

Heinz Kohut, though born in Vienna, spent most of his professional career in Chicago. At the peak of his career during the 1970s, he published books on the psychology of the self that ruffled the feathers of the psychoanalytic community and altered the flow of psychoanalytic thinking. His "Self Psychology" has become a methodology in its own right, differing enough from other Object Relations theorists that he is usually viewed as a "close cousin." Kohut's approach almost wipes out the functional importance of external objects, for their essential worth is simply to serve the development of one's self-concept and self-worth. Scharff and Scharff summarize the difference as follows: "the work of Kohut and his school focused exclusively on the use by one person's self of the self-object. In Object Relations Theory, we are interested in reciprocity, that is, wherever there is a self relating to an object, there is also an object relating to the self" (57–58). Kohut's work is particularly important to the understanding of narcissism.

Other important shapers of the field include Edith Jacobson, Harry Guntrip, Selma Fraiberg, James Grotstein, R. D. Laing, Sylvan Tomkins, and Wilfred Bion (who applied Object Relations Theory to group process). Recently, fewer "big" names seem to be emerging, until most recently with the brilliant and highly accessible work of Daniel Stern of the Cornell University Medical Center. Significant thinkers in the interface between Object Relations Theory and religious faith development include Ana-Maria Rizzuto, Benjamin Beit-Hallahmi, W. W. Meissner, Moshe Spero, Michael St. Clair, and John McDargh. These too will be discussed later in this chapter.

As this chapter unfolds, some of these writers will be cited by name and others will not. The problem is that while they are working in the same theoretical field, they do not always agree on even some of the basic concepts, and many tend to use technical vocabulary in a manner different from others in the same field. C. Ellis Nelson describes the literature on Object Relations Theory as "extensive, multifaceted, confusing." The literature is more complex than the familiar illustration of blind men explaining what an elephant is by feeling only one part of the animal. "It seems to be more like blind people feeling different parts of different animals" (26–27). As we move more deeply into an explanation of object relations, only those elements of the theory that are fairly widely accepted and useful to pastoral counseling and faith development will be explored.

The Development and Structure of the Object-Self

In the previous chapter on narrative, I quoted the following enigma from Roy Schafer's *Retelling a Life:*

> A male analysand says to his analyst: "I told my friend that whenever I catch myself exaggerating, I bombard myself with reproaches that I never tell the truth about myself, so that I end up feeling rotten inside, and even though I tell myself to cut it out, that there is more to me than that, that it is important for me to be truthful, I keep dumping on myself." (25)

The common usage of "I" and "myself" in casual English conversation obscures the careful distinctions necessary to distinguish the object relations concept of "self" and "ego" from the more widely known Freudian usages of the term. Ministry workers who deal with counseling issues of self-esteem and right relationship need to understand the significant distinctions.

The "I" or "self" most frequently referred to in Schafer's quotation is in Object Relations Theory called an "object-self," "self-representation," or "self-image." For our purposes here, the three terms will be understood as interchangeable. An object-self is a "snapshot," a moment in time, a scene in a script, a prototype of how one was and what happened in a particular relationship interaction within a particular context (and therefore how one should expect to be in the future anytime that or a similar context is encountered), or what Daniel Stern calls "a schema-of-being-with" (19). Michael St. Clair offers a succinct definition: "The *self representation* is the mental expression of the self as it is experienced in relationship with the objects or significant persons in the child's environment" (1986, 6). An object-self may be the result of an interaction with either an external other or an internal other, since even internally our "objects" remain in active dialogue with each other. Generally, object-selves referred to in situations like Schafer's reside in the conscious, although there are object-selves that also reside in the unconscious.

Object Relations theorist Daniel Stern identifies the three component parts of the "self" as a whole: "The self comprises: 1) the old-fashioned concept of the ego as an executive mechanism that modulates self-control through its control of motility, sphincters, and affect states, and that mediates relations with the outside world, 2) the internal objects, and 3) objects and parts of the ego bound together by the affects (feelings) appropriate to the child's experiences of these object relationships" (Stern, 7). In other words, the self as a whole includes the organizer, all internalized object–others, and the various object-selves, including the emotions that are attached to them, have been formed or constructed during childhood, and continue to determine the way we interact with others and what we expect out of relationships and life. Some of these aspects of the self reside in our conscious, and others in our unconscious, though all aspects reside internally, even though expressed externally. The self, even in its wholeness, is an internal image. Hamilton reminds us, "someone viewed by an outside observer is not a self, but a person. The self is private" (12).

D. W. Winnicott drew a helpful distinction between the True Self and the False Self. The True Self has a "Me" and a "Not-me" clearly established. If an infant's environment is not safe, however, it may respond with compliance. This compliance could lead to the isolation of the infant from its own spontaneous and life-giving core. The False Self—meaning "not true" rather than "bad"—develops at the earliest stage of object relations when there is not "good-enough mothering," when the primary parent does not meet and implement the infant's own sense of omnipotence. Should the infant's cues be repeatedly misread, the primary parent then substitutes another, unwanted gesture, which is met in turn by the infant's compliant response (St. Clair 1986, 71). The compliant False Self, designed to protect the True Self from rejection, hurt, or abandonment, can become the available mediator out of which one responds within relationship, a self designed to please and to "settle" for what is offered, as opposed to a deeper, more authentic self. Reclaiming the possibilities of the True Self involves owning its undesirable aspects as well as the desirable. This means accepting the child we had to become to survive, embracing both "the true self and the forms of false self organization which were necessary in order to protect the inner core of selfhood" (McDargh, 243).

Ultimately, the "self" in Object Relations Theory is an ephemeral concept, defying clear definition. Both theoretically and developmentally, the concept of self lags behind that of object, for the ability to see objects as different from one another precedes the ability to appreciate self as a separate entity. Perhaps this lack of clarity

explains the confusion in the earlier quote from Roy Schafer, which in fact speaks not of the self at all but of a series of self-objects: the Narcissistic Self (I catch myself exaggerating), the Punitive Self (I bombard myself), the Deceiving Self (I never tell the truth about myself), the Suffering Self (I feel rotten), the Self-Parenting Self (cut it out!), the Transcendent Self (there is more to me than that), the Ethical Self (it is important for me to be truthful), the Self-Defeating Self (I keep dumping on myself). These self-objects are obviously in dialogue with each other, and the client's explanation is but a verbal record of an active internal dialogue in which self-objects take turns being the speaker, the audience, and the subject of discussion. Behind these self-objects, many of which are surely "false" in Winnicott's sense, lies the "true," the whole, self.

Internalizing the Object-Other

The process by which impressions and information move from interpersonal (external relationality, between two persons) to intrapsychic (within one's own mind) is called "internalization." In order of ascending complexity and maturity, the three main forms of internalization are incorporation, introjection, and identification. The distinction among the three is determined by the developmental level of the incorporating self. Each of the three also has a parallel in Christian hymnody which, while hardly the point of object relations, will help readers in ministry to keep the three clearly separate.

Incorporation—from the Latin *corpus,* or body—is the manner of internalization typical within the intensely fused symbiotic relationship between a newborn and a nursing mother. Freud was even more specific in his nomenclature, referring to "oral incorporation." Gregory Hamilton explains, "Incorporation implies a psychological 'eating' prior to the development of clear self-other boundaries. The object is taken in and disappears inside the non-differentiated self-other matrix. A physiologic analogy is an infant sucking warm sweet milk at the breast. Milk comes in and disappears into the baby-mother symbiotic oneness" (68). Because the newborn has no sense that he and his mother are two separate persons, whatever is taken in by him seems simply to disappear without question or trace. Object Relations theorists presume that the infant believes he is taking the actual mother inside himself when he sucks in her milk. Christian readers might associate this with Richard Pynson's *Horae B. V. M.* Sarum 1514, "God be in my head and in my understanding; God be in my eyes . . . ; God be in my mouth. . . ." and so forth.

Introjection—a constructed term that is the inverse of projection (Latin for "throw forth")—assumes a level of internal differentiation, so that the internalized object can be held as an object–image rather than merged with the self-image. For something to be "thrown in," there must be both an object to take in from and a nascent self to take into. Introjection is thus possible only after an infant has learned to differentiate between itself and its primary parent. The infant's sense of "not-me" must have already begun to develop for introjection, as opposed to incorporation, to occur. But introjection also demands a certain lack of maturity; it can occur only in developmental stages wherein power and authority, real or fantasized, are still automatically attributed to what comes from outside. Thus, rather than being absorbed into the receiver, as is the case with incorporation,

an introjection tends to remain inside the receiver in an "unmetabolized" form.

Christian readers might associate this with Charles Wesley's "Author of Life Divine," in which he pleads, "Our needy souls sustain with fresh supplies of love." This Wesleyan theology seems to presume the introjection of unending quantities of eucharistic power and authority to sustain the weak. In contrast, in his *Totem and Taboo* (1913), Freud interpreted the taking-in of Eucharist elements as incorporation, implying that through communion the faithful believed they became wholly Christlike. Most eucharistic hymnody, however, including Wesley's, presumes that the faithful Christian is still quite capable of telling the difference between herself and Christ, even after receiving communion.

Identification is presumed possible only after a stable frame of object-self and object-others has been established. Identification is the ability to maintain a feeling of being distinct from important objects and yet attribute aspects of the object-image to the self-image. Throughout life, identification is a way to remain open to other people and allow them to influence us and help us change (Hamilton, 118–19). Christian readers might associate this with Lesbia Scott's "I Sing a Song of the Saints of God," which ends with the cry, "and I mean to be one too!" In general, theological themes of the *imitatio Christi* presume the same maturity level as does identification: the ability to internalize without foregoing one's own sense of self.

Daniel Stern differs somewhat in his understanding of the internalization process from most other Object Relations theorists (13, 19). He argues that while stimuli are external, the "objects" that come to represent the many early stimuli do not enter an infant from the outside but are created by the infant from inside. In this way, object relations are in fact a process in which two partners participate together. The primary parent imparts a "self" to the infant, but the infant responds to that imparting by creating from it an internal object representation. But, as has been stated, most infants begin the construction of object representations at the breast. Their immature level of development prevents them from comprehending a relationship with a primary parent as a whole person. Internalization begins with the relationship between an infant and just one part of another person.

Stern summarizes the key features of an infant's object representations (80–81):

1. They must be based on events that have feelings attached to them. Going to a restaurant is not per se an emotional experience. It only has feelings attached to it because it includes people with whom the infant is in object relationship.

2. They must be based on routine experiences, such as the ordinary daily interactions between the baby and its parents. These activities cluster around an infant's vital experiences, such as eating, sleeping, and playing. For example, object information cannot be gleaned from memories of what one had for dinner but, rather, from what it felt like to eat with daddy.

3. Object representations in infants are not internalized from outside, but are constructed from inside the infant's mind, from the self-experience of being with another. For example, when a baby imitates a parent, it is imitating not what a parent really does, but the baby's internally constructed impression of what is being done and its personal meaning.

4. Object representations are nonverbal. "They are less concerned with knowledge and more with doing and being."

Splitting

According to a familiar nursery rhyme, "There was a little girl, who had a little curl, right in the middle of her forehead; and when she was *good*, she was very very good, and when she was *bad*, she was horrid." The nursery rhyme doesn't tell us how old the little girl was, but perhaps she only had one curl because she was somewhere around eighteen months, or what Margaret Mahler calls the "rapprochement" phase of child development. At that age, a child is in the final stages of "splitting," or introjecting object-others by identifying them as either all good or all bad.

In the young child's environment before about the age of two, primary caretakers and their immediate support environment are observed and internalized as object-others. At first, because the infant has a limited capacity to internalize all aspects of people or interactions with these people, it can internalize only parts of objects. Partial objects are internalized in very crude, global mental representations. Typically such representations fall into an "all-good" or "all-bad" dichotomy. For example, a "good breast" is always there and always full, ready to satisfy the infant's need for nourishment or comfort. A "bad breast" is one that is not under the infant's omnipotent control, one that is too hard to suck or, worse, doesn't come when the infant cries. A good breast would never fail to show up when needed.

Perhaps that's as much information as a newborn can handle: the presence of a good breast and the absence of a bad one.

After the serenity of the womb, the infant experiences life "outside" as a buzzing, chaotic discontinuity. Splitting is related to processes that allow the infant to let in only as much of that environment as it can manage without being overwhelmed by the whole indigestible experience. Thus, early splitting refers to the maturational inability to synthesize incompatible experiences into a whole. The tendency to relate to part objects accounts in turn for the fantasy-like and unrealistic nature of the infant's relations to everything—to parts of its own body, to people, and to inanimate objects. The object world during the first two or three months of life consists only of gratifying and hostile and persecuting parts of the real world (St. Clair 1986, 39).

Since internalization begins at a preverbal level of development, infants will categorize their experiences based upon affective or feeling states. "Typically, feeling physically satiated or gratified, or psychologically satisfied, liked, rewarded, or loved is enough to store a trace-perception of what we adults would label 'good'; whereas feeling physical pain, non-gratification, psychological frustration, punishment, or not loved will be stored as 'bad'" (Magaletta, 23). In this manner, the infant internalizes interactions with the caretakers, as well as aspects or characteristics of these external objects, not necessarily as they are, but as they are felt and fantasized to be. In popular literature, splitting is illustrated not only by the little girl who was either very good or very bad, but also by classic novels such as Robert Louis Stevenson's *Doctor Jekyll and Mr. Hyde* or Oscar Wilde's *Picture of Dorian Gray*.

Splitting is not in itself pathological but part of normal human development.

Recent studies even suggest that it has both an epigenetic and a neurological basis. The act of being birthed is itself a splitting. Once this primal splitting is accepted, the infant can then *actively* conduct perceptual (and later, cognitive) splittings of his object world. Neurologically, splitting reflects the biological delay in the capacity of the two sides of the brain to be able to communicate with each other. In their 1978 study, Gazzaniga and LeDoux found that the corpus callosum and the deep cerebral commissures that unite the two cerebral hemispheres do not begin to myelinate (and therefore to function) until about three to four months of age, and do not complete myelination until adolescence. From this Grotstein concludes that "inborn splitting may be a method for achieving anesthesia of experience by keeping the two brain-minds from communicating with each other too quickly" (7).

It is not object-others alone that are split; developmentally we quickly learn also to split our developing sense of self. Early on we acquire the capacity to think not only of part-objects as good or bad, and then other persons as good or bad, but also of ourselves as good or bad. Initially we link our good selves with good objects, and our bad selves with bad objects. The good self and the good object are linked by positive feeling and mood; the bad self and the bad object are linked by negative feeling and mood. The linkage may be diagrammed as follows:

Self	Feeling or Mood	Object

This diagram suggests that we actually learn to speak on the basis of our initial object relations. A baby's first sentence might be diagrammed as follows:

Self	Affect	Object
I	Love	Mother
I	Want	Up
I	Want	Toast

An infant's speech, then, is simply the externalizing of sounds, and attaching of names, to a preexisting mental representation. This move is a concrete measure of the transition from nonverbal developmental phases to verbal.

The simplistic linking of good with good and bad with bad begins to break down sometime around age two, at the end of the rapprochement phase of child development. By then, the child should have begun to integrate split objects, creating single, cohesive representations of people in its environment that are not only good or only bad, but can be good and bad at the same time. The failure to integrate, however, can lead to more exaggerated splitting, termed "idealization and devaluation." Idealization exaggerates the good object to the extreme, just as devaluation exaggerates the bad object to the extreme. Exaggerated splitting creates larger-than-life people and larger-than-life objects, primarily because their opposites have been separated and cannot therefore provide a balance to the perceptions. This failure to integrate adequately can be diagrammed as follows (Hamilton, 82):

Split Object Relations Units
Good Self — Good Object
Bad Self — Bad Object
Idealized-Devalued Object Relations Units
Good Self — Bad Object
Bad Self — Good Object

Because extreme or excessive splitting is characterized by immiscibility (the inability to mix two opposites), when the good object becomes idealized, the linked self must become "bad" in order to preserve the polarization between the two. We shall see that this dynamic may show up when counseling survivors of sexual abuse.

As was stated, splitting is not in itself pathological; it is a normal part of child development. Splitting can equally be motivated by loyalty to good internal objects and the good people with whom we identify. Hamilton points out that "Splitting in the more global sense, then, is not only a destructive infantile failure to see the larger picture. It plays an important role in the establishment of love relationships, family fealty, loyal friendships, patriotism, and dedication to a cause. Splitting both binds societies together and tears them apart" (82). Some readers will be reminded of Carl Jung's theory that we learn only by dividing things into opposites, or of Alfred Adler's exploration of the role of "oppositional thinking" as a mark of immaturity. In all three schools of counseling—Object Relations, Jungian, or Adlerian—psychic maturity involves the integration of opposites, such that the inner world becomes increasingly synthesized and closer to reality.

Grotstein points out that it is not only objects which are split; we also can split ourselves, particularly in an effort to rid ourselves of object-selves that we do not know how to integrate (3). We can split off "good" object-selves or "bad" object-selves, depending upon what parts of ourselves make us uncomfortable. This is called "defensive splitting." When too many split selves attempt to coexist in the same mental space, we tend to rid ourselves of them by projecting them onto other objects, whether persons, things, or events. This projection usually leads to projective identification, a unique aspect of Object Relations Theory that will be explained in the next section of this chapter. We should note here, however, that any split self-object has the potential to function autonomously within our intrapsychic world, thus becoming a character within our intersubjective narratives.

Object relations concepts can at times seem ephemeral and difficult to ground in practice. Splitting is one such concept. Grotstein offers the following brief case description to illustrate the recognition and treatment of splitting in clinical practice:

> A twenty-two-year-old single female presented a dream in which I had come to her apartment in order to see her roommate rather than her. She was very upset and depressed about this. Her associations to her roommate were that she was more dependent and needy.
>
> I pointed out to the patient that the analysis was mobilizing her awareness of an aspect of herself with which she is not comfortable—a needy, dependent, infantile self which unabashedly needs the parent. This needy self is experienced, I told her, as a split-off self disenfranchised from her own sense of being, but now she needs to reenfranchise it so that she can become more comfortable with her dependent vulnerability, rather than continue to affect a disposition of a pseudomature, overaccomplishing, hyper-independent person—all of which characteristics comprised the "false self" which brought her into treatment. (63)

Other forms of splitting occur with frequency in the counseling process. Horner points out that a particularly common type of splitting is between "the good counselor" and "the bad spouse" (78). Day after day, the pastor hears how understanding and helpful he or she is while the congregant's spouse is portrayed as an insensitive, verbally abusive, and neglectful person. This form of splitting can be most difficult to sort out because the external situation may correspond to the split object relations to some degree. St. Clair remarks that beaten, abused children may see abusing parents as good and themselves as bad and deserving of beating. "The child would rather be bad him- or herself than have bad objects or be in a bad situation. The likely motive for a child becoming bad or delinquent is to make his or her objects 'good'" (1986, 54, 59). This of course is a prime example of idealization-devaluation, as described earlier.

Projection and Projective Identification

As already mentioned, when too many split selves attempt to coexist in the same mental space, we tend to rid ourselves of them by projecting them onto other objects, whether persons, things, or events. This projection usually leads to projective identification, a unique aspect of Object Relations Theory.

Projection, or expelling of the unwanted, is a natural human pattern. As Hamilton points out, "There are similarities between projection in the clinical situation and various behaviors in babies. An infant puckering up its face and spitting out an unpleasant mouthful of pureed spinach is considered to be an early behavioral equivalent of projection—getting the bad out of the self" (67). Such projection is the beginning of "projective identification," a term coined by Melanie Klein in her 1946 essay "Notes on Some Schizoid Mechanisms."

Projective identification can serve a positive or a negative purpose. Klein emphasized both. "The projection of good feelings and good parts of the self into the mother is essential for the infant's ability to develop good object relations and to integrate his ego" (Klein, 184). Projection is the result of splitting and incorporation: as Michael St. Clair observes, "The well-fed infant, filled with pleasure, turns this good feeling back into the object and believes the breast is good" (1986, 40). Projective identification, then, is a three-step process: a self-image or impulse is split off, then projected onto an object-other, and then reinternalized as though it were an accurate representation of the other person. In actuality, a person is simply responding to one of her own self-images as it is carried, temporarily or permanently, by the other person. Either "good" or "bad" self-images, or impulses or characteristics, can be projected. Most projective identification is defensive: a negative self-image that is split off, so that it can be controlled or abolished in the object-other who serves as the container for the projection.

In explaining projective identification, Gregory Hamilton offers the metaphor of a movie projector: "The crucial elements, film, light, and lens, are inside the apparatus, but the image is cast outside, onto a screen to create the appearance of an external reality. In our psychological lives we can see that which is within us in others" (63). Althea Horner suggests that this "movie screen" is actually more like a Rorschach blot, since it is being projected onto an object-other rather than a real person (63). An object-other bears what the self perceives. While each person has unique qualities, others respond differently to these qualities according to their own history, belief system, expectations, fears, wishes, and feelings. The Rorschach-like nature of projective identification is encapsulated in the adage "Beauty is in the eyes of the beholder." A beautiful self-image is split off, projected onto an object-other, and then internalized as a "work of art" by the beholder. To another, this "inkblot" might register as hideous. In this sense, projective identification is a form of transference.

Maggie Scarf cites the example of projective identification from therapists Berman, Lief, and Williams:

A woman who before her marriage had competently lived alone for a number of years, proud of her total independence, married a rather lonely, isolated man. The wife's perception of her husband was that he was a strong, powerful man—someone like her father—and she projected onto him all of her competence, allowing her hidden, helpless, dependent self to surface. Soon she found herself so dependent that she was unable to drive or make a shopping list. She insisted that she did not know why this was happening, but felt that she had simply "lost her nerve." She had, in fact, given over into her mate's keeping all of her former competence and assumed the burden of carrying his dependent needs for him.

The husband, in turn—because such projections involve a mutual "deal"—gave over to his wife all of his own unmet and disowned dependency needs; she expressed these needs for him by means of her utterly needful behavior.

Therefore, while objecting verbally to her dependency demands, he drove her everywhere, smiling indulgently about "my helpless little wife."

In effect, a projective trade-off had taken place. She took charge of the helplessness for the pair of them, enabling him to be in charge of the mastery and the competence. At the level of conscious awareness, the partners appeared to be very different people, but each held, for the other, a repudiated part of the self. (193–94)

The self-defensive nature of projective identification necessitates a blurring of boundaries between self and other. It also necessitates a "willing" container, an object-other who is willing to participate in the trade-off, however unconsciously. While projective identification plays some part in virtually every human relationship, its destructive character can be minimized when partners in relationship are each clear about their own boundaries. Clarity that draws the object-other closer to the reality of the real person necessarily reduces the power of the other's projected self-images and impulses.

Excessive projection leads quickly to overdependence. For example, when good self-images or good parts of the personality are split off frequently and projected onto another, the sense of self is impoverished. Very soon such processes extend to other people, and the result may be an overly strong dependence on these external representatives of one's own good parts (Klein, 184). Furthermore, when projection is forceful, its reinternalization will carry equal force. Klein points out that an aggressive projective self may cause another to feel invaded (185). The other may respond with a matching or even greater response. This may lead to the fear that not only the body but also the mind is controlled from outside by hostile people. Of course, the first self is simply responding to its own aggression, whose reinternalization may be even more uncomfortable.

Projective identification is a highly significant dynamic in ministry relationships. Ministers function as "movie screens" or Rorschach blots for their congregants. Every minister presents a particular "shape," unique qualities of style, as well as gender, age, and so on, to which people respond differently, according to their own history, belief system, expectations, fears, wishes, and feelings. This differential response, the *meaning* to the parishioner of what is perceived *about* the minister, is transference. It is further complicated by the power and authority usually attributed to ministers. Projective identification refers not only to the parishioner's *reactions* to the minister, based on meaning attributed to his or her behavior or demeanor, but also to the parishioner's *way of relating* to the minister when this way of relating is predominantly determined by unconscious or conscious expectations or defenses. Hamilton describes a case of projective identification that some ministers will have seen in parish work (153): A counselee could not tolerate the hostility she experienced when she was frustrated. Thus, she would project this hostility into her image and perception of the counselor. She would then reintroject it into her self-image, saying, "I am angry because he is angry." Thereby she split off her anger. Through the use of projective identification, she entered an all-bad self-object state, resulting in intense and inappropriate anger toward the counselor.

The parishioner may project onto the minister (1) his or her own thoughts or feelings, such as believing the minister is angry when it is the parishioner who is actually angry, (2) thoughts or feelings characteristic of a parent with the expectation that the minister is taking the same stance as the parent does now or did in the past, such as disapproval of a certain kind of behavior, or (3) a complete image of the self or of an important other (self and object representations) from the inner world of object relations.

But, as Grotstein points out,

> In its more positive sense, projective identification is responsible for vicarious introspection and, in its most sublimated form, for empathy. It can be seen to operate in such processes as anthropomorphization and personification; it is active in romantic experience; and from it issues the impact of warnings, advice, and persuasion. As a primitive mechanism of communication it exists first between preverbal infants and their mothers, but is also residual in adult life as a form of affective communication. It is of prime importance to authors, educators, ministers, artists, as well as psychoanalysts. (123)

Projective identification is probably the primary psychological explanation for the pastoral empathy implied in "You shall love your neighbor as yourself."

The Holding Environment

Object relations are created within a specific interpersonal space. Donald Winnicott called this space "the holding environment," a concept that generally parallels what Wilfred Bion called "the container." The purpose of both the holding environment and the container is to facilitate the health and eventual object-integration of an anxious or traumatized object-other.

The holding environment or container is first experienced between a primary parent and an infant. "Holding" should not only be interpreted literally: as Michael St. Clair points out, "Holding includes the whole routine of care throughout the day, especially physical holding of the infant, a form of loving. Some adults do not know how to hold an infant, and the infant feels insecure and often cries" (1986, 75). The holding environment does not have to be perfect; it has only to be "good-enough," as Winnicott explained in his 1955 essay "Transitional Objects and Transitional Phenomena: A Study of the First Not-Me Possession."

Part of what makes a holding environment good-enough is "the good-enough mother," a term coined by Winnicott in his 1962 essay "Ego Integration in Child Development." The good-enough mother provides enough holding but not too much. She is neither neglectful nor intrusive and overcontrolling. "Good-enough" is not intended to imply perfectionism, for no parent can avoid occasional lapses, misjudgments, and flawed decisions. Winnicott wished rather to emphasize consistency of age-appropriate patterns, values, and loving attitudes, and above all that the infant's developmental needs be placed uppermost in the parent's priorities. Hamilton points out, however, that "Some children and mothers who might be otherwise adequate to the developmental tasks facing them are simply a poor match" (53).

A good-enough holding environment is the container for an infant's earliest projective identifications. The infant projects its anxiety, panic, trauma, fear of annihilation, or feelings of being overwhelmed by stimuli too large for it to handle. Hamilton explains that the good-enough parent internalizes the child's projected feeling, contains it, modulates and alters it, and then gives the transformed affect back to the child in the form of holding behavior or a comment such as, "Oh, I know. It really hurts when you skin your knee. Ouch!" (239). The child can reintroject the transformed affect and thereby alter its internal experience. The parent thereby helps the infant to sort out (split into more utilizable components) those external stimuli that are at first inchoately emotional (Grotstein, 5), returning the unmodulated projection in a more manageable, tolerable form.

Containment relies upon the ability of the infant's parents and environment to adapt. The infant's needs and maturational processes are central, and it is the primary parent's responsibility to adapt to them. Over a period of time, the parents tend gradually toward what St. Clair calls "de-adaptation," a reassertion of their own independence (1986, 69).

The concept of a holding environment or container is very useful for those in ministry. Pastoral caregivers are called upon to "contain" people cognitively, emotionally, and spiritually (though pastoral ethics require people not to hold or "contain" parishioners physically). The holding environment does not have to be perfect, but "good-enough," just as a minister does not have to be perfect, but "good-enough." Particularly in the case of anxious or panicked parishioners, or of a traumatized congregation, the minister is expected to take in the projected or communicated feelings, modulate them, transform them, give them meaning, and return them to the congregants. If ministry is successful, the pastoral caregiver should be able to move gradually from adaptation to deadaptation, thus reempowering the disempowered or emotionally paralyzed object-parishioners. This process occurs most commonly within pastoral care and counseling, spiritual direction, and possibly within the weekly sequence of sermons.

Mirroring and Cueing

As good object relations are created *within* a good container, so they are created *by* mirroring and cueing. Donald Winnicott developed a theory of mirroring in his essay "Mirror-role of the Mother and Family in Child Development." His ideas were later echoed by Heinz Kohut as "the mirroring environment." Subsequent object relations theorists speak of the interactional "mirroring relation."

Michael St. Clair explains:

> What the baby sees when he or she looks at the mother's face is him- or herself. For when the mother looks at her baby, her appearance is related to what she sees in the baby (for example, her pleasure in her child is reflected in her face, and the infant sees that joy and feels like he or she is joyful and good). The mother gives back to the baby the baby's own self. It is as if the baby, in looking at the mother's face, looks in a mirror and sees itself. "When I look I am seen and so I exist." Thus, in the early stages of emotional development, a vital part is played by the environment that, in fact, is not yet distinguished from the infant by the infant. (1986, 75–76)

What the infant sees in the parent's face, as if in a mirror, is the parent's image of the infant—how the parent sees, feels about, and judges the child; what the parent wishes and hopes for not only in the child, but also for the relationship that is beginning between them (Howe, 100). Stern points out that these "nonverbal behaviors that make up a great part of this relationship are not communications about, nor comments upon, nor interpretations of the relationship; they *are* the relationship" (63).

Winnicott explained the purpose of mirroring as enhancing "the baby's legitimate experience of omnipotence" (112). When the infant is mirrored well by the parent, the infant feels as if this parent-object is a subjective object, created by the infant. In infant omnipotence, then, lie the early foundations of self-confidence and self-esteem. The baby sees itself as a subject not merely of gazing, but also of interest, regard, care, and protection. The reverse can also happen: the infant can be consigned to seeing itself as merely a source for the other's content or misery, or as something somehow contemptible.

Mirroring does not go only one way. It is reciprocal and is therefore based on cues between both partners in the dyad. St. Clair, relying heavily on the work of Margaret Mahler, emphasizes the correspondence between mirroring, cueing, and self-esteem:

> *Mutual cueing* is a form of mother-child interaction and develops into mutual verbal communication. The infant gives cues to needs, pleasures, and tensions, and the mother responds selectively to only some of these cues. The infant gradually alters behavior in response to the mother's selective response. The unconscious needs of the mother activate out of the infant's potential those characteristics that make the infant the unique child of this particular mother. The mother conveys a mirroring frame of reference to which the primitive self of the infant adjusts. From these circular interactions emerge the characteristics of the child's personality. If the mother's mirroring is unpredictable or hostile, then the child has an unreliable frame of reference to check back to. This can disturb the child's self-esteem. (1986, 107–8)

The reciprocal nature of interactive mirroring is actually a biblical concept. According to Proverbs 27:19, "Just as water reflects the face, so one human heart reflects another."

Mutual mirroring and cueing will remind Christian readers of the power of the creating word. As parents call their infants into unique personhood through mirroring and cueing, at the same time infants call primary parents into more effective motherhood and fatherhood. Just as God "calls into existence the things that do not exist" (Romans 4:17), so mirroring and cueing are a reflection of divine generativity.

Leroy Howe believes that insufficient emphasis has been placed on the infant's capacity to "notice" whether it is being mirrored and whether its cues are being read and responded to adequately (99). Further, Howe wishes to emphasize that not only are parents selective in their response to infant cues; infants also exercise selectivity in responding to the parent's cues and mirroring: "the infant's capacity for noticing is *activated* by, but it is not *created* in, the experience of being regarded. And even when the capacity is activated, we cannot be certain that a particular infant will *exercise* the power to allow herself or himself to be regarded, held, nurtured, and inspired. A loving face may shine brightly upon the infant's, but the infant may let it go unnoticed" (100). Howe's argument implies that infants have the capacity to make choices at a quite early age, even as young as two or three months. And indeed, as Stern points out, choosing to respond or not is one of the few ways that infants have to exercise control within relationships: "What else can the baby do? His hand-eye and hand-to-hand coordination is not yet good enough for him to be interested in the world of inanimate objects or to reach for or manipulate them. He cannot get up and crawl or walk away. By his nature he is a kind of prisoner to the face-to-face situation, for better or worse" (72).

Emphasis on the reciprocity of mirroring and cueing raises interesting questions about what happens when an infant is not mirrored, or when the parent-infant dyad miscues each other. Winnicott observes that some infants "look and do not see themselves" (112–13). All they see in the parent's face is the parent's face. The infant then must exercise its creativity to see if it can generate another way of getting some reflection back from its environment. If the infant is unsuccessful, its creativity will ultimately begin to atrophy. Some babies do not give up hope. Tantalized by this type of relative maternal failure, they study the variable parental face in an attempt to predict the parent's mood, in the same manner that we learn to study the weather. The baby learns quickly to make a forecast: "Just now it is safe to forget mother's mood and to be spontaneous, but any minute mother's face will become fixed or her mood will dominate, and my own personal needs must then be withdrawn; otherwise my central self may suffer insult." This type of unpredictability in the infant's most intimate environment can easily lead to adult personality disorders, particularly the borderline and narcissistic.

Miscuing raises a further question about infant identity and the nature versus nurture controversy. If we begin with the possibility that sexual orientation is somehow genetically determined, we must ask if a primary parent can read the cues of pre-heterosexual children and pre-homosexual children equally skillfully. If cueing is a mutual "stimulus-response" sequence, then we must wonder how much miscuing goes on between, for example, a heterosexual parent and a pre-homosexual child. Understanding pre- and nonverbal cueing as a form of

"cross-cultural" communication absolves us from any desire to "blame" parents for their children's sexual behavior, or homosexual adults for the shame and self-esteem distortions that they carry as an inheritance from their rearing. A pre-homosexual child being raised by heterosexual parents will necessarily not get all its needs and pleasures met because the parents will misinterpret too many cues. The struggle to claim "normalcy," so painful for many gay adults, may simply be the result of being raised by parents who were "constitutionally" incapable of understanding them, no matter how much they were loved.

Mirroring and cueing presume a face-to-face relationship. While the important theological metaphor of "face" is too complex to explore here, two examples will illustrate the similarity between Winnicott's ideas and the biblical matrix. Exodus 33:11 explains that the intimacy between God and Moses was both unique and magical because God spoke to Moses "face-to-face." The Aaronic Blessing in Numbers 6:25 teaches that to wish someone well is to pray that God will mirror them: "May the Lord make his face to shine upon you." The exercise of free will can be explained as a parallel to the infant's choice to respond selectively to its parent's mirroring. But we are left to wonder how else we humans miss God's cues, and how often God misses ours.

The Inner World of the Primary Parent

Daniel Stern has written brilliantly on the object world that develops within the primary parent's mind as he or she relates to the infant. Stern identifies three groupings of representations, or object configurations, or what he calls "representations-of-being-with" (19). In this analysis, we find repeated

connections as well to Family Systems Theory and Narrative Counseling Theory.

1. *The Object-Infant.* Stern contrasts the
real infant with the infant whom the primary parent perceives:

> There is the real baby in the mother's
> arms, and there is the imagined baby in
> her mind. There is also the real mother
> holding the baby, and there is her imag-
> ined self-as-mother at that moment. And
> finally, there is the real action of holding
> the baby, and there is the imagined action
> of that particular holding. (18)

The object-infant is related to within three
simultaneous time frames: past, present, and
future. The infant's past is present in the
object-infant, for a child is born into a story
that is already being told about it. Perhaps
an infant's story begins when its mother was
a little girl, practicing to be a mother by
playing with her dolls. Before conception
the parents have begun the narrative about
how it will be to have children. At conception, the narrative of this unique infant
begins: who it will be, what it will need,
what it will want. The object-infant has a
long prehistory. Postpartum, this narrative is
adjusted to reflect the object-infant as it is
perceived in the present: who it is, what it
needs, what it wants. In turn, the present
narrative is shaped by expectations of the
future, and indeed, the elaboration of the
object "baby" continues for the rest of the
mother's life.

2. *The Parent's Object-Self.* Winnicott and
Wilfred Bion identified the mother's inner
object life as one of the most significant factors shaping an infant's identity, going far
beyond the limits of simply the mother's
representation of the infant-object. Her
reveries, preoccupations, fantasies, and projective identifications became of great inter-

est to the psychic development of the
infant. According to Stern, "Selma Fraiberg
revolutionized the perception of this situation by placing maternal fantasies and
memories at the very center—practically
(that is, clinically) speaking—of a pathogen-
ic process that results in a disturbed parent-
infant relationship or in the formation of an
infant symptom" (22). Fraiberg's theories
demand that any family systems work that
involves an infant focus heavily on the
internal object life of the primary parents as
well as that of the members of their specific
support system.

Fraiberg illustrates her theory with the
striking metaphor of "the ghost in the nursery," a mother's memory of a previous
infant who died. The new infant is haunted
by this ghost in that the mother summons it
repeatedly to dwell in between herself and
her new object-infant. A family systems
genogram will often record stillbirths and
spontaneous abortions in order to access
these "ghosts."

The presence of a new infant also causes
the mother to reshape her own object-self.
Stern explains:

> The networks of schemas that undergo
> reworking are the mother's self as woman,
> mother, wife, career-person, friend, daugh-
> ter, granddaughter; her role in society; her
> place in her family of origin; her legal sta-
> tus; herself as the person with cardinal
> responsibility for the life and growth of
> someone else; as the possessor of a different
> body; as a person "on call" 24 hours a day;
> as an adventurer in life, a creator, a player in
> evolution's grand scheme, and so on—in
> short, almost every aspect of her life. All
> these networks are thrown by events into
> the postpartum crucible, potentially to be
> reforged. It will happen again with the
> second and third babies, but with less

intensity and usually with less mutation in the representational world. (24)

The same dynamics hold true for fathers, though Stern points out that society's lesser expectations of fathers, and fathers' less frequent contact with infants, delay the full impact of this object-self revision until the child is older.

3. *The Object-Parent of the Object-Self.* Stern also emphasizes the importance in the mother-infant dyad of the mother's memories and object-representations of her own mother's way of mothering her. He argues that the nature of the mother's current representation of her own mother-as-mother may be the single best predictor of the pattern of attachment (secure, ambivalent, avoidant, or disorganized) that the mother will establish with her own infant by twelve months of age (28). Further, a long series of studies suggests that the pattern of attachment seen at twelve months is one of the best predictors of a child's general adaptation during the preschool and early school years. Stern's research underlines the truth of a systems theory concept: that the primary determinant of the way we parent is our own memories and representations of the way we were parented.

The Infant's World and Transitional Phenomena

As the mother is busy making and reshaping a whole series of object-infants and object-self images, at the same time the infant is busy making and reshaping object representations of the primary parents. The infant is turning the primary parent into a parent and forcing the construction of new representational networks. These object representations formed by both infant and parent are guides to what to expect, how to act, perceive, and feel, and how to interpret the dyadic relationship between them.

As I have explained, an infant's object representations are chaotic and fragmented, at least until the age of two. Frustration in the parent-child relationship keeps the infant from integrating these psychological building blocks, and so these units of self images and object images remain "undigested." As undigested aspects of the childish self, they can return in adults as primitive feeling states and unintegrated emotions (St. Clair 1986, 17). This is particularly true of adults who have not developed adequate self-comforting skills or for whom childhood deprivation has produced personality disorders.

In a 1953 essay, Donald Winnicott outlined the manner by which infants create vehicles for comforting themselves:

Out of all this (if we study any one infant) there may emerge some thing or some phenomenon—perhaps a bundle of wool or the corner of a blanket or eiderdown, or a word or tune, or a mannerism—that becomes vitally important to the infant for use at the time of going to sleep, and is a defense against anxiety, especially anxiety of depressive type. Perhaps some soft object or other type of object has been found and used by the infant, and this then becomes what I am calling a *transitional object*. This object goes on being important. The parents get to know its value and carry it round when traveling. The mother lets it get dirty and even smelly, knowing that by washing it she introduces a break in continuity in the infant's experience, a break that may destroy the meaning and value of the object to the infant. (4)

Transitional objects are one part of a larger category that Winnicott called "transitional phenomena." The larger category may include some part of the child's own body, another's mannerisms, a particular bedtime routine or lullaby, a special food, a certain book or disc, or a specific set of words.

The word *transitional* should not be used in a developmental sense, that is, a transition from one stage to the next. Rather, "transitional" here is used to describe the way an infant creates a mediating reality between inner and outer realities. Although this created reality relates to inner and outer experience, it is a separate reality, almost in the sense of a geographical place. The infant's first "transitional object" is its own fist, which it puts in its mouth to comfort its yearnings. At this stage, the infant does not recognize the fist as its own; it is simply an object that is present in the environment and available whenever the infant needs it. Though there are many variations in the sequence of events, this fist-in-mouth activity leads eventually to a child's attachment to a teddy bear, a soft doll, or a "blankie." The transitional object is the child's first "Not-me" possession and thus a critical step toward individuation.

Transitional phenomena are created within the holding environment, building upon the infant's creativity and sense of omnipotence. Winnicott explains that this early stage in child development "is made possible by the mother's special capacity for making adaptation to the needs of her infant, thus allowing the infant the illusion that what the infant creates really exists" (14). A transitional object, then, is partly subjective and partly reality-oriented. The blanket is a real, objectively perceived thing, but serves like the comforting breast that the infant in its omnipotence has "called into being." To maintain the infant's neces-sary illusion of omnipotent creating, the infant must sense its control over the transitional object. Nelson describes this sense of manipulability:

> When babies are old enough to build a tower with blocks, they very often knock it down. Building the tower was play, it was a creation of the self. After the tower stood for a few minutes, the child began to see it as a physical object outside the child's control. By knocking it down children enhance the self's authority to do what it wants to do. (31)

In fact, the infant does not create the transitional object alone; it is a joint creation of both infant and primary parent. Parents accept a blanket or teddy bear as something the infant cares about and allow the infant control over the object. As Winnicott points out, the parents get to know its value and make sure the infant has the object when they go out or when the infant is placed in the crib (4). They may even postpone washing or cleaning it, comprehending intuitively that the infant's access to means of self-comfort transcends their standards of hygiene and propriety.

Winnicott observed that there was no significant gender difference between what infant girls and infant boys adopted as transitional objects (4). More recent research suggests that by adolescence a significant difference in choice of transitional objects exists between young males and young females. While "treasured possessions" serve adolescents of both genders to secure their self-identity, young males prefer transitional objects with some entertainment or instrumental value, while young females prefer those with relational or interpersonal value. Kamptner's research showed that a significant number of fourteen- to eighteen-year-olds still own some of their transitional objects from infancy, though they are not used any longer. Their place has been taken by "treasured possessions" such as, for boys, motor vehicles, sports equipment, and music, and, for girls, motor vehicles, jewelry, and stuffed animals. While the nature of our transitional objects may change greatly between infancy and adulthood, our need for them seems never to disappear.

The human ability to think in and cherish symbols begins with transitional objects. Christians find in transitional phenomena an explanation for the affective power of our unique customs. A cross worn around the neck, the crucifix on the wall of the bedroom, the words of familiar prayers, the ritual and elements of the Eucharist, and the rhythm of the liturgical year are all transitional objects, mediating the gap between the elusive worlds of inner subjectivity and external reality. We hang on to these "treasured possessions" as sources of self-comfort in the face of frustration, emotional disintegration, anxiety, and the untested. In addition to offering us satisfaction, stability, and some sense of control, they offer a direct link between our past as we have learned to represent it and a future that we do not yet know. The things of the playroom are the prototypes of the adult Christian's world of faith.

Connecting Narrative and Object Relations

When my children were young, they not only cherished their transitional objects, they told stories to and about those dolls and teddy bears, held tea parties in their honor, and were convinced that their dolls and teddy bears really could sing and dance. Strikingly, the dolls and teddy bears also had grandparents, and weddings, and arguments.

My children were externalizing parts of their internal object narrative through the convenient "actors" that were their transitional objects.

In his book *The Motherhood Constellation*, Daniel Stern identifies a number of clinical models useful in categorizing types of object representation, both in infants and in their primary parents. Three of Stern's clinical models coincide with the narrative models presented in this and the previous chapter.

What Stern calls "The Dominant Theme Model" complements what I have called Family Narratives. Stern writes, "the baby is represented in the mother's eyes as taking part in and being woven into themes that have been ongoing, conflictual, and problematic throughout the mother's life or that at least predate the life of the baby" (35–36). The mother is herself a part of a larger systemic narrative, for as she tells the story of the object-infant, she also tells the story of the infant's father, her parents and his parents, and the story of the mother's extended support system (which is itself an object). Stern illustrates his point by naming some common dominant themes:

> There is the baby who is needed as an antidepressant to activate and animate a depressed mother. There is the baby who will provide unconditional love. The baby may be seen as avenger, as family saviour, as gift, as marital glue or, conversely, as a marital wedge. There is the baby whom one of the parents can narcissistically identify with. The theme may be the baby as a stranger, or the baby who was switched with another baby right after birth; the baby as companion, or complement to an older sib; the baby as a "normal" child or a "perfect" child or as a genius, and so on.

Stern raises the serious problem that these themes may be so dominant that they command too much of the parents' behavior. How much representational room is left to view the baby in the many possible ways the baby offers, other than the ways dictated by the dominant theme?

Both infant and mother in Stern's illustration are parts of a family. R. D. Laing introduced the concept of an object-family in his 1967 essay "The Family or 'The Family'?" He wrote, "The 'family,' the family as a fantasy structure, entails a type of relationship between family members of a different order from the relationships of those who do not share that 'family' inside each other" (5). A family's boundaries and identity, claims Laing, are defined by the specific number of people who share the same object-family representation with each other. The group-owned object-family takes on its own life, shaping the representations and interactions of the individual members of the family, and even serving to police members so that their behaviors and dreams continue to conform to the object-family's needs. Even here the family-of-origin system of each adult is relevant, for those raw materials are "transformed by internalization, partitioning, and other operations, into the 'family' and [then] mapped back onto the family" (Laing, 3).

What Stern calls "The Narrative Coherence Model" complements what I have called the Self-Defining Narrative. Stern writes:

> In this view, the story that one constructs, believes, and tells about the past has a "narrative coherence" that is thought to have more of an influence on current psychological life than does the "historical truth," which can be known only by way

of the narrative anyway. . . . The predictive power is not whether the mother's representation is true or distorted or dominated by a particular theme. It is the coherence, comprehensibility, continuity, consistency, plausibility, and emotional balance of the narrative told—that is, of the representation as narrated. (37)

Stern's definition of this model is supported by his analysis of mothers' stories of their own mothers: "The aspect of the mother's representation of her own mother that is most predictive of her future maternal behavior is not necessarily what happened in the past—whether she had a good or bad mothering experience—but rather the way in which she thinks and talks about her own mother now" (28–29). In other words, the form of the telling may be as important as—or even more important than—the story's content. The narrative of the past history may be more relevant than the past history itself, and the narrative is one exposition of the representation.

What Stern calls "The Protonarrative Envelope" (90–91) is similar to what I have called the Intersubjective Narrative, at least as it relates to the infant's object representations. Stern describes this "envelope" as a significant component of the infant's representational world. The protonarrative is a subjective construction that includes an agent, an action, an instrumentality, a goal, and a context, and it tracks a progression of events toward an end resolution. Stern believes that such narrative-like structures are already being created by infants during the preverbal phase and certainly can be articulated by any child old enough to structure a sequence of events. Stern's argument supports what I have already claimed: that the object representations in our heads take on a life of their own, carry on conversations with each other and thus shape each other, develop their own plots and action-lines, suffer crises, and reach their own unique denouements on a regular basis. In this intersubjective drama (or at other times, comedy) there is not a consistent audience or a predictable storyteller. The multiple object-selves combine with myriad object-others (infants, children, marital partners, siblings, parents, members of our extended support group, employers, and colleagues) to structure a rich and endless theatrical work, and we spend a great deal of our lives, both waking and dreaming, standing on the stage in the midst of the action.

When Family Systems theorist Murray Bowen did marriage counseling, he focused not so much on how a couple *feels* during a verbal exchange, but what they are *thinking* as they listen to each other talk. Bowen calls the intersubjective narrative our "private thinking world" (314), and observes that however much we know about our marital partner's feelings, we do not actually know much at all about our marital partner until we become privy to our partner's private thoughts. For Bowen, the private thinking world is peopled almost exclusively with memories, messages, and lessons from the past, specifically from each person's family of origin. He does not posit object representations per se. But in the intersubjective narrative, we now find the confluence of Family Systems Theory, Narrative Counseling Theory, and Object Relations Theory. Family Narratives and Self-Defining Narratives can be viewed simply as the externalization and verbalization of microscopic portions of our rich Intersubjective Narrative. All are shaped by our family of origin

as well as our present, and meaning is made of each by superimposing a coherent narrative plot. As on the stage, so in our minds: no character is real, but we are convinced that they are.

Object Relations and Christian Faith

The psychotherapeutic application of Object Relations Theory is too difficult for all ministers except those who have specialized training. As should already be obvious, however, the theory itself serves as crucial backgrounding for all types of "people work," from pastoral care to pastoral counseling, from homiletics to conflict resolution. In particular, Object Relations Theory bears direct significance for the processes of religious education, Christian formation, and spiritual direction.

Pastoral theologian Robert Wicks observes: "When people are interested in 'the spiritual life' they are, de facto, saying: 'I deeply value relationships'—relationships with themselves, others and God. Spirituality and appreciation of the relationships they have go hand in hand" (St. Clair 1994, 1). Relationality is the foundation of the Christian faith, particularly as summarized in Jesus' response to the young lawyer: "You shall love the Lord your God with all your heart and with all your soul and with all your mind . . . [and] you shall love your neighbor as yourself" (Matt. 22:37-39). What is it that inspires us to exercise our drive toward human relationships in loving ways? Christians answer, in the words of 1 John 4:19, that "We love because [God] loved us first." God loves us first, and we see that love reflected in a tangible manner in the faces of human beings around us. Leroy Howe, and Object Relations theorists in general, are not fully satisfied with the simplest explanation, but correctly wish to explore the psychology behind such an assertion. Howe asks, "In specific, can the love shining on a *human* face somehow 'be' for another also the very face of God? How? Is it not more likely that the love that makes growth possible comes to us *only* on human faces? When we speak of the face of God at all, do we not have in mind simply a particular human face? Are not human faces, after all, *all* there 'is' to God? . . . Could it be that we create God in our own image, and then deceive ourselves with the belief that the process is actually the reverse?" (90–91).

Object Relations Theory, which puts the nature of personal relationships at the very center of human inquiry about the meaning of existence, is the most frequent point at which faith, theology, and psychology achieve rapprochement. Used skillfully, this is the proper path to spiritual maturity for most Christians.

A Trinity of Gods

Michael St. Clair makes the distinction between "the idea of God" and the "God representation" (1994, 23). The idea of God is the concept that exists at a conscious level of thinking, "the God of scholars and theologians, the God which may not move us emotionally." I would like to call this "the subject-God," for theology is that portion of our religious commitment which is shaped by our conscious mind and informed thinking about the God who stimulates our intellects as a subject of discourse. St. Clair describes "the God representation" as "made up of images, feelings, and memories from early childhood" (1994, 22)—in other words, what we would call "the object-God," the God who is the product of our relationships with significant

object-others throughout our lifetime. Some Object Relations theorists would prefer to stop at this point, arguing that what Christians call God is simply an externalization of a complex set of highly subjective mental representations.

The method of all psychoanalytic theory, however, including object relations, is archaeological. "It serves the psyche as evolutionary theory serves geology, and therefore cannot claim reliable commentary on the legitimacy or potency of the Absolute Other. While it can track effects and describe their historic antecedents, it can never confirm or deny God's life" (Schmidt, 233). Since psychological theory cannot prove or disprove God's existence, some Object Relations theorists, including Ana-Maria Rizzuto, John McDargh, Harry Guntrip, W. W. Meissner, Moshe Spero, and Benjamin Beit-Hallahmi, are eager to assert the existence of a God who is beyond human capacity, beyond the subject-God and the object-God. I will call this "the God Beyond," the One who constantly reminds us, "my thoughts are not your thoughts, nor are your ways my ways" (Isa. 55:8).

We might then diagram the "three" Gods under discussion (see diagram on the following page). In our daily lives, the subject-God stands as the corrective to our object-God, in order to allow us to approach God as mature Christians rather than through childish superstition. Behind both stands the God Beyond, the God toward whom we move in our spiritual journey through life, but who is not available to us until we understand that the subject-God and the object-God are both human creations that can never capture the truth of the Source of Our Being. To comprehend the God Beyond, we must each

The Subject-God	The God of belief, of rational and intellectual discourse, "the God of theologians and scholars."
The Object-God	The God of faith, for "faith is a reasoning of the heart by means of personal images" (McDargh in St. Clair 1994, 29), the God whom we perceive only through the eyes of our internalized object-others.
The God Beyond	The God Who Is, the God of Kierkegaard's "infinite resignation: the movement of the soul in which one strips oneself of all finite consolations and wish fulfillments in order to enter into a relationship with the absolute that is God" (McDargh, 57).

integrate and then transcend the subject-God and the object-God.

C. Ellis Nelson describes the durability of the object-God:

> The god image is also unique among the objects represented in the infant's self because it endures throughout the life span. This comes about because most parents—and society generally—reinforce the god image and negate other images. Although the god image is created at a time when the infant may internalize a mental image of ghosts, monsters, witches, or Santa Claus, these images are slowly suppressed by caregivers and society. The god image is encouraged or is allowed to be whatever the infant says it is on the theory the infant will "out-grow" the primitive image of god.... Some people are able to give up childish ways in religion as the Apostle Paul admonished them to do so that they would be able to reason like an adult (1 Cor. 13:11). But many people are not able to overcome fear, loneliness, or lack of self-confidence characterizing their private god image without the help of psychotherapy. (35–36)

Like all other object representations in our mental landscape, our object-God becomes a character within our intersubjective narrative. We dialogue internally with God, ignore God, bargain with God, manipulate God, fear God, seek God's comfort, and merge with God symbiotically. The dialogue and emotional relationships between various object-selves and the object-God are like those that exist between two persons. The relationship can be friendly, supportive, judgmental, forgiving, suggesting as to how to act, or some combination of the above, depending on the circumstances the self is facing. The self can also resist, reject, or deny any relation to the god image. Even atheists have an image of God in which they do not believe but continue to carry internally and dialogue with (Nelson 33, 36).

Because this "primitive image of God," the object-God, is the most durable image throughout our lives as Christians, and the one so difficult to free from the shackles of human projection, it is to the process of forming and then deconstructing the object-God that the rest of this chapter will be devoted. Along the way we may have to face uncomfortable truths about the way we image God and what we assume about faith. To some readers it may feel that we are disempowering or even destroying God. But as Carrie Doehring reminds us, "This disengaged and underpowered figure is reminiscent of images of the crucified Christ" (118–19). As disciples of Christ we must not fear powerlessness, for it is there that God is most present, even the God whom we fear we have disempowered.

Human Infancy and the Object-God

The first three years of a child's life are the most significant for the formation of an object-God. From myriad object images, cues, gestures, instructions, reprimands, and routines the young child begins the process that Rizzuto calls "The Birth of the Living God." Leroy Howe captures the tiny moments whose repetition creates the mental representation for a young baby of who God must be, beginning with the primary parent's mirroring:

> The substance out of which children begin, very early in life, to compose for themselves such a comforting, sustaining, encouraging, and encompassing idea of God, is parental countenance, the expressions on their faces by which parents gently communicate to their children what life is and can be like. Hopefully, what will show on parents' faces consistently is the kind of confidence about life and its possibilities that will arouse in each infant an abiding level of trust. If their children choose to catch such a vision and make it their own, then throughout all their lives their anxieties can give way to feelings of security, their frustrations can become

challenges rather than calamities, the pain of absence can become the opportunity to create cherished memories, and reaching out to the benevolent faces of those who love them will be only the beginning of a process that intends the embrace of all creation. Infants so blessed are able to gather up their experiences of benign, powerful, parental regard and weave them into the rich texture of an image of God and of themselves gazing upon the face of that God without fear, savoring God's kindly face perpetually shining with grace and peace. (105–6)

The particular way the parent starts the self-development of the infant is through eye contact and reflecting back to the child a sense of the child's status as beloved. This mirroring is but part of the larger environment that feeds the creation of the object-God.

The infant's primitive object-God is unique for each person because each person's experience as a baby differs so from everyone else's. In this sense, we can say that an object-God is private. The young child's God-image is formed from two sources: (a) the internalized images and feeling states from relations with parents, siblings, and playmates, plus the social, economic, and religious situation in which the family lives; and (b) the instructions and other verbal messages about God that parents give their children (Nelson, 35). Because the infant's object-God is so influenced by parental interaction, the parents' God images must also be taken into account, for they influence parenting style, both nonverbally and verbally (among the places we are called to live out our faith is in the nursery). The parents' God-representations will be passed on in

• unconsciously communicated attitudes, hints, and behaviors,

- family myths and stories,
- recounted details of the child's naming,
- the more overt religious practices of the family, such as mealtime grace, bedtime prayers, admonishments, and moral and ethical behavioral instructions,

as the child's inner representations of self, God, and the self-God relation begin to form.

The child does not consciously create the image of God out of fantasy, but rather out of the concrete experiences of family prayer, stories, or questions asked of parents. The child's sense and image of God are thus, in a complex way, closely connected with the child's own parents. In terms of projection, the continuity may be direct between the parents as a basis and the object-God, or the object-God might be quite opposite, so that God in this scenario may be utterly good and protecting while the parents get devalued (St. Clair 1994, 12). Whatever the case, children will collect bits and pieces of what they are told in order to construct a God-image that is essentially in place by the end of the child's third year. Though a child's object-God is repeatedly questioned and revised throughout the rest of life, it is this primitive God that a person is likely to fall back on in times of emotional or relational crisis.

Rizzuto, Doehring, Schmidt, St. Clair, and Beit-Hallahmi disagree over whether the mother or the father is a more important source of God representations. Certainly in Christianity, the God representation still has predominantly paternal characteristics. For the vast majority of infants, however, the first object-others are created in symbiosis at the mother's breast and in frequent interaction with a female parent. The solution to the theorists' disagreement is probably that an infant creates multiple mother-representations and father-representations during the first three years. While a Christian upbringing may teach a child to refer to God as male, the specific representations to which the masculine vocabulary are attached are probably in large part drawn from the infant's repertoire of both object-mothers and object-fathers. At any rate, in the early years a child's representations are primarily feeling complexes rather than sexualized "photographs" of object-others. Schmidt reminds us not to succumb to identifying simple parallels between God representations and respective persons in an individual's life (233). Rather, God representations are as complex as any object-other. What must receive greater attention is the *process* of forming and transforming representations, rather than rooting objects in a particular gendered parent. At the same time, St. Clair observes that during the oedipal phase, the object-God representation may become as gendered and sexualized as the object-parents become (1994, 42–43). The earliest object-others, and hence the earliest God representations, are based on the absorption of part objects, which are more easily split into all-good and all-bad camps.

Splitting, in general, is probably the source of many of the insidious dualisms that infect Christianity. Fauteux suggested that early infancy splitting of the mother into good/bad objects is reflected in religious belief systems about God and the devil (Beit-Hallahmi, 260). God may be idealized and things not having to do with God devalued (with the concomitant devaluation or idealization of the self). Body and soul may be split, with the bodily (and sexual) needs seen as all bad, deserving of suppression or punishment, and the soul's needs as all good, worthy of indulgence at any cost, as if the soul needs no disciplining. As early as 1939, Roheim interpreted the ancient ritual of covenanting through the cutting of a victim through the middle, mentioned in Genesis 15:7-21 but also known from other cultures, by offering an object relations explanation. The fantasy of opening up the mother's body, appearing in an analysand's free associations, is tied to a fantasy of finding "good body contents" inside (Beit-Hallahmi, 259).

As has been mentioned, the formation of transitional objects is probably the origin of the human ability to construct and cherish symbols. The earliest transitional object, according to Winnicott, is the baby's own hand. As Howe points out, "The infant whose use of his own hand Winnicott saw as a bold move toward self-pacification and separation from the mother's breast also was discovering what the hand of God is for, and the meaning it has for becoming what truly loving parents want their children to be above all else: creatures who can 'handle' life on their own" (106). Melanie Klein, however, in her seminal essay "The Importance of Symbol Formation in the Development of the Ego," points out that transitional objects as well as certain object-others are constructed by the infant in order to reduce anxiety (97–98). (This helps us to understand the theological usefulness of anxiety, as did Paul Tillich.) Another important aspect of the analogies between transitional objects and our ideas of God has to do with the "presence" that transitional objects mediate. In transitional objects we experience the presence of God in a "place" that is neither wholly outside nor inside us, neither solely real nor solely fan-

tasized (Howe, 112). Herein lies the affective power for Christians of symbols such as the cross and the Eucharist.

The "Pet God" and Faith Development

By age three, we have each constructed what Ana-Maria Rizzuto calls "our pet God," based on parental object-others and accumulated messages about God and faith from our environment. This object-God is constructed long before most children begin religious education in local congregations. Children in our youngest Sunday school classes, then, do not present themselves as a tabula rasa, for as Rizzuto puts it: "No child arrives at the house of God without his pet God under his arm" (167). The power of this infantile object-God is apparent when we examine the words of certain popular hymns. Nelson writes:

> During the first seven or eight months the infant has experiences related to caregivers of a physical nature such as being fed, bathed, held, looking at the mother's face, hearing sounds and music. Experiences of this type continue throughout infancy and are preserved as memories. They may be later linked to a particular god image and may result in a good feeling when singing "Safe in the Arms of Jesus," "O Love That Will Not Let Me Go," "God Will Take Care of You," "Jesus, Lover of My Soul, Let Me to Thy Bosom Fly." . . . Later, when individuals develop the ability to reason abstractly, there may be an effort to bring these early feelings states into harmony with reason; but this is difficult to accomplish. (33–34)

As a child enters formal religious education, particularly between ages three and six, the object-God of the child and the subject-God of church teaching face each other, so that through the child's reshaping and rethinking there is a blending, a "second birth" of God. Yet, however much religious education may add to the representation of God that has already been formed, it never undoes the infantile object-God completely.

Moving with the individual through the epigenetic phases of the developmental sequence, the God representation will, ideally, adapt with and reflect the more or less satisfactory integration of derivatives of all developmental phases. It may be friendly, supportive, forgiving, judgmental, or demanding in its relation to the self. The self may, in turn, welcome, resist, acquiesce to its demands, or reject and deny any relation to it. For some children, early intrapsychic dynamics or even religious instruction may create a rigid God figure unable to undergo correlative evolution with the changing self-object, cognitive and conceptual development, or accumulating life experience. John Shea describes this rigid object-God as "The Superego God." Transcendent and distant, exercising absolute authority, it demands moral obedience and orthodoxy of belief in relations characterized by conditional acceptance, benevolent domination, and providence. This is the God of power abuse and conformity who provides refuge from the struggle and pain of making our own choices. Trust and comfort become mixed with ambivalence, anxiety, doubt, and isolating guilt. Self and God representations in this structure are frozen and constrained by the superego's demands. Doehring reminds us how easily these rigid object-Gods become idolatrous when they are presumed to be an accurate representation of the God Beyond (112).

St. Clair offers one possible schema of faith development (1994, 35–46). It should be noted that St. Clair's schema differs sig-nificantly from the developmental schemas suggested by Margaret Mahler, Jean Piaget, James Fowler, and Erik Erikson. St. Clair's schema is based on the relationship between the growth of object representational stages and the derivative faith perceptions they enable. All are intended to point to ways in which growing Christians move from an infantile object-God to a perception of the God Beyond.

1. *Fusion*. If the infant's earliest object-representation is of an idealized parental image or object, then it follows, as Rizzuto suggests, that the prevailing characteristics of the God representation share in the characteristics of the parents' representations. Developmentally the first God representation is made from the real or wished-for good parent of a small child. This God is a kind and loving presence who is always available.

2. *Early Psychological Differentiation*. In Kohutian terms, parents serve as self-objects; that is, they play an important role in fostering the child's self-esteem and well-being by "mirroring" (showing joyful appreciation of the child) and allowing the child to idealize them (when the child attributes to them unrealistic status and power). Cognition and affect are still somewhat confused, while the feeling quality of the experience usually predominates over the rational and logical. God is felt, more than thought of, in animistic and magical terms as the omnipotent and omniscient presence of force. To depend on such an omnipotent and idealized God creates conflicted feelings that might get resolved by masochistic submission and superstitious placation.

3. *Integration*. Oedipal issues seem important because of the intense feelings involved.

The God representation that had already included aspects of both parents may become sexualized. If oedipal conflicts are resolved and the parental representation is desexualized and exalted into a Godhead, the individual may have a most pleasant and satisfying relationship with God. During the elementary school years the child becomes aware of a clearer distinction between God and parents.

4. *Latency and Puberty*. Children of latency age (from about seven to ten) tend to view God as more universal, and these children begin to dissociate the image of father from the image of God. God-images remain anthropomorphic—a magnified human— but the individual's ideas of God are progressing in the direction of a more spiritualized Godhead. W. W. Meissner believes this is the point at which most people's faith stops growing, and that they continue to act out their faith for the rest of their lives on the basis of a vaguely anthropomorphic God who is only slightly dissociated from their own object-father (St. Clair 1994, 45). Previous argument in this chapter would suggest that the object-God remains infused with significant representations of the believer's object-mothers as well. But the issue of arrested faith development is an interesting one, in that it is at approximately this same stage and age that James Fowler believes most people's faith stops growing (61–62, the Synthetic-Conventional Stage). By consulting Erik Erikson's developmental schema, we discover that pubertal mentality is highly dependent upon peer group conformity, and "in-group/out-group" splitting, a dichotomization typical of much Christian anxiety about boundaries, inclusiveness, and theological pluralism (1980, 129, 135).

5. *Adolescence*. By the end of adolescence, the God representation has acquired the basic traits that are to last for life, though some new additions and transformations are still possible. At this point the God representation is complex and made from the many exchanges between the individual and the parents.

Despite the claim that the object-God's traits are firmly in place by the end of adolescence, St. Clair, Nelson, and Doehring all agree that we continue to form potent object representations throughout our lives. "Transformative life events can change existing images of God, self, and significant others and add new images of God, self, and others" (Doehring, 110).

As a Christian matures toward more autonomy and independence, an authority-pleasing self relating to a private, authority-figure object-God may need to draw on other resources in order to engage the necessary adjustments of the inner world. New intellectual or philosophical resources may help move an oppressively immanent God toward more distant abstract representations that allow greater freedom. Conversely, a distant, transcendent God may become a closer, personal figure to whom the self relates in a more permissive mutuality. As Howe points out, "Those who are capable of mature religious belief renew their God representation to make it compatible with their emotional, conscious, and unconscious situation, as well as their cognitive and object-related development" (104).

St. Clair puts forward a comprehensive definition of spiritual maturity from an Object Relations point of view:

> A person of mature spiritual and psychological life is able to embrace, affirm and somehow resolve the tensions of life, to

integrate them in a more balanced faith orientation and faith existence. Such an individual can look upon religious belief systems and their traditions in increasingly realistic terms which enables the individual to tolerate inherent tensions and ambiguities. Such an individual can affirm and hold to the beliefs, ritual symbols and ceremonial of a religious community in all their relativity, partiality, limitations and particularity. At the same time this knowing through faith is able to acknowledge the existence and validity of other faith traditions adhered to by different persons and different cultures. (1994, 47)

In the Christian journey, some people will not be able to progress beyond their infantile needs for comfort or for a god who bears the image of their object-parents. Others will be able to mature in relation to their God representation just as they mature in relation to their parents. Faith relationships both will be and must be congruent with one's capacity for human relationships. As one grows, the other must grow. If either stalemates, the other will stalemate with it.

Moving beyond the usual growth arrest at a pubertal stage of faith to Christian maturity, including the integration of an object-God with the God Beyond, requires considerable soul searching, self-scrutiny, and internal re-elaboration of representations. The primary God-image, which is deeply influenced by parents, must undergo a secondary process in order to become a theologically informed image. Some secondary influences will be effective during childhood and early adolescence, such as the substance and nature of instruction in religion, the religious beliefs and practices of the family, and the religious ethos of the community. But a secondary reimaging of the object-God will not have the full

resources of the self until about age sixteen, when a person ordinarily develops the ability to reason abstractly. From that point on, individuals should be mentally equipped to reconcile their personal God-image with a theologically informed image (Nelson, 22).

Conclusion

Leroy Howe argues that Object Relations are ultimately the proving ground for our comprehension of God's love:

> Encounters with caring persons, and the relationships with them that transitional objects make possible, themselves are profoundly symbolic. As we have learned, transitional objects help us to sustain a sense of the presence of other caring creatures who with us bear God's image. In this way, they aid us in maintaining relationships. From the perspective of faith, being held and nurtured by someone who loves us as unconditionally as human beings are capable of loving is itself a representation of our most archaic (namely, origin-ating) relationship of all, being held and nurtured by the One who even now is creating us and calling us to fulfill our destiny. This suggests that one purpose for all our finite relationships is to prepare us for a loving relationship with God. And indeed, for faith, the most important transition in all of life does involve detaching our loyalties and affections from the things of this world, even from those who mediate the love of God to us, in order that we can devote them to their proper "object." (114)

Of course, not all relationships are expressed externally through Christian deeds and random acts of kindness. Object Relations reminds us that our external relationships are directly shaped by those intersubjective narratives which play out in our heads. In this sense it could be claimed that of the three psychotherapeutic systems upon which this book is based, Object Relations is most closely related to Christian character formation and ultimately, therefore, to Christian wholeness. We can connect character formation to the saying of Jesus at Matthew 5:21-22. There Jesus cites the social and religious prescription against murder, but goes on to say that angry thinking—a powerful plot within the intersubjective narrative—is as abhorrent to God as is an act of murder. Like all biblical passages, this dominical innovation needs to be treated carefully. It is not an encouragement to suppress our own emotional literacy but a challenge that the repeated analysis and healing of our intersubjective narrative is as imperative for Christians as is disciplined behavior.

Object Relations lays the foundation for ultimate intimacy with the God Beyond; equally it lays the foundation for dysfunctional social relationships, as we respond to the object-others we have constructed rather than to people as they understand themselves. Once again we see that the finest Christian hope lies buried deeply within the shadows of the human psyche.

BIBLIOGRAPHY

American Psychiatric Association. *Diagnostic and Statistical Manual of Mental Disorders, Fourth Edition (DSM-IV)*. Washington, D.C.: American Psychiatric Association, 1994.

Atkinson, Peter. "Object Relations Theory and the Necessary Cost of Theological Deconstruction." Unpublished essay, St. John's Theological College, Auckland, New Zealand, October 8, 1996.

Beit-Hallahmi, Benjamin. "Object Relations Theory and Religious Experience." In *Handbook of Religious Experience*. Ralph W. Hood Jr., ed. 254–68. Birmingham, Ala.: Religious Education Press, 1995.

Bowen, Murray. *Family Therapy in Clinical Practice*. New York: Jason Aronson, 1978.

Bowlby, John. *A Secure Base: Parent-Child Attachments and Healthy Human Development*. New York: Basic, 1988.

Doehring, Carrie. *Taking Care: Monitoring Power Dynamics and Relational Boundaries in Pastoral Care and Counseling*. Nashville: Abingdon, 1995.

Erikson, Erik. *Insight and Responsibility: Lectures on the Ethical Implications of Psychoanalytic Thought*. New York: W. W. Norton, 1964.

———. *Identity and the Life Cycle*. New York: W. W. Norton, 1980.

Fowler, James W. *Becoming Adult, Becoming Christian: Adult Development and Christian Faith*. San Francisco: HarperSanFrancisco, 1984.

Fraiberg, Selma, Edna Adelson, and Vivian Shapiro. "Ghosts in the Nursery: A Psychoanalytic Approach to the Problems of Impaired Infant-Mother Relationship." *Journal of the American Academy of Child Psychiatry* 14 (1975): 387–421.

Gazzaniga, M., and J. LeDoux. *The Integrated Mind*. New York: Plenum, 1978.

Grotstein, James. *Splitting and Projective Identification*. Northvale, N.J.: Jason Aronson, 1985.

Hamilton, N. Gregory. *Self and Others: Object Relations Theory in Practice*. Northvale, N.J.: Jason Aronson, 1990.

Horner, Althea. *Psycho-Analytic Object Relations Therapy*. Northvale: Jason Aronson, 1991.

Howe, Leroy. *The Image of God: A Theology for Pastoral Care and Counseling.* Nashville: Abingdon, 1995.

Kamptner, N. Laura. "Treasured Possessions and Their Meanings in Adolescent Males and Females." *Adolescence* 30:118 (summer 1995): 301–18.

Klein, Melanie. *The Selected Melanie Klein.* Mitchell, Juliet, ed. New York: Free Press, 1986. Includes "The Psychological Principles of Infant Analysis" (1926), 57–68; "The Importance of Symbol Formation in the Development of the Ego" (1930), 95–111; "Notes on Some Schizoid Mechanisms" (1946), 174–200; and "The Origins of Transference" (1952), 201–10.

Kosek, Robert. "The Contribution of Object Relations Theory in Pastoral Counseling." *Journal of Pastoral Care* 50:4 (winter 1996): 371–81.

Laing, R. D. *The Politics of the Family and Other Essays.* New York: Vintage, 1971.

Magaletta, Philip. "An Object Relations Paradigm for Spiritual Development with Highlights from Merton's Spiritual Journey." *Pastoral Psychology* 45:1 (1996): 21–28.

Mahler, Margaret. *Separation-Individuation.* The Selected Papers of Margaret S. Mahler, Vol. 2. Northvale, N.J.: Jason Aronson, 1979.

McDargh, John. *Psychoanalytic Object Relations Theory and the Study of Religion.* Lanham, Md.: University Press of America, 1983.

McWilliams, Nancy. *Psychoanalytic Diagnosis: Understanding Personality Structure in the Clinical Process.* New York: Guilford, 1994.

Nelson, C. Ellis. "Formation of a God Representation." *Religious Education* 91:1 (winter 1996): 22–39.

Parker, Don. "Melanie Klein." Unpublished lecture, St. John's Theological College, Auckland, New Zealand, May 19, 1996.

Rizzuto, Ana-Maria. *The Birth of the Living God.* Chicago: University of Chicago Press, 1979.

Sayers, Janet. *Mothers of Psychoanalysis: Helene Deutsch, Karen Horney, Anna Freud, and Melanie Klein.* New York: W. W. Norton, 1991.

Scarf, Maggie. *Intimate Partners: Patterns in Love and Marriage.* New York: Ballantine, 1987.

Schafer, Roy. *Retelling a Life: Narration and Dialogue in Psychoanalysis.* New York: Basic, 1992.

Scharff, Jill Savege, and David E. Scharff. *Scharff Notes: A Primer of Object Relations Therapy.* Northvale, N.J.: Jason Aronson, 1992.

Schmidt, William. Review of *Object Relations Theory and Religion: Clinical Applications,* edited by Mark Finn and John Gartner. *Journal of Supervision and Training in Ministry* 16 (1995): 230–34.

Shea, John. "The Superego God." *Pastoral Psychology* 43 (1995): 333–51.

St. Clair, Michael. *Object Relations and Self Psychology: An Introduction.* Monterey: Brooks/Cole, 1986.

———. *Human Relationships and the Experience of God: Object Relations and Religion.* New York: Paulist, 1994.

Stern, Daniel. *The Motherhood Constellation: A Unified View of Parent-Infant Psychotherapy.* New York: Basic, 1995.

Winnicott, D. W. *Playing and Reality.* London: Routledge, 1971.

Part Two

~

The Application

4. Premarital Counseling

"The pastoral pre-wedding task is to link the legacies from their families of origin with the values of the couple and the stories of the Christian tradition in order to understand more clearly their influence and to plan a wedding that symbolizes how they want to become married." (Herbert Anderson and Robert Cotton Fite, 6)

Current statistics suggest that a very low percentage of engaged couples seek any form of premarital counseling prior to their wedding (McGoldrick 1989, 222). Since in Europe, England, and Australasia, more people marry outside the church than in it, we can presume the truth of this statement for much of Western Christianity. In the United States, though many couples also live together without marrying, the majority of those who marry still have church weddings, and most denominations require some form of premarital counseling.

Most denominations leave the form and content of premarital counseling up to the individual minister. Styles and approaches vary widely, but the current divorce rate among both clergy and Christian parishioners would suggest that premarital counseling has more often been done badly than well. This is not to claim, of course, that effective premarital counseling can guarantee a stable and happy marriage. It can be claimed, however, that effective premarital counseling provides the opportunity to reduce significantly misunderstandings and tensions in the subsequent relationships, and thereby to reduce the level of unhappy marriages, if not divorces.

It would appear that the most common approach to premarital counseling takes the form of having the couple fill out various questionnaires or "inventories" in the hopes that they will identify potential issues between them. Yet, "becoming a couple" is one of the most complex and difficult transitions that anyone undergoes during the course of the life cycle (McGoldrick 1989, 209), and few questionnaires are designed to uncover these psychological processes of transition. While an inventory may provide a fairly accurate profile of the way each partner within the couple acts and thinks, it does not address the more critical issues of *why* they think and act the way they do. Nor does a questionnaire address the issue of one's separating from the family of origin and creating a new family, with its own rules, expectations, and allegiances.

The actual wedding day is but a fleeting moment in time. We have exaggerated and romanticized it to the point that it overshadows the year leading up to the wedding and the year following the wedding. Yet, it is not the perfect wedding day that makes a happy marriage but, rather, successfully navigating the pitfalls of the year leading up to the wedding and the year following. These are the more appropriate focus of the minister's attention, in spite of how easy it is to get distracted with the endless planning that seems to accompany most American church weddings.

This chapter will set out a program of premarital counseling that takes seriously the developmental and psychological tasks necessary for a couple to build a new life together that is their own, and not simply an extension of one or both partners' family of origin. The suggestions set forth here are based on Family Systems Theory, Narrative

Counseling Theory, and Object Relations Theory. By focusing on the theoretical basis of premarital work and the process leading up to the formal wedding ceremony, ministers more effectively equip a couple for the complex task of "getting married," a stage of becoming that more correctly describes the first few years of marriage than it does the wedding day itself.

Who Needs Premarital Counseling?

In much of the church's earlier history, premarital counseling was not required. For example, although the Episcopal Church in the United States first began to formulate its canon (ecclesiastical) law in 1789, it was not until nearly 150 years later, in 1931, that the canons required a clergyperson to provide premarital counseling to a couple (White and Dykman, 1.406).

Today virtually all denominations agree that every couple who plans to marry needs premarital counseling, whether they marry in the church or not. The minister should make it clear that the couple cannot be married in the church unless they have undergone a specific period of marital preparation. Yet, it would seem that not everyone can immediately see the benefits of premarital counseling.

In many Western countries today, the number of couples who are establishing long-term partnerships without marrying exceeds the number of couples who marry legally. In England, Europe, and Australasia, these couples may seek to participate in parish life fully, and "the jury is still out" concerning their acceptance, particularly in more conservative congregations. In congregations where such de facto partnerships are accepted, the materials laid out in this chapter may serve as a basis not only for premarital counseling, but also for pre-relationship counseling. As well, much of this material would be appropriate to use with couples who come to the church for a blessing on their previous civil marriage, for those who had less than optimal premarital counseling earlier and seek to improve their relationship skills, and for those who wish to renew their marriage vows on the occasion of an important anniversary.

Further, there is disagreement within and between denominations about whether those who are not already "churched" should have the opportunity to marry within the church. The dilemma is not new; pastoral counselor Martin Parsons struggled with it thirty years ago:

> We can fully sympathize with the desire to confine the use of Christian services to Christian people. The difficulty is in judging who is a Christian and who is not. If we demand that a person be a regular communicant, we have to define what we mean by "regular." . . . It seems better to take the more traditional view of giving our ministry to those who ask for it. . . . This gives us the opportunity of teaching them why a marriage service in church is "different," as they so often express it. (3)

In other words, Parsons sees weddings as an opportunity for evangelization, assuming that the couple, even though not both Christian, are willing to undergo the complete sequence of premarital counseling sessions.

Some couples will resist any suggestion to examine their relationship with seriousness or candor. As Mitchell and Anderson point out, "People who want to marry tend to regard it as not in their best interest to reveal anything that might lead anyone to doubt the sincerity of their love or the viability of their relationship" (73). Such people may have trouble being frank or honest about dysfunction within their family of origin, wanting only to present themselves to their potential partner in the best possible light. Enough psychological concepts have entered common parlance that to reveal family misery or family secrets may engender fear of possible rejection. Ministers need to emphasize that any family-of-origin issue that is guarded from examination is a potential land mine within the coming marital relationship.

Yet others will be cynical or, at the very least, skeptical. This seems more true for couples that have cohabited for a significant period of time, despite the fact that statistics indicate that couples who have lived together prior to marriage have a higher divorce rate than those who have not (Carter and McGoldrick, 211; Dornbusch, Herman, and Liu, 32). Such people may presume that cohabiting has already taught them all they need to know about being married, thereby making premarital counseling superfluous. Ministers need to help the couple understand that marriage is *not* the same as living together, and that a lengthy period of cohabitation before marriage may in fact indicate significant problems to come. Interpreting the reluctance to marry as indicating a failure to individuate adequately from one's birth family, Mitchell and Anderson remark, "Living together, no matter on how intimate or serious a basis, is not the same as being married, nor does it necessarily hasten the process of leaving home. Indeed, the resistance to marriage displayed by a substantial proportion of cohabiting couples often represents—the couple's proclamations of independence not withstanding—

the inability of one or the other or both to leave home effectively" (75).

One obvious difference is symbolized by the change in titles associated with roles. On the day of the wedding, a boyfriend or girlfriend, a lover, a partner suddenly becomes a "husband" or a "wife." Each person has grown up with a significant set of associations that define the terms *husband* and *wife,* based on our experiences as children. However much we may attempt to free ourselves from this childhood baggage, once we bear the title of "husband," we begin to behave in the way we think a husband does, and our partner begins to behave toward us in the same manner that she was taught to behave toward her "husband model," her father. The same reactivity holds true in relation to the title "wife." Such reactions easily lead to the charge "You're not the person I married," or perhaps "Marriage has ruined our perfectly good relationship," for the behavioral changes that accompany the title changes indeed mean that marriage is a very different relationship from cohabitation.

Another group will have trouble focusing on the task at hand. Some people in love simply cannot think clearly, as counselors have known for a long time. They see what they want to see and hear what they want to hear, and whatever is not focused on their new partner in passion is often simply tuned out. George Bernard Shaw put it succinctly: "you cannot devote your life to two divinities: God and the person you are married to" (Preface, 51). Anderson, Hogue, and McCarthy put it a different way: "The initial promises in marriage are made without knowing fully what they will mean or what they will cost" (80). These couples walk through premarital counseling as though it were simply "dues-payable" before they can get on with the business of living happily ever after. In order to distract them from their dreams and seduce them back to reality, a pastor must find some conversational venue that engages them.

For these and the many other types of couples who come to the church for premarital counseling, psychometric instruments and questionnaires feel tedious and seem to threaten their security or the "specialness" that they attribute to their relationship. Ministers need to develop an approach to premarital counseling that emphasizes the unique nature of these two people in relationship and offers them the means for exploring new ground. Something must rescue the church's standard practices of pre-marriage work from tedium and apparent pointlessness. We need to rediscover methodologies that engage the heart, and not simply the head (Webber, 204). One of the quickest ways to engage people's hearts is to ask them to talk about themselves: where they came from and why they are who they are.

The goal of premarital counseling is to create an atmosphere within which couples can leave their families of origin—psychologically and emotionally, though not always literally—as they move toward creating a new family unit. Effective use of this intimate time between a pastor and a couple will also lay the foundation for the couple's return to the pastor for further assistance when problems arise in the future.

When to Schedule Premarital Counseling

Many experienced clergy suggest that premarital counseling begin far enough in advance of the wedding that if something comes up between the couple that suggests they not marry at this time, it is not too late to notify guests that the wedding is being postponed or canceled. Most pastors also believe that at least one of the premarital sessions needs to be conducted before the pastor even agrees to officiate at the wedding. An astute pastor will be able to judge relatively quickly, within that first hour's appointment, whether the circumstances and chemistry between the couple "feel" right enough for the pastor to officiate without compromising the pastor's personal integrity.

One way to begin to ascertain this information is to ask the couple, during the initial session, to tell the story of their courtship. This will give the pastor a great deal of insight into the couple and will lay the foundation for the narrative approach to which the pastor will return in sessions 3 to 6. Once the couple have told their story, the pastor should ask why they have decided to marry now, as opposed to last month or next year, for example. What has happened to them that lets them know this is the correct moment to further their commitment to each other (Mitchell and Anderson, 76)? Such a question will lay the foundation for the genogram work to which the pastor will return, for in many instances the couple's decision to marry has been precipitated by events elsewhere in their larger family systems. As they tell their story and answer the questions, the pastor should observe how they communicate, who dominates, whether they tell "the same story" or whether their versions are quite different, and something about each person's temperament. This material, too, will indicate to the pastor whether or not to proceed with a further involvement with the couple.

As Anderson and Fite point out, "there is an inevitable gate-keeping function in all pre-wedding work" (62). When a couple has no interest in exploring the relationship between their individual family stories, the story of their love for each other, and the Christian story, it is probably appropriate to suggest that they marry outside the church. For some couples, this will be the first opportunity for them to clarify the place of faith and commitment to a parish in their future life together. If there is little place for faith and prayer in their lives, then marriage in the church makes no sense. If the couple is unwilling to follow the customs of the local parish, the dictates of good taste and decency, or the restrictions of the national denomination, they should be referred elsewhere. If there is any sign that one will do harm to the other, whether physical or emotional, the minister should refer the couple for psychological counseling before proceeding further with premarital work.

The counseling pattern laid out in the rest of this chapter implies a structured series of seven sixty- to ninety-minute sessions. Session 1 would be the initial meeting between the minister and the couple seeking to marry. The discussion above suggests the agenda for that initial meeting: to determine whether the minister is emotionally and ecclesiologically comfortable officiating at the wedding, and whether the couple is comfortable with the minister. Only after this initial session has been completed should the minister decide whether or not to proceed with the rest of the premarital preparation. Session 2 would focus on the arrangements for the wedding and for the reception if it is also to be held in the church. Some of the critical issues for the second session will be discussed below. Sessions 3 through 6 should adopt a systems approach to the psychological preparation for becoming a couple. As we shall see, this is often referred to as "leaving and cleaving." Finally, session 7 should address the Christian theology of marriage, and how the couple can interweave their own stories with the church's story. By this time, the minister will have gained enough intimate knowledge of the couple to help them realize how they are already living out the great theological themes of repentance and forgiveness, blessing and redemption, the kingdom of God and future hope.

This pattern, of course, is only a suggestion. Each minister will need to find a pattern that fits his or her own personal style and parish and denominational expectations. But if the component parts just described are followed, and two weeks are allowed between each session, then counseling would have to begin a minimum of fourteen weeks prior to the wedding service. Some ministers will prefer an even longer period, perhaps up to six months prior to the service.

In a highly mobile society, some couples may not be resident in the city or town where the wedding will take place and thus will not be available to the minister for premarital counseling. In that case, the pastor should insist that session 1 occurs in his or her presence, following which the pastor should contact a minister in the town where the couple currently resides. A phone conversation can make it clear what content the pastor expects to be included in the preparation, and the couple should be advised that the pastor will not proceed with the actual wedding unless assured that the required premarital counseling has been completed. On some occasions, the pastor may find that both members of the couple do not presently live in the same location. In that case, following session 1, each would be required to undergo premarital counseling alone, though this situation is certainly far from optimal.

Session 2: Taking Care of Business

A book written to serve the needs of a variety of Christian denominations cannot in a short space cover all the options available in planning a wedding service. Some denominations require that a standardized prayer book service be used and provide little chance for deviation. Other denominations take a completely free-form approach to the service structure, tailoring it to the desires of the bride and groom. In all circumstances, the bride and groom also bring unique wishes and circumstances to a wedding so that no two services are ever identical, even in denominations that require the use of a standardized prayer book liturgy.

Regardless of these denominational distinctions, certain decisions should always be made in consultation with the minister and not simply left to the discretion of the bride and groom. There are many things that can go wrong with a wedding service, and many popular elements of taste that actually contradict Christian tradition, such that the minister needs to pay detailed attention to all aspects of planning. In extreme circumstances, these details may prove so non-negotiable between the minister and the marrying couple that the minister may be forced to decline the couple's request to marry them. Among the many items that need the pastor's attention are:

• whether the wedding will take place in the church or in some other location. Many denominations now have an official

policy forbidding clergy to participate in weddings that do not take place in a church building. In this instance, as in several others that follow, the elemental question is why this couple desires a church wedding rather than going the more common route of being married by a justice of the peace or other secular marriage celebrant. Adequate reasons do not ordinarily include that "this is such a pretty church."

• whether the couple can marry legally according to state law. If either the bride or groom has been divorced from a previous marriage, the pastor must see the actual divorce papers and must check for any irregularities. Information in those divorce papers will prove useful in future counseling sessions as well. Nor can ministers, at least in most countries, marry people outside the requirements of civil law. For example, some years ago an older couple in my parish asked me to marry them "in the eyes of the church" but not "in the eyes of the state," for both stood to lose sizeable retirement benefits by remarrying. Of course, the answer was no. Any minister who is an agent of the state can no longer perform marriages that ignore the requirements of the state or national jurisdiction. A minister may not officiate at the marriage of anyone who is under age (without parental consent), and cannot marry anyone unless the state-issued marriage license is physically present and has been seen in advance of the wedding.

• whether the couple can marry according to ecclesiastical law. Each denomination has its specific requirements in this area, and the minister is obliged to be familiar with them. Most denominations require that at least one of the two partners be previously baptized, and that both parties give free, full, and competent consent to such a union, without fraud, coercion, mistaken identity, or mental reservation.

- if the minister has not done the premarital counseling, he or she must be fully satisfied that it has been done and that it has included instruction in some Christian doctrine of marriage.

- whether the plans for the wedding ceremony truly reflect the desires of the bride and groom and have not been unduly or inappropriately influenced by the wishes of the parents of either partner, the former children of either, or any other person.

- whether there are circumstances, even at the last moment, under which a minister will not officiate at the marriage. For example, if the bride is a half-hour late, or if the groom is too drunk to speak clearly, will the minister proceed as planned or will the gathered congregation be sent home?

- that the bride and groom will each wear clothing deemed appropriate and tasteful by the standards of the parish. Not everything that is in fashion necessarily befits the joy and solemnity that define a Christian wedding service. The minister needs to inquire about the specifics of what the bride and groom will wear.

- that colors have been coordinated, so that the liturgical fixtures of the church (for example, paraments, the altar frontal) do not clash with the colors chosen for the bridal party. In many churches this will necessitate the minister's or the couple's consulting with the chairperson of the altar guild or its equivalent organization. A growing number of churches restrict the number of floral arrangements at a wedding, as a witness to Christian stewardship, and the number of candles, in keeping with local fire codes.

- that the music chosen for the wedding is also appropriate and tasteful by the standards of the parish. Many congregations restrict the choice of organ music and vocal solos to those which have been approved by the organist, a music committee, or a pastor. They further restrict outsiders from being the "guest organist" at a wedding and limit instrumental music to standards from the classical or religious repertoire.

- that symbols other than those rooted in Christian tradition be thought through carefully. Ministers may find themselves under pressure to add "pop symbols" to the ritual. One example would be "The Unity Candle," a single candle on the altar lit by both members of the wedding party. This symbol has no foundation in Christian liturgical history, and its message must be considered critically. As will be discussed in the following chapter, boundaries between married people must be carefully respected to safeguard a healthy relationship, yet the Unity Candle suggests the destruction of those precious boundaries. In this manner, the Candle witnesses against the unique incarnational character of each Christian man or woman. Mitchell and Anderson speak even more bluntly, that the "marriage candle," lit after two individual candles are snuffed out, symbolizes "a brutal violation of self for the sake of marriage" and stands for "a process psychologically unhealthy and theologically unwise" (76). The psychological import of this and many other "modern" symbols must be scrutinized carefully before a minister agrees to their use.

- that a clear policy concerning photographs be set forth early on. Flash cameras, roving camcorders, and the like have no place in a service of worship, which is the nature of a wedding liturgy. Ministers should set rules for when cameras and electronic recording devices may be used and when they may not. No matter how much planning has gone into a wedding, it is still not a performance; it is a worship service invoking God's blessing on the future life of a couple.

• that spiritual needs and sensitivities be given special attention when a Christian is marrying a non-Christian. Mixed-religion couples are becoming increasingly common and placing unexpected demands on the creativity and theological flexibility of pastors. If one member of the couple is of a non-Christian faith, the wedding ritual needs to be adjusted so as not to cause offense.

• whether the wedding ceremony will include a celebration of communion. Many clergy claim that including communion in a wedding makes little sense unless both bride and groom are, or plan to become, committed members of the parish where the wedding is taking place. In mixed marriages, communion is almost always inappropriate.

• whether the bride will be "given away." Most contemporary prayer books and officially-sanctioned marriage rituals have now dropped this part of the wedding service. If anyone is "given away," it should be both bride and groom who are presented by their respective families. Even in such a case, the psychological implications need to be examined critically. "Giving away" implies some form of ownership, and few people these days understand themselves as being "owned' by their parents. If the couple insist that the bride be given away, the pastor can turn the moment to good use. At the rehearsal, as the father departs from the bride and places her hand in her husband's, the pastor can explain that never again shall family members come between this man and woman.

In general the words to be used in the service should be talked through carefully with the couple to make sure that they comprehend them and that they have no reservations. One case in point is the more traditional use of the word *obey*. Another case in point is the traditional prayers that a couple sire children, a request that an increasing number of people find inappropriate.

• whether, should the wedding reception be held on church property, alcohol will be served and in what quantity. Several American denominations have official national policies regarding alcohol, as a part of their social concern and responsibility for human health. For example, in the Episcopal church, wine at a wedding reception is ordinarily restricted to two glasses per person, and a nonalcoholic alternative must always be prominently displayed, presented in a manner that is at least as attractive as the wine.

• which of the various social occasions surrounding the wedding will be attended by the minister, whether the minister's partner and/or children are also invited, and whether the minister is expected to present the couple with a gift. In parishes where many marriages are performed, the clergy will ultimately need to limit their attendance to only one social function (the "rehearsal dinner" or the reception, but not both) due to the need to balance professional life with private life. In many areas of the world, it is no longer customary for the clergy spouse to be invited to such social occasions, and a growing number of clergy spouses find their time already committed elsewhere.

These are but a few of the details that need the minister's attention in the introductory session or in session 2. Increasingly it is the practice in parishes that a "customary" be drawn up, laying out several of the above matters, along with a fee schedule for being married in the church and contact phone numbers. A sample customary is attached to the end of this chapter.

Sessions 3–6: And the Two Shall Be One

"Two" what? Systemically, a marriage is the merger of two homes or, more specifically, the merger of two family systems. Everyone has a set of associations with the word *home*. For a few these associations are primarily positive, and for a few they are primarily negative. For most people these associations are an ever-fluctuating mix of positives and negatives. But for virtually all, these associations define the term *normal family life*.

According to 1 Corinthians 13, as adults (old enough to marry), we have put away childish things. But have we? Maggie Scarf writes:

> To some small or large degree, when we attain adult status, most of us have not put our childhood things behind us. In the very process of choosing our mates, and of being chosen—and then, in elaborating upon our separate, past lives in the life we create together—we are deeply influenced by the pattern for being that we observed and learned about very early in life and that lives on inside our heads. The fact that there may be other options, other systems for being in an intimate relationship, often doesn't occur to us, because we don't realize that we are operating from within a system, one which was internalized in our original families. What has been, and what we've known, seems to be "the way of the world"; it is reality itself. (1987, 52)

In the family in which each of us grew up, or spent the most time as a child, we were powerfully shaped and molded, and the family "handed" us a long and comprehensive list of ways to view the world and human relationships. We were taught, both consciously and unconsciously, what a family is, what it is not, how it functions, how to behave in it, and how to find the place in it that we were expected to maintain. The list of ways to be part of a relationship include:

- rules of conduct
- expectations for what we will receive and not receive
- the roles we and other family members play (for example, mascot, autocrat, servant, lost child, clown, switchboard, prevaricator, song-and-dance man, sweet young thing)
- our entitlements (what is "due" us because of our role or gender or birth position)
- how we will be disappointed or abused
- emotions that are allowable and the ways of expressing them
- responsibilities (who cooks, does laundry, changes the oil on the car, gets up in the night with a sick child, pays the bills, and so forth)
- the way money is used
- the way power and authority are used
- ways of apologizing or asking forgiveness
- what we are allowed to wish or hope for
- the permeability of family boundaries
- how secrets function, who keeps them, and the penalties for revealing them
- rewards and punishments
- the place and discipline of children of various ages
- the treatment of strangers
- the place of prayer and religious conversation, and other spiritual matters

- style and frequency of family recreation
- how much space and privacy each person should have
- attitudes about race and ethnicity, other faiths, and sexuality
- the respect and attention due to in-laws and extended family
- the right ways to disagree privately and to disagree publicly
- how often and how far one should travel away from home
- methods of expressing intimacy
- and finally, how attached you should remain to your family/home of origin after you have married and established a home of your own.

Our understandings about these many ways of relating to others are formed in our home or family of origin, and the way we learned to do or not do them there are what we each define uniquely as "normal." We might call this our dowry or our inheritance; certainly it is an integral part of our identity, woven into the very fabric of our being. Or, to explore another metaphor, we might call it our overweight or oversize baggage that we haul around with us, the furniture from the home we grew up in, which we are carrying and looking for a new home in which to deposit it. We operate on the presumption that if we could just find a new home to set it in, we would be immediately comfortable, for things there would be just like the home we left. But the shock is that when we find that new home by marrying, our new partner also has furniture of his or her own. The new home doesn't have room for two complete sets of furniture. We have to figure out how to combine it all so that we can both be equally happy.

My wife and I were married late in January. It didn't take until the following December for us to have our first fight, but our first Christmas together produced a doozie. When we came to decorate the Christmas tree, we discovered that I'd grown up in a family that put the lights on first, then the angel at the top, and then all the rest of the baubles. She'd grown up in a family that put the angel on first, the baubles on second, and the lights on last. We were both stubbornly convinced that our families had done it the "right" way and therefore the way we wanted to perpetuate in our new home together. It was a real "Showdown at the OK Corral" experience to see which one of us would stand aside.

Another word for marrying is "cleaving," a word we know from the New Testament. "To cleave means to be attached or united closely in interest or affection, or to adhere with strong attachment. Cleaving is like clinging or sticking" (Anderson and Fite, 14). In Mark 10:7-8 (and parallels) we read: "For this reason a man shall leave his father and mother and be joined to his wife, and the two shall become one flesh." We note the order of the first two verbs, that "leave" comes before "cleave." Hence the systems theory approach for premarital counseling suggested for sessions 3 to 6 is built upon the hypothesis that one must leave before one can cleave. "Leaving in order to cleave presumes the formation of a new family in which individual uniqueness is honored and encouraged, in which clear boundaries make for solid bonds, in which community and autonomy are both valued, and in which everyone has 'a room of one's own'" (Anderson and Fite, 30).

It is not always necessary to define the word *leave* in a literal manner. "Leaving home" refers to differentiation from the family of origin, not to the physical process of moving elsewhere. In most white Western cultures it does literally mean to leave home and establish an identity of one's own, separate from the family of origin, prior to getting married. But in many communal cultures, it is offensive to leave home before one marries and sometimes even after the marriage. A couple in Tonga, for example, may simply move into the house next door to the groom's parents. If they are modern, they may plant a hibiscus hedge between the two houses to symbolize gently a new boundary, but the two houses usually remain completely accessible to all members of the multigenerational family.

> Viewed from the perspective of cultures that give primacy to the family living within a larger social context, leaving itself is an ethically complex action....We need to be careful about prematurely labeling a decision to remain at home as a sign of emotional stuckness. (Anderson and Mitchell, 127)

"Leave," then, needs to be defined in terms of psychological rather than physical disengagement, and "individuation" in terms of relationship maturity rather than geography (Karpel).

> Leaving home means a readiness, willingness, and ability to make one's own decisions, and to make one's way in the world without undue emotional dependence on the home one has come from. Leaving home also involves a change in status or role in one's family of origin that makes it possible for parents and children to be adults together. (Anderson and Mitchell, 26)

Anderson and Mitchell define a variety of ways of leaving home (72–79):
- *Unnoticed departure:* the entire family behaves as though paying attention to the

process will stop it or make it worse. At some point, the family may suddenly start to behave as though the leaver were still a child in the family who has temporarily "gone out to the store."
- *Hidden departure:* announcing from a distance that one has left. This kind of leaving avoids both the grieving process and the potential conflict in the same way that unnoticed leaving does. There is a kind of "elephant in the living room" quality, for the process of leaving home had to be planned and executed in secret.
- *Leaving angry:* the departure is not explained as appropriate, but as "you people drive me crazy." The most serious problem with leaving angry is that it places a major roadblock in the way of going home again. A variation is when the leaver is "thrown out of the house."
- *Pretended leaving:* this may look like several of the above, but within a very brief period of time the leaver is once again a member of the family system in precisely the same role that he or she carried before.
- *Unaccepted leaving:* when a child leaves home and the parents do not accept it, they will struggle to treat the departed son or daughter as if he or she were still living at home.
- *Matter-of-fact leaving:* the entire process is out in the open and acknowledged; there is little or no conflict connected with it. Information and plans are shared with all parties affected. The cluster of feelings we call grief is recognized as appropriate, though not always dealt with well.

Psychological and emotional health are much less likely in persons who have left home in any manner other than the "matter-of-fact" leaving. Health is achievable, both in the present and in the future, by individuals and families who process the departure in an open and acknowledged way, and who are not afraid to name both the grief and the creative possibilities that leaving offers to all involved. Unfortunately, many people do not leave so successfully. As one young student remarked, "I didn't leave when I left; I left when I stayed; and before I finally left for the last time, I was already gone" (Anderson and Mitchell, 82). The responsible pastor must be on the lookout for manifestations of continued enmeshment and unfinished business.

The Psychology of "Leaving"

A leaving that serves the needs of all family members involved will include both grieving and blessing. It is a paradox that we have children so that they can leave, and we love them best by letting them go. But families grieve when a child leaves home to make a new family of his or her own because the familiar will never be the same again. Most families have at least some difficulty letting children go; some families have such difficulty that they cannot grieve until the moment of the wedding, thereby creating a very difficult pastoral dynamic. Anderson and Mitchell list five of the many reasons for which a family may have trouble letting one or more of its children go: "when a family role is lost, when the grief is too much, when the family is so close that the boundaries are not clear, when fear of the empty nest or parental dread of abandonment by their children in the future is present, and when a blessing is absent" (99).

Grief that is dealt with prior to the wedding has less chance of intruding on the wedding day. It is not easy for a family to be a sending community. "Parents want their children to grow up—but not too big—and go away—but not too far" (Anderson and Mitchell, 144). Of course, Christian parents will have already been signaled that their children are not their own, for infant baptism and child dedication are warning signs that our children belong to God and to themselves, and not to us. Change is part of a creation that God has declared to be good.

A leaving may be softened for the family if the child can be given the family's blessing. A blessing conveys a wish for the leaver's success and may take many forms, including inheriting a valuable piece of family memorabilia, a promise of financial support during the transition, or a more formal ritual involving the family or perhaps the church community. Sometimes a child will receive something special: some of grandmother's jewelry, a favorite uncle's treasured library, a sister's baseball mitt, or a brother's stamp collection. The blessing is implicit in the symbol, and the pastor may help a couple examine what implicit gifts they have been given by their own families. For financial support to be a blessing, it must be given in such a way that respects the dignity and autonomy of the receiver. Money with "strings" attached is not a blessing but a covert means of preventing the recipient from leaving home.

In many instances, some sort of ritual marking of the leave-taking will give the most closure to both the family and the one leaving. Anderson and Mitchell enumerate the essential components of a blessing ritual (107):
• I (we), having authority in this family,
• recognizing that a change is imminent,
• wishing for your happiness without reservation,
• placing you under God's constant protection,
• celebrating your gifts,

• confirming your separateness, and
• reaffirming our enduring connectedness.

As mentioned earlier, some pastoral theologians interpret the part of the marriage service in which the father "gives away" the bride as symbolizing this sort of blessing. Ever thereafter, the family should not come between the couple. But the emotional complexity of contemporary reactions to that part of the marriage service suggests that a ritual, informal or formal, with each family, long before the wedding day, is to be preferred.

The blessing of one's leaving may take place in the home, or in the parish church with the congregation present. Few if any liturgies exist for such a blessing, but the outline suggested by Anderson and Mitchell above provides a skeleton around which such a rite of passage might be constructed.

For most people, leaving is a lifelong process in which steps have to be repeated with regularity. The journey to mature individuation begins when we are born; it may still be going on when we are middle-aged and sometimes even after our parents have died. Leaving is a job we must do for ourselves, for no one can complete our developmental tasks of childhood and adolescence for us. As we move through the various developmental stages, we learn ultimately that "home" is not a physical location but an inner disposition that must be nourished. This is Dorothy's lesson in *The Wizard of Oz*: "home" is not Auntie Em's in Kansas, but Dorothy's own newfound sense of self at the end of her adventures.

Leaving must not be regarded as an end intrinsic to itself. Leaving also allows us to establish a home of our own, to form a family, to make our own choices about living and loving, and to accept the mystery of God's call to develop our unique gifts. Anderson and Mitchell link leaving home with the Christian tradition in three ways (134):

1. Leaving home is a *religious* act because it implies transcendence. It presumes that we are open to the new thing that God is doing in our lives.

2. Leaving home is an *ethical* act because it implies discipleship or vocation. It enables us to discover, foster, and utilize our particular gifts for ends beyond the meeting of our own particular needs.

3. Leaving home is a *sacramental* act because it implies reconciliation. We leave home so we can go home again. The freedom to go back depends in turn upon the promise of forgiveness and the possibility of reconciliation and reunion.

Leaving home also means making our own mature intentional choices about the rules, roles, expectations, and so forth that we mentioned earlier in the chapter. But these are very powerful, as we can see because we define them as normal. The failure to make truly mature intentional choices, the failure to "leave home," and the failure to communicate and negotiate these with our marital partner are major reasons why so many marriages end in bitter divorce or hostile stalemate (McGoldrick 1989, 227). Where does the power of these roles and rules and expectations come from?

Genograms

Our early lessons in love and our developmental history shape the expectations we bring into marriage. We are more often aware of disappointed hopes. But we also bring into marriage the unconscious longings and the unfinished business of childhood, and promoted by the past, we make demands on our marriage, unaware that we do. (Viorst, 212)

We inherited our dowry from our parents, who inherited theirs from their parents, who inherited theirs from their parents, and so on. Our dowry is so powerful because its contents have been inherited cumulatively down through many generations. This intergenerational repetition is one of the several senses of "system" or vertical networking referred to by the title Family Systems Theory. A basic principle of Systems Theory is that we will simply repeat the dysfunctions that are part of our systemic dowry over and over again until we (a) find them; (b) name them as something we have not chosen; and (c) make our own individual choice about whether to repudiate these ways of being and to break their power. One way we find and trace these dysfunctions is through constructing a genogram, which has now for many pastors become an indispensable part of the premarital counseling process. Constructing a genogram has already been explained in chapter 2.

Once a genogram has been laid out on paper, the next phase is to analyze it, in order to identify patterns of strength, compensation, and dysfunction. Scarf describes a genogram as "a road map laying out the important emotional attachments of each of the partners—attachments that lead backward in time, to the parents' and grandparents' generations, and forward to the new one, the children (if any) of the present union" (1987, 6). Emotional attachment is not the only theme one looks for in analyzing a genogram, though it is certainly a theme that indicates how successfully people "leave home" within the larger inherited family system. Analysis may indeed reveal that leaving home has been mishandled in

several successive generations. Other themes commonly sought in genogram analysis for the purposes of premarital counseling include cross-generational triangulation (sometimes called "invisible loyalties"), naming patterns that signal attached expectations or enmeshment, patterns of imbalance created by new marriages (no two families merge equally; for all practical purposes, one marital partner gets absorbed into the other partner's larger system, creating an imbalance), patterns of religious commitment and gender-role responsibility, systems roles (is the youngest child always the "clown"?) and rituals (how many generations has Christmas dinner been held at the maternal grandmother's home?), and so forth. An excellent source of discussion topics is the exercises at the end of each chapter in Grenz and Glover's *The Marriage Journey*.

Without the help of a genogram, we may miss some of the critical issues that may emerge down the road in a relationship, and we may even miss the reasons that people get married. According to Lederer and Jackson, it is a myth that people marry only because they are so deeply in love (39–84). Rather, in addition to being in love, people marry because (a) they have a natural desire to mate; (b) society expects people to marry; (c) they are responding to parental pressure; (d) romantic images in the media make marriage look easy; (e) they are lonely and believe marrying will fix that; (f) they seek economic security (for example, virtually every Western country gives a tax break to married couples); (g) they wish to get ahead in life (for example, married clergy are more easily employed than single clergy); (h) they need a partner to reinforce their personal neuroses; or (i) they need a parent substitute. Harville Hendrix, in the best-selling *Getting the Love You Want*, makes a claim that echoes this last reason. He claims that *all* people who marry are unconsciously seeking to establish a relationship in which they can work through issues they were never able to complete with their parents. We might reinterpret Hendrix's claim by saying that people marry that part of home that they have not found the courage to leave. These and similar issues will often show up in a careful analysis of a couple's genograms.

Another source of information that becomes apparent on a genogram is Sibling Position Theory. As both Toman and Sulloway point out, some significant portion of our personality, our expectations, and our sense of entitlement is formed by where we fit in the order of siblings in our family of origin. While the theory is too complex to summarize here, it can be illustrated by a generalization: marriages have a greater chance of success if the two partners come from opposite sibling positions. For example, an oldest child who is marrying a youngest child will find the smoother way, for one is used to taking care of a younger brother or sister, and the other is used to being taken care of by an older brother or sister. Two eldest children may have a rocky time, for they will compete for the role of caretaker. Two youngest children may have a rocky time, for they will both expect to be taken care of by their partner.

Pastors in marital counseling will find a bare-bones genogram easy to construct through casual conversation with couples. If the couple wishes to pursue this methodology on their own, a basic template should be made and then copied, so that one copy can be used to trace, for example, patterns of alcohol addiction, another copy to trace patterns of marital affairs, another copy to trace the typical tension between fathers and sons, another copy to identify areas of continuing enmeshment with the family of origin, and so on.

Of course any analysis of a genogram is ultimately hypothetical, for we are always dealing with interpretation as opposed to hard facts. But genograms provide the pastor with additional opportunities for ministry. One partner may be troubled by his mother's seeming lack of parenting skills. Instead of focusing anger on the fact that he did not have "a good-enough mother" (see chapter 3), the young man can be helped to understand that his mother reflected the mothering that she in turn received. As Samuel Osherson points out, "wounded fathers," or not-good-enough fathers, are themselves products of wounded fathers who were products of wounded fathers (30–31). Discussion of such issues may lead the members of the couple to forgive their parents, perhaps for the first time. Part of leaving home is being able to forgive our parents for not being all that we needed them to be. Anderson and Mitchell point out:

> Forgiveness is particularly necessary for family survival because buried anger, unresolved conflicts, and unforgiven violations of intimate trust are so disruptive to the human community. Accumulating grievances and resentments is one sure way to undermine the vitality of family living.
>
> Forgiveness works both ways in families. Children forgive and are forgiven. Parents are forgiven as well as forgiving. Children are not always what we wish them to be—neither are parents. (149)

For a genogram to be effective, the couple must have some sense of being part of a larger system. In other words they need at least a basic comprehension of how they relate to the larger system into which they were born. They must also realize that genogram work isn't so much about who they are as individuals but as family members and, ultimately, will be as a couple. Genograms are a tool for understanding the expectations each individual brings to the marriage based on his or her family of origin.

Family Narratives

One of the many inheritances that genograms easily uncover is family myths and stories. Anderson and Fite define marriage as "a wedding of stories" (37–38). Family stories convey information about family experiences, generational relationships, and family themes. What is important in the study of family stories is how life experiences are handed down from generation to generation (Martin, 46). Doing a genogram initiates a process of storytelling that is intended to extend far beyond the period of premarital preparation, for each of us carries so many stories that they cannot be told in a short space of time. As was explained in chapter 3, each of us has been created by the stories we were born into in our family of origin, and in turn we shaped those stories just as they shaped us. Stories convey our values and fears, our aspirations and disappointments, our dreams and fears, and so they must be told. Telling stories to each other is not only a source of information but a form of intimacy that can serve the couple for a lifetime.

Genograms often need illustration. Some pastors ask couples to bring photo albums or other important memorabilia to the premarital counseling sessions. Leafing through albums can provide new and important material in the construction of a genogram. In turn, photos examined after the construction of a genogram may convey new messages and new insights, as stories are "told" in the faces of those in the pictures.

Some pastors also find it useful, once a genogram has been constructed, to ask each marital partner to come up with a motto for their family tree, a pithy saying that captures the essence of their intergenerational heritage. Examples might include "Love does not conquer all" (*omnia non vincit amor*) or "To thine own self be true, in spite of parental expectations." Another analytic tool would be to ask each partner to draw a family coat of arms, perhaps a shield divided into quadrants, with each quadrant holding an important symbol. These imaginary coats of arms should be compared, and the couple should discuss whether the comparison suggests any significant trouble spots in the future.

Personality Type Inventories

With the wide availability in the church of the Myers-Briggs Type Indicator, more and more premarital counselors are administering the test to the couple as part of the preparation process. The MBTI is based on Carl Jung's theory of "psychological types" or "function types." Beginning in the early 1960s, the MBTI suggested ways in which these basic Jungian types might be applied to the everyday life of interested individuals. The MBTI breaks human psychological functioning into eight categories: Extroversion (E), Introversion (I), Sensing (S), Intuition (N), Thinking (T), Feeling (F), Judgment (J), and Perception (P). After an analytical test, each person is usually assigned four of those eight as a profile of his or her preferred method of functioning. That does not mean, for example, that an E person is always extroverted; in various settings, she may function as an introvert, depending on the particular circumstances. The test profile indicates only that in the majority of cases, she will function as an extrovert.

Isabel Briggs Myers, who pioneered the MBTI, reports that of 375 married couples that she studied, nearly 70 percent held two or three of their four preferences in common (124ff.). Of those, the most common was an SN husband married to an SN wife. The most troublesome differences were an E married to an I, and a F married to a T. But even where husband and wife share two or three preferences in common, a smooth conjugal road is not guaranteed. For example, two introverts may have extreme difficulty with communication, as they typically are so busy processing things internally that they don't make the time to process with the partner. Myers suggests that no matter how much a couple holds in common, the marriage will not work without understanding, appreciation, and respect for each other's psychological type differences. She observes, "Hostility can sometimes flare up suddenly between two people who love each other and neither may know why. Such clashes hurt less if both understand about the shadow side, which is visible to the partner but not to the possessor" (127–28). The shadow side is what Naomi Quenk calls one's "hidden personality."

Understanding, appreciation, and respect for a partner's dominant characteristics does not automatically mean the same respect for the partner's shadow, "hidden," auxiliary, or nondominant personality types. A T husband may be very respectful of, and even grateful for, his F wife's feelings but be caught completely by surprise when his wife operates out of her T. Because her T is her nondominant function, it is necessarily less developed or mature (Quenk, 211). It is all the more likely, then, that the logical conclusions in her T will not match the logical conclusions of his T (hers being less mature in this case), and his impatience with her immature thinking will lead to even greater misunderstanding between them. She may not even be aware that she is operating out of her T, though it will be painfully apparent to her husband.

Myers writes:

> In any marriage, a type difference may at times produce an outright conflict between opposite points of view. When this happens, the partners have a choice. One or both can assume that it is wrong of the other to be different—and be righteously indignant, which diminishes the partner. They can assume that it is wrong of themselves to be different—and be depressed, which is self-diminishing. Or they can acknowledge that each is justifiably and interestingly different from the other—and be amused. Their amusement may be warm or detached, wry or tender, according to their types, but it will help in working out the situation and keeping intact each partner's dignity and the precious fabric of their marriage. (130)

Working with a couple's MBTI can be a significant investment in their future happiness and reciprocal understanding. For this reason it is an appropriate tool, either as a complement to or a substitute for a genogram in sessions 3 through 6.

~

The next seven subjects are issues that should arise out of the use of genograms, family narratives, or the MBTI in premarital counseling. If they do not arise naturally, the minister should focus the couple's attention on them. These seven can also be successfully addressed in a premarital group with other couples and under the leadership of skilled lay ministers.

Power, Authority, and Intimacy

The struggle to share (or not to share) power pervades almost every aspect of marital life, involving issues such as who does the housework, who cares for the children, whose family tradition predominates, how leisure time is spent, or who writes the Christmas letter. Above all, power and authority struggles are most frequently worked out in the bedroom and in the availability and use of money. As Anderson and Fite point out, "Even under the most positive circumstances, sharing power in marriage is determined by many factors: by the individual's needs and fears, by values from our families of origin, by our understanding of gendered roles, and by the particular cultures within which we have been raised" (129). When power is not shared, one partner in the marriage will wind up feeling trapped, angry, or depressed. The women's movement feels threatening to many husbands because of the way it has empowered their wives, which explains why marriage has come to be so distrusted by both men and women in younger generations. Both partners may fear the loss of power and may attempt to compensate by overexerting their personal authority in the relationship.

Some couples enter the marriage relationship believing that their felt intimacy will negate the need to address issues of power sharing in relationship. Intimacy seems so easy in the weeks leading up to a wedding; besotted by romance and blinded by projection of themselves onto each other, the young couple will have difficulty comprehending the types of intimacy needed for the long haul. Among those types are:

- emotional intimacy (being tuned to each other's wavelength)
- intellectual intimacy (closeness in the world of ideas)
- aesthetic intimacy (sharing experiences of beauty)
- creative intimacy (sharing acts of creating)
- recreational intimacy (relating in experiences of fun and play)
- work intimacy (sharing common tasks and goals)
- crisis intimacy (closeness in coping with problems and pain)
- conflict intimacy (facing and struggling with differences)
- commitment intimacy (mutuality derived from common self-investment)
- spiritual intimacy (the we-ness in sharing ultimate concerns: God, life, death, and so on)
- sexual intimacy.

A discussion of intimacy is highly appropriate as a part of the premarital process.

Intimacy is closely connected with nurture. Again, gender roles are a complication in our understanding of how nurture works. A distinction needs to be drawn between the ways in which women have nurtured traditionally and men have nurtured traditionally. It has been assumed that women nurture in ways which we term "maternal," including devotion to childraising, self-sacrifice of career aspirations, and primary responsibility for homemaking.

Men's traditional ways of nurturing, while not always recognized as such, have included providing the family with a secure income, making decisions that are good for the whole family unit, and protecting family members from threat and danger. These distinctions are no longer so sharp as gender roles soften and change, but the historical backgrounding remains important in avoiding future misunderstandings.

Mammon

As mammon is a complex symbol in the New Testament, so finances and budgeting are complex symbols in a marriage. Betty Carter and Joan Peters state their version of the Golden Rule: "Whoever has the gold makes the rules" (9–10). Mitchell and Anderson state the same thing more softly: "Withholding money, like withholding sex, is a way of exercising power in a relationship. In addition, the money issue is often the key to understanding issues of dependence and independence in a marriage" (85).

Nearly every marriage goes through several years of imbalance in incomes, particularly during the childrearing period. Women especially are often disempowered to negotiate financial issues and, as an extension, many other domestic issues. Elizabeth Ridgely relates this case study:

> A young couple with two small children were discussing the financial arrangements in the family [with their therapist]. The husband said that this was absolutely no problem. They had a joint bank account into which he put his paycheck and she took out what she needed to run the household. He was working full-time and she had reduced her work to part-time because of the children. The presenting problem was marital dissatisfaction

and not feeling as together as a couple as they did before the birth of children. Their love story had become diminished by fatigue, additional responsibilities, babysitters and very different gendered lives.

> As the male therapist continued the discussion of money, the wife proclaimed dissatisfaction that she could not write the check to pay the mortgage. The husband immediately answered that they would lose the house if she were in charge of the mortgage. It was essential that the mortgage be paid by him directly. The [therapist], a male psychiatric resident married to a professional woman who earned twice the salary that he did, stated that he absolutely understood the husband's position and he too paid the house mortgage in his marriage. This was the man's job— to provide shelter. (Haber, 75)

Not only is this an excellent illustration of how a pastoral counselor can conspire with one marital partner at the expense of the other, but it also illustrates how much the way money is used in a marriage is influenced by gender-role assumptions, deeply ingrained from our childhoods.

Money is the great idol of Western society. "Having money is having power. Learning how to balance a joint checking account is a beneficial lesson in sharing power. Learning how to live within a budget when money is tight is a necessary lesson in shared power" (Anderson and Fite, 128). Because money holds so much power, it needs special attention as a metaphor, including within the premarital process. Each couple must find its own way to say to mammon, "You don't own me; I own you."

It is often the case that middle-income families have the most conflict in this area. Poor families know where their money must go, and wealthy families have enough money to do as they please. Middle-income families must make choices, and it is the process of making mutually agreeable choices that arouses the most conflict. Genograms and family narratives might come in handy here. The counselor could ask: When your parents argued over money, what was the issue? Who kept the books and wrote the checks in your family of origin? Was money used in the family to win favors and patch up quarrels? How would you like to handle money differently from the way your family of origin did?

Decision Making and Conflict Management

"Marriage requires that two people renegotiate together a myriad of issues they have previously defined individually, or that were defined by their families of origin, such as when and how to eat, sleep, talk, have sex, fight, work, and relax" (McGoldrick 1989, 209). Negotiations certainly indicate decision making and from time to time result in significant conflict. Even the Romantic Type of marriage, as discussed in the next chapter, will have moments of heated argument and hurtful misunderstanding.

Models of conflict management that people carry from their childhood can usually be identified through the use of the genograms and family narratives. Mitchell and Anderson try to establish how conflict was acted out in each family of origin. "We do not ask whether parents fought; we ask how they fought, and how they resolved their differences. When someone says that they never saw their parents fight, it is clear that for them family conflict was a matter reserved for times when parents could express differences away from the children. Some people grow up seeing open conflict but seldom seeing its resolution" (81).

Whatever the family pattern has been, it is important to know that each individual brings a set of scripts and rituals to the expression of conflict and its resolution.

Some pastoral counselors work with a couple to try to set "Rules for Fair Fighting." In this instance a list of rules is often made, with the proviso that nothing goes on the list unless the bride, the groom, and the counselor mutually agree that it is a good addition. Other pastors routinely refer people to a "handbook" for marital disagreement, such as Bach and Wyden's *The Intimate Enemy*. However the issue is addressed, it must be an integral part of any pastor's plan for effective premarital counseling. Most pastors agree that one of the most important goals of premarital work is to get the couple to trust the pastor enough that they will return for further counseling before their marriage is in so much trouble that it cannot be saved.

When discussing these issues with a couple, the pastor should use the term *conflict management* rather than *conflict resolution*. Resolution implies that a difference of opinion will disappear, but in some cases this is simply not realistic. Sometimes all that can be hoped for is that the couple will agree to disagree.

Sex

Most pastors shy away from this subject, as if it were somehow "dirty," and yet virtually every manual in pastoral counseling agrees that a marriage cannot be happy unless the couples have a mutually satisfying sex life for the duration of their relationship. How "mutually satisfying" is to be defined can vary widely from couple to couple. Approximately one-quarter of all married couples have intercourse once a month or less, yet of these many still define their relationship as sexually satisfying. Sexual satisfaction in marriage, then, clearly must not be limited to frequency of or proficiency in intercourse. We must beware of assuming that there is any "right" way to be sexually active in marriage, or any agreed standard to live up to. The emphasis in defining a good marital sex life should be the mutuality of satisfaction.

Anderson and Fite write: "Physical intimacy is the delightful companion of emotional intimacy; but sex becomes distorted and ultimately disappointing when it is cut off from emotional closeness. While sexual attraction may be what draws people together, it is rarely what keeps them together" (127). These words should remind us as counselors that we cannot even assume that sexually active couples understand the emotional intimacy that is the necessary complement to a healthy sex life in marriage.

Discussing sex during premarital counseling may make pastors uncomfortable. Hiebert offers a list of six counselor attitudes that may help nervous pastors relax (242–44):

1. *Warm permissiveness.* The pastor should convey that he or she is perfectly comfortable with this subject, and that it is as natural a topic as "the theology of marriage" to include in premarital counseling.

2. *Active listening.* The pastor should convey to the couple that he or she is genuinely concerned with their future happiness, without any suggestion of voyeurism or prurience.

3. *Thoughtful responses.* The subject of sex in marriage needs to be treated with the respect and dignity that befit the Christian understanding that sexuality is a gift from God. The pastor should speak slowly and carefully, as if addressing a great mystery. Sex is sacramental, in that it is an outward sign of an inner and spiritual intimacy between two people.

4. *Depersonalization.* A couple may be much more comfortable discussing sex and sexuality in more general terms, rather than talking about the specifics of their intimate life with each other.

5. *Acceptance.* The pastor must create a climate in which it is OK for each partner to express feelings and fears to the other. The pastor must not sit in judgment on sexual preferences or practices, or attempt to cause the couple to conform to external standards that are not their own.

6. *Meet them at their level.* Some people who come to the church to be married have a great deal of sexual experience, and others have almost none. The pastor should be sensitive to each partner's stage of psychosexual development.

If the pastor cannot find a way to be comfortable with direct conversation about sex, the genogram may provide an appropriate entry. According to Mitchell and Anderson:

> Attitudes about sexuality are generally formed initially in our families of origin, even when sexuality was a taboo topic. . . . Asking how affection was shown in one's family of origin often identifies patterns that have already begun to show in the new relationship. This focus on attitudes toward sexuality in families of origin effectively circumvents much embarrassment in discussing the couple's present sexual activity. . . . Whether a couple is sexually active before marriage is less determinative of the quality of their relationship in the marriage than the attitudes they brought with them from their families of origin. (84)

Sexuality in marriage is more a process than a state or a craft. It is a process through which both partners learn to contribute to what is, for them, a mutually satisfying shared experience. As with so many other aspects of marriage, a couple does not become expert after a few sessions of premarital counseling, but with luck they may begin healthy patterns of communication that can serve them for the rest of their lives together.

~

I have suggested a great deal of material to be covered in sessions 3 through 6. It is unlikely that a pastor will be able to cover it all, even in four ninety-minute appointments. The choice of material and approaches should be dictated both by the pastor's skills and by the couple's needs.

Session 7: The Theology of Marriage

The pastor might begin this session by asking the couple what has moved them to seek God's blessing on their union. This same question may have been asked in session 1, but since much has happened in the intervening sessions, the question merits repeating. We in the church have both the right and the duty to expect a fairly clear answer to this question. Is the couple marrying in the church because it is "the thing to do"? Have they come to the church because of tradition rather than faith? Are they seeking some magical circumnavigation of the reality of marriage that they hope will, because of the church's blessing, enable them to avoid the conflict and pain of marriage? How do we keep the mystery of the marital union intact while removing from it any suggestion of a "magical" aspect?

In beginning this discussion, the pastor may again find the genogram useful. Mitchell and Anderson comment, "A shared faith commitment and a set of common values are stabilizing factors in marriage. Since it is difficult, however, to ask the couple about religious matters without eliciting either defensiveness or artificial agreement, it is again more beneficial to begin by asking about the role of religion in each family of origin" (85). Once the theological issues have been opened up in this manner, the pastor may proceed with creating a climate in which each partner can comfortably claim a personal faith space in the presence of the other.

As the discussion of the theology of marriage continues, the pastor should present the developmental process of marriage realistically. Few people find marriage easy. "Marriage is, as sociologists Peter Berger and Hansfried Kellner have observed, 'a dramatic act in which two strangers come together and re-define themselves'" (Scarf 1987, 36). But as painful as self-redefinition may be at times, the Christian vision is that a marriage will be provided the opportunity to transcend the hard times through both faith and prayer. Thomas Moore writes:

> It's easy to be cynical about marriage, or to come up with yet another plan for making marriages "work." It's more difficult to look at marriage as we actually experience it, taking note of its deep fantasies, its hidden emotions, and its place in the life of the soul; not looking for perfection, but asking what the soul is doing when it entices us toward such a demanding form of relationship. (46)

In Moore's understanding, then, it is the soul which propels us toward Christian marriage, and in the dialogue between two committed souls lies the key to making marriage a vehicle of God's grace.

The broader theology of marriage differs significantly from one denomination to the next. For example, for Baptists marriage is an ordinance, while for Anglicans and Roman Catholics it is a sacrament. The nuancing of the theology of marriage will also be affected by the particular life experiences of the pastor and of each partner within his or her family of origin. It may, for example, be difficult to teach the innate goodness of God's will within marriage to one who has grown up in a highly abusive home. But whatever the various differences, Christian theologies of marriage hold certain core values in common:

- Marriage is a choice made by mature adults of their own free will.
- Marriage is one of the several vehicles intended by God to be a channel of grace and a vehicle of witness to the rest of the world.
- Marriage is intended to be a monogamous, lifelong commitment.
- Marriage should bring about the fulfillment of both partners and enable their fuller Christian ministry.
- Children brought up in a Christian marriage should be trained in Christian thought, disciplines, and values.
- Faith and prayer make a difference in the nature of a marital relationship.
- Marriage should be honored by the church community.
- Much about why Christian marriages work remains among the divine mysteries.

For these reasons, it is not pastors or ministers who make a Christian marriage, but the couple themselves. A wedding does not make a marriage, for, as will be explained in the following chapter, "becoming married" is a process that extends over many years. Rather, "the wedding is . . . a commitment that two people make to each other in the company of family and friends and community and in the presence of God that enhances the process of becoming married" (Anderson and Fite, 2). God is present in that process, nourishing and challenging the souls of each partner. Thomas Moore summarizes:

> Marriage is not only the expression of love between two people, it is also a profound evocation of one of life's greatest mysteries, the weaving together of many different strands of soul. Because marriage touches upon issues charged with emotion and connected to absolute meaning, it is filled with paradoxical feelings, far-flung fantasies, profound despair, blissful epiphanies, and bitter struggle—all signs of the active presence of the soul. (45)

Who Should Be Present in Premarital Sessions?

In most circumstances, premarital counseling sessions include only the pastor and the couple seeking to be married. In certain instances, however, and with the couple's permission, the pastor may wish to invite others to join all or a part of a session. For instance, when dealing with genograms, the couple should be encouraged to do their own research between sessions, but when dealing with family narratives, a pastor may wish to invite the parents of one or both marital partners to join the session. This can be particularly effective when addressing issues of intergenerational forgiveness or grief. Having parents present may also present the pastor with the opportunity to help one or the other partner complete some of the unfinished business of leaving home.

Children of former marriages are also likely candidates for inclusion in one or more premarital sessions. Anderson, Hogue, and McCarthy remind us that children have an enormous personal investment in discovering what a parental remarriage will mean for them: "talking with children about their fears, hopes, and ideas about new families is essential for those with children who choose to marry again" (104). These children may be carrying grief from the previous divorce, or have been handed dire predictions about their new life from some of their peer group, or even may have taken quite literally the archetypal fairy-tale character of "the wicked stepmother." Providing them a voice within premarital counseling is a way to pastor a whole family system rather than simply the couple planning to marry.

A third possibility is to invite a minister or pastor of the opposite gender to join one or more premarital sessions, so that a couple speaks to a couple. Again, this must not be done without the couple's prior permission, and a clear reason must be given them. For example, if a pastor sees that a coming session will deal with power and authority, or with marital sex, she may wish to invite a male pastor to join her for that session to make the gender representation around sensitive issues in the counseling room as balanced and as safe as possible.

Remarriage

Couples in which one or both partners have been previously married need a structure quite similar to the seven-session structure already outlined, but with some additional attention to certain areas. This is true whether the previous marriage ended in divorce or in death. There is no certainty that people who married before actually "left home" enough to become married. In some cases, leaving a first marriage is itself a differentiating act, perhaps compensating for the failure to differentiate completely from the family of origin. Therefore the genogram and family narrative work are just as critical the second time around, though it may now be even more complex. The genogram work may need to include a basic genogram of a former spouse, particularly if the children involved divide their time between mother's new family unit and father's. Family narrative work needs to include not only stories from both families of origin, but also stories from the first marriages of previously married partners. "Previous marriages are part of the individual stories we bring to form a new family. They need to be told with candor and clarity" (Anderson, Hogue, and McCarthy, 112).

Another task in preparing couples for a second marriage is to explore the need for clear—but not fixed or impenetrable—boundaries between the generations or between the members of the first family and the members of the second. The ghosts of former spouses may haunt second marriages unless they and their histories are brought out into the open for full discussion. Naming the ghosts provides some new opportunities to grieve vows broken, and for the divorced partners present to take clear responsibility for their own role in the breakup of the former relationship. In some instances, these same principles will apply to partners who had a previous long unmarried relationship before entering their new engagement.

Anderson, Hogue, and McCarthy offer a checklist to identify what pastors must be alert to in second marriages so that the act of "promising again" will endure (106–8):

• Former relationships have been grieved.

- Newly formed couples develop an openness to the reality of the former relationships.
- A new marital relationship has a developmental cycle of its own.
- Increasingly, a new community is being formed around the new couple.
- Members of the new family become realistic about the differences between this family and former families.
- Children are free to develop and maintain full relationships with both biological parents.
- A body of new rituals is formed.
- There is allowance for the time that it takes to form a new family.
- An openness to experimentation and a sense of humor are critical.
- Couples who marry again may decide to have children of their own.

Where one or both of the partners has been divorced, the pastor will also need to address sensitively the theology of remarriage. Vows have been broken, and to some it will seem that God failed to be adequately present. A pastor can help the couple see that a second marriage after divorce is a sign that sin and guilt are part of the human condition. Even if the first marriage that ended with the death of a spouse was happy, there are vestiges of imperfection in our memory (Anderson, Hogue, and McCarthy, 115). The inclusion in the marriage service of words seeking God's forgiveness, and hearing God's acceptance of the truly penitent, can strengthen the new couple's faith and their life together. The couple can take comfort in the God who promises, "Behold, I make all things new" (Rev. 21:5).

Conclusion

One of the most common symbols in the early church was that of a ship. The symbol's frequent use may have been inspired by the many fishing scenarios at the Sea of Galilee or by Paul's several voyages, but it had particular appeal as Christianity engaged its missionary task around and across the Mediterranean. Early Christian pilgrims grafittied pictures of ships in the caves and tombs, and the journey of the Christian soul was often described as a ship leaving port in order to arrive safely at its new destination. Edwin Friedman seems to tap into this pool of ancient imagery when he describes premarital counseling: "The idea, of course, is not just to get them married but, rather, to launch them in an attitude that will also be good for the whole trip" (286).

A ship leaves home and returns home. A ship can sail more than once and, if its journey is badly begun, can correct its course or even return to port to start over. A ship and its crew never know what to expect, but depend on the vessel's sound structure and the skill and cooperation of the sailors. And so the metaphor of premarital counseling as the beginning of a long and potentially dangerous voyage still holds. The Christian pastor is among the many who prepare the ship for its voyage, stocking it with practical provisions that will be needed along the way, no matter what storms may assault it. And when the ship at last reaches a safe port at the end of its journey, the pastor who has done a good job of preparing each couple can stand among the crowd of many who are thanked for making the voyage a success.

BIBLIOGRAPHY

Anderson, Herbert, and Kenneth R. Mitchell. *Leaving Home.* Louisville: Westminster/John Knox, 1993.

Anderson, Herbert, and Robert Cotton Fite. *Becoming Married*. Louisville: Westminster/John Knox, 1993.

Anderson, Herbert, David Hogue, and Marie McCarthy. *Promising Again*. Louisville: Westminster/John Knox, 1995.

Bach, George, and Peter Wyden. *The Intimate Enemy: How to Fight Fair in Love and Marriage*. New York: Avon, 1981.

Bowen, Murray. *Family Therapy in Clinical Practice*. New York: Jason Aronson, 1978.

Carter, Betty, and Joan K. Peters. *Love, Honor, and Negotiate: Making Your Marriage Work*. New York: Pocket Books, 1996.

Carter, Betty, and Monica McGoldrick, eds. *The Changing Family Life Cycle*. 2d ed. Boston: Allyn and Bacon, 1989.

Commission on Marriage, Diocese of North Carolina. *Clergy Resource Manual for Marriage Preparation and Counseling*. 1987.

Dornbusch, Sanford, Melissa Herman, and I-Chun Liu. "Single Parenthood." *Society* 33 (July 1996): 30–32.

Friedman, Edwin. "Churches and Synagogues." In *Practicing Family Therapy in Diverse Settings*. Michael Berger, Gregory Jurkovic, and Associates, eds. 271–300. San Francisco: Jossey-Bass, 1984.

Grenz, Linda, and Delbert Glover. *The Marriage Journey: Preparation and Provisions for Life Together*. Cambridge, Mass.: Cowley Publications, 1996.

Haber, Russell. *Dimensions of Psychotherapy Supervision: Maps and Means*. New York: W. W. Norton, 1996.

Hiebert, William. "Talking with Clients about Sexual Problems." In Stahmann and Hiebert, 240–49.

Karpel, Mark. "Individuation: From Fusion to Dialogue." *Family Process* 15 (1976): 65–82.

Keirsey, David, and Marilyn Bates. *Please Understand Me: Character and Temperament Types*. Del Mar, Calif.: Prometheus Nemesis Book Co., 1984.

Lederer, William, and Don Jackson. *The Mirages of Marriage*. New York: W. W. Norton, 1968.

Martin, Peter. "Family Stories." *Journal of Marriage and the Family* 50 (May 1988): 533–41.

McGoldrick, Monica. "The Joining of Families through Marriage: The New Couple." In Carter and McGoldrick (1989), 209–33.

———. *You Can Go Home Again: Reconnecting with Your Family*. New York: W. W. Norton, 1995.

McGoldrick, Monica, and Betty Carter. "Forming a Remarried Family." In Carter and McGoldrick (1989), 399–429.

McGoldrick, Monica, and Randy Gerson. *Genograms in Family Assessment*. New York: W. W. Norton, 1985.

Mitchell, Kenneth R., and Herbert Anderson. "You Must Leave before You Cleave: A Family Systems Approach to Premarital Pastoral Work." *Pastoral Psychology* 30:2 (winter 1981): 71–88.

Moore, Thomas. *Soul Mates: Honoring the Mysteries of Love and Relationship*. New York: HarperCollins, 1994.

Myers, Isabel Briggs. *Introduction to Type*. Palo Alto: Consulting Psychologists Press, 1993.

Myers, Isabel Briggs, with Peter B. Myers. *Gifts Differing: Understanding Personality Type*. Palo Alto: Davies-Black, 1995.

Osherson, Samuel. *Finding Our Fathers: The Unfinished Business of Manhood*. New York: Free Press, 1986.

Parsons, Martin. *Marriage Preparation*. London: SPCK, 1967.

Quenk, Naomi. *Beside Ourselves: Our Hidden Personality in Everyday Life*. Palo Alto: Davies-Black, 1993.

Scarf, Maggie. *Intimate Partners: Patterns in Love and Marriage*. New York: Ballantine, 1987.

————. *Intimate Worlds: Life Inside the Family*. New York: Random House, 1995.

Scott, Kieran, and Michael Warren, eds. *Perspectives on Marriage: A Reader*. New York: Oxford University Press, 1993.

Shaw, George Bernard. *Androcles and the Lion*. London: Constable & Co., 1930.

Smith, Veon. "Helping Couples to Differentiate from Their Families of Origin." In *Questions and Answers in the Practice of Family Therapy*. Alan S. Gurman, ed. 359–64. New York: Brunner/Mazel, 1981.

Stahmann, Robert, and William Hiebert, eds. *Counseling in Marital and Sexual Problems: A Clinician's Handbook*. 2d ed. Baltimore: Williams and Wilkins, 1977.

Sulloway, Frank. *Born to Rebel: Birth Order, Family Dynamics, and Creative Lives*. New York: Pantheon, 1996.

Toman, Walter. *Family Therapy and Sibling Position*. Northvale: Jason Aronson, 1993.

Vande Kemp, Hendrika. "Courtship and Counseling." *Theology, News and Notes* 35 (June 1988): 14–16, 26.

Viorst, Judith. *Necessary Losses*. New York: Fawcett Gold Medal, 1986.

Webber, Christopher. *Re-Inventing Marriage: A Re-View and Re-Vision*. Harrisburg: Morehouse, 1994.

White, Edwin A., and Jackson A. Dykman. *Annotated Constitution and Canons for the Government of the Protestant Episcopal Church in the United States of America, Otherwise Known as The Episcopal Church*. New York: Seabury, 1981.

Whitehead, Evelyn E., and James D. Whitehead. "Sexuality and Intimacy in Marriage." In Scott and Warren, 198–206.

A CUSTOMARY FOR WEDDINGS AT CHRIST CHURCH

Christ Church parish welcomes the use of its facilities for weddings by its members and others. A marriage service is a time that combines solemnity with joy. A wedding is a sacrament, that is, a service in which words and outwardly visible actions convey inward and spiritual meanings and transformations. The bride and the groom are the *ministers of the sacrament:* it is they who represent their physical and spiritual giving of themselves to each other by making promises, by giving and receiving a ring or rings, by taking hands, by prayer, and by the Kiss of Peace. The priest and people are present as witnesses but, more importantly, to offer their support and prayers, and to ask God's blessing on what the bride and groom are doing.

Couples planning to marry will naturally wish to meet with the rector or other clergyperson to share their thoughts and plans. The matters discussed below are simply "housekeeping details" and are not intended to take the place of premarital discussions and counsel. It is not required that persons seeking to be married in Christ Church be members of this parish, or of the Episcopal Church in general, but at least one of the pair must have received the sacrament of baptism. Both should agree with the teaching of the church that marriage is intended to be monogamous and lifelong.

In special situations, the church recognizes that marriages sometimes fail, and that divorce may, in some cases, be necessary. Persons who have been divorced may be married in the church, after appropriate consultation with the rector and after appealing to the bishop of the diocese for special dispensation. Persons who have contracted civil marriages may wish to have their marriages blessed in the presence of their friends in the church. The church also provides a service, which may be combined with a wedding, for the acceptance or adoption of children.

The Wedding Service

Except under unusual circumstances, the solemnization and blessing of a marriage should take place in church, assuming of course that the bride and groom have or intend to have a meaningful involvement with this parish or some other Christian community. Ordinarily the rector or one of the associates officiates, but of course clergy from other churches are welcome to collaborate in the services or, with the permission of the rector, to officiate. No announcement of the date or time of the wedding should be made until after consultation with the rector.

The 1979 Book of Common Prayer provides for considerable flexibility in the form and wording of the service, which may be very simple or very rich in its content and structure.

Ordinarily, if there is to be music, the regular organist of the parish will be in charge of it. Arrangements for special music by qualified musicians may of course be made in consultation with the organist and rector. The music should be appropriate to the joyfulness and the solemnity of the occasion. The fee for ordinary services of the organist is $100.

The chair of the altar guild should be consulted about appropriate flowers, if they are desired. Flowers are ordinarily obtained through approved local merchants.

Members of Christ Church parish may use the church for their weddings without charge, although they will be asked to underwrite any extra custodial services required, and to pay the standard fee for the organist. Nonmembers who do not contribute to the upkeep of the parish will be charged a standard fee for the use of the building. The parish secretary (775-2501, weekday mornings) will be able to put interested couples in touch with the rector, the organist, and the chair of the altar guild, and to discuss financial details.

The use of flash equipment for photography is *not* allowed during the service, which means from the time the bride enters until the wedding party has withdrawn. The wedding party may wish to return *after* the service for flash photographs. Noisy non-flash cameras should not be used during the service. If in doubt about parish policies, please check with the clergy.

Please inform the ushers and guests that confetti or other difficult-to-clean-up materials may not be used at the end of the service. Rice, which birds will eat up, may be thrown, but not in the church, the vestibule, or the parish hall.

Receptions

The parish hall, in the rear of the church, is available for rental for receptions of up to 300 persons (standing) or up to 120 for a sit-down dinner. The parish secretary will provide the name of the chairperson of the Fellowship-Parish Life Commission, who should be consulted about the use of the kitchen and other matters, and who will have information about rental charges and the returnable damage-deposit.

Dancing is not usually permitted, to avoid scuffing the hardwood floors. Care must be taken, especially when windows are open, not to disturb our neighbors with too much noise. An alcoholic punch or wine is permissible, in moderation, but no hard liquor may be served, and nonalcoholic beverages must be equally available and presented in an equally attractive manner.

Cleanup is the responsibility of the renters and must be accomplished at the end of the rental period, *not* on the following day. Failure to clean up adequately will result in the forfeiture of some or all of the damage deposit.

A Prayer for Those Betrothed

God of tenderness and strength, you have brought our paths together. Be with us now as we travel through good times, through trouble, or through change. Bless our home, our partings and our meetings. Make us worthy of each other's best, and tender with each other's dreams, trusting in your love in Jesus Christ. Amen.

(Adapted from *A New Zealand Prayer Book / He Karakia Mihinare o Aotearoa* [Auckland: The Church of the Province of New Zealand, 1989], 803)

5. Marriage Counseling

"Marriage is the most complex of all human relationships." (Carl Jung)

～

Twenty-five years ago, when I was in seminary and before I myself was married, our fairly perfunctory required lectures in pastoral care left me with the impression that all marital problems boiled down to three basic issues: money, sex, and in-laws. If complications could be avoided in these three areas, a marriage otherwise could be expected to go quite smoothly. The subsequent thirty years as an Anglican priest taught me a very different set of lessons. The first lesson was that there are more unhealthy marriages among the faithful than healthy marriages; the second was that there are a lot more complications within the marital relationship than the three I had been taught; and the third lesson was that most people fail to seek marriage counseling until it is almost too late, if they ask at all.

The preponderance of unhealthy marriages is notorious. That explains why so many comedians and television sitcoms base their appeal on complaints about one partner's dissatisfaction with the other. In the excellent book *The Good Marriage*, sociologist Judith Wallerstein describes the derisive reaction she received when she announced that she was going to conduct a systematic study of healthy marriages:

> On a raw spring morning in 1991, I shared my earliest thoughts about this book with a group of some one hundred professional women—all friends and colleagues—who meet each month to discuss our works in progress.

> "I'm interested in learning about good marriages—about what makes a marriage succeed," I said cheerfully. "As far as our knowledge is concerned, a happy marriage might as well be the dark side of the moon. And so I've decided to study a group of long-lasting marriages that are genuinely satisfying for both husband and wife." I looked around the room at these attractive, highly educated women—women who had achieved success in our high-tech, competitive society and who appeared to have it all. "Would any of you, along with your husbands, like to volunteer as participants in the study?" I asked.

> The room exploded with laughter. (Wallerstein and Blakeslee, 3)

The institution of marriage has undergone radical changes within the past two decades, so it is no wonder that pastors find themselves in a briar patch when it comes to helping a quarreling couple sort out the issues. For the first time in history, the decision to marry or, more importantly to stay married, has become completely voluntary. The transformation of our social fabric has meant that the forces that once held marriage together—a clear division of gender roles, the responsibility to have and raise children, contractual arrangements pertaining to property and status, the preservation of our obligations to our families of origin—have become the same forces that now seem to tear marriages apart. Where once divorce was considered dangerous, now premarital sex and de facto relationships are considered by many to be safe and normal, while marriage is considered dangerous!

We're very schizophrenic about marriage. We want "Caroline in the City" and "The Single Guy" to find a mate; we hold our breath to see if Clark Kent and Lois Lane will get married, or if Ross and

Rachel will ever become more than just "Friends." Though we know that half of all marriages end in divorce, and that the home is the place where women and children are most likely to be abused, beaten, or killed, we still push people toward marriage. Even when Wallerstein interviewed one hundred people who professed to be quite happily married, only 5 percent said they wanted to have a marriage like their parents'. The church sits within a culture of divorce and, I suspect because it is still stuck somewhere in the past, remains a party to the exaggerated expectations that are brought to marriage and has little to offer most couples who are in trouble. Perhaps Jung was correct when he said that marriage is the most complex of human relationships (Jung, 189).

The Witness of Scripture and History

Scripture provides us with several models of marriage, though most are unsuited for the present decade. Many of the patriarchs and kings of Israel had multiple wives. Comments on marriage in the Pauline or pseudo-Pauline literature are very heavily influenced by the structure of the hierarchical society in which the authors lived and by the imminent expectation of the Second Coming. The four Gospels record only one specific saying by Jesus about marriage (Mark 10:2-12 and parallels), and while Matthew, Mark, and Luke agree that his response forbade divorce, they disagree as to whether certain circumstances override that prohibition. The narrowest reading leaves the question about God's will for marriage unanswered.

In the Hellenistic world of the early church, life expectancies were short and the infant mortality rate was high. It was therefore a civic duty, expected of every good citizen of the Roman Empire, to marry and have as many children as possible, in the hope that some of them would live long enough to provide in turn the next generation to replace those who had died from poverty, disease, and the frequent wars that beset the empire. For Christians, the constant threat of martyrdom and, in time, the obvious crumbling of the empire left little energy for or interest in the construction of a theology of long-term relationships. It is only within our past few decades that infant mortality has been controlled, puberty begins earlier and earlier, and people live to ages inconceivable to the early Christian community. We have no systematic theology to service a golden anniversary because until quite recently such longevity wasn't possible.

Actually, the early church was of two minds about marriage. St. Paul clearly preferred celibacy, and St. Augustine wasn't sure whether women had any purpose in creation other than procreation. In his commentary on Genesis (*The Literal Meaning of Genesis* IX.5.9), Augustine wrote:

> Now if Eve was not made for Adam to be his helper in begetting children, what good was she to him? She was not to till the earth with him, for there was not yet any toil to make help necessary. If there were any such need, a male helper would be better, and the same could be said of the comfort of another's presence if Adam were perhaps weary of solitude. How much more agreeably could two male friends, rather than a man and a woman, enjoy companionship and conversation in a life shared together.

Celibacy, particularly as it prepared the faithful to be in a state of purity at the eschaton, was considered by most of the patristic writers to be preferable. If marriage could be dissociated from the civic obligations to raise up children, its purpose as a vehicle for ensuring the future of humanity became meaningless: there was no identifiable future to the worldly order once Christ reappeared. What the early Christians were saying when they commended celibacy was, "The resurrection of Christ has changed our values so radically that we no longer depend on marriage and posterity to give our lives meaning. Christ gives our lives eternal value—so who needs children?" (Webber, 183–84). For those who could not contain themselves until the dawn of the New Order, Paul conceded that it was better to marry than to burn (1 Cor. 7:9).

Is There a "Right" Way to Be Married?

Marriage and the creation of a family traditionally fulfilled six purposes: to control sexual access and relations; to provide an orderly context for reproduction; to nurture and socialize children; to provide a context for economic activity; to ascribe social status to its members; and to provide emotional support for its adult members. Without exception each of these functions is now being challenged (Nelson in Scott and Warren, 106). The challenge has brought about a new understanding of the several types of marriage into which we Christians enter and has raised questions about whether there is any such thing as one "right" way to be married. Judith Wallerstein and Sandra Blakeslee define four different types of marriage, each of which can be quite healthy, and each of which can degenerate, if not tended with care, into what they call an "antimarriage."

Romantic Marriage. At its core is a lasting and passionately sensuous relationship, enlivened by cherished memories. While many marriage counselors believe that the romantic glow of courtship is impossible to maintain for long, a few couples do seem to glow for years with excitement in each other's presence. These are good marriages, witnessed by the inability to stop touching each other tenderly and the desire to spend long evenings of intimacy together. However, because romantic marriages are often built on a sense of mutual complementarity— each partner seeing in the other something that fills some gap or lack in one's own sense of identity—commitment can degenerate into collusion, with each partner trapped in fulfilling the other's adolescent indulgent fantasies, a gamesmanship that often avoids mature adult responsibility.

Rescue Marriage. Of course every good marriage should provide a sense of comfort and healing for past unhappinesses. If most adults do not wish to emulate their parents' marital style, then we must assume that nearly everyone has grown up with some gnawing fundamental sense of unhappiness that will seek healing within a different kind of marriage. But rescue marriages meet the needs of those who have had particularly traumatic past experiences. People who have been abused or molested as children or adolescents still grow up to marry, apparently in the hope that healthy relationships are possible and that they might even erase, or at least compensate for, the pain of the past. People who have divorced marry again in the same sort of hope (in this sense, most second marriages would qualify as rescue marriages). As Wallerstein and Blakeslee point out:

> Each supports the other in working to prevent a repetition of old scenarios. They calm each other and gain a feeling of confidence they have never known before.

Their relationship teaches them that they can close the door on the past and affirm their deepest hopes. The effect can be electrifying. (106)

The rescue "antimarriage" is a codependent relationship in which partners keep each other's negative memories alive for the purposes of holding them together. Personalities regress, symptoms become frozen, and the marriage partners focus away from each other onto "the awful past" rather than turning toward each other in the healing hopefulness of love.

Companionate Marriage. As the product of rapidly changing gender roles in our society and new opportunities for women in the economic marketplace, the companionate marriage is quickly becoming the most common type of marriage for couples under the age of forty. Each partner is struggling to balance career responsibilities and family responsibilities. In a partnership of equals, all roles, all rules and obligations are negotiable. Most people in companionate marriages have no expectation that things will be easy, but such relationships carry the excitement of pioneering a new model better suited to the new values of the young. The inherent danger, the potential "antimarriage" within this type, is that in their individual autonomy, the necessary work of maintaining marital intimacy may be ignored. The couple may wind up simply as two highly motivated individuals living under the same roof, like brother and sister. Children may present a further complication: even though a couple may agree to share nurturing responsibilities equally, both come with unique and often conflicting assumptions about the "right" way to wean, discipline, or comfort a child, inherited from their own family-of-origin experi-

ences. The ideal of two successful professionals coparenting does not translate easily into the world of midnight earaches or nannies with the flu.

Traditional Marriage. The older tradition of marriage is one of separate spheres of responsibility: the husband for the family's financial security and the wife for the family's domestic health. This is the model around which "family values" and the American dream have been built, but interestingly, according to Wallerstein, even young couples who choose a traditional marital style do not wish to live it out in the way their parents did. The ground rules of the traditional marriage have begun to shift. Men's and women's roles are less rigidly demarcated, and mothers and fathers are experientially more sensitive to the stresses and frustrations each experiences within their spheres of responsibility. Of the four types of marriage that Wallerstein and Blakeslee identify, this is the one most under strain. Fewer families can afford to live on one income, and since wives do not gain extensive professional experience in this type, "traditional family values" can be maintained only if the economic climate of the nation assures the working husband of an exceptionally high degree of job stability. If the breadwinner becomes unemployed or disabled, the whole family's future collapses almost immediately. The antimarriage inherent in this type is a family so narrowly focused on the children that the two adults view each other only as "mom and dad," and when the children grow up and leave home, this couple may have little left to say to each other.

Of course there are also hybrid forms, such as the romantic-rescue, the traditional-rescue, or the romantic-companionate.

Relationships rarely fit neatly into tidy schemas. But the value of realizing that marriage comes in a variety of types is that the pastor can then "counsel to type," that is, counsel a couple to fulfill the type that they have already chosen for themselves, rather than producing a cognitive dissonance by, for example, counseling a traditional couple to espouse the values of companionate marriage.

The Destructive Power of Unresolved Issues

Most psychodynamic counseling theories, which seek to understand how people relate in the present based on their past experiences, realize that marriage is like an "open stage" upon which people play out unfinished "scripts" from their past. When people marry, there are many conscious decisions they must make, both individually and corporately, about what they will keep and what they will discard from their pasts. This of course is the primary task of premarital counseling, as described in the previous chapter. But many of the "scripts" that people act out in marriage are unconscious ones, formed early in their childhoods and carried unrecognized and unfinished through two or three decades before the marriage. No premarital counseling can address all the thousands of assumptions and expectations that each couple brings into a relationship, nor can a premarital counselor easily judge a couple's skills in naming, articulating, and resolving the conflicts that naturally arise when those expectations and assumptions clash. Nor *should* all such conflicts be resolved; where these expectations do not cause damage to the partner or relationship, they may indeed be kept as an expression of the individual freedom necessary within every healthy marriage.

Marriage counselors are fond of telling their clients that there are six people in the marital bedroom, not just two. At all moments of vulnerability or need, each person's parents are very much present, however invisible. Yet even this claim may be simplistic, for within the natural boundaries of every relationship there reside not only the parents of the two people involved, but also the opinions and values of their intimate friends, their experience with previous relationships, their personal values derived from life experience, their religious values, the standards of their immediate community, and the values of their society. Often this tangled skein of influences is too emotionally invested to be rational and too individualistic to be predictable, and few of these influences are rooted in an objective truth. As Wallerstein and Blakeslee point out:

> One child will say, "My mother hits me because she can't help it." Another says, "My mother hits me because I deserve it." The objective truth may have little to do with what the child feels. . . . It is the child's inner experience that becomes the lasting reality. (40)

That is why Anderson and Fite describe a marriage as "a wedding of stories" (43), for stories are always simultaneously truth and fantasy: each partner is negotiating with the other how to retain those inner experiences which are the building blocks of one's personal identity. Much of that "inner experience that becomes the lasting reality" is so deeply woven into the fabric of our personal identity that we cannot renegotiate or discard it without a significant element of pain.

This explains why disagreement and conflict are inevitable within marriage

(Schillebeeckx describes marriage as "a vocation, a commission to be realized despite and through a host of obstacles"). Each partner enters the relationship with the question: "How can I get my spouse to conform to my basic needs as I presently perceive them?" In long-term marriages, those basic needs may grow more closely matched, so that a couple has less need to quarrel. Rather, in a good marriage, both partners will eventually have a strong sense of what the other needs and values and will voluntarily attempt to meet those needs to the degree possible. In marriages that are not so good or generous, the drive toward self-protection and self-pleasure overrides the commitment, originally undertaken mutually, to build a lasting marriage of comfort, nurturance, and support. Present sociological studies do not show a correlation between deprivation or abuse in childhood and marital failure; the stronger correlate with marital success or failure is the maturity level of both partners, particularly when measured against the values of sacrifice, justice, reconciliation, hospitality, and joy (Anderson and Fite, 151). Even people from unstable families of origin are quite capable of conducting healthy relationships, as long as they feel emotionally and physically safe.

Marriage as a Developmental Process

A serious obstacle to a healthy relationship is viewing marriage either as a "thing" or as a state of being. In actuality, marriage is best viewed as a developmental process full of challenges, transitions, and accomplishments, and in need of frequent renegotiation. While sociologists and marital therapists offer a variety of definitions of the developmental stages of marriage, one of the best known is the schema described by Carol Nadelson, Derek Polonsky, and Mary Alice Mathews (Scarf, 13). According to these three authors, a marriage passes through at least five predictable stages.

Idealization. These are the early weeks and months of marriage, when a couple are so deeply in love. Most counseling psychologists would agree that each partner is in love with the other as an object-other or a projection of the partner him- or herself. That is to say, few people in this early stage confront the radical otherness of the other, but see only those parts of the self which have not been integrated and hence are projected onto the other as if the other were a blank screen. In the romantic type of marriage, feelings and memories from this stage continue to feed the couple throughout the duration of their relationship. Most other couples eventually run into a stone wall of differentness—what Wayne Booth calls "the otherness that bites" (70)—and are tempted to pack their bags and move back home to mother, figuratively if not literally.

Disappointment and Disenchantment. The second stage of marital development begins with facing the otherness of the other, realizing that no one really knows well the person he or she marries. A disillusionment sets in when one partner realizes that the other will *not* meet all of his or her needs, that marriage is not forever the idyllic bliss portrayed in the movies, and that marriage demands negotiation, compromise, and a flexibility previously unimagined. This stage in the evolving relationship is a normal one, though it is not often explained enough to a couple in order to avoid its terrible shock. Some marriages get stuck in this phase and are never able to move on, instead expending great amounts of energy on how to process the disappointment of one or the other partner.

Productivity. Settling into a more realistic appraisal of each other, a committed couple will enter a stage of productivity. In many marriages, this still means parenting children as well as embarking on a professional career. Because this is the next logical stage of marriage development, people who cannot have children may feel there is no point in continuing the relationship. Some may be assisted by finding other outlets into which to channel their productivity, whether increased professional commitment or involvement in issues of social service and social justice. Some couples in companionate marriages consciously choose not to have children. A counselor may be called upon to help a companionate couple defend themselves against family pressures to produce grandchildren. The increased number of intentionally childless couples suggests that more traditional viewpoints that define the purpose of marriage as procreation are not creative enough in identifying "productivity" to meet the evolving new types of marriage.

Redefinition and Child Launching. At midlife the original task of marriage—separating from the families of origin and establishing new connections—must be solved anew. These couples, once their family is no longer so focused on residential children, face many of the same questions as do newlyweds: "How much emotional investment do we make in us as a couple? How much time will we spend in activities with other people or in individual pursuits?" These decisions will determine the quality of a couple's relational health over the following decades (Wallerstein and Blakeslee, 274).

Reintegration and Post-Parenting. A shift toward greater empathy, companionship, and sharing may be discerned during this phase as the couple redefines itself as a twosome. This may be most difficult for those in a traditional marriage, for they often have had less contact with each other than in the other three types due to the sharp boundaries separating the work sphere from the domestic. The arrival of grandchildren inserts an extra generation between the senior and junior members of the extended family; because many grandparents do not have primary charge of their young grandchildren, they may find post-parenting much more pleasant than parenting. On the other hand, a couple in their final decades may have increased anxiety about being abandoned through the death of one partner or, worse, of being miserably lonely in a marriage that was not rebuilt or renegotiated in its due season.

Mel Krantzler speaks of "marriages within a marriage" (37), and indeed this would be an accurate description of the various stages through which a marriage proceeds. Each stage has its own task, challenges, disappointments and rewards. As a couple proceeds from stage to stage, they need to revision their relationship, and perhaps even more formally to celebrate the past and the future by renewing their marriage vows.

Viewing marriage as a series of developmental stages rather than as a state of being emphasizes how little a couple should take each other for granted and how important a role the ability to adapt plays for both partners. In this sense, marriage witnesses to a God who exclaims, "Behold, I am making all things new" (Rev. 21:5). Anderson and Fite point out that one may fall in love, but one does not fall into marriage; a marriage is built, step by step, and a happily married couple can rejoice in this mutual project because of the rewards it brings them (8). Building a marriage is rather like building a house; it must proceed according to a well thought out plan.

The Nine Tasks in a Healthy Marriage

Throughout the course of these developmental stages, certain tasks need to be accomplished. Most developmental schemas attach identified tasks to be accomplished at each stage. For example, Erik Erikson identifies "trust" as the task necessary to the first six months of life. Wallerstein and Blakeslee describe nine tasks to be accomplished over the developmental course of a marriage. They do not attach the tasks to particular stages in a marriage, but argue that over the course of a relationship's life, these tasks need to be mastered and frequently renegotiated. The tasks are not necessarily sequential and several may need to be revisited as the couple's external circumstances change. For instance, a couple that has lived near one or the other set of parents and then undertakes a move to a distant location may have to renegotiate the shape of loyalties to one or both of the families of origin. When a parent dies, an adult child may need to redefine his or her independence in relation to the surviving widowed parent. These constant renegotiations, too, are a part of marriage as a process.

1. The initial task toward building a healthy marital relationship is for both partners to detach emotionally from their families of childhood, commit to the relationship, and build connections to their new extended family (Wallerstein and Blakeslee, 331–32). Emotional detachment from family of origin should not mean severing the relationship, but redefining it to make room for new loyalties and responsibilities. Love of and loyalty to the new marriage must now become the first priority. Much of this work is accomplished internally or psychologically, though a variety of symbols may accompany it. Neither partner should be expected to do this for the other; adult individuation is a personal responsibility, though partners can be a source of important support for this task which may occasionally feel wrenching. Our loyalties to our parents are deeply ingrained and usually contain a great deal of unconscious bonding (attachment patterns) and unresolved conflict. Redefinition may evoke feelings of guilt and anxiety, so that this task may take several years, at work simultaneously with the successive tasks.

2. The second marital task is to build togetherness through intimacy and expand the sense of self to include the other, while each individual carves out an area of autonomy (Wallerstein and Blakeslee, 332). The new sense of "us," however, must not completely destroy the "I." A marital relationship needs to make room for each partner to retain his or her own sense of individual identity. Wallerstein and Blakeslee call this "creating a room of one's own" (67–68). Poet Kahlil Gibran described this healthy tension between togetherness and autonomy as being like "two pillars which hold up a common roof." The usual psychological term for it is "interdependence," a stance halfway between dependence and independence. Differences must be acknowledged, allowed for, and even welcomed, all of which necessitates frequent open communication of one's innermost feelings. The balance between togetherness and autonomy is usually not achieved easily or quickly.

Marriage and family therapist Stuart Johnson has devised a five-point schema to describe the couple's move toward relational interdependence, noting that many couples plateau at some stage that leaves them too emotionally entangled to individuate well (Scarf, 390-405). Progress through these stages of interdependence can often be measured by a couple's inability to process conflict or tolerate difference. Those who marry late may have increased difficulty in relinquishing the independence to which they have become particularly accustomed.

3. The third task is to expand the circle to include children, taking on the daunting roles of parenthood from infancy to the time the child leaves home, while maintaining the emotional richness of marriage (Wallerstein and Blakeslee, 332). This is the only task of the nine that is not always applicable, for a significant number of marriages cannot or choose not to include children as a part of the marital expression. Counselors should be prepared to talk this responsibility through with couples; possessing the proper genital equipment is no guarantee that a couple will make good parents. The childrearing stage of a marriage is one of ebb and flow, as parents successively turn toward the children and then back toward each other. What matters is holding on to the recognition that parenting is only part of a marriage, not the whole of it. Each partner should be available to help the other in the process of parenting, but also be ready to help each other and the marriage recover from the tensions and worries that naturally accompany nurturing children.

4. The fourth marital task is to confront the inevitable developmental challenges and the unpredictable adversities of life, including illness, death, and natural disasters, in ways that enhance the relationship rather than undermining it (Wallerstein and Blakeslee, 332). Coping with crisis evokes anxieties and emotional responses that normally lie dormant in a marriage, and so it may demand that either partner draw on personal resources deep within their identity. Wallerstein and Blakeslee believe that five characteristics mark a couple's ability to keep their marriage strong in the face of adversity (122–23):

- They tried their best to realistically acknowledge and think about the consequences of the crisis.
- They protected each other by not blaming, in spite of the great temptation to do so.
- They took steps to allow some degree of pleasure and humor back into their lives by keeping things in proper perspective.
- They didn't play martyr or pretend to be saintly. Fear makes everyone cranky and difficult.... But they were usually able to ... stay in control because they saw the connection between the crisis and the inappropriate hurtful response.... They made a great effort to keep destructive tendencies from getting out of control and harming the marriage.
- They blocked whatever crises that they could see coming in advance.

Because a couple has created a joint identity, a crisis that affects one affects both, as well as affecting the overall health of the relationship.

5. The fifth task is to make the relationship safe for expressing difference, anger, and conflict, which are inevitable in any marriage. A "conflict-free" marriage is an oxymoron; no two people have similar enough backgrounds in their families of

origin to avoid disagreements, particularly if the marriage is structured around mutual empowerment. But a couple needs to learn *how* to disagree without violating each other's boundaries of respect and safety. As Wallerstein and Blakeslee point out, "some remarks, once said, cannot be unsaid. Some actions, once done, cannot be undone" (146). Safety is an indispensable quality of a good marriage. Each partner must feel that inside the boundary around their togetherness, personal boundaries are also safe, including the physical, sexual, emotional, intellectual, volitional, and spiritual boundaries of the Wholeness Wheel. A couple may be helped by distinguishing thoughtfully between non-issues and issues that justify open disagreement.

6. The Greeks had at least three words for love: *eros* or sensual desire, *phileo* or friendship, and *agape* or devoted affection. All three must be present in a healthy marriage, and so the sixth task is to establish an imaginative and pleasurable sex life. A mutually satisfying sexual relationship is not simply a fringe benefit to a marriage, it is absolutely essential. But we are vulnerable in our sexual activity, so this aspect of marriage requires special attention and sensitive protection to keep it alive. Even as early as the year 600, Pope Gregory the Great was aware of the importance of an active sexual life in marriage. In his *Book of Pastoral Rule* III.27, he encouraged married couples never to deny themselves to each other. St. Augustine charged marital partners to pleasure each other sexually, even when they were "almost corpselike" (Hunter, 104). Both were quite clear that such joyous responsibilities had nothing to do with procreation, but with the society and charity natural to two people who had committed themselves to each other. Of course, sexual desire waxes and wanes over time, for "Sex is remarkably sensitive to what's happening in all areas of individual and family life. Illness, especially surgery, as well as depression, worry, fatigue, and stress at work can affect a man and woman's intimate life" (Wallerstein and Blakeslee, 192). Each partner's sexual needs are as individualized as a thumbprint, shaped by childhood and previous relationship experiences, so that discrepant needs require frequent communication and negotiation. But the church fathers and modern marriage counselors agree that long periods of sexual inactivity in a marriage must occur only if mutually agreed upon, and always increase the possibility of marital infidelity.

7. The seventh task is to share laughter and humor and to keep interest alive in the relationship. Little is as deadly to a marriage as monotony and boredom. Laughter provides a great relief of tension and easily encourages forgiveness. A good marriage is alternately playful and serious, sometimes flirtatious, sometimes difficult and cranky, but always full of life (Wallerstein and Blakeslee, 132).

8. The eighth marital task is to provide the emotional nurturance and encouragement that all adults need throughout their lives, especially in today's isolating urban communities. This may particularly hold true in rescue marriages and in companionate relationships in which two demanding professionals are always on the firing line. Partners need to be free from "performance evaluation" at home, with the space to be vulnerable to each other and to have their self-esteem supported and restored. Some counselors believe that poor self-esteem, often accompanied by persistent low-grade depression, is the "common cold" of con-

temporary mental health. No one should have to plead to have his or her self-esteem boosted, and no one should assume that a partner's sense of self-worth is so secure that it needs no stroking!

9. The popular Beatles' song asked, "Will you still need me . . . when I'm sixty-four?" The ninth task is to sustain the innermost core of a relationship by drawing sustenance and renewal from the images and fantasies of courtship and early marriage, and to maintain that joyful glow over a lifetime (Wallerstein and Blakeslee, 132). Past images and present realities are balanced so that both keep the other in perspective. Laugh wrinkles around a partner's eyes are not the ravages of time but proof of what a pleasure this person has been to be married to. A couple keeps the treasure of their early years alive by telling stories again and again and by marking their shared stages with toasts, flowers, and anniversaries. The stories they tell are unique to their relationship. No one else can tell them in the same way, and if they are not told, a little piece of human history dies.

These nine tasks form a tall order, perhaps, but they also underline that "marriage" cannot be taken for granted, and "being married" is an intentionally shaped process that, while commanding a lifetime of work, also yields a strength, a joy, and a shelter that transcend the individual limitations of the two partners.

The Characteristics of a Good Marriage

A casual observer does not need to tick off these nine points in order to recognize a good marriage. Healthy marriages are usually quite obvious to the outside world because of the characteristics they exhibit. These qualities are described in various ways in the counseling literature. Some authors opt for more "cold realism" than do Wallerstein and Blakeslee. For example, Lederer and Jackson, whose book *The Mirages of Marriage* has long been considered a classic, define marital satisfaction in this way:

> The happy, workable, productive marriage does not require love as defined in this book, or even the practice of the Golden Rule. To maintain continuously a union based on love is not feasible for most people. Nor is it possible to live in a permanent state of romance. Normal people should not be frustrated or disappointed if they are not in a constant state of love. If they experience the joy of love (or imagine they do) for ten per cent of the time they are married, attempt to treat each other with as much courtesy as they do distinguished strangers, and attempt to make the marriage a workable affair—one where there are some practical advantages and satisfactions for each—the chances are that the marriage will endure longer and with more strength than the so-called love matches. (59)

Such a definition seems to preclude the "romantic" type of marriage described above, but Lederer and Jackson are probably correct in their observation that most marriages are not held together by the sleepless nights, mindless obsessions, and fairytale daydreams that characterize romantic courtship.

British literary critic Nigel Nicolson, describing the marriage of Virginia and Leonard Woolf, portrays a relationship of deep commitment to and respect for the other that sounds very much like modern companionate marriage:

> When two people of independent minds marry, they must be able to rely upon each other's tolerance, affection and support.

Each must encourage, without jealousy, the full development of the other's gifts, each allow the other privacy, different interests, different friends. But they must share an intellectual and moral base. One of them cannot be philistine if the other is constantly breasting new ideas. They cannot disagree on what is right and wrong. Above all, their love must grow as passion fades. ("Introduction," xiii)

Harry Stack Sullivan, one of the great counseling theoreticians of the 1930s, defined marriage in a manner reminiscent of the biblical "Golden Rule": "When the satisfaction or the security of another person becomes as significant as one's own satisfaction or security, then the state of love exists" (Lederer and Jackson, 42). Sometimes in my pastoral theology classes I have defined the primary characteristic of a good marriage as "the unconditional rejoicing in the otherness of the other." Yet another commonly cited list of qualities of a good marriage is

1. tolerance and humor about one's own idiosyncrasies and those of the partner;

2. respect for the right of each partner to change and grow;

3. constructive honesty and open communication, which does not include physical, emotional, or verbal violence, and which does include joy at the opportunity constantly to renegotiate family rules and expectations;

4. deep commitment and desire to stay together for mutual advantage (adapted from Lederer and Jackson, 198–99).

However we choose to articulate the characteristics, pastors and counselors have learned from their experience that not every marriage is a healthy one, but once achieved through attention to both process

and task, a good marriage radiates a special warmth that enriches the lives of all who come in contact with it. James Nelson, among others, would call this radiance "grace": "Grace is the name for the meeting between two who are very different, be it human and God or human and human. Grace is also the name for when it works" (Scott and Warren, 72).

What Makes a Marriage Christian?

Historian Peter Brown writes: "Lacking the clear ritual boundaries provided in Judaism by circumcision and dietary laws, [early] Christians tended to make their exceptional sexual discipline bear the full burden of expressing the difference between themselves and the pagan world" (Trigg, 21). Some Christians would like to make a similar clear boundary between Christian marriage and non-Christian marriage. The case would be more convincing if the statistics revealed that marriages were healthier inside the church or ended in divorce less often. I would not like to push the distinction between Christian marriage and non-Christian marriage too hard (nor would St. Paul, who cautioned Christian spouses to remain with their unbelieving partners, rather than seeking a new Christian partner). As well, we know that the domestic abuse of women has been too often justified by twisting the meaning of certain biblical passages should as, "Wives, be subject to your husbands" (Col. 3:18). However, neither should the positive influence of a strong religious faith and practice be underestimated.

One of the complications in formulating a concept of Christian marriage as being distinctive from non-Christian marriages is that the church has not historically been clear whether a marriage is created by the church or blessed by the church. Until the medieval period, clergy attended marriages but rarely presided at them; they were there simply to add the church's blessing to the public legal declarations of a civil official. Over the course of time, marriage ceremonies were slowly incorporated more centrally into the life of local congregations, and around 1100, Peter Lombard included "marriage" in his list of seven catholic sacraments. A century and a half later, Thomas Aquinas agreed with Peter Lombard only grudgingly:

> Matrimony according as it is ordered to animal life, is a function of nature. But in so far as it has something spiritual it is a sacrament. And because it has the least amount of spirituality it is placed last. (Webber, 104)

Aquinas seems to recognize that it is human nature to seek a marital partner, but not all marriages—even between believing Christians—reach the level at which their spiritual content qualifies them for clear inclusion alongside the other dominical sacraments.

The sacramental definition of marriage was boldly rejected by the Protestant reformers. Martin Luther objected:

> There is no evidence that Christ determined any special ceremony for its making, or gave any special promise of grace to one who takes a wife. . . . Marriage is outside the church. . . . It is a civil matter, and therefore should belong to the government. . . . We have enough work in our proper office. (Webber, 108, 112)

Hence Protestantism has generally classified marriage as an "ordinance," a distinctly legal definition that differs markedly from a sacrament. Marriage in the medieval and Reformation periods, so formative to our present theologies, was primarily an economic partnership designed to facilitate survival in a harsh world, to ensure the retention of property ownership and status, and to provide structured control of social relations. All three purposes were informed by a calculated interplay of power, empowerment, and disempowerment. Today we raise hard questions about the use and abuse of power in interpersonal relationships and these questions have directly affected the way we understand relational health within marriage. An increasing number of couples find the original social justifications for marriage to be irrelevant.

The definition of marriage as a relationship of two mutually empowered people has a history that stretches back to the early church. John Chrysostom, commenting on Ephesians 5:25, wrote:

> She who is your life's partner, the mother of your children, the very reason for your happiness . . . must not be restrained by fears and threats, but by love and a gentle disposition. What sort of union is it, when the wife trembles before the husband? What sort of pleasure will the husband himself enjoy, if he lives with a wife who is more a slave than a free woman? (Homily 20 on Ephesians in Hunter, 80)

While Chrysostom's understanding of mutuality may not match our own, we can measure his recognition that wives have an unquestionable right to respect and dignity within a marriage.

In our own time, the church has moved toward defining marriage as a relationship between equals, entered into with full adult consent, and designed to set people free to love rather than confine them. Ten years ago, the Anglican Consultative Council issued this position statement on marriage:

We affirm the institution of marriage as a vocation of fundamental importance, but not of necessity for personal development. Marriage is a part of God's creation, but like all other relationships, it needs redeeming. The ingredients of Christian marriage are fidelity, trust, acceptance, commitment, an intention of permanence, mutual service and empowerment. It is unreasonable and unrealistic to expect marriage to meet all individual emotional needs. Disappointment at this point may lead to breakdown. (In Nichols, Clarke, and Hogan, 63–64)

What often needs redeeming in a relationship is the way that power is used by one partner against another. Yet, power is a great gift in marriage when shared. Sharing power in marriage is determined by many factors: by the individual's needs and fears, by values from our families of origin, by our understanding of gendered roles, and by the particular cultures within which we have been raised. Power is hoarded or shared within the everyday exchanges of marital life: use of leisure time, the family budget, the cycle of holiday visits to relatives, the claiming of priorities. Power approached as a scarce commodity may lead to a marital dynamic of resentment, competition, and "preemptive strikes"; power understood as one of God's generous gifts to humanity can lead to each partner's desire further to empower the other.

Spirituality may be difficult to measure in objective terms but is a critical component of any relationship, including a Christian marriage. Sharing power as a justice issue is just one way marriages exhibit their Christian character. Other ways include voluntary sacrifice (though I do not imply self-negation); reconciliation, particularly in generous acts of forgiveness and charity;

hospitality of home and heart; respect for the dignity of each partner as a living image of God; and shared opportunities for home prayer, quiet meditation, and formal worship.

Counseling Skills for Effective Ministry

In the Introduction we examined the "Wholeness Wheel" as a standard for measuring holistic adult health. As each individual should seek health in all six areas of the wheel—physical, social, intellectual or mental, volitional, emotional, and spiritual—so a marital relationship, in that it is a sum larger than its two component parts, must also grow toward health in each of these areas if it is to be whole. Most of the component parts have already been alluded to:

- *physical wholeness:* the sensual and erotic nature of the marital relationship
- *social wholeness:* the larger social network of which a relationship is one part and to which it is connected by careful construction
- *intellectual or mental wholeness:* the humor, vitality, and spontaneity of a relationship, and the ability to rejoice in the past as an integral part of the present
- *volitional wholeness:* the autonomy within togetherness, the "room of one's own in the home"
- *emotional wholeness:* the ability to be vulnerable, to find support and affirmation, and to weather crises
- *spiritual wholeness:* the spiritual and Christian understandings of justice, sacrifice, reconciliation, hospitality, respect, and prayer.

But on the way to wholeness, marriages may falter. In the case of Christian marriages, the pastoral practitioner is often the first avenue of help. In such cases, the pastor may occupy a position of privilege, for he or she may already know a great deal about the couple, their family, and their extended family. For this reason, pastoral counselors need to be familiar with some quite specific avenues of approach, whether counseling the couple themselves or making an appropriate referral.

The most difficult decision in marital counseling is often *whom* to counsel. Pastors should be aware that to counsel extensively only one partner of the two appears, according to our present statistical information, to increase significantly the chances of eventual divorce. As therapist Carl Rogers observed, "If growth towards self-hood occurs only in one partner, and fails to be encouraged or fostered in the other, then the increasing distance can become awesome, and the partnership, without some sort of near miracle, is headed straight for the rocks" (214). A pastor is often approached by only one of the two partners (statistically this is likely to be the female partner), but should proceed with great caution if both partners are not willing to attend counseling together. Ultimately this is an ethical issue, for, having been warned, the pastor is then in the position of being an accomplice to potential divorce.

Cultural definitions and expectations are indispensable background for marital counseling. Each partner is shaped by his or her culture of origin, and the marriage is shaped by the culture in which the partner is presently living. Partners from individualistic cultures may experience difficulty conceptualizing the obligations of togetherness; partners from communal cultures may experience difficulty conceptualizing the opportunities for autonomy. People from cultures that prize the closeness of large extended families may experience problems with "leaving to cleave"; even those who have been married quite some time may have left this task unfinished. Those from highly verbal cultures may have trouble understanding the boundaries of privacy; those from highly emotional cultures may have trouble respecting reserve. In such instances, a minister may be called upon to act as a proponent and translator of one culture to the other, in terms that the other can understand.

Bascue and Lewis outline some of the several more common approaches to marital therapy. Most are premised on a belief that a family is an organized social and psychological system with self-reinforcing operational principles, and that a family "whole" is usually greater than the sum of its parts. When it is no longer appropriate for the pastor to proceed with counseling, for whatever reason, the pastor should refer the couple to a therapist who specializes in the counseling approach best suited to the couple's taste and the issues presented.

Psychotherapy. Practitioners, who in America are carefully regulated by licensing, focus generally on the psychodynamics of one or more individual family members, in the hope that a change in one member will facilitate change in other family members. Of particular interest is the way that a family member's unconscious wishes and needs block open communication and healthy functioning within the larger system. Psychotherapy normally involves long-term and frequent contact with a professional counselor and should not be attempted by a minister or pastoral counselor.

Intergenerational or systems therapy. Some therapists are concerned with the influence of family patterns on successive generations. In the church, this approach was popularized by Edwin Friedman's best-selling *Generation to Generation: Family Process in Church and Synagogue*. Ivan Boszormenyi-Nagy and D. Ulrich describe the "inherited" dysfunction within a family system:

> At any point in time, at least three generations overlap. Even if the grandparents are absent or dead, their influence continues. Psychological, transactional, and ethical aspects lose crucial meanings if they are not seen in this perspective. (Bascue and Lewis, 270–71)

Intergenerational or systems therapists often insist on seeing more than one person in a counseling situation, preferably covering at least two generations. Treatment success is dependent upon a family's ability to differentiate itself from the generations that preceded. An increasing number of pastors report some success in using this approach, even after a fairly short course of specialized training.

Communication therapy. Communication therapy attends to the variety of ways in which two partners communicate with each other, including both verbally and nonverbally. Effective problem solving and interpersonal conflict resolution are often the result of communication therapy. One of the most important founders of this approach was Virginia Satir, particularly known for her books *Conjoint Family Therapy* and *People-Making.* Couples might more simply benefit from a weekend course in communication skills, particularly as they relate to processing anger and difference of opinion.

Structural therapy. The underlying assumption of structural therapy is that by identifying and changing the "physical structure" of a relationship system, the psychological relations among members will also change. Structural therapists seek to identify how partners seize or relinquish power by sitting in a certain position in relation to each other, or analyze sleep patterns and habits as an entry into a family interpersonal problems.

Behavioral therapy. Behaviorists, drawing inspiration from social learning theory, seek to identify the "reward system" at work in a family unit that encourages dysfunctional behavior. They also examine social environmental forces at work both inside and outside the family on the presumption that a family member will persist in destructive behavior because it is being reinforced from some source of authority.

Other relevant techniques. Several other specialized approaches complement these five schools of therapy. Sex therapy is almost categorically outside the bounds of propriety for pastors, though as we have seen, the sexual aspect of marriage is critical to its long-term health and should not escape the inquiry of a caring minister. Parent Effectiveness Training may take several forms, all of which are premised on improving family health by training parents in specific relational techniques. Marital Enhancement programs such as Marriage Enrichment or Marriage Encounter are not designed to help marriages under stress (and should not be used as a referral in such circumstances), but are effective at enriching marriages that are already generally healthy. Conflict resolution workshops, particularly those based on the model of Bach and Wyden, may improve a couple's ability to disagree without harming each other through verbal or emotional violence. Certain marital partners would also benefit from an Assertiveness Training program.

Conclusion

Marriage—even a Christian one—can be a source of destruction, tedium, or delight. Ministers and pastoral counselors may find themselves overwhelmed by the complexity of the marital dynamic. When marriage is reinterpreted as a fluid process with specific tasks to be accomplished and identifiable characteristics of health, new possibilities for effective pastoral assistance emerge. Marriage counseling is a crucial training area for pastors, and the qualities of a good Christian marriage should form the content of regular sermons and adult education programs in local parishes.

BIBLIOGRAPHY

Anderson, Herbert, and Robert Cotton Fite. *Becoming Married*. Louisville: Westminster/John Knox, 1993.

Bascue, Loy O., and Roy Lewis. "Marital and Family Therapy Skills for Pastoral Therapists." In *Clinical Handbook of Pastoral Counseling,* vol. 1, expanded ed. Robert Wicks, Richard Parsons, and Donald Capps, eds. 267–78. New York: Paulist, 1993.

Booth, Wayne. *The Company We Keep: An Ethics of Fiction*. Berkeley: University of California Press, 1990.

Friedman, Edwin. *Generation to Generation: Family Process in Church and Synagogue*. New York: Guilford, 1985.

Hunter, David G. *Marriage in the Early Church*. Minneapolis: Fortress, 1992.

Jung, Carl. "Marriage as a Psychological Relationship." In *Collected Works*, vol. 17, *The Development of Personality*. R. F. C Hull, trans. 189–201. London: Routledge and Kegan Paul, 1954.

Karpel, Mark. "Individuation: From Fusion to Dialogue." *Family Process* 15 (1976): 65–82.

Krantzler, Mel. *Creative Marriage*. New York: McGraw-Hill, 1981.

Lederer, William, and Don Jackson. *The Mirages of Marriage*. New York: W. W. Norton, 1968.

Martos, Joseph. *Doors to the Sacred*. Garden City, N.Y.: Doubleday, 1981.

McGoldrick, Monica. "Ethnicity and the Family Life Cycle." In *The Changing Family Life Cycle*. Betty Carter and Monica McGoldrick, eds. 69–90. Boston: Alyn and Bacon, 1989.

Nadelson, Carol, Derek Polonsky, and Mary Alice Mathews. "Marriage as a Developmental Process." In *Marriage and Divorce: A Contemporary Perspective*. Carol C. Nadelson and Derek C. Polonsky, eds. 127–41. New York: Guilford, 1984.

Nelson, James. "Varied Meanings of Marriage and Fidelity." *Journal of Current Social Issues* 15:1 (spring 1978): 14–22.

Nichols, Alan, Joan Clarke, and Trevor Hogan. *Transforming Families and Communities: Christian Hope in a World of Change*. London: Anglican Consultative Council, 1987.

Nicolson, Nigel. *The Letters of Virginia Woolf,* Vol. 2: 1912–22. New York: Harcourt Brace Jovanovich, 1976.

Rogers, Carl. *Becoming Partners: Marriage and Its Alternatives*. London: Constable, 1973.

Ruether, Rosemary Radford. "An Unrealized Revolution: Searching Scripture for a Model of the Family." *Christianity and Crisis* (October 31, 1983): 399–404.

Scarf, Maggie. *Intimate Partners: Patterns in Love and Marriage*. New York: Ballantine, 1987.

Schillebeeckx, Edward. *Marriage: Human Reality and Saving Mystery*. London: Sheed and Ward, 1965.

Scott, Kieran, and Michael Warren, eds. *Perspectives on Marriage: A Reader*. New York: Oxford University Press, 1993.

St. Gregory the Great: Pastoral Care. Henry Davis, trans. New York: Newman, 1950.

Trigg, Joseph. "What Do the Church Fathers Have to Tell Us about Sex?" *Anglican Theological Review* 74:1 (winter 1992): 18–24.

Wallerstein, Judith S., and Sandra Blakeslee. *The Good Marriage: How and Why Love Lasts.* Boston and New York: Houghton Mifflin, 1995.

Webber, Christopher. *Re-Inventing Marriage: A Re-View and Re-Vision.* Harrisburg: Morehouse, 1994.

6. Divorce Counseling

"Marriage is obviously more insane than taking flying lessons or collecting beer cans." (Carl Whitaker and David Keith, 29)

In addition to the issues of human sexuality and power abuse in ministry, among the most troubling issues for the contemporary church is the extraordinary rise in the divorce rate over the past two decades. Those who would define "family values" in its narrowest sense view divorce as a sinful occurrence and look for someone or something to blame. Those who understand increased divorce rates as reflecting the opening up of new opportunities for self-definition, and a restructuring of an institution often seen as impossibly patriarchal, are less quick to name divorce as a sin or to cast blame in any direction. Yet, both points of view hold correctly that divorce almost always brings a great deal of pain to all parties involved and quite often necessitates the intervention of counseling support and mediation in order to move all parties concerned toward greater emotional and spiritual health.

Whether the dissolution of the marriage is brought about because of abuse (physical or emotional), by the uneven growth of the partners, or by the decision of one partner, marriages do end. Unfortunately, many couples are left on their own to work through the painful process of separating, divorcing, and caring for children. At least, they often must undergo these transformations without the help of the community of faith, who have seen it as their obligation only to keep people together, and who are not available to help those for whom continuation in marriage is no longer possible (Anderson, Hogue, and McCarthy, 94).

Counselors who address issues of separation and divorce—whether with adults or children—need a sound knowledge of counseling psychology, conflict resolution, family law, gender constructions, and recent sociological research. Unfortunately, most of the available sociological research has been done on middle- to upper-middle-class white men and women. Statistics further blind us to cultural diversity. For example, the 48 percent overall national divorce rate in America masks the fact that 38 percent of white children, but 75 percent of African American children, will experience at least one parental divorce. When discussing divorce, therefore, it is important to look critically at gender assumptions and the tendency to universalize our own racial and socioeconomic experiences.

The Shock of Marriage

The initial promises in marriage are made without the partners' knowing fully what they will mean or what they will cost (Anderson, Hogue, and McCarthy, 80). We learn what our marriage promises mean as we live them out. For some the rewards of marriage outweigh the deficits, though these rewards are as often economic security and social respectability as they are emotional fulfillment. For others the reality of marriage falls far short of expectations. Anderson, Hogue, and McCarthy ask a simple but profound question: "To Whom Was This Promise Made?" (86)

• Some have made the promise to their first lover or a secretly beloved person other than their spouse.

- Some have promised to an ideal spouse—to someone they imagined their partner would become.
- Some make promises more to their parents or to the image of the person their parents expected them to marry.
- Others make career commitments that require them to marry certain kinds of spouses for the sake of their success.
- Still others "marry the owner's daughter" in order to assure themselves a steady job.

In any of these cases, the promise is not truly made to the partner, but to someone or something else.

Perhaps this is even more true for women than for men; the statistic that more women file for divorce than men would appear to suggest this. Betty Carter articulates the dream handed on to young girls as part of their gender construction:

> Women have always been taught that marriage is the solution to their problems of living, and were not taught to develop autonomy or to identify personal life goals other than marriage. Therefore, they have traditionally looked forward to marriage tremendously, only to become disillusioned and depressed when they discover that often they are not taken care of in marriage and family life, but rather are expected to take care of everyone else. (254)

But men, too, bring unrealistic expectations to marriage, perhaps the most common being that marriage will cure their loneliness or will provide them with a wife who will care for them in much the same way as did their mother.

As remarked in the previous chapter, marriage is a process, not a state of being. The romantic notions about marriage that are so much a part of both male and female gender construction focus on that "false" state of being and rarely address the complicated and often painful process of learning to share our life fully with another person. Theologian Karl Barth observed: "Two people may be formally married and fail to live a life which can seriously be regarded as married life. And it may happen that two people are not married and yet in their precarious way live under the law of marriage. A wedding is only the regulative confirmation and legitimation of a marriage before and by society. It does not constitute marriage" (Borrowdale, 69). Only when both partners participate actively and intentionally in building a relationship will a wedding become a marriage. As with all processes, things go wrong along the way.

The Reasons for Divorce

In predominantly white Western societies, two-thirds of divorces take place between the fifth and fifteenth year of marriage. People opt for divorce for complex motives, some of which have little relation to marital incompatibility. Customarily, one partner wants to get out of the marriage with a great deal more urgency than the other. For instance, in Wallerstein and Kelly's study, women took the final step to terminate the marriage in three-fourths of the cases, while nearly half the husbands strongly opposed their decision (the statistics for the United States, England, and Europe are almost identical in this case) (16–17). The same study revealed that divorcing families included not only those suffering from loneliness and isolation, with each family member going his or her own way, hardly communicating and rarely touching, but also families whose members shared a rich history, common recreational interests, and religious beliefs (13). We might then claim that it is nearly impossible to predict which marriages will last and which will end in divorce. The reasons given for divorce, however, generally fall into fourteen categories. The first four are those most commonly cited in the counseling literature.

1. *Miscommunication.* This may take many forms, possibly the most common being simply failing to make sufficient time to communicate clearly. Gender assumptions and gendered styles of communication may also play a part: he shows his feelings with actions, she speaks her emotions; he says things once, she repeats things for emphasis. Too often we assume that our partner should understand us just because he or she loves us.

2. *The inability to manage conflict.* Arlene Brewster cites the research of Howard Markman to claim that certain behavior patterns result in the impending collapse of the marriage: when one spouse withdraws from conflict, the continuous escalation of conflict, the inability to stop fights before they get ugly, and the tendency to invalidate the relationship by hurling insults at each other. Giblin comments that conflict styles are often instinctually destructive rather than constructive (318). A partner may choose fighting, flight, submission, or freezing, rather than face-to-face, collaborative problem solving. Conflict is viewed as win-lose, interests appear to be mutually exclusive, and the need is to change the other. Problems are often unclearly defined. Person and problem become indistinguishable. Couples attack each other rather than the issue at hand.

John Gottman identifies what he calls the Four Horsemen of the Apocalypse—criticism, contempt, defensiveness, and with-drawal—as the most corrosive factors in marriage over time (Hetherington and Stanley-Hagan, 199). Relatedly, a pursuer-distancer pattern where one spouse wants to confront and talk about problems and the other to avoid such discussions and conflict is a common precursor of divorce. He notes that a distressed spouse who feels emotionally flooded by the unexpected and unprovoked negative emotions expressed by the other spouse may experience an overwhelming need to escape or avoid flooding. This flooding can cause the person to become hypervigilant for potential negative cues in the partner's behavior, and leads to the interpretation of even ambiguous or neutral cues as negative. Over time, the ongoing strain leads to emotional disengagement from the spouse and from the marriage itself.

To complicate matters further, men and women have often been socialized to deal with conflict in different ways (Smith, Goslen, Byrd, and Reece, 27–29). Of the two moral perspectives identified by Carol Gilligan, males are more often socialized to emphasize an individual rights perspective and to de-emphasize the care perspective. In so doing, men lean so much toward individual rights that the care perspective is not developed beyond the level of exclusion of others (care for self first). Women, on the other hand, are socialized to emphasize the care perspective and are reinforced to reach the level of inclusion of others to the exclusion of self (care for others first). In so doing, women de-emphasize the perspective in which individual rights are emphasized. Yet both men and women have been socialized to think they are doing what is morally right. This will guarantee unsatisfactory relationships and make negotiation even more elusive.

Giblin emphasizes the power of projective identification in marital conflict (316). Feelings of anger, shame, guilt, and sadness are experienced as "the enemy" and are defended against, often by splitting them off from the self and projecting them onto one's partner: "He is the bad one"; "She is the angry one." The partners may feel defensive, protective, out of awareness, reactive, or drained of energy. Quarreling partners often need rescuing from both themselves and each other, and pastors would do well to gain training in conflict management. The choice of the term *conflict management* over *conflict resolution* is intentional, since within marriage, many conflicts are not resolvable but can be managed.

3. *The inability to tolerate difference.* Difference in choices over how to parent, fealty to birth parents, work schedules, levels of independence and dependence, sleeping patterns, use of financial resources, whose career takes precedence, and other such potential differences are the day-to-day material of married life. Marriage means constant negotiation and compromise, but the family-of-origin "dowry" may mean that these differences result in nonnegotiable polarization and ultimately divorce.

4. *Unresolved past issues.* In his best-selling book *Getting the Love You Want*, Harville Hendrix argues that *all* people who marry are unconsciously seeking to establish a relationship in which they can work through issues they were never able to complete with their own parents. Hence Giblin and many others can claim that chronic marital conflict generally stems from unresolved family-of-origin issues, that is, "debits," "undifferentiation," "childhood wounds/imago transference" (317). Essential psychological tasks of childhood

necessary for healthy adult functioning and especially the capacity for intimacy sometimes fail to be completed within the family of origin. One's choice of a marital partner is powerfully and unconsciously influenced by efforts to rework those unresolved issues; we tend to be attracted to and marry partners that replicate the positive and, in particular, the negative traits of our primary caretakers. In cases of chronic marital conflict partners remain excessively dependent upon and need to control the other in order to maintain a wounded and fragile sense of self.

5. *The stifling of self-expression.* Erik Erikson has observed that human beings learn fidelity—the ability to remain faithful to promises they make—during adolescence. Some marital partners, particularly women, discover somewhere in the marriage that they have been faithful to everyone but themselves. Instead of locating their hopes and dreams in marriage and spouse, they begin to relocate within themselves a drive for self-development and self-expression that stands in contradiction to the compromises and demands of marriage (Carter, 258). Pastoral responsibility demands that people who remain in marriages out of requirement, rather than choice, be supported in taking charge of their own lives, even if in some cases this means divorce.

Anderson and Stewart's study discovered that some women chose to leave their traditional roles because the roles never really fit them (115–16). In doing so, they were leaving more than their marriages: they were choosing to leave the safety of well-established lives to try their "wings" in unfamiliar skies. These women may have experienced early doubts or had always had alternative dreams of their own competing for their attention. Their decisions to marry represented detours from these early dreams; getting divorced—while painful—often simultaneously felt like getting "back on track."

6. *Death of the commitment.* Robert Gordis describes a loveless marriage as one in which God is no longer present:

> Once it becomes clear that the marriage is beyond remedy, Judaism recognizes that the union has lost its sanction and its sanctity, for love and mutual respect are the only marks of God's presence in a home. When these conditions do not obtain, the husband and wife are no longer joined together by God in any meaningful sense, and society stultifies itself by trying to ignore the truth. (120)

Many understand the vow "till death do us part" to allow for separation when love has died between two people, beyond hope for repair.

7. *Power struggles, including physical and emotional abuse.* Adolescent fights with parents for independence and control are often repeated in marriage. As well, people who have been emotionally, physically, or sexually abused in their past and have not yet undergone some sort of therapeutic healing may bring their former abuser into the marriage with them, so that there are always three persons present rather than just two. A power struggle may also go on between a flesh-and-blood person and an invisible, but still very present, former spouse.

8. *Unrealistic expectations.* Expecting a spouse to supply the kind of unconditional love and support one wanted from parents is unrealistic and leads to disappointment. Lack of shared interests is often a danger signal in marriage, and yet neither partner should expect the other to share all of his or her interests.

9. *Romantic illusions.* Ignoring the faults of a potential mate leads us to marry our own romantic creation rather than a real person. Object Relations Theory provides an excellent way to understand why some people marry partners who seem so inappropriate.

10. *Sexual incompatibility.* According to Hetherington and Stanley-Hagan, about one-third of men and women who later divorce complain about their sexual relationship, but men complain about quantity and women about quality (200). This pattern may be changing, however. Some of the recent counseling literature shows that as women become more self-assured, they are also complaining more frequently that their sexual drive exceeds their husbands' capacity to satisfy them.

11. *Parental marriage patterns.* Although we may *want* a very different marriage than our parents had, we often unconsciously follow their example and choose a mate with whom we can duplicate their relationship.

12. *External influences.* Some decisions to divorce are made under the influence of a therapist, physician, women's or men's group, or minister. Factors external to a relationship may also provide so much stress that the marriage crumbles. Such experiences might include the unexpected death of a parent or grandparent, the diagnosis of a mortal illness, the death of or serious injury to a child, or even a job loss. The decision to divorce in such instances is often the result of what Murray Bowen called "the emotional shock wave," as will be explained in chapter 8.

13. *Extramarital affairs.* Studies show that extramarital affairs are quite far down on the list of reasons that people divorce, for many marriages survive such a breach of trust. Affairs must not be defined only sexually, for any secret, deeply affectional relationship

with someone outside the marriage can threaten destruction. Infidelity is most often a consequence, not the primary cause, of persons going outside the marital bond to seek fulfillment, appreciation, and pleasure. For couples to get past hurt and blame, two things are required simultaneously: a confession and admission of betrayal and an exploration of circumstances that contributed to either brokenness in the relationship or a lingering dissatisfaction in the marriage. (Anderson, Hogue, and McCarthy, 91)

14. *Lack of other options.* For some, having tried all other options, the only rational choice left is to walk away from the marriage.

Understanding the interpersonal dynamics of a divorce may be as complicated as understanding the interpersonal dynamics of a marriage. Furthermore, the two separating partners may understand the reasons for their divorce very differently. The astute pastor may discover more about what went wrong in a marriage by comparing the narratives of its decline: his, hers, and theirs.

Divorce Narratives

Just as an object is the product of some sort of relationship, thus being created through an event or interaction, and is invested with a particular emotional energy such as love, hate, or fear, so narratives usually have some sort of affective core. Divorce narratives are structured around a person-specific set of emotions and peopled with projected objects. Hence each divorce narrative will differ markedly from the next, and it is extremely rare that a separated couple can agree on the narrative that describes the extended process leading up to their divorce. The experiences of husbands and wives in marriage and their perceptions of their relationship are so divergent that we

should talk of "his and hers" marriages. Research findings suggest that just as there are his and her marriages, there are his and her divorces (Hetherington and Stanley-Hagan, 199).

Divorce narratives are heavily influenced by gender construction. Although men and women often voice similar complaints about their marriage, the salience of these complaints differs. Lack of communication, affection, and shared interests are the most common complaints of women, whereas for men their wives' nagging, whining, and fault finding, followed closely by their immaturity and irresponsibility, are prime grievances. Less important contributors to the decision to divorce for both men and women are economic factors, infidelity, alcoholism, and abuse (Hetherington and Stanley-Hagan, 200). Furthermore, it has been found that many men are unaware of even the possibility of divorce prior to the decision to divorce and that the decision is more commonly made by women. In giving reasons for the divorce, women are more likely to list specific problems, but men are more likely to report lack of knowledge concerning reasons for the divorce, or to report that their wives left simply to gain freedom (Diedrick, 37).

Themes of agency and victimization in divorce narratives often reveal the narrator's level of self-esteem. Patricia Diedrick's research indicates that women fare better after divorce emotionally—though not always economically—when they are the initiators of the divorce, thereby claiming their own power and agency (39–40). After separation and divorce, men report more suicidal thoughts than do women. Anxiety and thoughts of suicide are further correlates of low self-esteem. Healing for both men and women may mean finding the sense of agency within their particular divorce narrative and letting go of a "victim" script or a culturally or religiously determined sense of obligation.

In addition to the "his and hers" narratives, there will be a third set in any marriage: "their" narrative, whether this refers to a parent of either the husband or the wife, a child of either, or close friends. Susan Engel has written particularly effectively about the way in which young children shape narratives to reflect their personal concerns for survival. When someone in a congregation divorces, including the chief pastor, a variety of contradictory narratives will spring up to explain what happened. Some narratives need to be taken more seriously than others—for example, the "his," "hers," and "theirs" narratives of any nuclear family that is dissolving—but the pastor must remember that any narrative tells us more about the narrator than it does about the "facts." "Theirs" may match neither "his" nor "hers"; a narrative describes a *constructed* reality only. The narrative, however, *is* reality for the narrator. The pastor should listen to each narrative, but ask, "What does this tell me about the narrator?" rather than "What does this tell me about the other characters in the story?"

Divorce within Family Systems

Marriages that have the most potential for growth occur between partners who have made it out of their families of origin, achieved individual adequacy, and lived on their own. Family Systems Theory provides several other useful insights into whether people have really "left home" before marrying, why and how they divorce, and how successfully they adjust afterwards. Even

when there are no children from the marriage, divorce is felt throughout a multigenerational system. Whitaker and Keith describe the systemic dynamics involved in marriage that in turn can lead to divorce:

> A form of delusional thinking which is seen in family or marital therapy is the statement, "I did not marry your family." Marriage is the union of two families and the two families help to make it work or help to facilitate the divorce. Divorce is a 3-generational problem until proven otherwise. . . . Usually the marital dyad is in the foreground but they are in fact embedded in a complex mix of intergenerational battles, traditional family-governed sex roles, and childrearing practices. (70–71)

Whitaker and Keith thereby emphasize the symbiotic character of many marriages, understanding divorce as a backlash against such symbiosis, or "bilateral, nonautonomous, system-controlled living."

Systems theory also cautions us to watch for ways in which a post-divorce family reconfiguration recapitulates the pathology of a pre-divorce family. This seems particularly to hold true for those coming out of abusive relationships. Chances of a woman entering a second abusive relationship very similar to the first one are quite high unless she has undergone some sort of therapeutic intervention, such as counseling treatment in a women's shelter. Even worse, the post-divorce parent may structure the new family reconfiguration in a way that perpetuates the abuse. Wallerstein and Kelly offer the following illustration:

> One eleven-year-old girl told us that when she misbehaved her mother instructed her eighteen-year-old brother to spank her. This solution was startling,

because central to the mother's complaint against the father was his physical abuse of her and the children. Yet she had arranged for the spankings to continue via her delegation of authority to the oldest boy. (113)

Use of a genogram in pre- or post-divorce counseling may reveal that divorce is a systemic "acceptable solution," a way of coping that a system has learned to absorb without upsetting its homeostasis too badly. It may uncover some trauma in the recent past, such as the death of an authority figure in the extended system, again underlining the importance of Murray Bowen's "emotional shock waves." Or a genogram may reveal the undue impact of particular in-laws on the marriage, senses of entitlement that contribute to marital tension, or divorce as a "copycat" solution. Use of a genogram may lead each partner to understand present affect in relation to the past and the family of origin. When the mystery of a couple's woundedness can be uncovered, they are enabled to acknowledge and understand the frustrated longings each partner brought into the marriage (Giblin, 319).

Whitaker and Keith suggest that pre- or post-divorce counseling should begin with the counselor's taking a history of the marriage (74–75). Why is the couple choosing to divorce now? Why not six months ago? Why not wait six more months? They also suggest exploring how in-laws felt about the marriage and how much they have interfered with the relationship. Because parents are often quite involved in what Whitaker and Keith call "de-courting," they suggest bringing in-laws into the counseling room. "It is uncanny how much the husband's mother resembles his wife in her manner of speaking, how often the

marital fight is a transplantation of an undone parent-child fight as demonstrated earlier" (77). Another example of the system-controlled marriage is the forbidden marriage that becomes committed to rigid pseudomutuality as a way to avoid the "I told you so" confrontation with the parents. The two authors also suggest the judicious use of paradoxical but deliberately confrontational statements, such as : "How long do you think it will be before she remarries?" "Will you try to find someone with more money?" "Do you think your parents will let you come back and live with them? Will you get your old room back?"

Research by Susan Holloway and Sandra Machida suggests that overinterference by the intergenerational family members may delay the healing processes necessary in a post-divorce reconfigured family.

> It appears that women who relied on their own family for assistance or companionship were less able to maintain authoritative relations with their children than were women who relied on friends. Social support by relatives was also associated with less use of coping strategies and particularly with less use of problem solving. These findings are supported by other studies finding that the assistance or companionship of relatives may not always have a positive impact. (196)

Pastoral support should be shaped by the goal of encouraging divorced women and men to reestablish their sense of healthy singleness and autonomy again, as quickly as is emotionally appropriate. Divorced women and men should generally be discouraged from either rushing back home or rushing into the arms of someone else. The insistence upon doing either may well reveal the systemic pathology that brought about the divorce in the first place. Instead, they should be encouraged to invest themselves in improving relationships with their children, parents, and other family members, and in expanding their social network and its level of intimacy and support.

Cultural Factors in Divorce

Pastoral ministry with divorcing or divorced families should always be tempered by a sensitivity to the cultural expectations placed upon single-again men and women, particularly if they have children. In many cultures, including the Samoan, parents who are not pleased with a son-in-law or daughter-in-law can force the couple to divorce, even against their own wishes (Afoa, 194). In Asian cultures, a woman can be divorced, either by her husband or by her in-laws, (a) if she does not serve her parents-in-law well; (2) if she cannot produce children, particularly male; (3) if she is lecherous; (4) if she is too jealous; (5) if she has an incurable disease; (6) if she talks too much; or (7) if she steals (Song, 221–22). The daughter is usually expected to return home to live with her parents in such instances, though sons are usually given greater freedom of choice. In these cases, in spite of the differing fate of daughters and sons, both divorced partners may be emotionally devastated by experiencing a divorce that neither of them chose. Some cultures exert quite overt social pressure on divorced people to marry immediately by classifying the divorced, especially women, as social nonpersons; other cultures do not even have vocabulary words to express the status of "single adult."

Many cultures dictate the fate of children of divorce, presuming that cultural norms are necessarily the best criteria for ensuring the children's happiness. In some cultures, children of divorce are automatically sent to live with grandparents rather than with a single parent: in matrilineal cultures this would be the maternal grandparents, in patrilineal cultures the paternal grandparents. In other cultures, such as Orthodox Judaism, all children under the age of five live with their mothers; after five, girls live with their mothers and boys with their fathers. White Western cultures generally presume that the legal system responsibly determines "the best interest of the children," although, as will be discussed, most current literature shows that in fact the legal system is at least as destructive of children's good as is the disintegrating family itself. The pastor, *after* having become fully attuned to cultural norms, may feel compelled to question whether those norms are always necessarily the best choice for the future happiness and security of all adults and children involved. In every culture it is reasonable to suppose that God can work in a marriage or a divorce in different ways that are contextually appropriate. We should not assume that there is one universal style of "Christian marriage" or "just divorce" (Borrowdale, 74–75).

The Stages of Divorce

For both adults and children, divorce is not a single event. It is a chain of events—a series of legal, social, psychological, economic, and sexual changes, strung complexly together and extending over time. Divorce is a process that begins with the escalating distress of the marriage, often peaks at the separation and legal filing, and then ushers in several years of transition and disequilibrium before the adults are able to gain, or to regain, a sense of continuity and confidence in their new roles and relationships (Wallerstein and Kelly, 4). As with all psychological developmental processes, a person can get stuck at some stage, or can leave the tasks of a given stage so unfinished that it must be returned to again and again before the person can move on to new health. This "unfinished business" of divorce will be discussed later in the chapter.

The chain of events begins long before either marital partner has decided to separate or divorce, and usually extends for several years after the legal decree of marriage dissolution. Various writers schematize the pre- and post-divorce process, with few agreeing on specific identifiable stages. The stages described here are based on the work of Judith Wallerstein and Sandra Blakeslee, whose ongoing work with the California Children of Divorce Project constitutes the oldest and largest longitudinal study of the effect of divorce on middle-class American families (278–81).

Ending the Marriage. As has already been stated, a divorce actually begins long before the legal separation and divorce decree. So, however, does the anticipatory adjustment to being single again or at least free from the stress of a relationship that feels personally destructive. Long before this, the couple may have stopped having sexual relations, stopped sleeping in the same bed, perhaps ceased eating together, and have begun to develop new friendships and postponed interests outside the relationship. Emotional divorce begins long before the legal event occurs.

Many marriages teeter on the brink of divorce year after year, held together only by the stalemated mutual accusations of what Bach and Wyden call "exit fight rituals" (321). Such fights are the ultimate in round-robin battles. Among the reasons why they drone on and on and why these sterile partnerships don't break up faster are (a) each partner may want the other to assume the responsibility and guilt for the actual breakup and final rejection of the other; (b) one or both may be excessively afraid of loneliness; (c) their separation anxiety may be pathologically extreme because of deep-rooted fears of being abandoned like orphans.

Most couples wait too long to seek help with their marital problems. Unfortunately, they think of therapy or pastoral counseling as a last-ditch effort to save their marriage rather than as the first line of defense. Once they arrive at the stage of legal divorce, things are so bad between them that a "friendly" divorce is impossible. Legal mediation may be necessary to end a protracted and adversarial relationship. Property settlement, custody of children, and other important matters are all decided far too quickly, with everyone living for years with the consequences of decisions made in the heat of the moment. But divorce seems better than remaining together while destroying each other.

Mourning the Loss. The initial stage immediately post-separation is euphoric for many people. Free from bickering and stress for perhaps the first time in years, they may enter what Stephen Johnson and others call "crazy time." The person may experience a kind of roller-coaster emotional life—feeling free and on top of the world at one moment, down and in despair at the next.

Divorcing adults often exhibit anger, anxiety and depression, and antisocial and impulsive behavior, and are overrepresented among suicides and homicides. Furthermore, even controlling for factors such as initial health and health habits, divorcing men and women appear to experience disruptions in immune system functioning and a corresponding increased risk of recurring and severe physical disorders (Hetherington and Stanley-Hagan, 197). Others experience regrets off and on during the first year of separation, wishing they had worked harder on the problems in the marriage. As Whitaker and Keith observe in a pointed metaphor, "Divorce is leaving part of the self behind, like the rabbit who escapes the trap by gnawing one leg off" (71).

Others experience profound loneliness in this initial post-divorce stage. The larger social structure of their life, which normally accompanies marriage, seems to have vanished. Friends are conflicted about which spouse to phone, and according to Wallerstein and Kelly, women have a particular tendency to allow this to occur (33). It is true that people abandon the divorcing, in part out of anxiety for their own marriages, and in part because they are unsure how to express the needed solace. Ironically, this is a time for divorcing persons when friends are particularly important for support as they work through what went wrong.

Reclaiming Oneself. Eventually, having talked through the crisis again and again, the marital partners need to accept their own part in the breakup and work toward a more amicable agreement on custody, visitation, and financial arrangements that will benefit all family members as much as possible. Without adequately working through these issues, restabilization cannot occur.

One part of this stage in which a counselor can be helpful is in rehearsing with a divorcing spouse how to inform friends. This can be done actively, or the person can wait passively for the news to spread, though the first choice is healthier. As well, new friends must be formed, new daily routines structured, and personal and financial security must be begun anew. While women statistically survive divorce in better emotional shape, they suffer a reduced standard of living much more often than men following divorce. Even if a woman is not poor, is well educated, and has a career, she may still tend to suffer the emotional distress of feeling unprepared to go on alone because of the pervasive influence of the female socialization process that trains her for dependency. Reclaiming oneself means finding a way to secure the future both financially and emotionally.

The heart of the emotional process of divorce is to retrieve one's self from the marriage, that is, to give up as finished the hopes, dreams, and expectations that one had invested in the spouse and the marriage, and to reinvest these hopes and expectations in one's own self (Carter, 256–57). For women in particular, this degree of self-direction goes against the grain of most of what they have been taught to believe about themselves.

Resolving or Containing Passions. Many people are emotionally numb after divorce, and as well, Miller and Jackson describe them as "intimacy numb" (364).

Intimacy is by its nature an intensely private and discreet human activity. Intimacy may entail sexual activity, but needs not to be defined that way solely. Emotional intimacy is perhaps an even more basic need than sexual intimacy. Adult sexual needs must be tended to, however, and to this end Karen LeBacqz has proposed a sexual ethic for singles that she calls "appropriate vulnerability." In developing her argument, she leans heavily on the insight captured in the biblical account of creation in Genesis 2:25: "The man and his wife were both naked, and were not ashamed." To be "naked," she argues, is a metaphor for being vulnerable, and to "not be ashamed" is a metaphor for appropriateness. Moral and ethical choices in this area of recovery would be appropriate topics for pastoral conversation.

Wallerstein and Kelly point out that many adults have had few emotionally significant relationships with other adults during the marriage (105). Therefore, at the collapse of the marriage, they may turn to their children, who become new sources of support and love. Both younger and older children may be pressed into being advisers, practical helpers, buffers against loneliness and despair, replacements for other adults—in other words, parents for their own parents. The technical name for this process, which can also happen within a marriage, is "parentification," and it robs children of whatever age of essential parts of the natural childhood development.

A preoccupation with sex on the part of the adults can spill into the parent-child relationship. The phenomenon of fluid boundaries between the psychological repercussions within the parent and the inappropriate involvement of the children occurs frequently at the time of divorce. Some parents have sexual fantasies about their children's relationship with the opposite partner. In Wallerstein and Kelly's study, mothers in particular became concerned with the child's continued contact with the father, which the mother suddenly perceived (without visible or new evidence of any kind) as dangerously seductive. If a pastor becomes concerned about inappropriate sexual contact between a child and either parent, assistance should be sought to have the child examined medically and psychologically.

Venturing Forth Again. Miller and Jackson describe this phase as the expression of "autonomous adulthood" (363). Having redefined oneself as a single, individual, worthwhile person, one is ready to advance again on life. Reaching this phase may take much longer than anticipated. Song cites various studies that estimate that two to five years will elapse after separation before the individuals are "fully themselves again," with the average recovery time closer to the four-year mark (224). Carol Tavris, however, cites other studies that show that even after ten years, half of divorced women and one-third of divorced men are still intensely angry at their former spouses (300). Children watched their already divorced parents continue to hit, scream at, and abuse one another.

Rebuilding. Sixty-five percent of American women and 70 percent of American men remarry (Carter, 256). Unfortunately, the divorce rate for second marriages is almost twice as high as for first marriages. For this and other reasons, one-third of all divorced adults choose not to remarry, and many of these continue to raise families alone. These families go through one additional phase of the family life cycle and may restabilize permanently in intentionally configured single-parent families. All the members of a post-divorce family must do the emotional work of mourning the loss of the intact family and giving up fantasies of reunion. Men and women who choose to remarry require the negotiation of a second additional phase of the family life cycle, in which they adequately work through new and complicated emotional processes. In this additional phase, the family emotional process consists of struggling with everyone's fears regarding a new family, dealing with hostile and upset reactions to the new marriage, and trying to discover or invent a new paradigm of family that will allow for the complex new roles and relationships.

Divorce Counseling and Divorce Mediation

While divorce counseling has often been ignored within the field of pastoral training, it is potentially one of the church's most important healing ministries. In divorce counseling, divorcing parties meet with an impartial third party to identify, discuss, and hopefully settle the disputes that result from marital dissolution. Whitaker and Keith define the reasons for pastoral intervention with dissolving marriages as (1) to help the partners get back as much of their original investment as possible by helping them to "de-court" and (2) to straighten out the issues of parenting when there are children involved (71). But counseling divorce situations can be tricky, so the pastor needs to be alerted to a number of potential pitfalls. In general, relationship counseling raises special issues and difficulties beyond those encountered in individual counseling. These include privacy of information between partners, the counselor's transition from individual to joint counseling, maintaining balanced attention to both partners and a sense of equity, and dealing with an uncooperative partner.

The pastor who is approached to do divorce counseling must first ascertain whether both partners see divorce as the only solution left open to them. In some instances, one of the spouses comes to

divorce counseling professing to want to do the "decent thing," even though he has already made up his mind about the outcome he wants. Another objective on the secret agenda may be to deposit the rejected spouse with a counselor to help cushion the blow of the other partner's unilateral decision to leave. Some people may not actually want the divorce but may be using a divorce threat—rather like a suicide gesture—as a way of getting their spouse to recognize the seriousness of their discontent. Pleading, defending, criticizing, placating, demanding, crying, hinting, or complaining is not the same as stating, from a position of entitlement, what one wants. It is important that the pastor explore carefully whether a man or woman wants to leave the marriage or wants help in learning to confront the partner and to negotiate a different way of being together.

If divorce seems inevitable, in order to keep matters as amicable as possible from the beginning some pastors would be tempted to urge a "no-fault" divorce on the couple. Betty Carter points out the fatal flaw in such advice:

> The no-fault divorce laws are an excellent example of a well-intentioned attempt to be fair, based on a false assumption. If a wife has no income, no skills to earn sufficient income, and bears all or most of the responsibility to raise the children as well, then any arrangement that does not take these facts into account can never be remotely fair or equitable, much less equal. (255)

When property settlement, custody of children, and other important matters are all decided far too quickly, everyone lives for years with the consequences of decisions made in the heat of the moment. Rather than rushing to judgment or attempting to resolve quickly any ambivalence, it is better for the pastor to suggest that the couple enter into joint mediation with a professionally trained mediator.

Mediation generally refers to the process whereby a third party helps the two spouses to separate as amicably as possible, including the negotiation of post-divorce parenting and the division of jointly held property. Divorce mediation should reduce the adversarial nature of the divorce process, encourage cooperation, and promote the subsequent exploration of options other than traditional custody and visitation arrangements. Research shows that the use of divorce mediation as opposed to litigation leads to more satisfaction with respect to custody arrangements, financial settlement, and the decision to divorce in general. Divorce mediation could be central to a package of policies aimed at promoting post-divorce paternal involvement and financial responsibility (Arditti, 115–16). In the United States, a few states require divorce mediation, and many others make it available.

A pastor may discover that the division of property in divorce mediation perks along quite nicely and then suddenly gets stuck on some particular possession that both spouses claim and neither will agree to negotiate. The pastor will then understand that the possession fought over is in fact a "transitional object," in object relations vocabulary: an item that has become symbolic of the relationship, the loss of which both partners understand, individually and subconsciously, as the final sign that the relationship is over. Even couples quarreling bitterly, and apparently seeking to damage each other as much as possible, can get stuck

on a symbolic possession in which undue emotion is invested, such as a family pet, the sterling silver, or an oil painting.

If the pastor is involved in divorce mediation with a couple, everything may be negotiated but nothing should be finalized without legal consultation.

In the course of assisting a couple toward a smoother separation, the pastor should not lose sight of the many other people affected by the particular divorce. Pastoral care should also be directed toward any children involved and, where appropriate, toward parents and other relatives, and perhaps even close friends. As Giblin points out, "The pastor should no more hesitate to speak directly with a child than with an adult member of the church who is in personal crisis" (79).

Telling the Kids

One aspect of divorce that can be effectively rehearsed or "coached" within the pastoral relationship is how parents will inform their children of the impending divorce. Among the issues through which parents should be coached are when and how to tell the children, what should be included in the telling, post-divorce parental relationships with each other and the children, and custody and visitation arrangements. Parents need help in understanding that telling the children about the divorce provides a signal opportunity to help the child cope with the crisis, and that the telling is not an act apart but a central component in the supportive role of the parent.

Children's fundamental response to parental divorce is separation anxiety. Separation anxiety is defined as "a threat to instinctual need which is symbolically linked to earlier threats that resulted in vulnerability and conflict" (Giblin, 72). The temporary or permanent loss of a parent causes the child's basic sense of trust, security, and self-identity to be seriously threatened. How this anxiety manifests itself will depend upon the child's developmental level and social environment and the actions of significant persons, including the parents themselves. How a child will react also depends upon age, custody arrangements, coping mechanisms, and the relationship between father and mother.

Wallerstein and Blakeslee have summarized the process of informing children about an impending divorce:

> Parents should take very seriously what they say to their children and how they say it, for what they say or fail to say will long be remembered. . . . If possible, both parents should tell the children together. By representing unity, they convey the sense that a rational, mature decision has been made. . . . It is better to tell all the children at once than each separately. . . . Children in divorced families can genuinely help one another. . . . Children should be told about the divorce when it has become a firm decision. They should know within a few days or a week or two beforehand of one parent's intention to leave the home. . . . When it is time to discuss the decision, parents should offer a clear explanation of what is going on in the family. . . . Children have the right to understand why the divorce is happening. . . . In essence, the divorce is presented as a solution that the parents have come to reluctantly, only after exploring a range of other options. . . . In this way, in this best of all possible worlds, the goal is to present the child with models of parents who admit they made a serious mistake, tried to rectify the mistake, and are now embarking on a moral, socially acceptable

remedy. The parents are responsible people who remain committed to the family and to the children even though they have decided to go their separate ways. . . . If true, parents can say that the children have been one of the greatest pleasures of the marriage. . . . Courage is a good word to use. . . . Children feel powerless at divorce and should be invited to make suggestions that the adults will consider seriously. . . . Finally, parents need to give the children permission to love both parents. (285–88)

Even after taking pains to follow the best parental practice as described, however, parents should not be too bewildered if a child responds, "OK. Can I go outside and play now?" Like adults, children need the luxury of entering into denial for a temporary period, in order better to control the impact of unwanted information. This does not mean that the child is indifferent, but that the thought of a major family disruption is too overwhelming for the child to accept (Giblin, 73).

Divorce and Object Relations Theory

Divorced partners selectively perceive the negative in the other and the good in the self, highlighting differences between self and other, attributing blame and ill motivation to the other. Partners' "automatic thoughts" or "internal communications" are typically characterized by cognitive distortions such as tunnel vision, selective perception, overgeneralization, polarized thinking magnification, mind reading, and a tyranny of "shoulds." Such distortions usually result in all-encompassing negative expectations and beliefs about self, other, and both marriage and divorce (Giblin, 317). To comprehend the importance of Object Relations Theory in explaining post-divorce relations between ex-spouses, we must bear in mind the defensive function of various object relations mechanisms, for the splitting, idealization, projective identification, and objectification that characterize many "bitter" divorces are ultimately defensive in nature.

The longitudinal study reported by Wallerstein and Kelly revealed that four-fifths of divorced men and an even higher proportion of women expressed anger and bitterness toward their ex-spouses (26). The most common form of this post-divorce hostility was the denigration of the other spouse. One of the central complaints of the youngsters in the study was the "bad-mouthing" and "backbiting" by their parents of each other. They had good reason to complain. More than half of the mothers and almost as many fathers were extremely critical and abusive in all their comments about the other parent. According to their analysis of their own study, the defensive function of this anger was to ward off a potentially even more devastating depression. The raging tirades and complex angry behavior had an organizing influence on these shattered adults. For the same reason, each parent was tempted to hold tightly to the children in an effort to maintain self-esteem and to ward off self-criticism. As the investigators observe, "litigation over custody thus may reflect the dependence of the adult on the child, and the adult's need to hold on to the child to maintain his or her psychic balance" (103).

David Schuldberg and Shan Guisinger discovered that no recent study has examined the perceptions of the formerly married of each other. The vast majority of the men they interviewed significantly devalued their ex-wives, in some cases many years after the divorce. Schuldberg and Guisinger attribute this phenomenon to splitting. First, the husband might contrast himself and his former wife, with the former wife being seen as all bad: "I really tried to make the marriage work; she was just too self-centered for the give-and-take of marriage." A contrast between two others occurs when the former wife is perceived as very difficult from the present wife: "They are as unlike as night and day; my first wife was a real witch; my second wife is an angel." In either instance, one party has been devalued and the other party idealized. But their study also revealed that the devaluation of an ex-wife occurs relatively often even when the husband does not seem to be idealizing himself or his second wife. The authors attributed this phenomenon to selective memory:

> It is highly likely that the former wives sometimes *were* "emotional," "defensive," and "demanding" in *situations* where they dealt with the former husband and his new partner. The stress of marital separation and divorce often elicits atypical behavior, and divorce researchers have well chronicled the uncharacteristic behavior, sexual activity, child neglect, drug and alcohol abuse, and even violence of separating marital partners.... The husbands may also have now forgotten their own post-divorce behavior while still vividly remembering the spouse's. It is also possible that the devaluation of the former wife serves a defensive function and helps to protect the integrity of the remarried family. (71)

The distinction must then be made between normal splitting (selective memory, protection of the reconfigured family) and pathological splitting (devaluation and idealization, revealing a personal inability to integrate good and bad aspects into one person). Hetherington and Stanley-Hagan (200) and Carter (270) suggest that pathological splitting is a continuation of some pathological objectification existing in the marriage prior to the divorce. The disturbing element in the studies of both Schuldberg and Guisinger (72) and Wallerstein and Kelly (26) is that angry feelings between alienated partners can continue for ten years or more after a divorce. A husband's devaluation of his ex-wife is usually passed along to his new wife, thus creating a ghost who haunts the new relationship. The exaggerated devaluation of a former spouse can only occur with a concomitant idealization, and such idealization often signals that the new relationship is already on the verge of disintegration.

Projection is present in divorce as well as in marriage. Anderson and Stewart document their counseling work with a divorced woman who was bearing a crippling sense of failure because her husband divorced her (107). The woman eventually "came to understand that the shame she felt when her husband left her actually belonged to *him*, the person who could not live up to his commitments." In this instance, it was apparently more comfortable for the husband to dump (project) his own shame and then leave. Post-divorce anger can sometimes be understood this way as well. Is a divorced woman carrying her own anger or the projected anger of her ex-husband?

Of course, an "ex-wife" is an object-other, the mental representation of some sort of relationship, thus being created through some event or interaction, and is invested with a particular emotional energy such as love, hate, or fear. Apparently the trauma of divorce creates a number of new object-others. The social role of "ex-hus-band" and "ex-wife" clearly reveals that we are dealing with archetypes, with raised or lowered social standing, rather than with people. Wallerstein and Kelly point out how children can also become object-others in post-divorce situations (101). They may suddenly be marked off as "his" or "hers," as if one were setting up competing teams inside the former family. Children are then treated differently in accord with these differing, relatively new perceptions. The preferred child was treated well; the rejected child, shabbily. The children whose attachments to the parents did not reflect these preferences or choices were bewildered. Often they all suffered intensely—those who were elected felt guilty, those who were rejected were acutely unhappy.

An ex-husband is also an object-other, which may explain a startling revelation about divorced men and child support payments. Joyce Arditti's study of non-compliant fathers uncovered a significant discrepancy between fathers' and mothers' reports on child support payments. Seventy-two percent of the fathers they surveyed reported that they always paid their child support on time, while less than half of the mothers (41 percent) reported that they received their support on time. This statistic is problematic, because nearly all the U. S. Census Bureau statistics on divorce and child support are based solely on interviews with mothers, without any consultation with fathers at all. Subsequently, most of the statistics used by researchers, policymakers, and the media may be inaccurate or at least reinforce a particularly dim picture of child support compliance and visitation patterns. Such discrepancy can only suggest that the non-compliant father is also an object-other, which may or may not correspond with reality.

Because of the significant presence of object-others within the divorce system, a minister must be extremely reluctant to take sides. Object-others capture subjective reality but never objective reality and, without care, the minister may be drawn into the subjective world of a divorcing partner, all the while forming an opinion about what is happening on the basis of information that is minimally correct at best. In such situations the pastor would do better to focus his or her attention on healing the interparental hostility by bringing a greater congruence between an object-other and reality. Interparental hostility has negative implications for child adjustment in general and contributes to lessened contact with the noncustodial parent in divorcing families. For the sake of the children involved, the feelings of anger toward an ex-spouse must be offered up for healing.

In her book on anger, Carol Tavris affirms a number of studies that show that women who vent their anger and humiliation do not register as high on mental health scales as do women who hold it in (302). While anger is perhaps appropriate as a temporary symptom during divorce, its long-term nurture is apparently quite destructive of women and those in their care. Tavris and others attribute this ongoing anger to the divorced person's intersubjective dialogue, the continued invisible conversation between him- or herself and the object-other ex-partner who resides in the head. Tavris remarks, "chances are that the spouses are continually saying things to themselves that are keeping [the humiliation and anger] alive. They are rehearsing a script, playing the part of the wronged wife or misunderstood husband over and over" (303). This continued anger is often linked

to low self-esteem. The anger may help them leave a marriage, or feel righteously betrayed if they are left, but it does not cure their low self-regard. If they didn't hate their ex-spouses they would have to hate themselves, which is intolerable. The best cure for persistent anger, then, is improved self-regard. A pastor can help a bitter divorced person understand that hate is an optional emotion, not a mandatory one. The healing of emotions is one of pastoral ministry's greatest gifts.

The Effect of Divorce on Children

Much of what we know about the effects of divorce on children comes from Judith Wallerstein's "California Children of Divorce Project." She followed sixty divorcing families, with a total of 131 children, since 1971, thereby collecting an enormous amount of direct information on children's adjustment. The bias in her research needs to be kept in mind, however, in that the majority of her children came from white American middle-class families.

Wallerstein's research does not support many popular assumptions about divorce and children's mental health. For example, she writes:

> Thus the conventional wisdom of yesteryear was that unhappily married people should remain married "for the good of the children." Today's conventional wisdom holds, with equal vigor, that a marriage that is unhappy for the adults is unhappy for the children and, furthermore, that a divorce that promotes the happiness of the adults will inevitably benefit the children as well. (Wallerstein and Kelly, 10)

She concludes: "There is considerable evidence in this study that divorce was highly beneficial for many of the adults. There is, however, no comparable evidence regarding the experience of the children. There is, in fact, no supporting evidence that divorce is overall better for children than an unhappy marriage or, for its opposite argument, that living within an unhappy marriage is by and large more beneficial or less detrimental than living in the divorce family" (306–7). Nor is there any evidence that children feel relieved when an unhappy marriage ends in divorce, even after years of anticipation that it will. Above all, the most significant factor in children's adjustment was their parents' behavior toward each other. Wallerstein's study showed clearly (Wallerstein and Blakeslee, 305) that children in emotionally or physically violent homes were much more damaged than were the children of a relatively civilized divorce.

During the course of her research, Wallerstein discovered that children's responses to divorce divided neatly into broad and distinguishable age-related categories, namely, preschool children (approximately three to five and one-half years old); young school-age children (six to eight years old); older school-age children (nine to twelve years old); and adolescents (Wallerstein and Kelly, 51–52). Subsequent research by Black and Sprenkle would add a fifth category, of university-age students. Divorce adjustment is a constructive process influenced by many factors: individual coping skills, systemic family coping skills, quality of family relationships, support networks available to parents and children, and societal and cultural norms regarding divorce. In addition, the way a child adjusts is directly influenced by the child's age, maturity level, and gender.

Preschool children were developmentally the least able to understand that "divorce is a grown-up problem." These children's fears reflected confusion about their future relationship with their parents, in large part because their psychological and emotional needs had been ignored or overlooked by both parents. Not unreasonably the children concluded that if the marital tie could dissolve, the parent–child relationship could dissolve too (Wallerstein and Kelly, 45). Unfortunately, angry or grieving mothers contributed to the child's sense of abandonment by exclaiming, "He left *us*. He no longer cares about *us*. He does not love *us*." Even in situations where the child's fears were not exacerbated, they still took divorce personally. Giblin points out:

> Adults, including the affected spouses, will primarily view the crisis as *husband* and *wife* no longer living together. The child will see what is happening as "Mommy and Daddy no longer live with me." The difference is not one of semantics. . . . Failure of parents and counselors to grasp this essential point may be a major contributor to the inability of both parents and counselors to grasp that divorce is a major life trauma in the lives of children. (70)

Thus, while all children need a clear explanation of why the divorce is occurring, the youngest children need special attention, with explanations that frame the divorce as a problem between the adults, accompanied by frequent reassurance of the children's access to both parents once they no longer live together. Sadly, Wallerstein's research showed that three-quarters of the children received no help from grandparents or other relatives, and only 5 percent received any support from a minister. When support did come for these children of divorce, it came either from their schools or from parents of some of their friends (Wallerstein and Kelly, 43–44).

Older schoolchildren, adolescents, and university-age students seem best equipped to understand that the divorce was not caused by them and that they are not being personally abandoned. Apparently parental divorce and family structure, in and of themselves, are of little importance to adolescent adjustment. Again the key factor seems to be parental discord (Dusek, 287–88). In Black and Sprenkle's study, university-age students who experienced parental divorce and those whose parents are married to each other were not found to differ significantly in their readiness to marry and their attitudes toward divorce. The only significant difference between the two groups was that children of divorce were nearly twice as favorable toward cohabitation.

A child can survive divorce without long-term emotional or psychological damage if the divorce is explained as a serious and carefully considered remedy for an important problem, when the divorce appears purposefully and rationally undertaken, and indeed succeeds in bringing relief and a happier outcome for one or both parents. Thus virtually all researchers agree on the need for a well-rehearsed, coherent, and age-appropriate true explanation of the parents' reasons for separating. Wallerstein and Kelly found, however, that a number of parents did not bear in mind the age-appropriate factor (102). Some addressed their children, even very young children, as if they were adults, able to understand complex confessions or to process hurtful and immoral behavior by a parent. Parents sometimes even brought children into their beds to provide the lonely parent with companionship, a potentially very damaging form of parentification. "These parents, who were usually socially isolated and in profound psychological turmoil, maintained stoutly that their young children were fully able to understand them and endowed with unusual capacity to provide wise counsel."

While virtually all children studied showed some reaction to this traumatic event in their lives, some acted out more vigorously than others. Adults can understand that change is gradual, painful, and often extends over several years. However, two or three years of instability represent a significant part of a child's entire life experience—one-half the life of a kindergarten girl or a third of the life of a nine-year-old boy (Wallerstein and Kelly, 4). Adults, then, should not expect children to adjust to divorce at the same rate, or indeed on any schedule other than their own. The transition from a married family to a post-divorce family is complicated because children have little control over the changes in their lives. Not only must they often adjust to new locations, new and more stringent economic situations, and the changed availability of the mother, but there are the more difficult adjustments that they must make to the changed attitudes and behavior of their parents. Accordingly, youngsters' initial responses to their parents' divorce must be seen and understood in this context. They are not responding just to the structural change of the family itself, but to the whole complex, sometimes tragic drama precipitated and set in motion by the decision to divorce and its often long-lasting aftermath (Wallerstein and Kelly, 34). These children are responding primarily to the event of divorce rather than to their two parents. Because they need an "address" for their anger and fear, however, they may turn angrily on the parent who least deserves it or, conversely, shower an abusive parent with demonstrations of support and affection. Again, adult logic is not always particularly useful in understanding how children react to trauma.

Jerome Dusek nominates six psychological tasks that a child must accomplish in adapting to parental divorce (285):

1. *Acknowledging the reality of the marital rupture.* The child must come to grips with fears and fantasies about how difficult things will be and must learn that the parents will not live together again. This is especially difficult for young children.

2. *Disengaging from parental conflict and distress and resuming customary pursuits.* Children must learn to distance themselves from the parental difficulties, often with little help from the parents, and go about living a normal life conducive to healthy growth. Children also must not let the parental separation be completely consuming. As children get older this task does not get easier.

3. *Resolution of loss.* The child, who at this point may feel "unlovable," must come to grips with feelings of rejection and worthlessness. This may be especially difficult to do if mother is the one who leaves the house. This task is the most difficult and may take many years to resolve.

4. *Resolving anger and self-blame.* The child must overcome anger over the parents' decision to separate rather than stay together as the child wishes. The younger child especially must come to realize that he or she was not responsible for the divorce.

5. *Accepting the permanence of the divorce.* Children must overcome fantasies and hopes about parental reconciliation. This may be more difficult for younger children because of their lack of mature understanding of the nature and meaning of divorce.

6. *Achieving realistic hope regarding relationships.* This is primarily a task of the adolescent years. The adolescent must learn to trust others in intimate relationships and to develop the capacity to love and be loved by others.

Dusek believes that girls generally accomplish this task more easily than boys, though conversely, girls have a more difficult time adjusting to a subsequent stepparent (286). Wallerstein and Kelly find, however, that while girls adjust initially more easily, after five years there is no significant difference in adjustment between girls and boys (313).

There are specific gender difficulties along the road to adjustment that a minister needs to be aware of. The Wallerstein study showed that a father's anger and bitterness are more anxiety-producing than a mother's. Parents tended to favor the children of their own gender, mothers favoring their daughters and fathers favoring their sons, much to the pain of the excluded children. Of all the relationships the mother-son relationship remains the most troubled. In studies by Hetherington and Stanley-Hagan and by Dusek, the majority of mothers, even six years after divorce, still used less effective rearing techniques and did not show a great deal of warmth toward their sons (Dusek 286).

Five years after divorce, according to Wallerstein's study, while most of the adults approved of their decision to divorce, over one-half of the children did not regard the divorced family as an improvement over their pre-divorce family (Wallerstein and Kelly, 305). In some instances, this may have been due to the increased poverty of the custodial mother. Dusek cautions us in the use of our assumptions about divorce and poverty:

> Poverty, in and of itself, does not cause developmental difficulties. Rather, research shows that poverty negatively influences marital quality, feelings of efficacy in the parenthood role, and parental emotional health. These lowered feelings of ability as a parent and of self-worth are related to poorer parenting skills which, in turn, are related to poorer childhood outcomes. (284)

For the most part, however, after an initial rocky year during which their normal developmental progress was impeded, the majority of the children in Wallerstein's study had adjusted to divorce and resumed their developmental progress. Only one-quarter of the children continued to show moderate or severe developmental inhibition or regression after the first year of adjustment. On the other hand, one-quarter of the children experienced a significant developmental spurt consequent to the divorce. "In the main, this group consisted of those children we described who were separated by divorce from psychiatrically disturbed fathers and whose custodial mothers were competent and psychologically stable" (Wallerstein and Kelly, 177–78).

In sum, when divorce is undertaken thoughtfully by parents who have carefully considered alternatives; when the parents have recognized the psychological, social, and economic consequences that can be expected for themselves and for the children; when they have taken reasonable measures to provide comfort and appropriate understanding to the children; where they have made arrangements to maintain good parent-child relationships with both parents—then those children are not likely to suffer developmental interference or enduring psychological distress as a consequence of the divorce.

Alternatively, if the divorce is undertaken primarily as a unilateral decision that humiliates, angers, or grieves the other partner, and these feelings continue to dominate the post-divorce relationships of the divorced partners; if the divorce fails to bring relief from marital stress or to improve the quality of life for the divorcing adults; if the children are poorly supported and poorly informed or co-opted as allies or fought over in the continuing battle and viewed as extensions of the adults; if the relationship with one or both parents is impoverished or disrupted, and the child feels rejected; if the stresses and deprivation of the post-divorce family are no less than those of the failed marriage—then the most likely outcome for the children is developmental interference and depression (Wallerstein and Kelly, 316–17).

Post-Divorce Parenting
As already mentioned, parenting skills apparently decline during the first year post-divorce. Each member of the divorcing couple tends to be so wrapped up in his or her own pain, disappointment, and mustering of new resources that there is little energy left over for effective parenting. They are more likely than parents from intact families to report feeling angry at their children and having little tolerance of misbehavior (Holloway and Machida, 180). Mavis Hetherington and Margaret Stanley-Hagan report that newly divorced fathers and mothers both face the same set of problems: feeling overloaded, socially isolated,

and worried about their parenting competence (205). However, there is no significant difference in competence, ultimately, between custodial mothers and custodial fathers. (About 20 percent of single-parent households in the United States are headed by a separated, divorced, or never-married father.) Noncustodial fathers, however, often are less competent than custodial fathers. Betty Carter suggests that they may need coaching in concrete issues such as having available adequate space for their children to visit them; being able to relate to children of various ages; and managing their relationships with children without excessive reliance on grandmothers, aunts, and girlfriends (261).

Traditional social opinion, and a legal system that trusts its own too-often-misguided wisdom, are the two biggest blocks to parents who wish to find a cooperative style of post-divorce parenting. Virtually all contemporary research supports some form of ongoing shared responsibility for children's upbringing. Wallerstein and Kelly make a sharp distinction between "shared physical custody" and the more traditional designation of a primary or "psychological" custodial parent (310). They define "shared physical custody" not as a precise apportioning of a child's life, or even an insistence that a child spend equal amounts of time with each parent, but rather as a concept of two committed parents, in two separate homes, caring for their youngsters in a post-divorce atmosphere of civilized, respectful exchange.

The legal tradition, however, supported by a mistaken popular "wisdom," is that "the best interests of the child" mean almost automatically that custody is awarded to a mother. This reward system is based on a now outdated assumption that mothers are psychologically more important to children than fathers, and that women should appropriately devote themselves to home and hearth. (When I divorced and sued for custody of my children, the judge looked me square in the eye and said sternly, "Young man, fathers work and mothers nurture.") Hetherington and Stanley-Hagan point out that even the experts cannot agree any longer on how to define "the best interests of the child," and that the whole idea of a "primary caretaker" contains an inherent bias against fathers (210). Even more pointedly, Joyce Arditti comments upon the irony that social pressure now demands that fathers participate fully in child rearing, and yet when marriages dissolve, the legal system denies any history of equal parenting (113). The court system paternalistically defines "the best interests of the child" without consulting the wishes of the father, and certainly not of the children, and at times not even of the mother.

The standard court award in the U.S. legal system remains sole custody to the mother and two weekends a month to the father, regardless of the parenting competence of either. This gives exaggerated power to custodial mothers, and almost completely disempowers noncustodial fathers. Resident mothers are empowered to act as gatekeepers after divorce, partially limiting fathers' contact with children and determining the circumstances under which contact can occur. If conflict is high between former spouses, mothers are more likely to close and lock the gate (Hetherington and Stanley-Hagan, 203). This power imbalance is the primary source of erosion in both a noncustodial father's child support payments and his efforts to stay in contact with his children.

It is perhaps a surprise, then, given the damage that the courts do to an already vulnerable broken family, that as many fathers pay child support as do. Citing U.S. 1984 Census statistics, James Dudley argues that 50 percent of custodial mothers receive their full child support payments, 26 percent receive partial payments, and 24 percent receive no payment at all (121–22). But, as has already been cited, these statistics are based on the self-reporting of custodial mothers and are not compared to the self-reporting of noncustodial fathers. Nor do such statistics reveal any further breakdown by race, economic class, or other contextual considerations. Mavis Hetherington and Margaret Stanley-Hagan dispute their male colleague's figures, and therewith his conclusions:

> Estimates of the number of nonresident fathers who pay the full amount of court-ordered child support range from 50% to 71% with a quarter paying nothing at all. It has been argued, however, that focusing on compliance with formal court-ordered support may give too pessimistic a picture of fathers' economic support. Many parents make informal agreements about support depending on the fathers' ability to pay support and the economic situations and needs of parents and children. (192)

Certainly, they argue, women below the poverty line deserve all the assistance they can get through mandatory deductions from the non-compliant father's paycheck. But, as Arditti points out, such a system, while perhaps benefiting those children whose fathers would not pay child support otherwise, overlooks those fathers who voluntarily comply and poses risks for individual privacy (116–17). Furthermore, universal enforcement does not address the psychological relationship between compliance and the impact of "child absence" on noncustodial parents.

While child support enforcement efforts may be necessary to hold noncustodial fathers accountable for their financial obligations to their children, these efforts should be seen as a last-resort measure, not the first and primary means of addressing the issue. Instead, prior steps that are preventative in nature and that encourage the father's voluntary participation should be given much more serious consideration (Dudley, 122). The most important preventative step, in the opinion of virtually all researchers in the field of divorce, is for the parents to find a way to facilitate each other's commitment to and involvement in the newly reconfigured family. Greater psychological involvement stemming out of joint custody arrangements may facilitate emotional closeness between divorced fathers and their children and thus more frequent and compliant child support payments. When noncustodial fathers feel they have little control over court decisions or what will happen to their children, or when conflict is ongoing, they are less likely to remain involved or to pay child support. To achieve a civilized post-divorce relationship between two parents should not be that difficult if both parents choose to commit themselves to their children in spite of what has occurred between them. Wallerstein and Kelly point out that even in very deprived and unhappy marriages, most couples find a way to maintain their parenting effectiveness within a relatively conflict-free sphere of behavior (15). If this is possible within a miserable relationship, why should it not be possible when the two adults are no longer living together and realize that their children's future health hangs on their ability to cooperate?

Hetherington and Stanley-Hagan describe three parenting patterns in sole or joint custody families:

> *Cooperative parents* talk with each other about their children, avoid arguments, and support rather than undermine each other's parenting efforts. *Conflicted parents* talk with each other about their children but with criticism, acrimony, defensiveness, and attempts to undermine each other's parenting. . . . *Disengaged parents* are both involved with their children but adopt what Furstenberg has termed a "parallel parenting" model. Each parent adopts his or her own style and does not interfere with the other's parenting. Communication with each other is avoided except perhaps through their children. This reduces the likelihood of direct conflict but also reduces cooperation. (208–9)

Although cooperative coparenting is associated with positive adjustment for children, in cases where both parents remain involved, the disengaged or parallel style of shared parenting is most common particularly when parenting adolescents. Although a disengaged coparenting style is not the ideal, children have been found to adjust well, provided their parents do not interfere with each other's parenting, conflict is low, and the children are not asked to act as go-betweens.

The primary argument for cooperative coparenting is that all studies show how much children continue to need quality access to both of their biological parents. Studies by Wallerstein and Kelly (307), Arditti (111), and many others reveal that a child's desire to spend quality time with his or her noncustodial parent does not diminish at all, even five or more years after the parents' divorce. If anything, as children approach adolescence, they increasingly chafe under restrictions on their own choice of which parent they will spend what time with (Wallerstein and Kelly, 138). The most pressing demand that children of divorce bring into counseling is for increased visitation time. Wallerstein and Kelly summarize poignantly:

> Even within remarriages, at least during the earlier years of these remarriages, though the stepfather often became very quickly a prominent figure to the children, the biological father's emotional significance did not greatly diminish, although his influence on the daily life of the child lessened. It has been, in fact, strikingly apparent through the years that whether or not the children maintained frequent or infrequent contact with the non-custodial parent the children would have considered the term "one parent family" a misnomer. Their self-images were firmly tied to their relationship with their parents and they thought of themselves as children with two parents who had elected to go their separate ways. (134)

Divorce and the Church

Having established the roles that parental animosity, societal assumptions, and misguided judicial judgments play in decreasing the chances of both children and parents surviving divorce, what should be the role of the church in providing support for families who are experiencing divorce?

The tradition of the church has legitimized only two options: marriage or celibacy. This "splitting," however, is not a part of the biblical tradition. The Bible says very little about marriage on the whole, nor does it say much about the single life as we know it today. Adrian Thatcher writes:

> Paul's claim that the lives of singles are less complicated than those of spouses and parents is based on his view of Christian conduct in light of the end [of the world]. He thinks husbands and wives are alike "concerned with worldly affairs" (1 Cor. 7:33–34). Unfortunately his view tells us nothing about the actual lives of single people today. Single people may also be concerned with worldly affairs (including children). Their concerns may be different from married people, but it does not follow that they are less. (13–14)

The normal age of marriage in biblical times was about twelve or thirteen, so the Bible also does not address issues of premarital sex or of sexual activity by single adults.

Nor does the Bible address divorce to any degree. Divorce figures in only three biblical passages. Deuteronomy 24:1ff. explains the process for a husband's terminating his relationship with a wife he finds sexually repugnant. At Malachi 2:16, God says, "I hate divorce," but as Ann Borrowdale points out, "There are also instances where God hates religious festivals (Amos 5:21) or usury (lending money at interest), which even fundamentalists rarely apply" (48). At Jeremiah 44:4 God appears to hate all whose allegiance is elsewhere, and at Jeremiah 12:8 God appears to hate his own followers. At Mark 10:11-12 (parallel Matt. 19:9 and Luke 16:18), the passage about "if a man divorces his wife and marries another . . . ," the issue at hand is remarriage, not divorce. Beyond this, as Collins points out, it is almost impossible to recover the original version of Jesus' saying (230). Ironically, while the Gospels suggest that remarriage is

a sin when one's previous spouse is still living, and the early church held the same opinion (see Jerome, Letter 77, paragraph 3), the church subsequently has condemned divorce and, at least recently, been quick to bless second marriages.

The divorce rate is very high in all first-world countries and is rising in most other cultures. The dedicated work of the religious right and, outside the church, of economic conservatives known as "new familialists" (Struening, 135) has little hope of swinging the tide in the near future, if at all. In the meantime, other voices in the church are asking why we are abandoning such a large part of our population that stands in critical need of pastoral care.

Episcopal bishop Jack Spong believes that the necessary stance for the church today is to take both marriage and divorce seriously. "The church should recognize and state quite openly that divorce is not an unforgivable sin, nor is it always tragic; indeed, in some instances divorce is and can be positive and good. After having done all it can to fulfill its vow to support the marriage, the church also needs to undergird divorcing persons when they make that decision. Passive, benign rejection is neither helpful nor compassionate" (63).

Rejection, however, has been the usual policy of the church as a whole and of most congregations. In many denominations, divorce by a pastor automatically bars him or her from exercising ministry until a new marital partner is found, in spite of the irony noted about the sin of remarriage in the Gospels. Being married or being celibate are the only two options available to those in ministry. This split standard is stricter for the ordained. As Thatcher comments: "Those whom God calls to priesthood (at least in 'unreformed' churches) or to the religious life must be single (and celibate). Those who have children must be married. Those who are neither called nor married are defined by what they are not" (24). But perhaps Thatcher is too generous. Lay ministers, and indeed the laity as a whole, usually must undergo the transformations of divorce without the help of the community of faith, who have seen it as their obligation only to keep people together, and who are not available to help those for whom continuation in the marriage is no longer possible (Anderson, Hogue, and McCarthy, 94). Giblin asks what message we are giving our children, the next generation of the faithful:

> With families who have regularly attended the same church, the divorce of parents will usually result in one parent's dropping out of that church. Churches, even the more "liberal" ones, have been unable to convey to both divorced parents that they are accepted and welcome. . . . What does that say about a child's view of the church as the family of God? (77)

Normalizing Divorce

New voices in sociological and psychological research are asking whether it is not time for a paradigm shift. Hetherington and Stanley-Hagan (191), Carter (262), and Wallerstein and Blakeslee (297) all point out that if we look realistically at what is happening with American families, divorce is just one of several stages in a family's life-cycle development. In this paradigm, divorce is not a single event but is a process that is part of a continuum that begins in an unhappy marriage and extends through the separation, the divorce, and any remarriages or second divorces. "Divorce is not the culprit; it may be

no more than one of the many experiences that occur in this broad continuum" (Wallerstein and Blakeslee, 297). It is a trauma, but not a tragedy.

Our era is perhaps the first time in Western history that marriage has come close to being an option for women instead of either a necessity or a demand. But we must not let the changing roles of women mask the fact that "family" has always been a term that describes a whole variety of human relational organization. Here we must be careful to distinguish between religious heritage and cultural heritage, in the same way that Niebuhr analyzed the relationship between Christ and Culture. The American nuclear family is a cultural value, but not a religious value. It is cultural arrogance to represent the American nuclear family as the ultimate will of God, or the only "true" form of family life.

Changing patterns of family life are not necessarily evidence of a moral crisis. In fact, as Anne Borrowdale argues, the presence of diversity ought to be one of the joys of any social community.

> St. Paul's image of a body with many working parts [1 Cor. 12:12-31] captures this sense of diversity in unity. The call for Christian family values is often linked with insistence on the nuclear family of once-married parents and their biological children. However, as I have shown, family takes many different forms for different people and at different times of their lives. Christians cannot restrict themselves to valuing only one particular family form. Even for those Christians who oppose families formed after divorce, deliberately chosen single-parenthood, or gay and lesbian couples, there is still a rich variety of family form, to meet different people's needs at different times. People live alone

or with friends, extended families with elderly relations living in, non-residential extended families, step-families, or one-parent families formed after a former partner has died, foster families, and so on. (195–96)

It is the celebration of this diversity that the 1988 Lambeth Conference, the international gathering of all Anglican bishops in the world, had in mind when they refused to put boundaries around the definition of the family: "We believe that the family, whether a unit of one parent and children, an adult child and an elderly parent, adult relatives, a husband, wife and children, or *whatever other shape*, is the fundamental institution of human community" (Borrowdale, 42).

Perhaps one way for the church to claim its rightful ministry to the divorced is through the wider promotion of rituals that mark this traumatic and most significant event in the family life-cycle continuum. Carol Tavris points to the psychological healing that such rituals make possible:

> To overcome rage that doesn't subside, one must first recognize the ambivalence and attachment that contribute to it, and to move toward a sense of closure on the marriage. Anger is often prolonged after divorce because our culture offers no rituals of resolution, no way a community can help its members manage anger as it helps them manage grief. (304)

The church has begun to recognize that it is very good at being with people when they come together, but a miserable failure at being with them when they come apart. Slowly rituals have begun to develop that mark the end of a relationship as publicly and reverently as it was begun. James Lancaster describes one such ritual, which

includes counseling prior to the ceremony, much as premarital counseling sets the stage for a wedding; biblical readings about journeying into the unknown wilderness; expressions of grief, assurance of the resurrection, and the pledging of community support (39–42).

Spong also describes "A Service of Recognition of the End of a Marriage" (189–92). Designed to offer to God the pain of divorce, the prayers concluded as follows: "On behalf of the church which blessed your marriage, we now recognize the end of that marriage. We affirm you as single persons among us and we pledge you our support as you continue to seek God's help and guidance for the new life you have undertaken in faith." Such a service can bring the grace, love, and forgiveness of God to a common human experience of brokenness and grief. Spong claims that this sort of service would place the church where it ought to be: in the midst of human hurt and the sense of failure. He closes his description with the words of Christ at Mark 2:17, "Those who are well have no need of a physician."

Conclusion

Divorce has two purposes. The first is to dissolve a marriage that has grown intolerable for at least one person. The second is to build a new life. Everyone who initiates a divorce fervently hopes that something better will replace the failed marriage—and this second-life-building aspect of divorce turns out to be far more important than the crisis. It is the long haul of divorce that matters. How people succeed in translating the hope for a better life into a reality is the critical, unexamined issue in the post-divorce years (Wallerstein and Blakeslee, xi).

To speak quite personally: My god-daughter, when once considering a divorce, observed that one should never divorce unless it is the only option 'left open. As a divorced man myself, I heartily concur with her observation. As much as everyone longs for a "friendly" divorce, calm partings are rare animals indeed. The more common characteristics of divorce include acrimony, decrease in self-esteem, financial hardship, emotional turmoil, misuse of children, and loss of personal friends. The process is much longer than anyone ever anticipates, and more painful. When divorce is the unavoidable solution to a bad relationship, however, the pastor's role is to help stabilize all those involved, and to normalize the situation as skillfully as possible.

BIBLIOGRAPHY

Afoa, Ioane Asalele. "Marriage and Divorce among Samoan Couples." In *Counselling Issues and South Pacific Communities*. Philip Culbertson, ed. 189–213. Auckland: Snedden & Cervin, 1997.

Anderson, Carol, and Susan Stewart, with Sona Dimidjian. *Flying Solo: Single Women in Midlife*. New York: W. W. Norton, 1994.

Anderson, Herbert, David Hogue, and Marie McCarthy. *Promising Again*. Louisville: Westminster/John Knox, 1995.

Arditti, Joyce. "Child Support Noncompliance and Divorced Fathers: Rethinking the Role of Parental Involvement." In Volgy, 107–20.

Bach, George, and Peter Wyden. *The Intimate Enemy: How to Fight Fair in Love and Marriage*. New York: Avon, 1968.

Black, Leora, and Douglas Sprenkle. "Gender Differences in College Students' Attitudes Toward Divorce and Their Willingness to Marry." In Volgy, 47–60.

Blackwelder, David. "Single Parents: In Need of Pastoral Support." In *Clinical Handbook of Pastoral Counseling*, vol. 2. Robert Wicks and Richard Parsons, eds. 329–59. New York: Paulist, 1993.

Borrowdale, Anne. *Reconstructing Family Values*. London: SPCK, 1994.

Brewster, Arlene. "Review Essay." *Pastoral Psychology* 44:4 (March 1996): 265–68.

Burski, Krisanne. "Correlates of Women's Adjustment during the Separation and Divorce Process." In Volgy, 137–62.

Carter, Betty. "Divorce: His and Hers." In *The Invisible Web: Gender Patterns in Family Relationships*. Marianne Walters, Betty Carter, Peggy Papp, and Olga Silverstein, eds. 253–88. New York: Guilford, 1988.

Collins, Raymond. *Divorce in the New Testament*. Collegeville, Minn.: Liturgical, 1992.

Culbertson, Philip. *Counseling Men*. Minneapolis: Fortress, 1994.

Diedrick, Patricia. "Gender Differences in Divorce Adjustment." In Volgy, 33–46.

Dornbusch, Sanford, Melissa Herman, and I-Chun Liu. "Single Parenthood." *Society* 33 (July 1996): 30–32.

Dudley, James. "Exploring Ways to Get Divorced Fathers to Comply Willingly with Child Support Agreements." In Volgy, 121–36.

Dusek, Jerome. *Adolescent Development and Behavior*. 3d ed. Upper Saddle River, N.J.: Prentice-Hall, 1996.

Engel, Susan. *The Stories Children Tell: Making Sense of the Narratives of Childhood*. New York: W. H. Freeman, 1995.

Giblin, Paul. "Marital Conflict and Marital Spirituality." In *Clinical Handbook of Pastoral Counseling*, vol. 2. Robert Wicks and Richard Parsons, eds. 313–28. New York: Paulist, 1993.

Gilligan, Carol. *In a Different Voice: Psychological Theory and Women's Development*. Cambridge: Harvard University Press, 1982.

Gordis, Robert. *Love and Sex: A Modern Jewish Perspective*. New York: Farrar, Straus and Giroux, 1978.

Griffin, Benjamin. "Children Whose Parents Are Divorcing." In *When Children Suffer: A Sourcebook for Ministry with Children in Crisis*. Andrew Lester, ed. 69–81. Philadelphia: Westminster, 1987.

Hetherington, Mavis, and Margaret Stanley-Hagan. "The Effects of Divorce on Fathers and Their Children." In *The Role of the Father in Child Development*. Michael Lamb, ed. 191–226. New York: John Wiley and Sons, 1997.

Holloway, Susan, and Sandra Machida. "Child-Rearing Effectiveness of Divorced Mothers: Relationship to Coping Strategies and Social Support." In Volgy, 179–202.

Lancaster, James. "Ceremony of Dissolution." In *Equal Rites: Lesbian and Gay Worship, Ceremonies, and Celebrations*. Kittredge Cherry and Zalmon Sherwood, eds. 39–42. Louisville: Westminster/John Knox, 1995.

LeBacqz, Karen. "Appropriate Vulnerability—A Sexual Ethic for Singles." *The Christian Century* 105:5 (May 1987): 435–38.

Miller, William, and Kathleen Jackson. *Practical Psychology for Pastors*. Englewood Cliffs, N.J.: Prentice-Hall, 1985.

Mollenkott, Virginia Ramey. *Sensuous Spirituality: Out from Fundamentalism*. New York: Crossroad, 1992.

Palisi, Bartolomeo, Myron Orleans, David Caddell, and Bonnijean Korn. "Adjustment to Stepfatherhood: The Effects of Marital History and Relations with Children." In Volgy, 89–106.

Peterson, Karen. "Turmoil of Divorce Grows Over Time for Children, Study Finds." *USA Today*, June 3, 1997, 4D.

Schafer, Roy. *Retelling a Life: Narration and Dialogue in Psychoanalysis*. New York: Basic, 1992.

Schuldberg, David, and Shan Guisinger. "Divorced Fathers Describe Their Former Wives: Devaluation and Contrast." In Volgy, 61–88.

Smith, Rebecca, Mary Anne Goslen, Anne Justice Byrd, and Linda Reece. "Self-Other Orientation and Sex-Role Orientation of Men and Women Who Remarry." In Volgy, 3–32.

Song, Young. "Single Asian American Women as a Result of Divorce: Depressive Affect and Changes in Social Support." In Volgy, 219–30.

Spong, John Shelby. *Living in Sin? A Bishop Rethinks Human Sexuality*. San Francisco: Harper and Row, 1988.

Streuning, Karen. "Feminist Challenges to the New Familialism: Lifestyle Experimentation and the Freedom of Intimate Association." *Hypatia: Special Issue on the Family and Feminist Theory* 11 (1996): 135–54.

Tavris, Carol. *Anger: The Misunderstood Emotion*. New York: Simon & Schuster, 1989.

Thatcher, Adrian. "Singles and Families." *Theology and Sexuality* 4 (1996): 11–27.

Volgy, Sandra. *Women and Divorce/Men and Divorce: Gender Differences in Separation, Divorce and Remarriage*. New York: Haworth, 1991.

Wallerstein, Judith. "Children of Divorce: The Psychological Tasks of the Child." *American Journal of Orthopsychiatry* 53 (1983): 230–43.

Wallerstein, Judith, and Joan Kelly. *Surviving the Breakup: How Children and Parents Cope with Divorce*. New York: Basic, 1980.

Wallerstein, Judith, and Sandra Blakeslee. *Second Chances: Men, Women and Children a Decade after Divorce.* New York: Tichnor and Fields, 1989.

Whitaker, Carl, and David Keith. "Counseling the Dissolving Marriage." In *Counseling in Marital and Sexual Problems: A Clinician's Handbook.* Robert Stahmann and William Hiebert, eds. 2d ed. 65–78. Baltimore: Williams and Wilkins, 1977.

Worden, J. William. *Children and Grief: When a Parent Dies.* New York: Guilford, 1996.

7. Counseling Gays and Lesbians

"Homosexuality is assuredly no advantage, but it is nothing to be ashamed of, no vice, no degradation; it cannot be classified as an illness." (Sigmund Freud)

Perhaps there is no more divisive subject in any denomination today than the issue of homosexuality. The purpose of this chapter is not to enter directly into the heated argument about whether intimate same-sex relationships are "permitted" or even reflected in Scripture, nor to immerse myself in the murky politics of ecclesiology. The purpose is to help ministers and pastoral counselors understand the developmental issues that shape the identity of gays and lesbians, to cut through some of the confusion that most pastors feel when dealing with the relationship systems in which gays and lesbians live, and to foster a more sensitive, constructive, and healing attitude among caregivers toward gay Christians who cry out for pastoral assistance.

To some degree it is a surprise that there are any gay men and lesbian women left in the church. The debate in most denominations over whether there is a contradiction between being gay and being Christian, or being gay and being in a Christian leadership role, has been so drawn out and vitriolic that many gays and lesbians have simply left the church. Perhaps Masters and Johnson were correct to observe, "The available evidence certainly supports the homosexual population in their general contention that if they expected the worst from healthcare professionals, they would be rarely dis-

appointed" (247). From time to time, denominations, realizing that they are "killing their own walking wounded," have attempted to redress the destruction by issuing statements affirming their concern for gay Christians. For example, in 1977 the House of Bishops of the Episcopal church declared:

> We are mindful that homosexual persons as children of God have a full and equal claim with all other persons upon the love, acceptance, concern and pastoral care of the Church. Furthermore, they are entitled to equal protection under the law with all other citizens. We call upon our society to see that such protection is provided. We are deeply distressed that in parts of the world such persons are deprived of their civil rights and in some cases are subjected to the tragedy of humiliation, persecution and violence. The Gospel of Jesus Christ compels us to act against these injustices and affirm these persons as our brothers and sisters for whom Christ died.

In 1993, the Archbishop of Canterbury disassociated himself from a mission in London dedicated to healing homosexuality, saying, "I am not aware that homosexuality is a disease which is in need of healing." But most gays and lesbians who have remained within the church feel that in spite of their personal commitment, the church gives them double messages about their worth in the eyes of God and their welcome within the local community.

In the privacy of church offices across the United States, pastors and ministers continue to deal with gay men and lesbian women and their families as Christians in pain. To redress the church's history of making the lives of gays and lesbians a living hell, pastors must allow their commitment to the healing nature of God's grace and forgiveness to take a higher priority than arguments over the authority of Scripture or ecclesiastical policy.

Pastoral Attitudes and Counseling Skills

Neither Freud nor Jung considered homosexuality to be a problem per se; rather, they were concerned about the developmental and relational issues that faced gays and lesbians living in a society that defined heterosexuality as normative. It would be easy for us to interpret their opinions as though heterosexuality and homosexuality were two widely separated oppositional poles. Both Freud and Jung, however, understood the human being as inherently bisexual in nature, but the natural developmental processes socialized most people to be heterosexual in tendency, while for reasons that neither Freud nor Jung were able to argue consistently, some people wound up with a tendency toward homosexuality. The relationship between the two poles of sexuality was systematized in a famous 1948 study of American males. Alfred Kinsey devised a seven-point (0–6) scale. Those who were identified at the 0 end of the scale were considered exclusively heterosexual. Those who were identified at the 6 end of the scale were exclusively homosexual. Each person's sexual orientation fell somewhere on that scale, though in Kinsey's opinion there were very few people who were pure 0s or pure 6s. Over the period of an individual's lifetime, his or her sexuality reading on the Kinsey scale might vary slightly, or perhaps as much as a full point, but in general sexual identification remained stable throughout adulthood. In today's counseling world, the American Psychiatric Association of Social Workers, the American

Psychological Association, the National Association of Social Workers, and the National Association for Marriage and Family Therapy state that it is unethical for members to treat gayness as an emotional disorder or to discriminate in any way on the basis of sexual orientation.

Understanding human sexuality as a graded continuum rather than a bipolarity helps us understand the diversity of the gay and lesbian population within the church. It is difficult to make any broad generalizations about gay men and lesbian women. Homosexual men and women come in as many varieties and shapes as heterosexual men and women do. The majority of gay people cannot be identified on the basis of their looks, behavior, taste, or marital status. This will be particularly true of gay people in local congregations: because of the conflicted messages given them over the course of their lifetime, most gay men and lesbian women keep a low profile in the parish, and indeed, many present as happily married middle-class husbands and wives. Sometimes this is true because they have not yet come to terms with their sexuality; other times it is because a lifetime of discrimination or fear of being found out has convinced them to blend in as much as possible with their surroundings.

The most important pastoral tool in counseling men and women on issues of sexuality is an attitude of acceptance and respect. In his book *Embodiment*, pastoral theologian James Nelson presents a now-famous schematization of four possible counselor attitudes toward homosexuality. The first, which has prevailed in most of Christian history, Nelson calls the "rejecting-punitive" attitude or motif. At base, it is a vindictive prejudice, rooted in centuries of conditioning and fear of the "other"—in this case, the gay person. While occasionally expressed in the form of physical violence, this prejudice is more often expressed through forms of social exclusion, inequities in the workplace, sarcastic humor about gay people, prejudicial attitudes handed on to children around the dinner table through bigoted remarks, and so on. Somehow, being gay represents a tragedy and a stigma for these people. Some would even prefer a child who grows up a criminal to one who turns out to be gay.

Nelson calls the second common attitude the "rejecting non-punitive" motif. For example, Karl Barth holds that humanity comes into its fullness only in relation to persons of the opposite sex. To seek one's fulfillment in a person of the same sex is "physical, psychological and social sickness, the phenomenon of perversion, decadence and decay" (*Church Dogmatics* 3:166). Convinced that the central theme of the gospel is grace and forgiveness, however, Barth advocates the condemnation of homosexuality but the acceptance of the gay person, or, as it is sometimes expressed in a more banal manner, "hate the sin but love the sinner." This attitude is reflected in certain denominational positions that make a distinction between "orientation" and "activity" in the lives of gay persons. For example, the 1986 "Letter to the Bishops of the Catholic Church on the Pastoral Care of Homosexual Persons" from the Vatican Congregation of the Faith states:

> Although the particular inclination of the homosexual person is not a sin, it is a more or less strong tendency ordered toward an intrinsic moral evil; and thus the inclination itself must be seen as an objective disorder.... Special concern and pastoral attention should be directed toward those who have this condition, lest they be led to believe that the living out of this orientation in homosexual activity is a morally acceptable option. It is not.

(On the high failure rate of Christian ministries that seek to "cure" homosexuality, see Stafford.)

A third attitude Nelson terms "qualified acceptance." This option posits that while homosexuality is in some way against the order of creation, many gay people have not chosen their sexual orientation but seem to have been born with it. The ideal lifestyle for such individuals would be one of faithful abstinence from all sexual activity. If this proves impossible, then they should "structure their sexual relationships in an 'ethically responsible way' (in adult, fully-committed relationships). They should make the best of their painful situations without idealizing them or pretending that they are normal." A caricature of this position would run: "If they have to be that way, then let them at least model their relationships upon the norm of Christian heterosexual marriage and not flaunt their gayness as good."

Nelson identifies the fourth possible attitude as "full acceptance." Those who adopt this position accept fully the conclusions of medical and psychological research that same-sex orientation is given and then discovered, rather than being a choice or a preference. Christian theologians who advocate full acceptance interpret this "given" as "grace." It is part of the mystery of divine creation according to which God created each person in God's image. In this view, sexual attraction and its loving expression are intrinsic to the mystery of personal identity. Same-gender love, then, becomes a way of imaging God, just as heterosexual love images God (Byrne, 273).

Unless a pastor is fully committed to Nelson's fourth position as just described, he or she should not attempt pastoral work with gays and lesbians. To continue counseling, instead of making an appropriate referral, would be unethical from any point of view. The other three attitudes described by Nelson suggest a homophobia so destructive of the pastoral relationship in general that it can only interfere with the minister's ability to engage the careseeker fully enough to effect healing, as well as reinforcing the careseeker's own homophobia internalized from years of society's negative messages. Many gays and lesbians approach a minister already suspicious that he or she will call their very right to exist into question, and the gay community is rife with stories of the extensive damage done by ministers who misuse a cry for help as an opportunity to "cure" a gay man or woman of some imagined perversion. The pastor's attitude of acceptance and positive regard must be apparent enough to counteract these initial suspicions. As Richard Isay observes, "The proper application of [counseling] technique to the treatment of homosexuals demands that his sexuality, like the heterosexuality of a straight man, be perceived as normal for him" (8).

"Acceptance" of a gay or lesbian orientation, however, is not in itself enough to provide competent pastoral support. A pastor must also have some knowledge and understanding of the language, politics, values, stresses, and pertinent psychological theories of lesbian and gay identity. At the same time that lesbian women and gay men are indistinguishable from the majority population, being lesbian or gay influences and

permeates every aspect of a person's life, health, and relationships. A lesbian or gay person's sexual orientation must never be ignored; it is never irrelevant and it always makes counseling a different process from counseling a straight person. It is to the description of these particular theories, values, and stresses that the rest of this chapter is devoted, along with some possible pastoral interventions.

Coming Out as a Developmental Process

The foundation of counseling theory is developmental psychology. A number of theorists argue that gays and lesbians undergo a process for the development of their sexual identity that differs from the heterosexual developmental process. As in other schools of developmental psychology, these stages of gay developmental psychology assume that the locus for stability of, and change in, behavior lies in the interaction process that occurs between individuals and their environments.

Perhaps the best-known explanation of the unique nature of gay developmental psychology and sexual identity has been put forward by Australian psychologist Vivienne Cass. She argues that gays and lesbians move through six stages in the journey from initial discomfort to "fully integrated" sexual identity. The length of time taken to proceed through the stages will differ from person to person. At each stage, what Cass calls "identity foreclosure" is possible—that is, individuals may choose to arrest their development at least temporarily. Cass's model then assigns a person (P) an *active* role in the acquisition of a homosexual identity. Further, Cass makes a distinction between the private (personal) and public (social) aspects of identity. The two develop separately but in a related manner. Thus, an individual may have a private identity of being homosexual while maintaining a public identity of being heterosexual. This distinction is of crucial importance in understanding not only the coming out process, but also why pastors may find themselves dealing with gay parishioners whom they had always assumed to be happily married. Gay people are propelled through these developmental stages by the incongruency between what they know about themselves versus what they believe that their relationship network knows about or expects of them. A healthy sexual identity presumes a growing consistency between the private and public aspects.

Change and transition are universal adult experiences. Given recent changes in social expectations and the public perception of homosexuality, the developmental process will possibly flow more smoothly for younger men and women than for older, since the younger will have been given more room to actualize who they perceive themselves to be. It is not, however, the actual transitional event that creates difficulty for an individual, but rather the event's impact on one's relationships, routines, roles, and assumptions about oneself and the world. Cass's school of thought falls within what is generally known as "intrapersonal congruency theory," a way of viewing the interaction between individuals and their environment.

> P acts in accordance with the way P perceives the surrounding world. The social structure establishes P's interpersonal environment by regulating the way in which others behave toward P. From this environment P develops a perception of how P is regarded by others. This percep-

tion plays a crucial role in the maintenance of behavior patterns. The basic unit in the model, and the source of stability and change, is the intrapersonal matrix. This consists of three elements:

> 1. P's own perception of some characteristic that P attributes to self (S).
> 2. P's perception of P's own behavior directly as the result of that characteristic (B).
> 3. P's perception of another person's view of that characteristic (O).

> An intrapersonal matrix is a recurring functional relation between these three components. Each component has an affective element. The affect given to the component is either positive or negative. Each component also has a cognitive element since P will assign some value to perceptions. (Cass, 221)

Resolution of any incongruency among S, B, and O will be influenced by how severe the tension feels to P, whether the tension is felt between two or between three of the constituent elements, how deeply P values the opinion of others, and the number of options within the behavioral repertoire that P is able to identify and feel comfortable with.

Stage 1: Identity Confusion. Prior to this stage, P has held an image of self as being nonhomosexual and heterosexual, generally socialized by a society that holds those same values. Let us say, for example, that we are talking about a male. He sees himself (S) as heterosexual. He sees his behavior (B) as heterosexual. He sees others (O) viewing him as heterosexual. His sexual self-portrait is consistent, or *congruent* for heterosexuality. Then at some point in his life a change occurs. It might happen in childhood, in adolescence, in early adulthood, in middle age, or even very late in life. P's discomfort begins when he or she becomes consciously aware that same-sex information or stimulation precipitates a confusing sense of attraction. The more clearly P identifies this attraction as homosexual, the greater incongruency is created. P may adopt one of three possible tactics to defuse this new sense of personal alienation:

1. Accepting the self-labeling of the attraction as correct and beginning to make alterations to S. Exploration to resolve the incongruency often results in a progression to Stage 2.

2. Accepting the self-labeling of the attraction as correct but undesirable. This often results in an attempt to restore the original congruency through (a) becoming asexual, (b) exaggerating heterosexual behavior as a reassurance, or (c) more commonly, adopting the public position of an antihomosexual moral crusader.

3. Identifying the self-labeling of the attraction as both incorrect and undesirable. To do this, the content of the attraction needs to be reframed along with the meaning, so that, for example, a fascination with pornographic pictures becomes "a natural curiosity," or genital contact becomes "a mistake when I was drunk." Such a reframe is a typical form of Stage 1 identity foreclosure.

While identity confusion at Stage 1 is uncomfortable, it is usually not disturbing enough to precipitate revealing it to a friend or marital partner, or seeking counseling support. In some cases, the generating episode is processed and then deeply suppressed, justifying, for example, the self-righteousness of the moral crusader.

Stage 2: Identity Comparison. If identity foreclosure has not taken place in Stage 1, P now feels an increased incongruency

between S and B. Yet P is able, at the beginning of Stage 2, to state, "I may be homosexual." P can now examine the wider implications of that tentative commitment, perhaps by seeking to find some consistency between S and B. P becomes aware of the difference between P's perception of his or her own behavior and self and P's perception of how others view that behavior and self. In other words, increased congruency between the S and B components of the intrapersonal matrix results in greater incongruency between these two elements and the O component.

Accepting the self as "not heterosexual/homosexual" may lead P to feel alienated from society and from subgroups such as family and peers. This sense of "I am different" also creates a rupture between the comfortable past and an uncertain future. The resulting isolation may lead P to seek contact with a pastoral counselor, but will otherwise not yet produce significant changes in public behavior. Three stages for reducing incongruence are typical to Stage 2:

1. Passing as heterosexual, thereby allowing P to avoid a confrontation with others' negative evaluation of homosexuality and to take more time to think through a growing commitment to homosexual identity. This strategy reduces incongruency enough that P may pass along to Stage 3.

2. Accepting the homosexual meaning of P's behavior but refusing to claim a homosexual image. P may argue that his or her homosexuality is engendered by only one other "special case" person; adopt a self-definition as bisexual (that is, potentially heterosexual again); or claim personal innocence by blaming someone else for the homosexual identity ("if only my father had been more available . . .").

3. Accepting S as homosexual does not mean that B must be accepted as homosexual. A person may so despise homosexual behavior that, recognizing it in herself, she becomes the victim of her own deep-seated self-hatred. P may flee the church or move to another city to reduce the impact of others' perceived negative judgment. Even when identity foreclosure is the result, P is left with a terrible inner tension.

This stage may also be marked by a profound grief. If marriage and family are not in one's future, what is? What will there be to give form and structure to one's life? With the letting go of the perception of a self that is clearly heterosexual, one can experience a profound feeling of loss. As with any loss, the way to move beyond the grief is to acknowledge and express it. That means talking about it. Expressing grief over the loss of one's heterosexual status and all the fantasies about the future that went with it has not been a popular topic for dialogue in the gay and lesbian community. But, at this stage of identity development, grieving the loss of that heterosexual blueprint for life is an inescapable part of what is going on. The more it is acknowledged and talked about, the sooner it can be worked through and prevented from becoming a chronic, underlying theme in the person's intimate partnerships.

Stage 3: Identity Tolerance. P begins to tolerate a homosexual self-definition along with homosexual behavior, seeking out the company of other gays and lesbians and distancing from the intimate company of heterosexuals. The helplessness typical of Stage 2 begins to lessen and P begins to take responsibility for his or her own life situation. If P is married, this will probably be the stage at which the "secret" is revealed to the marital partner. Usually P will discover that investigation into more frequent homosexual social contacts will yield a mix of positive and negative experiences. If the positive experiences outweigh the negative, P will continue to move toward integration of the interpersonal matrix. If the negative experiences outweigh the positive, P will opt for identity foreclosure, leaving a negative mix of self-hatred and yet seeking the approval of heterosexual others.

Stage 4: Identity Acceptance. This stage is characterized by continued and increasing contacts with other homosexuals. These allow P to feel the impact of those features of the subculture that validate and "normalize" homosexuality as an identity and way of life. P discovers a preference for homosexual company and begins to develop a primary circle of friends there. The questions "Who am I?" and "Where do I belong?" generated in the early stages of development have now been answered.

Identity foreclosure will occur if P can find a comfort level at this stage. This comfort may include continuing to "pass" when necessary to avoid being confronted by others; selectively disclosing homosexual identity to significant heterosexual others; and decreasing contact with nonaffirming family members. On the other hand, maintaining contact with nonaffirming others may actually lead P toward Stage 5, as he or she seeks growing integration while attempting to stay in contact with heterosexuals toward whom she or he feels ties of love and duty.

Stage 5: Identity Pride. P dichotomizes the world into homosexuals (creditable and significant) and heterosexuals (discredited and insignificant). Commitment to the gay group is strong, generating a sense of group identity ("These are *my* people") and of belonging. With the devaluation of heterosexual others, P also rejects those values P classifies as heterosexual (such as marriage, gender-role structures) since they are seen to promote the concept of homosexual inferiority. The strong identification that P now has with the gay subculture provides an alternative and more satisfying set of values. P not only accepts a homosexual identity but prefers it to a heterosexual one.

With the rejection of the established institutions, P is now far less concerned about how heterosexuals perceive P. This in turn gives P the freedom to choose disclosure as a strategy for coping. Disclosure of a homosexual identity naturally brings about a reaction of some kind. P's perception of that reaction plays an important part in whether or not development continues. Perceived negative reaction is seen as consistent with P's intrapersonal matrix, and P is able to say, "This is what I expected to happen." Where reactions are perceived as positive, however, this is inconsistent with P's expectations. Attempts to handle this inconsistency lead P into the final stage of homosexual identity formation.

Stage 6: Identity Synthesis. P enters Stage 6 with an awareness that the "them and us" philosophy espoused in Sage 5, in which all heterosexuals were viewed negatively and all homosexuals positively, no longer holds true. With increasing contact between P and supportive heterosexuals, P comes to trust them more and to view them with greater favor. Unsupportive heterosexuals are further devalued. P still experiences the anger of Stage 5 but with less intensity because of the reduction in incongruency. Similarly, feelings of pride are still present but felt less strongly as P comes to see no clear dichotomy between the heterosexual and homosexual worlds. P accepts the possibility of considerable similarity between self and heterosexuals, as well as dissimilarity between self and homosexuals.

P's personal and public sexual identities become synthesized into one image of self receiving considerable support from P's interpersonal environment. With this development process completed, P is now able to integrate P's homosexual identity with all other aspects of self. Instead of being seen as *the* identity, it is now given the status of being merely one aspect of self. This awareness completes the homosexual identity formation process.

Orientation, Preference, or Behavior? Identity and Community

Cass's developmental schema suggests that the movement toward a healthy gay identity has many pitfalls along the way. Her Stages 1 to 6 form a sort of continuum, just as the Kinsey scale suggests that human sexuality in general is a continuum rather than a bipolarity. The issue of human sexuality is complicated even further by the fact that we do not understand where sexual identification begins. We do not know why some people understand their identity as heterosexual, while others do not. A person's sexual orientation may not be easily captured in a single word and it may change over time. Sexual orientation is a complex and dynamic concept rather than a simple, fixed label.

Some psychologists of human sexuality distinguish between orientation, preference, and behavior. To a degree, Cass's categories underline this distinction, for she makes it clear that people with a homosexual orientation may prefer partners of the opposite sex, or may choose whether or not to behave in a homosexual manner. We know, for example, that men in prison may have a heterosexual orientation, and even a heterosexual preference, but behave homosexually for periods of time. We also know that some people may have a homosexual orientation but behave heterosexually. As Bridges and Croteau point out, "A person's behavior may be totally at variance with all aspects of orientation, and the various parts of orientation might not all agree" (137).

For this reason, Richard Isay is tempted to truncate definitions by claiming, "I have found sexual fantasy to be a more clinically useful way of defining homosexuality than behavior.... Some gay men may not express their homoerotic impulses because of internal conflict, social bias, or personal choice" (39). I believe that Isay's definition is not useful for pastors. Rather, the pastor should begin work on the basis of the careseeker's self-definition. Sexual identity is too complicated to jump to simplistic conclusions.

Because sexual identity is so complex, it is difficult to categorize the types of gay people with which pastors will deal. Some will be publicly identified as gay, and others will be publicly identified as gay but choose to hide that from the pastor. Others will be in various stages of identity foreclosure as Cass describes it, or will choose to behave in a manner contradictory to their sensed orientation, such as a heterosexual preference and a homosexual orientation. While this obviously produces a state of incongruency in the careseeker, the pastor will probably not be a position to challenge that incongruency until the careseeker signals that he or she is ready for it to be challenged. The correct attitude then would be to remain focused on the careseeker's mental health, but be ready to move toward greater congruency at the speed dictated by the careseeker.

Gender issues further complicate sexual identity. Isay reports that because the male role is valued over the female role in this society, homosexuality is more threatening for men than for women, making the stigma attached to being gay more painful for men (94). Male heterosexuals often find themselves titillated by lesbian pornography but repulsed by gay male sex. This highly sexist differentiation serves to highlight the strong public resistance to homosexual expression in males and a general tendency to discount women's sexual expression as nonthreatening and even unimportant. These factors make it more difficult for males to come to terms with their homosexuality, though women's struggle should not be discounted, as will be explained later.

Public resistance to male homosexual identity is also complicated by stereotypes. Gay people may struggle hard to distance themselves from any overt signaling of their sexual identity. In these instances, fear of public reaction seems to overpower facts about the social and educational advantages enjoyed by other gay people. According to an extensive 1986 study of self-identified gay men in the United States, 43 percent had a four-year college degree or higher and 31 percent had served in the armed forces. (The same study revealed that 25 percent were or had been married to someone of the opposite sex, 19 percent had children, respondents first recognized their homosexual orientation at an average age of 12.5 years, and after recognizing their homosexual orientation it was an average of another eight years before a respondent told anyone about his/her sexual orientation; Bess, 49.) Thus it might be claimed that as a whole, gay men are better educated and more patriotic than heterosexual men in general, but this does not seem to have reduced the public stigma of homosexuality.

Literature emanating from conservative churches and politicians often speaks of a "gay lifestyle." There is, of course, no such thing, nor is there a single or homogeneous gay community. Gay people are as diverse as straight men and women, and what is a preferred lifestyle for one may be abhorrent to another. Gay lifestyles range from the late-night disco scene to quiet domesticity at home; the gay community can range from political action groups to the regulars at a local bar to the devout members of a local gay congregation. What is true, however, is that the percentage of gay people is larger in urban areas than in rural areas. Cities offer gay people greater employment opportunities free from discrimination and a chance to lead their own lives without the often intrusive familiarity of a small town. There are gay men and lesbian women in rural areas as well, though the isolation and their minority status sometimes makes it more difficult for them to find a supportive circle of like-minded friends.

The stereotypical images of gays and the stigmatization of homosexuality have led many people to lump gay people together in an offensive manner far more often than they would heterosexuals. An effective minister will approach each gay man or lesbian woman, and each man and woman exploring sexual identity issues, as a unique person and not as a caricature. Behavior, preference, orientation, gender expectations, the weight placed upon the opinion of others, the life history of positive and negative experiences, commitments that are natural barriers to claiming a more open identity,

occupational stability, marital status—these and many other factors combine in quite particular ways in the life of each gay man or lesbian woman who seeks help and counsel from the church.

Counseling Teens about Gay Identity

While an increasing number of secondary schools include sex education in their mandatory curriculum, the church and its ministers continue to be remiss in addressing openly the developmental and familial issues of gay identity in young men and women. For the church to leave its young adrift in this area is a failure bordering on sin. It is surely the result of ministers' embarrassment in dealing with sexuality issues in general, and for many pastors, an expression either of their own internalized homophobia or of the deep conflict they feel between concern for human beings and an overly dogmatic interpretation of Scripture and Christian tradition.

In the meantime, too many young men and women act out their pain in self-destructive ways. Guilt and secrecy, harmful and frustrating relationships, and unsafe sexual behavior are but a few of the fruits of the church's failure. Perhaps the most damning is the high teen suicide rate: most studies identify about 30 percent of all teen suicides as being due to the despair that results from struggling with a gay identity in an unsupportive and stigmatizing environment.

As discussed previously, sexual identity issues are complicated by the social construction of gender. When teens struggle through their developing sexual identity, they are confused and vulnerable anyway. When rigid or exaggerated expectations about how "real men" and "real women" should behave are overlaid on top of sexual identity, some young men and women despair of being able to succeed in becoming what they perceive to be "normal" (a singularly unhelpful word in the pastoral vocabulary). For example, Australia and New Zealand have among the highest rates of teen suicide in the world; they also both have unusually inflexible definitions of masculine gender behavior.

Pastors who counsel teenage and adult gays should be aware of a variety of distinctions between types of homosexuality, for these distinctions inform the choice of pastoral intervention.

(a) *Congenital homosexuality.* Many, though not all, gay people relate that they were aware of being "different" at a very young age, long before they became sexually active. Sometimes this type of homosexuality is termed "congenital" because it feels to gay people as though they were "born that way." We would now understand this as homosexual orientation, as opposed to homosexual preference or homosexual behavior. According to Cass's schema, the initial suspicion that one might be homosexual, then, can come at a very early age, thus extending movement through her developmental stages over as much as three decades.

(b) *Prepubertal homosexual behavior.* Many young men, whether eventually straight or gay, participate in some form of homosexual "child's play." Some men suppress these memories, though they may emerge again during adulthood, particularly during counseling or therapy. There is no indication that these early childhood experiences between young children "cause" homosexuality later in life, and a pastor should not take them overly seriously unless a counselee expresses undue distress at their memory.

(c) *Institutionalized homosexual behavior.* Some societies, even those in which Christianity has a strong influence, still include elements of institutionalized, or culturally mandated, homosexual behavior as a part of young men's rites of passage from childhood to adulthood. These behaviors may include the ingestion of semen from adult males, genital manipulation (often connected with adolescent circumcision), or even anal intercourse. In their social context, these behaviors are deemed normal; it is their omission that would be deemed abnormal. Again, there is no indication that such experiences "cause" adult homosexuality, or are connected in any way with what might be called a homosexual orientation.

(d) *Adolescent homosexuality.* There are two forms of adolescent homosexuality, one covert and the other usually overt. The covert form is sometimes called postpubertal bonding, and is common in both males and females. Parents would recognize this as the developmental stage in very young teenagers when boys and girls are inseparable from their same-sex favorite friends. While this covert bonding rarely includes any genital behavior, it is a form of psychic homosexuality that most schools of counseling theory consider to be a necessary transitional stage toward healthy heterosexuality. But there is also an overt form of adolescent homosexuality, when teenagers begin to claim an open identity as young gays and lesbians, as described in Cass's Stage 4. These teens may choose, sometimes with the support of pastoral counselors, to "come out" to their parents, their peers, or both. The inability to decide to come out, or a rejecting response by parents and peers, are two significant factors that may lead an adolescent to commit suicide. As indicated, this is a stage of homosexual identity formation that needs sensitive and courageous counseling from pastors.

(e) *Transitional homosexuality*. There is an adult form of the teenage covert homosexuality that is sometimes called "transitional" homosexuality, in that it is an interpsychic coming-to-terms with the internalized Jungian masculine. David Tacey describes this transition effectively as the shift from a deeply homophobic heterosexuality to a more secure, less threatened, more accepting form of heterosexuality that can celebrate the ambiguous character of sexuality in general.

(f) *Situational homosexual behavior*. In some situations men and women identify their orientation as heterosexual, but behave homosexually because there is no member of the opposite sex immediately available. Such behavior is well known in single-sex educational institutions, the military, and penal institutions.

(g) *Political homosexual behavior*. This form of homosexuality is much more common to women than to men, partly because the gender construction of femininity is less rigid in most societies than the construction of masculinity. Some women who are sexually abused as children opt for homosexual behavior as adults as a form either of protest or psychic defense against patriarchal violence.

The two biggest obstacles faced by teens who are exploring a gay identity are parental reaction and peer reaction, though both are compounded by society's attitudes toward homosexuality in general. A teenage male described the reaction he received upon telling his parents that he thought he might be gay:

> My mother tended to blame herself and thought she was at fault somehow with my upbringing. She then refused to accept it and subscribed to my father's view that I was too young to know and it was "a phase." (Stewart, 40)

Peers can be cruel and rejecting, though a structured support system can help most teens get through that phase. A negative response from parents, however, can tear an entire family apart because developmentally most teens—even highly rebellious ones—still desire a fair amount of parental approval. By the time that teens have addressed their sexual identity enough to declare it, parental rejection will feel to them like a vicious attack on their most basic sense of self. Pastoral counselor Felix Donnelly writes:

> Few parents are able to cope with the knowledge of their child's homosexuality alone, and should therefore seek support from someone who understands the orientation and will be sympathetic to their needs. Going to a fundamentalist religious minister usually only adds to the parents' problems. The son or daughter who is gay will usually need the support of their parents more than the rest of the family, and they are often closer because of this. (77)

Betty Berzon offers some tips for teens in how to open up a dialogue with their parents on their sexual identity (297–304; see also Myers):

1. Before you disclose, clarify to yourself *why* you are disclosing at *this* particular time. What are the factors in your personal circumstances that convince you that this is the moment to begin the conversation?

2. Disclose when *you* are ready to, but take into account what else is going on in the family situation.

3. Choose a quiet, private place for your conversation where you are unlikely to be

disturbed or distracted. Think carefully about which family members you want to have present at that moment.

4. Open the conversation positively. Don't begin, "I have something terrible to tell you. . . ." or "You're not going to like this, but. . . ."

5. Explain in as relaxed a manner as you can how you feel about being gay, and how you hope they will feel about it and about you. How long have you known you are gay? When did you first know? Have you tried to change? Does this mean you hate the opposite sex? Don't you want children? Are you happy? Do you think you will always be gay? Whom have you told or do you plan to tell?

6. Think carefully about whether you want to have your lover present with you or not. Consider both your needs and your parents' needs or possible responses. For some parents, this can make the situation more difficult to talk openly. It also opens up the possible response that if you terminated your relationship with your lover, you'd go back to being heterosexual.

7. Don't make your parents say it for you. What counts here is the affirming experience of announcing your sexual identity in your own voice, in your own words, to the face of someone important to you.

8. Be prepared realistically for a whole range of possible reactions. If your family did not know you were gay, you have told them something that is probably very unsettling. You have broken the contract of silence and changed the rules for the way you all relate to this important fact. They'll probably need some time to adjust. And different people adjust in different ways. Give them time and understanding. As Bess points out, your announcement has inter-

rupted the familiar family narrative, causing them to rethink their comfortable hopes, dreams, and aspirations (138). Your parents may need time to grieve.

9. Be available but not pushy. Keep your perspective: you have done this to improve family relations. Disclosure is a courageous act, and it is an expression of your willingness for your family to be an important part of your life.

The role of the pastoral counselor in assisting such a family cannot be overemphasized. Parents need a safe place to express their concerns, disappointment, and fears; information about relationship and lifestyle options available to gay men and lesbian women; reassurance and guidance; and perhaps confrontation if their response to their gay son or daughter is rejecting, overreactive, or otherwise inappropriate (Myers, 138–41).

Counseling Married Adults Who Are Coming Out

Perhaps an even more perplexing pastoral situation than dealing with gay teenagers is dealing with gays and lesbians who are heterosexually married. In most cases, the revelation of a spouse's homosexual identity, preference, or behavior comes as a terrible shock to the marital partner, and thus should be interpreted as a crisis ministry.

Cass's schema for the development of a gay identity notes that at any of the first five stages, P may opt for identity foreclosure—that is, to terminate any further development toward a fully healthy gay identity through repression, sublimation, or simply reframing. In such instances, it is quite possible that at a later stage in life the foreclosure will "wear off," and due to psychological or biological processes beyond P's conscious control, P will continue a move through at least some of the remaining stages of gay identity hitherto foreclosed. At this point, P will usually begin to behave in a homosexual manner for some time before breaking the news to the family. An emotional attachment to someone of the same sex, or a repeated set of encounters experienced as positive, are much more likely to trigger an interfamily revelation than are anonymous encounters. On the basis of case studies reported in the work of Buxton, Gochros, and others, it seems even more likely that the marital fabric will be rent when one partner falls in love with someone of the same sex. The power of the emotions involved forces a revelation of the extramarital activity and can be expected to precipitate a family crisis. The crisis is even more severe if P has been arrested while engaging in some illicit activity. The famous study by Episcopal priest and sociologist Laud Humphries proved that the majority of men who engage in sexual activity in public restrooms are married at the time, and his studies have repeatedly been proven correct.

Two options are available to P and his or her family: to remain married by negotiating a reconciliation and a new understanding, or to separate and probably divorce. Both of these options will be explored from a pastoral perspective, but first one must ask why some gay people marry in the first place.

The obvious answer would be that these gays and lesbians did not really realize that they were gay until well into the marriage. Most of the studies of such men and women, however, reveal that they had had homosexual stirrings, or even experience, before the marriage. Some marry hoping that the marriage will "make them normal";

such an unrealistic expectation is perhaps the product of internalized homophobia. This "compulsive heterosexuality," as Adrienne Rich has called it, is after all the primary message into which we are socialized. Others marry in the hopes that they will somehow be able to control themselves, and a small handful marry in the hopes that a "respectable" public front will mask their continued homosexual activity. But the majority seem to marry out of genuine love for their spouse, as would seem only obvious if we continue to consider human sexuality as a fluid spectrum. It is this deep love for their marital partners, however, that makes the breakup of a man or woman's marriage even more wrenching. It is crucial for a minister not to assume why a counselee got married, but to inquire why marriage looked like the best choice, and what P hoped to attain by marrying that could not be attained by an earlier declaration of a gay identity.

Married men and women who are facing a major upheaval in their sexual identity have four behavioral options open to them: heterosexuality, bisexuality, homosexuality, or celibacy. The cleanest resolution, though with the most complicated pastoral side effects, is when P "comes out" as gay or lesbian and leaves the marital relationship. It may even be that such a move is an attempt at a more integrated sexual identity (Isay, 65). Bisexual identity or behavior is an option in some cases, especially if the husband and wife have compelling reasons not to divorce. Such marital arrangements tend to be deeply hidden from public view. The husband or wife may choose to continue in their heterosexual behavior only and attempt to rebuild the marriage, though the incidence of depression and suicide increases dramatically in such instances. P may also opt for celibacy, either continuing in the marriage or leaving it, though when celibacy is "involuntarily" chosen rather than given as a spiritual gift the pastor would be correct to query P's continuing sexual integration and psychological wholeness.

The pastor working with married men and women who are leaving a marriage has three primary tasks: (a) to help the careseeker develop a positive homosexual identity, (b) to help the careseeker adapt to an eventual relationship with a same-sex partner, and (c) to help the careseeker deal with family and work-related issues arising from the changed life pattern (Bridges and Croteau, 136). The primary hindrance to a positive homosexual identity is what is called "internalized homophobia"—that is, negative beliefs about homosexuality or certain types of homosexuals, too narrow a definition of homosexual behavior, or a purposive refusal to recognize or claim a homosexual identity due to self-disgust or a fear of stigmatization. Since all gays and lesbians grow up in the midst of a heterosexual majority, every one of them will have internalized this socially pervasive homophobia to some degree or another. A significant task for the caregiver is to assist the careseeker in replacing negative images of gay identity with positive images.

Many other pastoral issues brought forth by gays and lesbians will be the same as those presented by heterosexual clients. But gay men and lesbian women also seek help for depression resulting from ended or unsatisfactory relationships, nonevents (expected events that do not occur; see Rosser and Ross, 91), estrangement from family, secrecy, shame, fear of disclosure, and guilt. The pressures of living in a homopho-bic world may also make feelings of suicide more common (Magnuson, Norem, and Skinner, 111). Lesbian counselees may fear being branded with a "double deviance"—lesbianism and single parenthood (Victor and Fish, 457).

Though accurate statistics are difficult to gain because of issues of social shame, most of the counseling literature estimates that about 20 to 30 percent of marital couples choose to remain together even after one of the partners has announced a homosexual orientation or behavior. Dr. Eli Coleman suggests that the following conditions are necessary if a marriage is to survive the shock of such a revelation (101–2):

1. Both people love each other.
2. Both people want to make the relationship work.
3. There is a high degree of communication in the relationship.
4. Both people have resolved feelings of guilt, blame, and resentment.
5. Physical contact is necessary. Each partner has to touch, and desire to touch, the other.
6. Each partner has a sense of worth outside the marriage.
7. If there is outside sexual contact, the other partner does not know about it, or the husband and wife have worked out an open-marriage contract.
8. The heterosexual partner is willing to work on understanding and accepting the homosexual partner's feelings.
9. The homosexual partner continues to work on his or her own sexual identity integration.

If a significant number of these factors are missing, the pastor should probably help the couple separate in as respectful and honorable a manner as possible, in order to preserve the integrity of each partner and the continued successful parenting of any children involved.

The counseling literature disagrees concerning the impact of parental homosexuality on children, and in particular the impact of coming out. The majority of the literature finds no significant negative long-term developmental impact on children, whether their parents remain married or separate. The minority voice, however, cautions that teens who learn they have a gay parent may go through an extended period of anger, for the information catches them at a time in their own lives when they are sorting through their sexual identity (Coleman and Ramafedi).

What seems to make more difference than a parent's declared sexual identity is whether or not the parent is in a long-term stable relationship. As Victor and Fish point out, "Higher self-esteem scores were obtained for children if their mothers currently lived with a partner than if she was single, regardless of the mother's sexual orientation. . . . A parent's sexuality does not appear to be a significant issue in a child's self-esteem or self-concept" (470). Some pastors may be concerned about the modeling offered by same-sex couples to children of the opposite sex. Pastoral counselor Howard Bess finds the worry unfounded:

> The family is only one of the many sources for role modeling for the growing and developing child. A typical child has an abundant exposure to a wide range of role models. Every child is exposed to teachers, coaches, Sunday School teachers, neighbors, ministers, etc. . . . The key to healthy homes is not gender but genuine honest love. (180)

Children are much more apt to survive a marital breakup for reasons of parental homosexuality if both parents portray same-sex relationships to their children as loving and committed relationships between two responsible adults.

The worst way for heterosexual spouses and other family members to deal with the issue of homosexuality within the nuclear family is for the whole rest of the family to go into hiding. Bess describes this reaction as "going into the closet," describing its tragic long-term effect:

> Their closet is just as rigid and dark as that of their homosexual sons, daughters, and friends. This particular group is huge. It is obviously much larger than the homosexual population itself. While the typical homosexual stays in the closet for an average of eight years, the typical parent, brother, sister, or friend stays in the closet for a lifetime.

The homosexual partner may be in agony over the impact of his or her largely involuntary identity shift upon the marriage, his or her deeply loved spouse, and their priceless children. The heterosexual partner may well be consumed with feelings of betrayal, shame, anger, helplessness, and confusion. Straight partners typically ask, "Why me? What did I do wrong?" The answer, of course, is "Nothing." To address the straight partner with God's forgiveness and grace is to affirm that the partner has indeed done something wrong. It is exactly because the straight partner has not done anything to cause the marital breakup that it is so painful for everyone involved. Identity issues are not rational choices, and sexual integrity cautions against the blanket wisdom of assuming a discipline of behavior that is incongruent with P's identity.

Homosexual partners who leave a marriage in order to explore more deeply a homosexual identity should be counseled against establishing a same-sex relationship too quickly. Repeated studies suggest that these "rebound" relationships are unlikely to last long. Any number of defenses against claiming a healthy gay identity or committing to a healthy gay relationship may have developed during the types of identity foreclosure that Cass has described. For example, the rationalization that "I can always go back to being heterosexual whenever I want to" (Cass's Stage 2) can prevent a gay man or lesbian woman from making the commitment necessary to a stable long-term same-sex relationship. Because gay people have the same basic needs for intimacy, dependability, and stability that everyone else has, most deeply desire to find someone to pledge themselves to for the long haul. A gay man or woman leaving a marriage, however, should be strongly encouraged to spend two or three years exploring the depths of his or her own sexual identity and socialization before attempting to establish a new relationship.

Counseling Gay Couples for Permanency

The forming of families by gay people is not surprising, if one reflects on their situation. All gay persons have grown up in some sort of family, and because they have grown up in families, family is just as natural to homosexual men and women as it is to heterosexual. In a previous chapter I have discussed what makes a good marriage. The same-sex couple is a lot like other families. The dominant themes in a same-sex union—caring, sharing, giving, and receiving—are the same as in the heterosexual union. Many of the same problems also apply: battering, the crisis of miscarriage, economic security, relationship boredom, and sexual maladjustment.

The heterosexual couple is generally accepted as a family for good reason. So, too, should same-sex couples be recognized as families (Bess, 173–76). As Hochstein remarks, "Family is no longer only two heterosexually married people, a man and a woman, with a child" (84). Ultimately we must expand our idea of the meaning of the word *family* to include two mothers, two fathers, one mother and no father, a father and no mother, unrelated people committed to each other and a child. We might conceive of a diversity of family forms arising in a diverse universe, each sharing common concerns for justice, love, and mutuality, though doing so in unique and particular ways. In order to grant stability to same-sex couples and their immediate families, for the sake of all involved, we need to grant them the same public recognition and social valuation accorded to heterosexual families.

It is also true that same-sex couples display significant differences from heterosexual couples. Because almost all gay people grew up in homes that implied, if not included, one male parent and one female parent, gay men and lesbian women may have little experience in choosing an appropriate life partner of the same sex. Therapist Betty Berzon offers the following criteria for making sure a choice:

Is this a person:
- who seems as if he/she will grow as an individual and not become overly dependent on me to make his/her life work?
- who is in touch with his/her feelings, who can talk about them freely, who is comfortable expressing anger as well as affection?
- who doesn't have to run away from conflict, who is willing and able to confront relationship problems and work on them?

- who listens when I talk, who gives me the feeling that I am being heard and understood?
- who can give as well as receive, who would be able to take care of me if I should have that need?
- who can receive as well as give, who is able to ask for what he/she needs, so that a relationship would afford the opportunity for both of us to give as well as receive?
- who functions on an intellectual level that is similar enough to mine so that one of us would not be chronically at a disadvantage with the other?
- whose life experience is similar enough to mine so that we can understand and respect each other's values and needs? (32)

Of course these criteria are as applicable to choosing a heterosexual partner as a homosexual one. It is simply that the gay man or lesbian woman may not be used to applying these criteria to someone of the same sex. Indeed, most of the criteria for identifying a good marriage listed in chapter 6 would also apply to a same-sex pairing.

Moreover, the effect of lifelong patterns of secrecy on the communication skills of a same-sex couple needs to be considered. Patterns of caution or reticence around self-revelation, developed in order to avoid stigmatization, may be compounded in same-sex relationships. Further compounding may result if both same-sex partners have trouble with the same relationship quality, such as emotional openness, competitiveness, or aggression.

Because we grow up in a society that values heterosexuality as normative, gays and lesbians may also have little experience in choosing an appropriate life partner of the same gender (as distinct from the same sex). Western society holds up few healthy models of a same-gender relationship; even intimate same-gender friendships seem to be consciously discouraged in adult men and women. Hochstein believes that gender role complications are much more influential in a gay relationship than sexual orientation issues (73), and Isay points out that gay people will often select a partner on the basis of their perception of socially acceptable opposite-gender relationships, including their parental models (88). Thus not only is the potential partner's sex at issue, but so is the way in which the potential partner lives out socially inherited gender expectations. So, for example, a gay man who is still concerned with the "manliness" of his own public presentation will be more likely to choose a partner who also lives out the same "manly" cultural construct, rather than a man who is more "feminine" in his social presentation. But the opposite may as well be the case. Because we are all trained in a relationship paradigm that assumes male-female complementarity, a very masculine-identified man may choose a partner who is very feminine-identified, and the two partners will then establish a relationship that mimics the traditionally accepted division of roles in a heterosexual marriage.

Such difficulties underline the struggle that each member in a gay relationship may face in maintaining individuality within a partnership. As Bridges and Croteau observe:

> A second difference between heterosexual marriages and lesbian relationships may lie in the negotiation of the delicate balance between autonomy and connection in relationships. Lesbian relationships are at greater risk for enmeshment or fusion than heterosexual marriages. . . . The balance between separation and closeness may be a different process in lesbian ver-

sus heterosexual couples due to the stigmatization and gender-role socialization factors. (137)

Unclear autonomy boundaries between two men or two women are much more likely than between a man and a woman. The tendency to fuse is increased if one or both partners have cut themselves off, or have been cut off, from their family of origin.

Gender identification should not be presumed to predict gender role comfortability. For example, a feminine-identified gay man may not be at all satisfied with playing the domestic roles usually assigned to women. A counselor may be called upon to help partners in a same-sex couple articulate and emphasize their needs and differences from one another in order to downplay the likelihood of identity fusion or confusion.

Unclear boundaries within the relationship are likely to be further complicated by unclear external boundaries that serve to protect the partners' identity as a couple. Because so much of the social context does not grant the same status of respect and privacy to gay couples as to heterosexual couples, a gay couple has to fight harder to ward off intrusions that would be less likely in a heterosexual couple. For instance, biological family members who are unwilling to recognize the validity of a gay couple's relationship may persist in inviting a gay man or woman home for dinner without inviting the partner, or they may refuse to cooperate in setting up arrangements for the disposition of family trusts, or act antagonistically in child custody negotiations. One would rarely find such dilemmas posed to a straight couple. Counselor Betty Berzon summarizes the dilemma of gay couples by asking, "You wouldn't let a destructive child run rampant and unchecked through your home. So why would you let a parent run rampant through your relationship?" (293).

Since at least 25 percent of "out" men and women have been previously married, children are likely to play a significant role in the lives of a gay couple. Many of the specifics of gender-role expectations are based on the assumption that males and females will grow up to pair off and produce children. Therefore, the same-sex pair bond may also strive to imitate the behaviors thought necessary for child rearing. Even where child custody issues have been smoothed by the cooperation of a previous marriage partner, a gay couple is still faced with significant issues such as the role and authority of the same-sex stepparent, helping children construct a positive self-image when coming from a "nonnormative" home, and the usual financial and legal responsibilities that apply to heterosexual adults and their children.

Because the public recognition and social valuation accorded to heterosexual couples are not generally accorded to gay couples, the breakdown of a gay relationship may go unnoticed. As Berzon remarks, "A heterosexual couple married *one hour* has more rights and privileges with regard to one another than does a homosexual couple living together in a committed relationship for twenty-five years" (11). The social isolation of a gay couple may result in no support being offered to either partner as a relationship comes to an end, and yet emotionally there is little difference between the end of a long-term gay relationship and the divorce that terminates a heterosexual marriage. Gay partners often grieve alone when their relationship ends, bearing their pain and disappointment without the public emotional and legal processes that divorcing heterosexual couples take for granted. The same isolation may hold true for those whose partners have died, particularly if they have died from AIDS.

Spiritual Direction with Gays and Lesbians

The attitudinal posture of ministers, described earlier in this chapter, applies also to spiritual directors. To provide care for lesbian women and gay men, the caregiver must confront his or her own attitudes toward homosexual orientation. Without honesty about where one orients him- or herself among the range of opinion about the psychological, theological, and moral status of homosexuality, much harm can occur in caregiving and spiritual direction (Graham, 97). Inasmuch as any human being, whether gay or straight, participates in embodied, incarnate, and concrete relationships, the image of God is reflected among them. Thus heterosexism and homophobia distort the image of God, injuring rather than healing, dividing rather than affirming right relationship. To provide spiritual direction to gays and lesbians, spiritual directors must confront their own internalized homophobia and heterosexism, be able to absorb lesbian and gay anger at the church and culture, and give space for gays and lesbians to work out their conflicts in a positive manner.

Shallenberger describes the typical journey of gay Christians as fourfold: childhood loneliness and attraction to the church, coming out, distancing, and questioning and deepening. Many gays and lesbians had positive experiences with the church in their childhood. Feeling different, out of place, and lonely, the church offered a haven, "a place where the harsh rules of life—how to be an 'appropriate' boy or girl—and the costs for not following those rules, did not apply" (Shallenberger, 88). These early memories should predispose gays and lesbians to spiritual direction, though they are often overlaid with later memories of betrayal by their beloved church. Perhaps as they grew into a fuller realization of their homosexual identity, they no longer felt welcome, or they were shaken by the conflict between their emerging identity and the professed beliefs of the institution. Coming out also meant struggling with bodies and sexual activity, but the church has so long ignored bodies that it has often been of little help to men and women working through their sexual identity, whether straight or gay. Spiritual directors may find an enormous amount of anger with the institutional church in their gay directees, and should be prepared to work through the sense of betrayal in order to recover the positive feelings of childhood, though it is unlikely that most congregations will ever again feel like safe havens for adult gays and lesbians.

Spiritual direction for lesbians and gays is most fully affirming when it is grounded in a doctrine of cocreation through which diverse forms of life emerge that must be regarded as intrinsically good. Yet oddly, in mistrusting their sexuality, gays and lesbians may have learned to distrust Creation (McNeill, 316). For the cosmos to have vitality, it must have diversity—the very diversity that is celebrated in the doctrine of the incarnation. However constructed, homosexual orientation is a part of this diversity that must be affirmed as good and protected from the destructiveness of others (Graham, 101–3). Incarnationalism, further, affirms the goodness of the human body. In the course of spiritual direction, human beings must be helped to claim a sexual expression regulated by the norms of care and justice, one that does not degrade, oppress, or destroy the image of God in others. Eros, the erotic love that describes God's own passion for connection, must be every bit as much a part of spiritual wholeness as is agape.

For some, the process of coming out is the peak experience on their spiritual journey. For these men and women, the movement through Cass's steps of homosexual identity development signaled the option to grow from brokenness to a new level of wholeness. Coming out was a process of cocreation with God, the creation of a home for their soul within their human bodies, a soul reflecting the grace of God's love for their particularity. To embrace one's sexuality without shame is a journey into freedom, creativity, vulnerability, and joy. This sort of erotic spirituality usually brings in its wake the desire to express that love in relationship and to offer that relationship to God. But here again the church has too often abandoned its own. Mary Borhek points out, with irony:

> A person who has spasmodic sexual encounters with someone of the same gender can go to confession, perform a penance, and thus remain in a right relationship with the church and thus by presumption with God. The person who is in a committed, monogamous relationship with a person of the same gender, however, does not have access to forgiveness unless he or she agrees to foreswear any sexual activity within the relationship. The peculiar unintended result of such a position is to give a kind of approval to the very activity that is most detrimental to

the person's physical, emotional, and spiritual well-being. (185)

Spiritual directors should be ready to listen to the pain and anger that surrounds the church's hypocrisy in addressing the fulfillment of committed same-sex relationships.

Spiritual directors who have written on their experience with gay directees mention four particular gifts that gays and lesbians bring to the process of spiritual direction:

1. *The gift of being mentored.* Many gays and lesbians remember the times in their lives when the caring words of just one person made the difference whether they should go on or give up. They may have been offered a key resource or a well-timed question to ponder, and from this they will have learned to listen carefully to those who meet them in love, concern, and acceptance.

2. *The gift of introspection.* The nature of coming to terms with sexual identity demands a great deal of introspection. In order to confront their own and others' internalized homophobia, gays and lesbians have had to go deeply inside themselves and to weigh the ethics and process of decision making. They may be more skilled at opening themselves up verbally than many straight people.

3. *The gift of discriminating insight.* Gays and lesbians may have a well-developed ability to see truth and hypocrisy in the institutional church and the more traditional methods of spiritual direction. Along the path to identity, they may also have learned to appreciate the nebulous, the ambiguous, and the paradoxical, thereby setting themselves up to cherish the complexity of God's self-revelation. Holding the natural tensions of the spiritual journey—between divinity

and humanity, free will and predestination, faith and intellect—is easier for one who has dealt with the ambiguity and paradox of being gay or lesbian.

4. *The gift of eclecticism.* As gays and lesbians discovered how judgmental their own Christian tradition could be of them, they may have struck out on new or less explored paths of spiritual identity. The nuancing of their Christian faith with these less common insights may have helped them move to a new stage of spiritual maturity, from what James Fowler calls, in his *Stages of Faith*, the synthetic-conventional (Stage 3) to the individuating-reflexive (Stage 4). The spiritual director should thus be prepared for the spiritual companionship of a gay man or lesbian woman to be rich and challenging, offering the opportunity to expand the boundaries of the more traditional forms of direction.

Following Cass's schema of gay identity development, there are stages in a gay man or woman's journey when spiritual direction will not be particularly helpful. At Stage 1, the directee may be not yet be able to address the complexities of incarnationalism, God's embodiment, and wholeness in gay relationships. At Stage 5, the politicization and intolerance characteristic of a newfound gay pride may predispose the directee against the richness of paradox and nuance that are so important to spiritual maturity. Chojnacki and Gelberg suggest that spiritual direction will be more helpful for people in Stages 2, 3, 4, and 6. They also raise the issue, as does much of the relevant literature, whether straight counselors or spiritual directors can be maximally effective with gay and lesbian clients. They wisely suggest that heterosexual counselors or directors work with gays and lesbians in

groups, so that other gay people may offset the director's internalized homophobia or inexperience in and ignorance of the diverse gay community. If a heterosexual pastor or director feels the need to work with gays and lesbians on an individual basis, the same balancing could be achieved by insuring that the gay careseeker is involved in one of the many support groups now available to gays and lesbians and their families. There are many such groups, with chapters in a wide variety of locations. They can be located through the phone book or by contacting the nearest chapter of the national organization PFLAG (Parents and Friends of Lesbians and Gays).

Conclusion

Howard Bess suggests a way ahead for the church, in spite of its dismal record in dealing with gay and lesbian issues:

> The largest failure of the churches in America over the past century is their inept handling of heavy drinkers and alcoholics. . . . The very existence of AA is an embarrassment to churches, and a painful reminder that churches were too slow in developing an understanding of alcoholism and never created a framework of ministry to this large segment of our population. (185)

But some parishes *have* become venues for AA meetings and a whole variety of related Twelve-Step programs. So with pastoral ministry to gays and lesbians and their families. An increasing number of denominations are affirming publicly the basic right of gays and lesbians to be full participants in parish life and recipients of the same frequency and quality of pastoral care offered to every Christian. With time, more and more congregations will become inclusive havens for those of any sexual orientation, offering refuge from rejection and abandonment elsewhere in Christendom. The hardest question raised by pastoral ministry among gays and lesbians is how any pastoral caregiver can justify denying pastoral care to any one of God's children.

BIBLIOGRAPHY

Back, Gloria Guss. *Are You Still My Mother?* New York: Warner Books, 1985.

Berzon, Betty. *Permanent Partners: Building Gay and Lesbian Relationships That Last.* New York: E. P. Dutton, 1988.

Bess, Howard. *Pastor, I Am Gay.* Palmer, Alaska: Palmer Publishing Company, 1995.

Borhek, Mary. *Coming Out to Parents: A Two-Way Survival Guide for Lesbians and Gay Men and Their Parents.* Cleveland: Pilgrim Press, rev. 1993.

Bridges, Karen, and James Croteau. "Once-married Lesbians: Facilitating Changing Life Patterns." *Journal of Counseling and Development* 73:1 (1994): 134–40.

Buxton, Amity Pierce. *The Other Side of the Closet: The Coming-Out Crisis for Straight Spouses and Families.* New York: John Wiley, 1994.

Byrne, Richard. "Pastoral Counseling of the Gay Male." In *Clinical Handbook of Pastoral Counseling,* vol. 2. Robert Wicks and Richard Parsons, eds. 267–94. New York: Paulist, 1993.

Cass, Vivienne C. "Homosexual Identity Formation: A Theoretical Model." *Journal of Homosexuality* 4 (1979): 219–35.

Chojnacki, Joseph, and Susan Gelberg. "The Facilitation of a Gay/Lesbian/Bisexual Support-Therapy Group by Heterosexual Counselors. *Journal of Counseling and Development* 73:2 (1995): 352–54.

Coleman, Eli. "Bisexual and Gay Men in Heterosexual Marriage: Conflicts and Resolutions in Therapy." In *A Guide to Psychotherapy with Gay and Lesbian Clients.* John Gonsiorek, ed. 93–103. New York: Harrington Park, 1985.

Coleman, E., and G. Ramafedi. "Gay, Lesbian and Bisexual Adolescents: A Critical Challenge to Counselors." *Journal of Counseling and Development* 68:1 (1989): 36–40.

Donnelly, Felix. *Who Cares?* Auckland: Australia and New Zealand Book Company, 1984.

Gochros, Jean Schaar. *When Husbands Come Out of the Closet.* New York: Harrington Park, 1989.

Graham, Larry Kent. "Caregiving and Spiritual Direction with Lesbian and Gay Persons: Common Themes and Sharp Divergencies." *Journal of Pastoral Care* 50:1 (spring 1996): 97–104.

Hochstein, Lorna. "What Pastoral Psychotherapists Need to Know about Lesbians and Gay Men in the 1990s." *Journal of Pastoral Care* 50:1 (spring 1996): 73–85.

Hopcke, Robert, Karin Lofthus Carrington, and Scott Wirth, eds. *Same-Sex Love and the Path to Wholeness.* Boston: Shambhala, 1993.

Humphries, Laud. *Tearoom Trade: Impersonal Sex in Public Places.* Chicago: Aldine, 1970.

Isay, Richard. *Being Homosexual: Gay Men and Their Development.* New York: Farrar, Straus and Giroux, 1989.

Magnuson, Sandy, Ken Norem, and Christopher Skinner. "Constructing Genograms with Lesbian Clients." *Family Journal* 3 (April 1995): 110–15.

Martinson, Roland. "Sexual Orientation: The History and Significance of an Idea." *Word and World: Theology for Christian Ministry* 14:3 (summer 1994): 239–45.

Masters, William, and Virginia Johnson. *Homosexuality in Perspective*. Boston: Little, Brown, 1979.

McNeill, John. "Tapping Deeper Roots: Integrating the Spiritual Dimension into Professional Practice with Lesbian and Gay Clients." *Journal of Pastoral Care* 48:4 (winter 1994): 313–24.

Money, John. *Gay, Straight, and In-Between: The Sexology of Erotic Orientation*. New York: Oxford University Press, 1988.

Myers, Michael. "Counseling the Parents of Young Homosexual Male Patients." In *A Guide to Psychotherapy with Gay and Lesbian Clients*. John Gonsiorek, ed. 131–42. New York: Harrington Park, 1985.

Nelson, James. *Embodiment: An Approach to Sexuality and Christian Theology*. Minneapolis: Augsburg, 1978.

———. "Reuniting Sexuality and Spirituality." *The Christian Century* 104:6 (February 25, 1987): 187–90.

Rich, Adrienne. "Compulsive Heterosexuality and Lesbian Existence." *Signs* 5 (1980): 631–60.

Rosser, Simon. "A Scientific Understanding of Sexual Orientation with Implications for Pastoral Ministry." *Word and World: Theology for Christian Ministry* 14:3 (summer 1994): 246–57.

Rosser, Simon, and Michael Ross. "A Gay Life Events Scale (GALES) for Homosexual Men." *Journal of Gay and Lesbian Psychotherapy* 1:2 (1989): 87–101.

Scroggs, Robin. *The New Testament and Homosexuality*. Philadelphia: Fortress, 1983.

Shallenberger, David. "Companions on a Gay Journey: Issues of Spiritual Counseling and Direction with Gay Men and Lesbian Women." *Journal of Pastoral Care* 50:1 (spring 1996): 87–95.

Stafford, Tim. "Coming Out." *Christianity Today* 33:11 (August 18, 1989): 16–21.

Stewart, Terry. *Invisible Families: A Resource for Family and Friends of Lesbian or Gay Daughters and Sons*. Dunedin: New Women's Press, 1993.

Tacey, David. "Homoeroticism and Homophobia in Heterosexual Male Initiation." In *Same-Sex Love and the Path to Wholeness*. Robert Hopcke, Karin Lofthus Carrington, and Scott Wirth, eds. 246–63. Boston: Shambhala, 1993.

Thatcher, Adrian. *Liberating Sex: A Christian Sexual Theology*. London: SPCK, 1993.

Victor, Sherri, and Marian Fish. "Lesbian Mothers and Their Children: A Review for School Psychologists." *School Psychology Review* 24:3 (January 1995): 456–79.

Appendix to Chapter 7: A Coming Out Chart

Based on the work of Vivienne Cass;
adapted by Paul Kinder for the New Zealand AIDS Foundation

The processes of homosexual identity development	Implications for the homosexual person	Guidelines for assisting
Identity confusion: Coming out begins when the individual becomes aware that his thoughts, feelings or behaviors conflict with how he has been taught to see himself (as heterosexual). His new feelings could be called homosexual or bisexual. He begins to see his homosexuality is personally relevant.	Because his feelings are in conflict with his previously imagined identity he will experience some confusion and turmoil. "Who am I?" is a burning question. He will have strong feelings of personal isolation and self-doubt. When he begins to accept these new feelings he may secretly seek out information. If he denies or resists his homosexuality, a negative or self-hating identity may begin to develop.	Because it is still unclear what the real problem is, and it is such an intensely personal matter, it is rare for people at this stage to tell others of their feelings or confusion. If he does tell you, provide: • reassurance that it is perfectly natural to feel confused about personal feelings that contradict how you have seen yourself, • basic value-free information, • further support if and when he wants it. Don't use labels he isn't ready for. He is seeking clarification of feelings, often wanting to be told it's OK to feel this way—not a definition of being gay.

Identity comparison: As he begins to accept his homosexuality he realizes the difference between himself and others. He will feel isolated from other people and feel a strong sense of not belonging to society, family or friends. He will feel lost and very alone as all his expectations about behavior and the future—that accompanied his presumed heterosexual identity—are in doubt. And there is no obvious alternative.	The question "Who am I?" is now joined by "Where do I belong?" Since being gay is often equated with perversion, effeminacy, mental illness etc., he may react against being gay. Most will be terrified at the expected negative reaction from friends and family. To lessen the intense loneliness, at this stage he may think of making contact with other gay people.	Provide an accepting environment for him to explore his feelings and personal beliefs. Also provide: • same support as stage 1, • reassurance that you won't reject him, • support for him to learn more about himself in his own time, • clear unequivocal support for the person he is, no matter what his sexual orientation.
Identity tolerance: His acceptance of his homosexuality has two consequences: 1) Confusion and turmoil lessens, allowing him to acknowledge his social, sexual and emotional needs, and 2) The difference between how he sees himself and how others see him grows. This increases his feeling of social isolation. He will usually try to make contact with other gay men and consider telling family and friends he is gay to lessen this isolation.	Telling others involves enormous personal risk. Many people live in terror for a long period, in fear of being "found out" and rejected. Personal suffering lessens, and self-esteem strengthens from positive reactions to telling others. Negative reactions make negative feelings worse and lower self-esteem. Telling others should be and is usually done one person at a time. This is less risky and easier to cope with. Building up positive reactions clears away the confusion, and allows the development of new social skills.	Support for his wish to explore his developing identity in the gay community, and among his family and social networks. Also provide: • gay community contacts, if available, • a safe place to return to if his exploration does not go according to plan, • support for the personal and social risks he is taking, • acknowledgment that it will take time, • help identify the key people who will most likely react positively, support his telling them first, • a reminder that many people, especially family, will take as long to accept his homosexuality as he did.

Identity acceptance: He has now come to see his gay identity in a positive way. Increased contact with gay people allows for the development of gay friends and meeting of partners. His identity though is not yet public and he adopts a strategy of fitting into society while also retaining a gay identity. This can be a comfortable and sensible compromise for many people, and large numbers of gay men choose to stay at this point.

Mixing with other gay and bisexual men offers a chance to have social support and role models, and learn to cope with discrimination. He can also now do the things he was unable to during adolescence due to social isolation, i.e., first loves. First relationships can be difficult, as there is no social support and few role models for them. His relationship with his family can be clearer as he is more confident with his identity. A three-way system develops between himself, his new gay family and his family of origin. How these interrelate will depend on levels of acceptance.

His relationships and friendships are just as meaningful and potentially fully loving as heterosexual relationships. They are more difficult for him to maintain due to a lack of social support and opportunities to develop social skills.

Provide:
- respect for his right and need to have support from, and belong to, a gay community,
- support for and acceptance of his new friends/partners in the same way you would for a heterosexual,
- opportunities for him to develop the new interpersonal skills required for relationships.

Identity pride: As he attempts to live openly and honestly as a gay person he will become more aware of society's expectations of him to be heterosexual or remain hidden. He will feel a conflict between a commitment to himself and other gay people, and society's denial of homosexuality. This may result in a feeling of gay pride. He may develop a strong commitment to gay culture and community and some anger at society's disapproval.

Increased openness about his sexual orientation will test the level of acceptance in the people and environments around him. There may be some anger and strong reactions, often for good reason, at the negative discrimination he encounters. Some family and friends will not understand or accept this stage. This may, in some situations, force choices of commitment.

At this stage he is able to work out what sort of support he needs, and choose where he gets it from. What often motivates this stage, other than the discrimination, is a resentment of the personal pain and loneliness he had to endure unnecessarily, and a concern that other gay people do not repeat the same. Clarification of the motives for actions may ensure they stay positively directed. Continue to provide the support and acceptance as outlined above.

Identity synthesis: Open contact with heterosexuals who accept his sexual identity allows him to extend his feeling of belonging to include society. Full integration into society is not possible when many social responses to homosexuality are still discriminatory, hurtful and stigmatizing. However, personal acceptance of self can be fully achieved. At this stage his identity becomes integrated with all other aspects of his self.

He may never tell his friends and family members about his homosexuality; others he tells will never come to accept it. This situation must be fully understood and accepted by him for personal development to be successful. At this stage being gay is no longer an issue—what is, is getting on with life. There may be times when he chooses not to disclose his sexual identity, though not out of fear of rejection, but for practical reasons of not wanting to bother with an ignorant person or an unnecessarily difficult situation.

Despite full personal acceptance of his gay identity, dealing with being gay is ongoing in a society that is less than fully accepting. Coming out is never fully complete. He has required a great deal of courage to reach this stage and will need more and continued personal and social support to stay here. The problem is not homosexuality but some people's lack of acceptance of it. If we wish to assist gays and lesbians we must make our community a healthier place for them.

8. Ministry with Those Who Mourn

"Grief is a circular staircase." (Linda Pastan, 62)

~

In her now-classic book *Necessary Losses*, Judith Viorst argues that the movement through human life from infancy to death follows stages of progressive maturation that necessarily involve losses as well as gains. Mourning and grief, then, are natural processes by which we adjust to living with any significant loss in our life course. Too often we associate grief and mourning only with death, when we are bereft of a loved one. Mourning, however, naturally follows the loss of anything meaningful—a broken engagement; marital separation; the loss of robust health; a shift from the familiar to a strange new place; the loss of a body part or a comfortable illusion; the disappearance of a job, self-respect, dignity, or independence; failing an exam; our children leaving home; the death of a pet; a car accident or a burglary; the loss of hope; the shattering of dreams. Viorst calls to our attention the sobering fact that we never fully finish with grieving. No sooner do we appear on the road to recovery from one loss than another comes along as we attend to the task of growing up and moving on.

We grieve whenever our equilibrium is upset and our customary coping mechanisms are thrown out of kilter. There is even what has been termed "the grief of new gains," such as receiving weighty new responsibilities at work or being "set free" from a relationship before we are ready (Creagh, 33). Not all mourning, then, is attached to loss, but in every case, people expect and deserve a sustaining presence from their pastors that will comfort them in their sadness and strengthen them for the tasks ahead.

So while almost anything can be mourned, ministers often face some of their most difficult pastoral challenges in dealing with those who are mourning the death of a loved one or family member. Grieving a death will therefore be the focus of this chapter, though it should be understood that many of the principles discussed here apply to the mourning of all other significant losses as well.

Normalizing Death

Dying is a natural part of the human condition, and even premature and tragic deaths must be understood as intrinsic to God's order of creation. We do not die because of sin or because of God's whim or arbitrary character. As Silverman and Cinnamon point out, "Those who die in war are not dead because of the will of God, but because of the will of men, governments, and nations. Those who die in a natural catastrophe do not die because God wills them to die, but because of the immutable laws of nature that are part of God's creation" (17). Death is as normal a part of human life as is living. Judaism and Christianity hold that part of our human task is to learn both to live well and to die well, and that both have significant potential meaning for the faithful. We sin against the Christian tradition if we argue otherwise.

Unfortunately, white Western culture, and American culture in particular, is death-denying. We speak of death in polite euphemisms that mask its inevitability, thereby dishonoring the central Christian belief that Christ has broken its sting. Charles Meyer lays bare both the heresy and the cruelty in the common euphemism "God took him," which presupposes divine caprice:

> This slogan makes God into a celestial body snatcher, or as one person said, "the great Hoover in the sky," randomly vacuuming people up off the earth. If true, it is no wonder survivors feel frustrated and angry at God. Rather than providing comfort, this statement often results in blame and resentment for God's alleged theft by appropriation. [In actuality,] the God of the Gospels is presented as one who welcomes and accepts us with open arms when our bodies quit working. (65)

Other similar euphemisms include "going to sleep," "passing away," "being called Home," and "going to live with Jesus," all of which are a disservice to both the good news and those who mourn. To fear death, or even simply to be resigned to it, is a sign that we still look upon death as "the enemy." Rather, death should be an act each Christian personally performs, not an experience to be endured. Death is a "yes," an "I do" (Creagh, 8).

Anticipatory, Normal, and Acute Grief

Grief is a regular feature of living because in this life none of us can have or hold all we want. We are always losing something. Adjusting to these losses is part of life. We have to learn to live without that thing or person. It is when we suffer our most serious losses that grief is most difficult.

It would seem that the intensity of our grief has to do with how significant the thing or person was in our life. We each determine for ourselves what is important to us, not outsiders. The death of the farm child's pet lamb can be quite a devastating loss of company to the child, while to the farmer it may simply represent the loss of profit. The child experiences grief. The farmer may hardly give it a second thought other than the effect on his child. But however painful, the child's grief is normal. John Hewett defines grief as "the feeling that comes in response to the experience of *amputation*, whether it be physical or emotional. It's your reaction to having part of your life cut off from you. Whether you lose an arm, or a close member of your family, the grief is similar: both are parts of *you*, and you mourn their loss with great sorrow and distress" (32).

In addition to this sort of grief, which Viorst reminds us we must experience over and over again in life, the pastor needs to be alert to both anticipatory and acute grief. Anticipatory grief follows the awareness of impending loss. It is a mourning of something yet to come. As with normal grief, in anticipatory grief we become aware of promises to oneself or another that may never be kept, intentions that have no future, and anger at how someone has lived or not lived. Our dreams seem to crumble slowly into ashes and we are powerless to stop them. Anticipatory grief is just as real as any other grief, and needs pastoral attention.

Walter Smith points out, however, that anticipatory grieving is not without its inherent liabilities. In cases of cancer or AIDS, for example, where the terminal period may be of considerable duration,

> it is possible that some persons could complete the grief work prior to the loved one's actual death. The implications for this are immediately obvious. Grieving has a predictable and time-limited course. Dying persons frequently express fears that they will die alone and abandoned. If those who are closest to them complete

their grieving prior to a loved one's actual death, there is the possibility that the dying person will sense the emotional distancing and disengagement. This may be perceived as rejection and abandonment. (1988, 164–65)

Anticipatory grief, then, runs the risk of depriving the dying of dignity and of leaving the mourners feeling empty and awkward, as the actual death becomes an anticlimax.

Sometimes loss or death comes very suddenly. Ronald Grimes describes acute grief as feeling that "Someone, somewhere in the universe, slipped a switch" (147). John Hewett describes it as "like a fist slamming into your chest" (32). The sudden death of one we love, the shock loss of something deeply valued when we least expected it, the demise of anyone whose years of greatest promise still lay ahead—all these generate the extreme shock that can easily produce acute grief. While all mourning necessitates the same basic tasks, acute grief seems to intensify the impact of those tasks and is much more likely to result in a pathological reaction that will need professional intervention. Such variability emphasizes the need for pastoral attention to both the ratio between grief and time—in anticipatory grief too much of the work is done before its time; in acute grief the time to address the tasks of grief work may be significantly extended—and the fact that each death, each loss, is both existentially and culturally unique. Mourning is never the proper subject for the application of stock techniques or formulaic approaches.

Death and Human Culture
Pastoral approaches to mourners and mourning must be built upon the contradiction of two widely held myths:

1. It is a myth that there is only one healthy way to grieve.
2. It is a myth that Western ways of mourning are superior to those of other cultures.

In mourning, we do the best we can to find our way through a difficult experience. Some paths are better than others in coping with loss, but in the end, not all persons are suited to the same paths, and not all even find their way. Thomas Attig describes a couple grieving the loss of their son: "Ed and Elise, as they grieve for their little Bobby, cringe when others say (as they far too often do) 'I know how you feel' or 'I know what it must be like for you.' How could anyone presume to know such a thing?" (16). What mourners need more than anything is understanding and respect for the uniqueness of their experiences. Attig describes the grieving process as "relearning the world" (17–18), and points out that no two of us learn an identical way of being our own person and living in the world. To appreciate the unique experience of each mourner, pastors must understand how the mourner was bonded to the deceased, for each human relationship is unique; how each mourner handles challenge and vulnerability; the mourner's unique perception of God, faith, and the afterlife; which culture or cultures shape the mourner's identity and expression of grief, and how the mourner feels about the influence and demands of that culture. Charles Meyer emphasizes how individualistic is each person's style of mourning:

People handle death the same way they handle any other difficulty in their lives. If the person is an aggressive problem solver, he or she will take on grief in the same way. A person who passively reacts to other life events will more passively respond to the death of a lover, hoping that some resolution eventually will present itself. (96)

Pastoral psychologists Miller and Jackson emphasize that "it is a myth that it is unhealthy for people to show relatively little emotional response during grief adjustment" (191), and David Crenshaw reminds us that everyone has the right to take a break from mourning and from culturally dictated methods of grieving: "No one can grieve all the time no matter how close the relationship" (36).

Laungani challenges us by writing: "It is a myth that the Western world sets a universal standard against which all other societies all over the world are to be evaluated. Consequently, those societies which come close to achieving (or mimicking) Western standards are to be applauded and those which don't, derided" ("Conclusions I," 225). In fact, cross-cultural studies of grieving practices show that Western cultures, which tend to discourage the overt expression of emotion at funerals, are "highly deviant" within the spectrum of the world's cultures (Parkes, Laungani, and Young, 5). Paul Rosenblatt describes the variety of culturally determined ways of mourning:

> In many societies, death rituals are far more elaborate and are extended over quite a bit more time than is common in Euro-American societies. The rituals occurring at the time of what Westerners might call physical death may last for days, weeks, months or years. They may require isolation of the bereaved, the wearing of special mourning clothing or special markings, and may require actions that seem to some outsiders to be pointlessly destructive or unpleasant—for example, tearing one's clothing, not bathing, tearing at one's skin, beating oneself or shaving one's head. (32)

A culture usually determines who is to be grieved. For example, in developing cultures with high infant mortality rates, the death of small children is grieved only briefly, whereas the death of an elder, the repository of wisdom and memory, is grieved elaborately. This is the inverse of the typical pattern in the United States, where a stillbirth or an infant death may generate extended grieving, while the death of an elder is viewed as timely and appropriate. A culture usually also determines who is to grieve. Family may be expected to grieve, but not friends; adults may be expected to grieve, but not children. For example, traditional Islam forbids children to attend or even be made aware of a funeral. If a parent or sibling dies, the children are to be sent to a neighbor's and allowed to return only after the immediate rituals of grieving have been completed (Jonker, 160).

Monica McGoldrick reminds us that cultural groups have specific beliefs about forms of mourning, and the pastor must find out from a family what it believes about death, the rituals that should surround it, and the afterlife (81–82). Because of the dominance of hospital personnel and funeral directors in the death process, more and more families have lost control of their traditions, yet, without the opportunity to express its grief according to particular cultural dictates, a family may become embedded in the mourning process without resolution. In an increasingly culture-sensitive church, McGoldrick's reminder helps to create new pastoral roles for both ministers and communities of faith.

Too many pastors treat grieving families according to some hypothetical "manual of procedure." "They operate with their theology, a theory about death that does not go beyond the familiar concepts of grief and mourning, and they tend to aim their help at the overt expression of grief. This may provide superficial help to a majority of people, but it misses the deeper process" (Bowen, 329). In order to support a grieving family in its vulnerability, many pastors will need to let go of their personal preferences about mourning and their sense of cultural imperialism. Rosenblatt writes:

> There are no pan-human categories for understanding death; how people think about death is everywhere culturally embedded. One reaction to find that one's own categories do not fit the realities of others might be to consider their ways to be uneducated, misinformed, superstitious, less developed, or in some other way faulty. But such ethnocentrism is unhelpful. In trying to offer understanding and assistance to people from societies other than one's own, there is no justification for privileging one's own reality over that of the people one wants to understand and help. The more useful course is to become adept at learning, respecting and dealing with another person's reality, no matter how discrepant it is from one's own. (31)

Effective pastoral care of mourners must take into account the specifics of their unique relationship with the deceased, the mourner's unique personality, characterological, and emotional structures, and the unique demands and expectations of the mourner's own culture.

Mourning Rituals

The cultural demands and expectations that each person brings to grief work include a sense of which rites and rituals are necessary for the deceased to be sent successfully to the next phase of his or her existence.

Deprived of this performance, many mourners are unable to proceed with their own post-trauma recovery.

In almost all cultures death is a transition not into nothingness but to some other state. To ensure that this process of transition proceeds unimpeded, it is incumbent upon the bereaved to perform the culturally determined rituals. This gives lie to the common Western assumption that "funerals are for the survivors." In fact, anthropologically, funerals are for the future security of the deceased; it is only our modern understandings of human psychology that have shifted the focus to the personal grief needs of the mourners. Cultural rituals may include many activities, but in every culture the primary rite is the funeral. Worden lists three primary benefits to mourners of the funeral: it provides (1) a means to acknowledge the death, (2) a way to honor the life of the deceased, and (3) a means of support and comfort for the bereaved (21). Combining traditional insights with more modern psychological ones, we can then claim that the performance of time-honored rituals not only ensures the successful transition of the deceased but also enables the bereaved to part from their dead in gradual stages.

Rituals can be understood in many different ways. According to Rosenblatt, the central purpose of funerals is to define: "They define the death, the cause of death, the dead person, the bereaved, the relationships of the bereaved with one another and with others, the meaning of life, and major societal values" (33). Not engaging in rituals or having them shortened or undermined can leave people at sea about how the death occurred, who or what the deceased is, how to relate to others, how to think of self, and much more. Ronald Grimes emphasizes the lasting effects when mourners avoid the culturally and psychologically dictated rituals, or when they are forced to bury their dead according to rites and assumptions that conflict with the mourners' culturally dictated identity:

> A funeral avoided leaves business unfinished, and there are few things worse than some ceremony's trying to work itself out through us when we are either resistant to it or unaware of its covert manipulation. A missed rite enacts and reenacts itself in surreal ways. If we flee a major transition, it will pursue us. If we don't do the work of passage, it will bird-dog us until we pay it proper attention. (131)

Proper pastoral care in a multicultural world demands sensitivity to the mourners' cultural needs. This sensitivity should define not only the liturgical rite used, but also the role of the local congregation.

An unqualified willingness by a host Christian community to respond sensitively to the fundamental values (religious, social, and familial) of different cultural groups, and actively to assist in their perpetuation rather than their destruction, is consistent with the Christian belief that God loves each person in his or her particularity and each culture in its diversity. To live out this ministry, it is necessary for persons of goodwill, compassion, and power from both sides of the cultural fence to come together in a desire to support and understand each other. Unless this is done, in the years to come the rituals, traditions, and customs that give each culture its unique identity and meaning will be swept aside, replaced by monolithic, homogeneous, pantheistic cultural arrangements. And that would mean the death of a culture. "The death of

a culture is a far greater loss to humanity than the death of an individual; the latter is inevitable, the former avoidable" (Laungani, "Hindu," 71). One role of a Christian host community, then, is to facilitate the effective playing out of funeral rites for neighboring cultural groups who have no "safe" place in which to carry on their traditions.

Serving dying and bereaved people from other races and creeds provides Christians with the privilege of learning from them. We should not expect that our expertise is greater than theirs but that does not mean that there is nothing we can do to help them. Death and bereavement are times when people need people and the mere presence of another person who cares is important. If, in addition, we have sufficient knowledge of and sympathy for the other person's culture to be able to understand what they need from us we shall have a great deal to offer (Parkes, Laungani, and Young, "Introduction," 7–8). When pastoral care of the bereaved is done well, with genuine care and thoughtfulness and without religious or cultural imperialism, many doors to acceptance and respect by the wider community are opened, trust is built, and the encompassing love of God is made physically manifest.

The Shape of Grief Work

During a certain period of training in pastoral ministry, it became an accepted truism that mourners, of whatever loss, went through identifiable and sequential stages of grief, and that it was the responsibility of pastors to move people through these smoothly and at a reasonable clip. This understanding was based on a simplistic misreading of the pioneering work of Elisabeth Kübler-Ross, particularly in her work

On Death and Dying. Kübler-Ross identified six phases of grief reaction: shock, denial, anger, depression, bargaining, and acceptance and decathexis. These six were subsequently reworked and expanded into ten, by way of Granger Westberg's famous book *Good Grief*: shock and denial, emotional instability, psychosomatic symptoms, depression and panic, guilt, anger, idealization, decathexis, acceptance, and normalization.

Obviously Kübler-Ross's system and Westberg's system do not easily match each other. Kübler-Ross was concerned about the grief reactions to one's own impending death. Westberg was more concerned with grief reactions to the death of another, though in both cases their work is applicable in either situation. Many others have also suggested stages or phases of grieving. In social-scientific and clinical writing, Erich Lindemann tells us that we grieve in three stages: shock and disbelief, acute mourning, and resolution. John Bowlby says we grieve in three phases: the urge to recover the lost object, disorganization and despair, and reorganization. George Engle's six-stage schema includes shock and disbelief, development of awareness, restitution, resolution of the loss, idealization, and outcome. Colin Murray Parkes modified Bowlby's idea (and Bowlby later accepted the modification) to describe four phases of grieving: numbness, yearning and searching, disorganization and despair, and reorganization (Attig, 42). Miller and Jackson suggest three: numbness and shock, emotional distress, and recovery (191), and Crenshaw suggests seven (20–25). There is no point in arguing which theory is better or more accurate. The point is that mourning is an extended period of varied intense emotional reaction, and both mourners and their pastors need to be prepared for almost anything. As one student expressed it beautifully in an essay on grief: "Our feelings surge in and out as the tide with unexpectedly large waves now and then" (Atkins, 266).

Neither Kübler-Ross nor Westberg intended their schema to describe an inevitable linear progression, though perhaps they were not as clear as might be preferred. More recent writers insist that we do not fall into lockstep as we grieve, for we do not lose our individuality. To suggest that there are predictable stages that everyone *must* pass through denigrates individuality and can even invoke further guilt for a mourner that he or she hasn't done things "right" or "well enough." Such ideas can also reinforce the mourner's feelings of helplessness and being out of control, and they encourage passivity in both mourners and their pastors. In place of stages or phases of grief, Charles Meyer (6–7), William Worden (12), and many others now speak of "grief work," a term first coined by Lindemann in 1944. Grief work suggests that there is a set of tasks to be accomplished within the grieving process, but the order of those tasks is unimportant, nor should anyone feel that every one of the tasks must be completed successfully by any certain date. Thomas Attig, however, finds even this reframing too demanding and "success oriented." He prefers the term "relearning the world" (107), by which he does not mean learning information *about* the world, but learning *how to be and act in* the world differently, in light of the mourner's loss.

In spite of these justifiable criticisms of virtually every approach offered, the caring pastor will benefit from a broad knowledge of the various "tasks" or reactions that characterize normal grief. For the sake of simple organization, a list resembling Westberg's will be explored here briefly. Again, pastoral response must take individual character and cultural expectations into account. Some cultures find the expression of some of the following responses to be tasteless or even offensive.

Shock and denial. Healthy psychological functioning depends upon the effective use of defense mechanisms. Studies of stress consistently identify the loss of a close family member or a deeply loved one as the most stressful event of everyday life. Shock protects us from some of the effects of this stress, and denial is a part of this protection. Maori novelist Witi Ihimaera expresses this sense of shock in a sharp metaphor, picturing a magnificent kauri tree (like a California redwood) struck down suddenly:

> I shut the door. . . . Mere starts to weep again. I put my arms around her. Dad used to cradle his children in this manner when they'd fallen asleep at a hui [tribal gathering]. No matter how tired his arms, he would have cradled us all like this even if the world was ending. He was a Kauri, my father. If there were storms I would shelter beneath his wide-spreading branches. But lightning has struck the tree. It has toppled to the ground with a cracking and splintering of branches. And I have no shelter now. (123)

Denial allows us to accept the shock of death without being overwhelmed. It takes time to assimilate new facts and their consequences. "Denial is a semideliberate, and perhaps psychologically necessary hesitation before we actively cope with loss" (Attig, 38). In healthy individuals denial is a temporary solution, not a permanent one. It

is a transitional state, a bridge between the world as it is and the world as it used to be or as we would like it to be. We wake up from sleep and are *sure* that the death of our loved one was only a bad dream. The majority of people utilize denial as a temporary retreat while they better prepare themselves for engagement with the facts and consequences of their illness. Some pastoral counselors experience difficulty in dealing with persons who deny the reality of their situation. It is important, however, to underscore the appropriateness, normality, and, for a number of people, the necessity of denial. But some pastors become confederates in denial. For example, when one is diagnosed with AIDS, a pastor, in the attempt to express positive support and to help maintain hope, may pretend that the person is not so sick, or may collude in the denial by other family members. In far too many situations, pastors speak constantly in euphemisms instead of the plain terms of death, or offer absolute assurances of physical healing if one only has enough "right" faith.

Emotional instability. At times the mourner seems to have mounted an emotional roller coaster. Pain is expressed through tears and wailing, anger and rage in violent outbursts of words or actions. One may laugh too loudly or chatter on and on. Repetitive activities such as making cups of tea over and over are attempts to regain external control, since the mourner's normal inner control seems to have disintegrated into chaos.

Psychosomatic symptoms. The word *psychosomatic* is not a medical put-down, nor is it meant to imply that one is simply imagining this illness. A psychosomatic symptom is simply a physical problem brought on by an emotional reaction, and is as real as any other physical symptom (Hewett, 38; and see the excellent study by Broom). Grief disturbs not only our thinking and feeling, but all our bodily rhythms are upset to some degree. Natural patterns of sleeping, eating, going to the toilet, menstruation, breathing, and heartbeat may be disturbed. The mourner is likely to be more susceptible to colds and other diseases. Those deep in grief may even take on "twin" symptoms that resemble the disease that killed their loved one.

Depression and panic. Affective expressions are a normal part of the bereavement process, and depression and panic are common responses to loss. They may be exaggerated by extenuating circumstances. For example, Attig's study of mourners found that those with high depression scores had significantly lower incomes and larger numbers of dependent children (39). Furthermore, he found that more women than men remained depressed after a year, though by the two-year anniversary there was no significant gender difference. Along with panic comes anxiety. In his study of children and grief, William Worden found two types of common anxiety: the fear of losing yet another loved one, particularly a surviving parent, and the child's fear that he or she too will die. Anxiety in children seemed to increase over time rather than decrease; the same could be surmised of widowed adults who over time face an increasingly uncertain future.

Kübler-Ross pointed out that many people in the midst of panic attempt to bargain with God. Terry Creagh points out how childish such bargaining may sound: "God, I promise to be good and to stop swearing if only you'll bring me out of this"

(30). He goes on to point out that caregivers should not take such vows too literally or too seriously but understand them as one manifestation of the fight for life and health.

Along with depression, panic, and bargaining may come the loss of self-esteem in those facing their own death or the loss of their independence. There are many things that affect self-esteem. A person's perceived inabilities to supply for his or her own basic physical and psychological needs can weaken self-esteem. In a culture in which a person's worth is defined as a function of what he or she is able to do, disability related to disease can have profound effects on self-esteem. Walter Smith observes that the loss of self-esteem is particularly acute in those facing a long slow death from AIDS (1993, 695).

Guilt. Both the dying and the mourning may feel guilty as a part of the grief. Bonnie Miller-McLemore analyzes the "struggle that many ill people face as they search for a reasonable cause for their fate and wonder what they have done to bring it upon themselves" (186). For centuries, some in the church argued that sickness and death were the consequence of sin. Freud's theory of the death instinct seems to support this idea that we bring our own destruction upon ourselves: we each die of our own "internal conflicts," the self-destructive death instinct killing us when our libido has been used up or fixated. In neither case is death seen as normal and natural, the logical outcome of the immutable laws of nature that are part of God's creation. Yet we continue to search for natural, external causes. In a death-denying culture we also hypothesize that illness might arise from problems such as character deficiencies, neurotic or aberrant behavior or misguided lifestyles, or from unjust, oppressive social systems that breed poverty, ignorance, and brutality or that fail to be fair in distributing scientific cures. We may no longer believe the religious tenet that because we sin we die. But we have replaced this idea with more insidiously punitive moralisms. Patients blame themselves for behaving or even thinking the wrong way. In a culture of punitive moralisms, how else can we explain why nonsmokers die of lung cancer? So guilt may rest heavily upon those grieving their own death, for they comprehend death as a sign of personal failure.

Mourners also may be wracked with guilt. Judith Viorst explains:

> The ambivalence that is present in even our deepest love relationships tainted our love for the dead while they were alive. We saw them as less than perfect and we loved them less than perfectly; we may even have fleetingly wished that they would die. But now that they are dead we are ashamed of our negative feelings and we start berating ourselves for being so bad. (241)

Perhaps we now seek forgiveness but have trouble feeling forgiven because the dead cannot speak to us. Children in Worden's study were particularly vulnerable to assuming that they somehow caused their parent's death, perhaps by not being good enough or not having taken on enough responsibility for the sick parent's care (61). Hewett highlights the heavy burden of guilt borne by spouses of suicides. Here the entire marriage is held up for public examination. The survivor imagines that others see the suicide as proof that she or he was a failure as a spouse (39–40).

Anger. Walter Smith points out that in its Scandinavian and Icelandic origins, the word *anger* means "grief" and "sorrow" (1993, 692). Thus we should not be surprised when mourners are angry. A pastoral counselor needs to find appropriate ways to respond to projections of anger no matter where they may be directed. Those who are dying may be angry with the disease or with those who gave it to them; with their attending health care professionals; with the medical profession in general; or with government agencies who regulate the availability of experimental medicines. They may direct their anger toward God, the church, or their pastoral caregivers. Those mourning the death of a loved one may be even more angry. According to Viorst, a great deal of the anger that we focus on those around us is the anger we feel, but won't let ourselves recognize, toward the dead (240). Sometimes, however, we do express it directly. "God damn you! God damn you for dying on me!" a widow recalls having said to her dead husband's photograph. "Like her, we love the dead, we miss and need and pine for our dead, but we also are angry at them for having abandoned us." Many students of grief work believe that once a mourner's anger has been worked through, he or she has begun the long slow climb back to recovery.

Idealization. "My wife was a saint," "My father was wiser than Solomon" allow us to keep our thoughts pure and to keep guilt at bay. It is also a way of repaying the dead, of making restitution, for all of the bad we have done—or imagined we've done—to them (Viorst, 242). Idealization is very natural, for we are all socially conditioned to speak well of the dead, though some cultures, such as the Maori of New Zealand, dictate that funeral speeches include both praise and a very frank recital of the deceased's faults. But idealization taken too far becomes "mummification" (Viorst, 250), the keeping of every object that the dead one once possessed exactly where and how he or she had kept them. Queen Victoria, for instance, when her beloved Prince Albert died, had his shaving equipment and clothes laid out every day, and all of his possessions remained the way he had arranged them in his lifetime. Rev. Patrick Brontë, father of Emily and Charlotte, treated his dead wife's possessions in the same way. Idealization should ring alarm bells for the pastoral caregiver, for no human being is without fault. Mummification is pathological and needs treatment by a specialist.

Decathexis is a technical word for the process by which one renounces old loves and old belongings in preparation for that which lies ahead and beyond. The dying decathect, as do mourners in the recovery process. Terry Creagh tells the story of his dying father's decathexis and how easily it was misunderstood:

> Too many relatives are unnecessarily hurt at this phase, feeling that their loved one has turned against them at last, rejecting them. During his final days, my father withdrew increasingly from some of his strongest interests in this world, which included his family. We were no longer *essential* to him, he was no longer *dependent* upon us; in a quite wonderful way he was looking ahead to the goal which lay before him, and the separating process was in motion; he let go of the old loyalties to assume his new responsibilities in the broader scheme of God's order.
>
> Far from rejecting us, he was witnessing to us. (31)

But those whose grief is beginning to heal also find themselves decathecting. In order to be able to begin to separate from the enmeshment of a loving relationship, the mourner needs to find a "place" where he or she can image the deceased as being safe. Worden calls this "constructing" or "locating" the deceased (27). For example, in his study of grieving children, he found that most of the children in the study (74 percent), regardless of religious orientation, were able to locate the deceased, often "in heaven," though adolescent girls were the most skeptical about identifying a specific place. The "constructing" of an absent loved one in a location where the mourner felt he or she had access to the deceased proved an important step in the continued relearning of the world. This constructing bears a strong resemblance to Object Relations Theory and will be discussed again later in this chapter.

Acceptance. Attig describes the process by which a mourner continues to separate from a beloved deceased by using the metaphor of ballroom dancing:

> Death does not end our caring or our loving but is compatible with our continuing and transforming our care and our love. As we grieve we struggle to learn the next figures of the dance and to find a meaningful way to continue caring about, and loving, the absent person even as our lives are transformed by our losses. As we grieve, we learn to love in separation. (170)

In an important sense, no one ever fully "recovers" from the death of a loved one. The deceased remains present with most mourners for years and years to come. "Acceptance" means learning to proceed with life by incorporating the absence of the deceased into one's daily life.

Normalization. The mourner resumes his or her daily life and begins again to relearn the world by exploring options, making choices, taking risks, and assuming new roles. Some cultures and religions prescribe an acceptable length of time by which normalization should be achieved. For example, Jewish tradition separates out six graduated periods of mourning over the course of one year, during which the mourner can gradually express feelings of grief. The periods are very structured and allow for expression of grief at times when it is most keenly felt (Levine, 112). These phases should not, however, be interpreted as marking a "right" way to grieve, for Jewish tradition recognizes that each person will grieve in his or her own way and time. Tongan culture dictates that mourners who have lost a parent wear black for a full year, and in Greek culture widows usually wear black for the rest of their lives. In Anglo-American cultures, the length of time it takes a mourner to move from shock to normalization should not be dictated, for each unique individual moves through grief work at his or her own pace, though the lack of bereavement support in those cultures means that mourners may feel great pressure to resume normal life too quickly. Charles Meyer raises the often ignored issue of the resumption of sexual activity. He writes:

> Feelings of intimacy do not die with the spouse or lover's death, though some temporary abatement will occur. Survivors will continue to be sexually active or intimate in some manner. Initially, and often permanently, this behavior will occur outside of marriage. (Often there are quite reasonable legal, insurance, property, medical, or emotional reasons for this.) The worst that may be said, morally, about this is that it is unfortunate. While marriage may be the desired goal, it is grossly unre-

alistic to demand it as a requirement for survivors. To do so is to be rigidly legalistic, unforgiving, and unmercifully critical. (89)

At the very least, those who are widowed often complain about the fact that no one touches them in an intimate way any longer. Discussion of such issues should not remain outside the purview of pastoral care. If we approach grieving Christians wholistically, we will not wish to ignore mourners' physical needs any more than we would ignore their spiritual needs.

Good Grief and Bad Grief

"Bereavement is Choiceless, but Grieving is Not," writes Thomas Attig (19). Although bereavement may be experienced as a "choiceless" event, those who mourn have many choices in how they grieve. Tasks and challenges may be attacked vigorously and time and energy invested in grief work. The mourner can also choose to take momentary or even frequent respite from rigors of the process. Silverman and Cinnamon tell a parable about the creation of new beauty from a distressing loss:

> A king once owned a large, beautiful, pure diamond of which he was justly proud, for it had no equal anywhere. One day, the diamond accidentally sustained a deep scratch. The king called in the most skilled diamond cutters and offered them a great reward if they would remove the imperfection from his treasured jewel. But none could repair the blemish. The king was sorely distressed.
>
> After a time a gifted lapidary came to the king and promised to make the rare diamond even more beautiful than it had been before. The king was impressed by his confidence and entrusted his precious stone to the lapidary's care. And the man kept his word.

With superb artistry he engraved a lovely rosebud around the imperfection. He had used the scratch to make the stem of a flower. (xii–xiii)

The shape of mourning is determined in large part by the act of one's will. "It is not what happens to us, but how we respond that ultimately matters and shapes who we are from inside out" (Bolen, 34). While bereavement is a choice that few would make, those who mourn can still choose their own responses to their emotional processes, to the holes left in their lives, to the tasks that lie ahead, to the other survivors who surround them, to the deceased, and even to God. Grieving as coping requires that mourners find the healthy balance between self-indulgence and active response.

To talk of "good" grief implies that there is bad grief, an unhealthy way of grieving that blocks the growth of personality and stagnates our life. Granger Westberg reminds us that "religious faith—at least the Jewish-Christian faith—has never said that a truly religious person does not grieve" (2). What both Judaism and Christianity emphasize is a redemptive way of dying and a constructive way of mourning. Not everyone can easily achieve redemptive dying and constructive mourning, however. Some people get stuck in their grief work in a way that leaves them permanently crippled.

Some discover that remaining in grief brings them "secondary rewards" (Attig, 39). Family, friends, and associates see their protracted longing, yearning, and searching, and these outward signs of grief bring at least attention and often sympathy, understanding, patience, and efforts to comfort and support that the bereaved unfortunately find gratifying. Others get stuck out of fear

of relearning the world in their own new ways. They fear that if they stop longing for those they have lost, they will stop loving them; if they stop living the way they had been living before their bereavement, they will have betrayed the deceased. As Meyer points out, "Just because the lover died doesn't mean that his or her wishes are always and forever to be followed for the rest of the survivor's life, especially since the survivor probably did not always do what the person wanted when the lover was alive" (100). All of these responses can be interpreted as pathological.

As important as it is to give mourners the time and permission to grieve each in his or her own way, it is not the case that *anything* is normal during this time. Miller and Jackson list some of the signs of abnormal and worrisome responses to grief: suicidal thoughts, ideas, or actions; continued weight loss, slowed movement, or pervasive guilt after one year; frequent crying, depression, sleeping problems, and unusual fatigue after two years (192–93). What is considered a grief pathology differs widely from culture to culture. No matter the culture, however, recent research indicates that about 14 percent of the bereaved population develops intense and enduring pathological grief responses (Crenshaw, 27). Even without such overt symptoms as just listed, the effects of bereavement can be quite long-term. Crenshaw reminds us that it is relatively common for couples to get a divorce within a year after the death of a child (26). Unable to deal with their grief, they displace their rage onto each other. Unexpressed resentments prior to the loss loom as significant divisive issues. A major goal of grief counseling is to prevent subsequent psychopathology by helping the

bereaved to mourn their loss fully. Crenshaw continues:

> In my practice, whenever adult patients
> share a plan to leave their spouse, to
> change jobs, to relocate, or to make any
> other major change in their lives, I always
> review with them any significant losses
> they have experienced over the past three
> years. Very often they will then describe
> the death of a parent, a close friend, a sib-
> ling, or perhaps a child for whom they
> were unable to mourn fully. I ask them to
> delay plans for major changes in their lives
> until they have completed the grief work.

Murray Bowen calls this the "emotional
shock wave" and observes that it occurs
most often after the death of a significant
family member such as the head of the
household (325). This idea will be explored
further in the following section on mourning and systems theory.

Some Dos and Don'ts of Caring for Mourners

The vulnerability that mourners exhibit
will tempt some pastors to be overly proac-
tive in their pastoral care, though ironically,
as mentioned before, the traditional understanding of phases of grief may encourage
others to be too passive. Terry Creagh
addresses the problem of activism:

> It is not so much a question of what we
> can do (activism) as who we are (the
> courage to be), and it is the lending of this
> kind of support that makes the difference
> for another between coping and not cop-
> ing. Just our presence introduces a needed
> structure and order at that precise
> moment when the afflicted person feels
> that his or her world is disintegrating. (62)

But "being" demands that pastors have
taken seriously the problem of ministry

congruency. "No issue is more ripe for
countertransference than that of death and
dying" (Crenshaw, 30). Hence, Creagh goes
on to remind us:

> A careless doctor can poison a patient by
> writing an incorrect formula; the "doctor
> of the soul," who is neither in tune with
> himself nor well versed in his resources,
> may just as easily contaminate a parish-
> ioner. It is rationalization, and wrong, to
> take the position that "Jesus is everything
> and I am nothing, so it doesn't matter to
> know myself." God seldom, if ever, oper-
> ates in spite of us; it is with us and *through*
> us that [God] acts upon the created order.
> (64)

Because issues of death are so ripe for
countertransference, it is imperative that
pastoral caregivers address their own attitudes about death—of others and of themselves. Meyer illustrates how easily we
project our own fears of death and mourning onto others:

> During a class on "Death and Dying"
> [Larry Bugen] had arranged to have as a
> guest speaker a woman who was termi-
> nally ill. Before she came into the room,
> he pre-tested the class, asking the students
> a list of questions that would indicate
> their comfort level with their own deaths.
> The woman then joined the class, spoke
> of her illness and impending death, and
> her feelings about dying. After she left, Dr.
> Bugen post-tested the class, asking ques-
> tions that would elicit how well the stu-
> dents thought the woman was coping
> with her situation.
>
> Not surprisingly, after comparing the
> two sets of responses, Dr. Bugen found
> that the students who saw themselves as
> having a very difficult time talking or
> thinking about their own deaths saw the
> woman as coping very poorly with her

death. The students who reported a level of relative comfort in discussing or planning for their own deaths thought the woman was handling her death quite appropriately and with courage. (23)

If caregivers have not addressed their own fears, anxieties, and insecurities about death, they will be ill equipped to judge correctly whether others are dealing with mourning in a healthy manner. As well, Walter Smith reminds us that the caregiver's attitudes about certain diseases need to be analyzed. Addressing the pastoral care of people with AIDS, Smith writes, "It is difficult to be effective in a helping relationship if one has strong negative feelings and judgments toward the individual seeking help. To attempt to provide care without attending to and resolving personal issues related to the individual is irresponsible" (1993, 689).

Caregiving for the dying and the mourning begins with three basic questions: Who are you? What has happened to you? What do you need? The establishment of an accepting and understanding relationship makes it possible for a pastor to begin assessing the person's inner resources (Smith, 1993, 696). From then on the minister must find that proper balance of "being" and "doing." Traditional Jewish mourning customs understand that both are important. For example, the laws and traditions surrounding behavior in a house of mourning are designed to allow the mourner to express his or her grief. When one visits a house of mourning, traditionally no greeting is given. Visitors wait for the mourner to speak and do not engage in idle chatter (Levine, 116). Meyer reminds us that pastoral "chatter" disempowers both the dying and the mourning (9). Some dying people will talk about their illness and some

won't; some mourners wish to talk a great deal and some only a little. Whatever the case, caregivers should listen to the other's agenda and follow it wherever it may lead, "from weather to whether or not they'll survive, from sports to life supports, from daily news to the latest news of their test results."

Judaism also defines "the visiting of the sick" in a highly practical way. The twelfth-century philosopher Maimonides points out that visitors should do everything possible to support those in need. Thus a visit to the sick might include sweeping the floor if it is dirty or preparing a meal. The rabbis also realized the reality and inevitability of death, however. Thus one should not only visit the ill, one should do whatever one can to aid the dying person's peace of mind. This may involve assisting in the preparation of a will, making funeral arrangements, disposition of property, and so forth (Levine, 102). All of these tasks provide pastoral opportunity, as long as they are undertaken in a manner that respects the dignity and individuality of those who are grieving.

The dying and the mourning have multiple needs, which good pastoral care treats holistically. The Wholeness Wheel helps us bear in mind that pastors need to be attentive to mourners' physical, psychological, intellectual, and social needs as well as their spiritual needs. This is true not only for those grieving a death, but also for those grieving their own aging, the loss of employment, an "empty nest," a geographical move, or the whole host of life's losses.

The pastoral care of mourners, conducted in humility and respect, can be greatly rewarding for caregivers. Sharing the grief of survivors makes the minister more sensitive, more responsive, more loving. But it has its pitfalls as well, which the caregiver must be careful to avoid. William Sloane Coffin wrote of the reactions he encountered from some fellow ministers during his last months of grief over the drowning death of his teenage son. Many offered "comforting words of Scripture" to suggest he find God's will or some blessing in the midst of tragedy. But "the reality of grief is the absence of God," he noted, and we must guard against words offered "for self-protection, to pretty up a situation whose bleakness [we] simply [cannot] face." As a bereaved person expresses his or her feelings some pastors become defensive, judgmental, and rejecting. These inappropriate and negative responses become additional burdens for a bereaved person. Because the individual is emotionally vulnerable, perceived attack and rejection by a pastor is experienced as a significant wound. In some cases, perceived rejection by a pastor may inhibit a bereaved individual's normal process of grieving (Sunderland, 71). At the least, respect requires that caregivers avoid exacerbating the vulnerability of those who grieve or interfering with them as they cope in their own individual ways. Even within the demands of a busy schedule of ministry, the pastoral caregiver must find ways to create a safe holding environment for those who mourn.

A safe holding environment often simply means the presence and attention of pastoral supporters. Not everyone who mourns needs a course of grief counseling, for the majority of those bereaved handle their grief adequately in their own way and time. Grief is not a psychiatric illness, though on occasion it may trigger other pathological systems as a result of preexistent personality disorders. Except in cases of

unexpected post-bereavement complications, there is presently no evidence that the majority of the bereaved adults need any extended counseling (Parkes, "Help," 213–14), nor do the majority of bereaved children (Worden, 139). They usually do, however, all need some direct pastoral attention, and virtually everyone needs interpersonal support and care in their grief. In many ways, the community of friends, neighbors, and church companions can provide support and care as good as, if not better than, many highly trained but overworked ordained clergy.

Creagh remarks on the poor job that churches do in preparing people *in advance* for bereavement: "Aside from funerals themselves, I cannot recall ever having heard a sermon preached, in the ordinary course of the church year, on grieving. The church must take seriously her preventive function, equipping people in advance so that they will cope better when crises come" (71). Much of the pastoral literature, including the work of William Amos (1988) and Ronald Sunderland (1993), recommends the development of congregationally based ministries to the bereaved, and then explains their implementation. Such active lay ministries are designed to serve the needs not only within the Christian community itself, but also to the dying, such as the destitute and persons with AIDS, whose needs otherwise go largely ignored. In this way, every congregation can share, much as do Mother Teresa's Missionaries of Charity, in the care of Christ's own beloved: the hungry, the thirsty, the stranger, the naked, the sick, and the imprisoned (Matt. 25:31-47).

Some supportive "secular" ministries to the bereaved already exist and in many cases can pick up some of the long-term work of supporting those who grieve. The largest organization in England is Cruse: Bereaved Care. Important work is done in the United States by Compassionate Friends and Parents Without Partners, to name just a few. In all of these the essential qualification for giving help to a bereaved person is the experience of personal bereavement oneself. No other training is thought necessary and no attempt is made to select counselors or to make a distinction between counselor and careseeker. All who come to the organization for help are expected to give as well as to receive. Thus these organizations are self-sustaining and make little or no use of professionals (Parkes, "Help," 213–14). Pastoral ministers should take care in referring people to these organizations, in that they are not set up to deal with cases of pathological grief or mental illness.

Mourning and Object Relations Theory

Object Relations Theory, as discussed in a previous chapter, provides significant insight into why and how people mourn. A subset of Object Relations Theory is called Attachment Theory and was pioneered by psychologist John Bowlby. According to his theories, human beings are innately programmed to seek and form attachments or enduring affectional bonds with others (1988). These behavioral and feeling tendencies are found in all social animals, some reptiles, most fish, and many insects. The urge to attachment, which is necessary to survival, develops in human babies and their parents during the first year of life in order to keep children safe in the world until they become capable of surviving without parental support. Infants attach to parents and parents to infants. But

we do not all attach in an equally healthy manner.

Bowlby identified four different attachment patterns, initially determined by how responsive the mother was to the infant seeking to attach. Bowlby categorized the types of attachment that are built between a mother and an infant as secure, ambivalent, avoidant, or disorganized. Alternatively, the work of Ainsworth, Blehar, Waters, and Wall identified three principal patterns of attachment: secure attachment (the mother is accessible and responsive to the infant as it seeks to attach), anxious/ambivalent or preoccupied (the mother is inconsistently responsive or helpful), and avoidant (the mother consistently rejects the infant's efforts to solicit caring and support) (Lopez, 12). Our specific attachment patterns are woven into those self-objects from which we form our sense of identity, and thus the relationship patterns are then repeated in all subsequent important emotional alliances, though they are also subject to modification. Attachment patterns can create positive as well as negative ties.

Initiating the attachment patterns, and then included within them as a modus operandi, is one's "seeking to attach." A child whose mother leaves will deny it and then begin to seek her. Depending on the child's developmental stage, its attachment patterns (even those with avoidant attachment will seek out the object they wish to avoid), and the achieved level of object constancy, children who are left become increasingly anxious the longer the mother is absent. Ultimately, this is overcome developmentally through object constancy, by establishing a "permanent mother within," who thus *feels* present even when she is absent. In the course of childhood, attachments are made to a wider and wider range of other people and, during adolescence and early adult life, the strong attachment to parents usually diminishes and a new strong attachment is made to a person who is not related by blood and is most often of the opposite sex. This attachment provides both partners with the mutual support they need in order to rear children of their own. Attachments need to be powerful if they are to keep us and our children safe.

The urge to seek for and to find those from whom we have become separated transcends most other drives and is felt as the most passionate of emotions, separation distress or pining. Loss by death, like other losses, evokes intense pining for the lost person and an urge to stop all other activities in order to find them (Laungani, "Conclusions I," 238–39). The death of a loved one revives childhood fears of abandonment, the ancient anguish of being little and left. Bowlby himself noted this phenomenon: "On the one hand is belief that death has occurred with the pain and hopeless yearning that that entails. On the other is disbelief that it has occurred, accompanied both by hope that all may yet be well and by an urge to search for and to recover the lost person" (Viorst, 242).

In his novel *Tangi* (a "weeping" or funeral), Witi Ihimaera portrays a young protagonist whose father's death revives memories of his having been left behind once as a small child:

> E pa, if I could I would grasp those ticking hands and force them back through all those yesterdays gone, just to be with you again. We had such good times together. It was good to feel your hand in mind.
>
> Do you remember, e pa, that time when you took me into town one crowded night so many years ago? I was only a little boy then, about five, I suppose.
>
> You wait here, you said. Then you disappeared with the crowd and left me waiting for you on the pavement.
>
> E pa, I waited and waited. But you didn't come back. Where did you go? I tried not to cry because you'd said that only babies cry.
>
> Are you lost, little boy? a lady asked me.
>
> No, I told her. My Daddy, he's just gone away for a while. He's coming back to get me, though. He told me to wait here.
>
> So the lady left me. I wanted to shout: Come back! But she was gone.
>
> I waited and waited, e pa. I was frightened. All those people, they jostled and pushed against me. They couldn't see me; I was so small. I felt as if I was in a land full of giants.
>
> In the end I cried, Dad. I couldn't help it. And some of the passers-by, they asked me if I was lost, just like that lady asked. But I pushed them away and decided I would find you.
>
> I wandered along the streets and everybody was laughing and having a good time. Where were you, Dad? . . .
>
> Then I saw you. You were looking for me just as I was looking for you. And I shouted:
>
> Dad! Dad!
>
> And you lifted me up and hugged me.
>
> Turi turi [hush, hush], Son. I'm here.
>
> I hit you hard.
>
> Don't leave me again, Dad. Don't you leave me again.
>
> You promised you wouldn't. (12–13)

And yet his father has left him now, in spite of that promise. The dialogue illustrates an irony typical to mourning: of both denial and acceptance, of seeking childishly for the lost yet realizing in an adult manner that the father is dead. In mourning we may seek our parents again, or we may seek the lover to whom we were attached.

The movement from shock to grief recovery involves the establishment of an "object constancy" relationship with the deceased. The mourner must internalize the one lost to death by now making the deceased a part of the mourner's *inner* world. In this sense the deceased achieves immortality, by living on in the memory of those who survive. As mentioned earlier, Worden calls this "constructing" or "locating" the deceased, so that the mourner's relationship can continue yet life can go on (27). But the road from shock to object constancy is a long and rocky one, and along the way many people need the assistance of transitional objects and transitional phenomena.

Something that belonged to the deceased may become a transitional object, suddenly taking on exaggerated importance. Worden's study of children and death revealed that nearly 80 percent of all children attach to something that their deceased parent had owned (30–31). For a widow or widower, the transitional object may be a wedding band or some other cherished symbol of the relationship.

An issue that may cause puzzlement to pastoral caregivers is transitional phenomena. Judith Viorst writes of the "seeking" that goes on after death:

> Searching for the dead we sometimes even summon them up: we "hear" their step in the driveway, their key in the lock. We "see" them on the street and eagerly follow them for a block; they turn and we confront . . . a stranger's face. Some of us may bring our dead back to life with hallucinations. Many of us bring our dead back to life in our dreams. (243)

Such phenomena are not uncommon, nor, within reason, unhealthy. The bereaved may "speak" to the deceased or may feel watched by them. Worden reports that such experiences can be quite disturbing for children, who sometimes decide they are "haunted" (28–29). A pastoral caregiver should attempt to normalize such experiences by reassuring children that they are signs of deep love and attachment.

During periods of stress, we tend to revert to the most childish of our attachment patterns. Certainly, little is more stressful than loss and grief. Sometimes the depth of attachment and its patterns are not clear until a loved one dies. Howe suggests that in certain cases the intensity of grief reactions may signal that a marriage was based on some form of dysfunctional attachment (145). For example, recent studies show that those with an "anxious" pattern tend to marry those with an "avoidant" attachment pattern, yielding a couple whose marriage is built on a "pursuer-distancer" dynamic and yet that is enmeshed in a most unhealthy manner (Lopez, 13). The death of one partner in such a marriage would yield more intense patterns of grieving (a pursuer without someone to pursue suffers major identity loss) than would partners who each attached "securely" and were thus able to exercise a relationship of comfortable interdependence.

Mourning and Family Systems Theory

Family Systems Theory provides a broader perspective on death than is possible with more traditional pastoral counseling theory, which focuses on death and mourning as processes within the individual. Knowledge of the total family configuration, the functioning position of the dying person in the family, and the overall level of life adaptation are important for anyone who attempts to help a family before, during, or after a death. To attempt to treat all deaths as the same can miss the mark. Some well-functioning families are able to adapt to approaching death before it occurs. To assume that such families need help can be an inept intrusion (Bowen, 328). On the other hand, some families do need pastoral intervention, so the caregiver needs a sophisticated understanding of what to watch for within the larger family system.

One of the most taboo subjects of discussion with family systems is death. To some degree this is cultural. American culture is notoriously death-denying. As further example, Tongan culture presumes that divulging a prognosis to someone dying will actually cause the patient to die; the family's task is to sit by the deathbed and promise the patient that he or she will recover very soon. But more problematic are individual family systems of communication. Murray Bowen divides family communication styles into "open" relationship systems and "closed" relationship systems:

> An "open" relationship system is one in which an individual is free to communicate a high percentage of inner thoughts, feelings, and fantasies to another who can reciprocate. No one ever has a completely open relationship with another, but it is a healthy state when a person can have one relationship in which a reasonable degree of openness is possible. . . . The most open relationship that most people have in their adults lives is in a courtship. After marriage, in the emotional interdependence of living together, each spouse becomes sensitive to subjects that upset the other. They instinctively avoid the sensitive sub-

> jects and the relationship shifts toward a more "closed" system. The closed communication system is an automatic emotional reflex to protect self from the anxiety in the other person, though most people say they avoid the taboo subjects to keep from upsetting the other person. (322)

Not only do families have open or closed communication styles; caregivers, nurses, and physicians also have styles that either encourage discussion of death in a healthy manner or discourage it dysfunctionally. If an individual is closed, a family is closed, and if the physician is so anxious about the issue of death that he or she cannot communicate effectively with the patient and the family, the patient will probably die isolated and locked into thoughts that cannot be communicated to others, and the long-term effect on the family system will be greatly exacerbated.

Families exist to give support to their members at times of danger and loss. Most of the time they will do this without much help from outsiders, but there are many situations when the family fails in its supportive function. It follows that an important task for the pastoral caregiver is to discover what familial and other supports exist for the bereaved family and its members. A crucial buffering and protective element in facing any stressful life event is a close, stable, and confiding relationship with at least one other person. Silverman and Cinnamon present a short parable and its moral:

> A small boy struggled to lift a heavy stone, but he could not budge it. The boy's father stopped to watch his efforts and said to his son, "Are you using all your strength?" "Yes, I am," the boy said with irritation. "No," the father said calmly,

"You're not. You have not asked me to help you."

You cannot do it all yourself. You need the help of your friends and dear ones. (6–7)

Just when the family is most needed it may become dysfunctional. It is at such times that the intervention of a pastoral caregiver or someone else from outside the family is most needed.

The length of time required for the family to establish a new emotional equilibrium depends on the emotional integration in the family and the intensity of the disturbance. A well-integrated family may show more overt reactiveness at the moment of change but adapt to it rather quickly. A less integrated family may show little reaction at the time and respond later with symptoms of physical illness, emotional illness, or social misbehavior. Bowen calls this delayed response "the emotional shock wave," describing it as a network of underground "aftershocks" that can occur anywhere in the extended family system in the months or years following serious emotional events in a family.

> It occurs most often after the death or the threatened death of a significant family member, but it can occur following losses of other types. It is not directly related to the usual grief or mourning reactions of people close to the one who died. It operates on an underground network of emotional dependence of family members on each other. The emotional dependence is denied, the serious life events appear to be unrelated, the family attempts to camouflage any connectedness between the events, and there is a vigorous emotional denial reaction, when anyone attempts to relate the events to each other. It occurs most often in families with a significant

degree of denied emotional "fusion" in which the families have been able to maintain a fair degree of asymptomatic emotional balance in the family system. (325–26)

The shock wave occurs most often after the death of what Bowen calls "head of the clan" (328), a power identification that may describe any significant family member, from elder statesperson to most powerful sibling to the favored grandchild and heir. The same shock response can be almost as severe after a threatened death or an unsuccessful suicide attempt.

Bowen continues:

> Symptoms can include the entire spectrum of physical illness from an increased incidence of colds and respiratory infections to the first appearance of chronic conditions, such as diabetes or allergies to acute medical and surgical illnesses. It is as if the shock wave is the stimulus that can trigger the physical process into activity. The symptoms can also include the full range of emotional symptoms from mild depression, to phobias, to psychotic episodes. The social dysfunctions can include drinking, failures in school or business, abortions and illegitimate births, an increase in accidents, and the full range of behavior disorders. (326)

These symptoms can appear anywhere in the identifiable family system. In systems thought, the family may develop a "designated mourner," much like an "identified patient," the one subconsciously chosen by the group to act out the grief of all the rest. Terry Creagh likens this to the British game of "pass the parcel" (69); Americans would be reminded of the game "hot potato," in which one does everything possible to avoid holding the unwanted object (or, in this case, emotion).

Just as all family systems have their games, so families in mourning may have their games as well. John Hewett lists the ten most common games played in a family after one member has committed suicide (53–59). Many of these same games are played in other mourning families too.

1. *Scapegoating.* Family members expend enormous amounts of time and energy deciding who should bear the blame for the suicide. In this game, finger-pointing is the favorite activity and "she drove him to it" is the motto.

2. *Keeping an Impossible Secret.* The stigma that suicide causes is more than some families can bear. They would rather actively attempt to cover up the fact of suicide, or adopt an attitude of "we know but we're not telling." Families get a lot of help in this camouflage from sympathetic doctors, reporters, coroners, and police.

3. *The Survival Myth.* This game is similar to Keeping an Impossible Secret, with one difference: in this game, family members themselves refuse to accept the fact of death by suicide. Even in the face of solid evidence, they choose to keep alive the possibility of accidental death or murder.

4. *Circle the Wagons.* Like the pioneer caravan in hostile territory, the family draws together in a defensive pattern. It becomes "us against them." The group feels threatened by rejection and stigmatizing by others. They develop a "family resistance system" that acts as a barrier against communication with those outside the family.

5. *King (or Queen) of the Mountain.* When a parent completes suicide, especially the father or a single parent, this game is likely to go into effect. In this pattern, family members jostle for leadership and power. As the new family leader emerges from this free-for-all, the anger begins to surface from the losers.

6. *The Silent Treatment.* This family game is sometimes called the "conspiracy of silence." It is a kind of "cold war" where most communication is cut off. Family members don't talk to each other. They don't touch. Each grieves alone, behind closed doors. They avoid each other's gaze, raising their eyes or staring down at the ground in passing.

7. *Who Loved/Was Loved the Most?* Some family members will fight each other for the coveted title of "Most Loved by the Deceased." This game has a flip side, played when the deceased was the source of much trouble in the family. This side, called "Who Was Treated the Worst?" is designed to gain sympathy from other family members.

8. *Let's Grieve Forever.* This game involves a perpetual state of mourning. Hewett calls it the "black armband" reaction. Family members wear their grief as a badge for all to see, and they do it without end. All this is seen as the only loving way to grieve over the deceased; anything less would be evidence of selfishness and lack of devotion.

9. *Halo and Pitchfork.* The halo placed over the suicide's life is the result of what psychiatrists call *idealization*. The pitchfork game works the same way, but with opposite intentions. Here the members come not to praise the deceased, but to bury him or her with insults and recriminations.

10. *Head for the Hills.* Running away is the point of this game. Here families pack up and move away from the "suicide house," usually within a year after the death. Myths 2, 3, 4, 6, and 9 would also be applicable in some families who have lost a close member to AIDS, given the unfortunate social stigma that still attaches to it.

Two other aspects of family systems need extra sensitivity by the pastoral caregiver: children and "invisible" mourners.

William Worden's extensive research with grieving children reveals how often they are neglected, not only by caregivers but by their own grieving parents. The loss of any significant person within a family system can unbalance everyone in the system, children included. Family members need to confront the death together so that the family as a whole can recover some sort of homeostatic equilibrium after the loss. Worden argues that mourning children need three things to help them cope with the disruption caused by death: emotional and behavioral support, intellectual and affectional nurturance, and a clear sense that the family will continue, with a connection between the past and the future (36). He also identifies four factors that can derail the healthy resolution of a child's mourning for a parent who has died: the dysfunctional level in the surviving parent, the discrepancy with which the parent misperceives the child's emotional needs, the consistency of discipline and responsibility within the remaining family, and the dating and remarriage of the surviving parent (78).

As the definition and structures of "family" change, pastoral caregivers must be sensitive to the existence of "invisible mourners." Ronald Grimes tells in a most touching manner how when his young son died, his ex-wife scheduled the funeral and made the arrangements without consulting him, provided no seating for him at the funeral, and omitted his name from the newspaper obituary (109). Cueing off the ex-wife, "The minister's prejudices, along with the insensitivity of the funeral directors, so incensed me that grief had to vie with anger for breathing room." Attig lists the people whose grief may be insufficiently recognized, or even ignored in cruel fashion:

> Few if any recognize the grieving itself of the parents of adult children, very elderly persons, young children, or retarded, demented, or otherwise mentally compromised individuals. In some instances people dismiss the significance of our relationships with the deceased or discount the value of what is lost, as we lose homosexual partners, extramarital heterosexual partners, stillborns, miscarried or aborted fetuses, loved ones who are severely afflicted or handicapped, pets, prisoners, . . . coworkers, public figures, or people from our past, including former spouses, companions, and friends. (82)

Invisible mourners within the extended family system deserve pastoral care and support as well. To argue for their inclusion may necessitate some delicate negotiation with more visibly related family members, but to fail this opportunity would be pastorally irresponsible.

Mourning and Narrative Counseling Theory

Do the dead have a place in our narratives? Silverman and Cinnamon quote Shalom Levy: "With the death of a husband or wife you lose your present; with the death of a parent the past; and with the death of a child you lose your future" (13–14). In the same vein, Attig writes that when our loved ones die, "We lose the presence of central characters in the ongoing stories of our lives" (172). The pastoral caregiver can help those who mourn to compensate for their losses by keeping the dead alive among those who survive them through narrative.

In *Tangi*, novelist Witi Ihimaera relates how the simplest rhythms of the day keep the protagonist's father alive in his memory:

It took a long time for Mum and Dad to make enough money to buy the farm. There were the wandering years, and then the years in Gisborne to be lived through. The wandering years however will always seem a long time in my memory. Or perhaps it only seems to have been a long time because of the loneliness and hard work of those days. Dad would wake early each morning and somewhere in my drifting dreams I'd hear the soft stamping of his feet and the clink and rustle of strange sounds. I'd hear him and Mum whispering to each other and then the rustle of her dressing gown as she moved round getting him some kai. A match would flare, casting a sudden light in the morning darkness. Then the light would begin to flicker from a candle or lamp in the room. Dad would light the fire and Mum would hang a billy of water on one of the wire hooks above the burning wood. Smoke would billow into the room when the wind gusted down the sheet-iron chimney. Mum would cough. There'd be more soft sounds as Dad had his kai and then the soft scraping of his chair when he'd finished. Perhaps Wiki would cry from her cradle. Dad would whisper to her for a moment. Then soft he would kiss her, Mere, Ripeka, and me.
—Goodbye, Daddy, Ripeka would say sleepily.
—Goodbye, Daddy, I would say too. I'd feel the touch of his lips.
—Look after Mum, Tama.
—Okay Dad.

The door would creak. Mum would curl her arms round Dad's neck. For a moment there'd be silence. Then the door would shut and far away in my dreams I'd hear Kuri and Tim barking as Dad untied

them. When I awoke Dad would be gone. Throughout the day I would sometimes find myself looking out the window or across the hills, waiting for him to come back again. . . .
All my days I will look out for Dad. He will not come back again. He is dead. One day I will stop looking for him. Yet he still whispers to me, for this is another morning beginning.
—Look after Mum, Tama. (41–42)

In this text we hear a family narrative developing: the framing of childhood memories, their continued presence many years later, and the creation of a vivid picture worth passing along to the next generation. In the framing of narratives about the dead, we see that meanings, purposes, and the love we thought lost is found again.

Unless a mourner is stuck in idealization of the deceased, memories retained and retrieved will be a mix of happy, sad, and painful. Idealization, unfortunately, destroys the accuracy of all memories, for it makes the deceased into one-dimensional saints, devoid of flaw but also devoid of humanity. In Greek mythology, the river Lethe is one of the five rivers of Hades, the netherworld, and according to some sources is located on the edge of the Elysian Fields. Lethe in Greek means "forgetfulness" and gives us the English word *lethargy*. The story is told of a woman who approached the river to be ferried across to the region of departed spirits:

Charon the ferryman reminded her that it was her privilege to drink of the waters of Lethe and thus forget the life she was leaving. This seemed to be a wonderful idea and she said, "I will forget how I have suffered." Added Charon, "Yes, but you will also forget how you have rejoiced."
She said, "I will forget my failures." The old ferryman added, "And also your vic-

tories." She continued, "I will forget how I have been hated." Charon hastened to add, "And also how you have been loved."

When she considered the matter, she decided not to drink the Lethe potion, but to retain her memory, even of the bad, that she might never forget the good. She now knew that to forget the heartache of sorrow is to forget the heartthrobs of joy and love.

The happy and the painful must be remembered together, for both are necessary to tell the full story of any human life.

Memories will need to be shared again and again. Stories will need to be told and retold. As with any good story, but especially with the intricate stories of human biography, if we *hear* them but once, we fail to capture the richness and fullness of the tales. As we review and retell stories repeatedly, they return new and unexpected rewards each time. We can always reinterpret the stories, and as we do so, we can deepen our appreciation of the values and meanings they reveal. We cannot completely and definitively interpret stories in principle, since each retelling comes at a different point in our lives, and we bring changing background experiences, perspectives, interests, needs, and desires to the interpretive context. As with any good stories, but again especially with the stories of a loved one's life, we can return to the stories deliberately for specific purposes (to refresh our memory or understanding or to seek new understanding) or as events in our lives remind us of them and of their continuing importance to us (Attig, 179–80).

Everyone is part of some story or another. Attig reminds us, "Some stories are far shorter than others, but even the life of an infant, a newborn, a stillborn, or a miscar-

ried child is a life with a history that we can find meaningful and in which we have typically invested much hope" (179). Children need to be told and retold the stories of their deceased parent, or grandparent, or sibling. As adults we draw strength and inspiration from repeating these family narratives, or perhaps we learn to laugh for the first time at the flaws and foibles of our deceased loved ones. As we grow older, these same narratives become our link with the past and part of the heritage that we bequeath to the future by passing them down to the generations that follow.

Narratives are also part of the grief work process. Ira Nerken emphasizes the role that intersubjective narrative plays, as one self talks to another inside our heads:

> Grief is, in fact, an extended conversation—with others, but primarily with the self. If grief is not suppressed, the griever eventually persuades the part of the self that fears it must stay behind—out of love for the one now dead—that the loved one's meaning and purpose is best preserved, albeit in new form, only if it will let go. (1093)

Intersubjective narratives become a source of healing, in that they allow us to decathect and to reframe our attachments to the deceased, and thereby to "construct" them in a location that is accessible yet gives us the freedom to move ahead in life.

Personal narratives also have a role within mourning, particularly for those who are grieving their own aging, and for those who are preparing for their own death. Psychologist Robert Butler introduced the concept of "life-review," the use of reminiscence by older people in the service of ego integrity. Butler describes the process of "life-review":

As the past marches in review, it is surveyed, observed, and reflected upon by the ego. Reconsideration of previous experiences and their meanings occurs, often with concomitant revised or expanded understanding. Such reorganization of past experiences may provide a more valid picture, giving new and significant meanings to one's life. It may also prepare one for death. (Kimble, 139)

A life-review may be summarized and framed shortly before one dies. Such a deathbed testimonium often includes narratives that recapitulate family history, particularly reflecting myths, events, and relationships that have shaped the identity of family members. It is not unusual for stories to be told on the deathbed; most families understand important events in the life cycle—courtship, weddings, births, illnesses—as opportunities to review where the family has come from and how members interact with one another. In Judaism, when a deathbed testimonium, oral or written, is designed to direct the religious and secular behavior of surviving children, it is called an "ethical will" (Abrahams, xix). This is a tradition as old as Jacob's blessing of his sons in Genesis 49 (Culbertson). Ethical wills are statements of the individual's hopes and dreams for his or her family, the values that he or she would like to pass on, and any other thoughts or messages that the individual would like his or her family to remember. Ethical wills are usually warmly and lovingly written, and can be a great comfort to the family once the individual has died (Levine, 100). In this same sense we might understand the Gospel of John, chapters 14–17, as a "constructed ethical will" for Jesus' "children," the followers in the early church who would keep his memory and teachings alive.

Mourning and Human Development

The way we mourn is directly affected by our developmental stage in life. Toddlers mourn differently from adolescents; young children mourn differently from adults; the middle-aged mourn differently from the elderly. The way we mourn is always shaped by our unique ego functioning and our personal cognitive, emotional, and social development. The pastor and others who support the grieving need to be sensitive to these differences and to specific issues connected to certain stages of life.

Children. Pastoral caregivers need to set aside special moments of attention to grieving children within families. If a parish has developed a grief ministry, the team should include ministers who are gifted in dealing with children's questions and emotions.

There has been a lengthy and often contradictory debate among professionals as to when children acquire the capacity to grieve. On one side, people such as Wolfenstein believe that the capacity to mourn is not acquired until adolescence, when the person is fully differentiated. On the other side of the debate, Bowlby posits that infants as young as six months experience grief reactions resembling those seen in adults. A middle position, represented by R. Furman, places the capacity to mourn at around three and a half to four years of age. Worden's exhaustive study of grieving children begins with the age of six.

In that same study, Worden identifies what he believes to be the ten particular bereavement needs of grieving children (140–46):

1. *Adequate Information.* Children need information that is clear and comprehensible. A child's understanding of death depends on his or her ability to deal con-

ceptually with abstractions, such as finality and irreversibility; one who has not developed the cognitive abstractions of irreversibility and finality will have difficulty accepting the reality of the loss. Children who are too young, or who have been given insufficient information, will often make up a story to fill in the gaps.

If at all possible, children should be informed about an impending death. They know something is taking place, even if they are not told directly. A lack of information can make a child feel anxious and less important; and in a worst-case scenario, the child can feel responsible for what is happening to the dying person. It is also helpful for children to have clear information about the cause of death. Helping them know that "Daddy died of cancer" and that they cannot "catch" cancer can be reassuring for some, particularly younger children.

Children need to be told about death in ways that are accurate and in language that is age-appropriate. Meyer cautions not to use euphemisms such as "passed away" or "gone to take care of other little boys and girls in heaven" (115). These phrases, and others like them, can be very unsettling and even threatening to the child, who usually takes them literally. Instead, tell the truth about death. The sooner the child realizes death is a normal, natural part of our life together, the sooner he or she will begin to seek accurate, realistic information about it and come to terms with it.

2. *Fears and Anxieties Addressed.* Children need to know they will be cared for. The death of a parent, which is one of the most fundamental losses a child can face, often elicits a primitive anxiety that one will not survive without one's parents (this same fear can also be experienced by adults). Many children who lose one parent fear that the other will die too. In Worden's study there was a significant increase in this type of fear during the first year of bereavement. Not only do children fear for their one remaining parent, but they fear for their own safety as well. These fears need to be directly addressed by those attending to the needs of these children and the appropriate reassurances given.

For the great majority of children, parents remain their most significant others— in effect, their partners in negotiating the essential developmental tasks that will take them to adulthood (Worden, 9). Worden's study revealed that children who lost a parent of the same gender were more likely to remain affectively attached to that parent. The most attached were children who lost mothers rather than fathers, and were more likely to be girls than boys. Many children with mother-loss suffer more emotional and behavioral problems than those with father-loss, though the impact of losing either parent should not be underestimated.

3. *Reassurance They Are Not to Blame.* Bereaved children may wonder, "Did I cause it to happen?" Children learn early that strong feelings can hurt another person, and sometimes they misconstrue these strong feelings as having contributed to their parent's death. These children need to know that they did not cause the death out of their anger or shortcomings.

4. *Careful Listening.* Children have the same emotional needs after tragedy as adults, but their hurts are rarely taken seriously. Their friends don't usually come to see them. Their playmates can't afford to send flowers. They get some words of comfort and silent hugs from adults, but usually they are ignored by those who come to

comfort the surviving adults (Hewett, 67). Children have fears, fantasies, and questions and need a person who will hear them out and not minimize their concerns. Many of the questions that arise around a death are complex, and it is important not to give children superficial answers, even though this can be awkward for adults. The listener may be someone other than a parent. This can be especially true in the case of teenagers who are dealing with issues of separation from family as part of their own development. These other listeners can be teachers, counselors, relatives, family friends, or parents of peers.

5. *Validation of Individual's Feelings.* Children need to express their thoughts and feelings in their own way. Parents need to be reminded that each child has a distinct personality and each had a different relationship with the deceased. What the deceased parent was to one child can be different from what he or she was to another. These differences in relationships depend primarily on the age and gender of the child and the parent's hopes and expectations for that child. Such differences in personality and in relationship will make for varying expressions of grief, or even a hesitation to express much overt feeling.

6. *Help with Overwhelming Feelings.* Children need help in dealing with emotions that are too intense to be expressed. Those between the ages of five and seven are a particularly vulnerable group. Their cognitive development enables them to understand something of the permanency of death but they still lack the ego and social skills to deal with the intensity of the feelings of loss.

The very strong feelings elicited by the death of a parent can become displaced as aberrant behavior patterns. While most children manage the tasks of mourning in a healthy fashion, one-third of the children in Worden's study were found to be at some degree of risk for high levels of emotional and behavioral problems during the first two years of adjustment.

7. *Involvement and Inclusion.* Children need to feel important and involved before the death as well as afterward. The youngest children in the family are frequently those who feel the least important and involved. One way to address this is to include children in funeral planning and in the funeral itself.

Ministers may be asked whether children should attend funerals. All the sources consulted here agree that they should be given the choice of attending, *but only* if they are properly prepared beforehand about what they will be seeing and experiencing. Creagh describes Maori custom in New Zealand in relation to children at a *tangi* (funeral):

> Children attend the funeral and tend to come and go at will, to play and to cry. They are taught early on that death is a part of life. I shall always remember the tangi for a Maori infant. One moment the children were outside playing on swings, the next inside kissing the body before the lid was fastened, and everything was done so naturally. Touching the body assists the process of separating from it. (59)

Other research indicates that children usually benefit from attending the funeral of a loved one, not only because it helps to promote their immediate mourning but also because, in later years, children often report that their participation was important, while others regret not having attended (Young and Papadatou, 199–200). Murray

Bowen argues that it is the anxiety of the survivors that may hurt young children, but not the funeral itself (332). He summarizes the importance of a funeral for the whole family system: "The goal is to bring the entire family system into the closest possible contact with death in the presence of the total friendship system and to lend a helping hand to the anxious people who would rather run than face a funeral."

Children, like adults, need rituals, but there are few rituals in our society that include children. Children can be asked if there is anything they would like to see buried with the person, a symbolic act related to transitional objects. Families can be encouraged to develop their own rituals around anniversaries of the loss, and around holidays, birthdays, or other times when it is appropriate to remember the deceased in a more formal way.

8. *Continued Routine Activities.* Children need to maintain age-appropriate interests and activities. Children worry about whether they will have to attend school the day of the funeral or who will accompany them to the bathroom. These and various other concerns are developmentally appropriate but they can be misunderstood by adults in the context of bereavement. It is axiomatic, but often overlooked, that a bereaved child is still a child and, as such, may do things that seem insensitive to adults.

To some degree, the nature of this adjustment is determined by the roles and relationships that the dead parent played in the child's life, as well as in the life of the family. For example, the mother is frequently the emotional caretaker of the family as well as the child's confidante. An aspect of the mourning process includes adapting to the loss of these roles that have died with the mother.

9. *Modeled Grief Behaviors.* Learning theory tells us that modeled behavior is one of the most potent sources of learning. A child's ability to process the pain of loss will be influenced by observing the adult's experience of this process. If the child sees an adult express grief without being overwhelmed, this can serve as a salutary model for the child. On the other hand, if children see adults dysfunctional with grief, they may be frightened of feelings in general and their own feelings in particular. Children learn how to mourn by observing mourning behavior in adults. They need to be with adults who can model appropriate grieving.

10. *Opportunities to Remember.* Children need to be able to remember and to memorialize the lost parent not only after the death but continuously as they go through the remaining stages of life. Silverman (1989) studied a group of college-age women who, at an earlier age, had lost a parent to death. These students reported that they were continually rethinking the loss and renegotiating their relationship to their dead parent as they matured from girls into women. What the parent was to the child at age eight was different from what the parent would become when the child reached adolescence or adulthood. Caretakers should note that mourning for a childhood loss can be revived at many other points in life as well, especially when important life events such as a wedding or the birth of a child reactivate the loss.

As stated earlier, the way we mourn is always shaped by our unique ego functioning and our personal cognitive, emotional, and social development. Adults mourn differently at different phases of their life.

Sometimes this mourning is overlooked or at least minimized. One type of mourning that often passes unnoticed is the grief adults feel in late middle-life or early old-life over the loss of physical vitality and the diminishment of future possibilities.

The Grief of Aging. Erik Erikson differentiated the tasks of the eighth and final stage of life as "integrity versus despair." Some cultures deal well with the aging, attributing to them wisdom and honor. Buddhist cultures, for example, foster detachment, humility, and the acceptance of God's will as virtues, thus easing the way for adults to make a smooth transition from late middle-age to early old-age (Laungani, "Conclusions I," 240–41). These same issues become particularly difficult for Westerners during the latter part of life. Those who are sick or aging can no longer compete with the young; their physical and mental status is declining and there are some who, having lost employment, think, with some justification, that they are on the "scrap heap" from the age of forty.

Obviously many older people in Western cultures survive the transition from the earlier stages of life to the final stages with many gifts and strengths, and with their ego-functioning well intact. But others do not. Erikson speaks of the personal mourning in the final stages, not only for time forfeited and space depleted but also for autonomy weakened, initiative lost, intimacy missed, generativity neglected, and identity potential bypassed or, indeed, an all too limiting identity lived. Melvin Kimble and Nancy Burgess both speak about the ageism and sexism that face older widowed women: "In the present 'graying of America,' women will be culturally defined as *older*—and *elderly*—over a longer period of time than men"

(Kimble, 142–43). Questions concerning the meaning of life and suffering, self-definition and worth, sexual and family roles, and attitudes toward caregiving and care-receiving are among the challenging questions that confront older women and those who would render pastoral care to them. Older men, however, may not fare well either, especially those widowers who have capitulated to "learned helplessness," the inability to take care of their own domestic *and* emotional needs due primarily to the gender-role conditioning of both men and women. The majority of older men in Robert Rubenstein's study were unable to return to any semblance of "normalcy" following the death of their wife, but instead found themselves marginalized, pathologically attached to their wife's memory, lethargic and lonely, and unable to comprehend how they suddenly became "so old."

Gender Differences in Mourning

Not only do we mourn differently depending on our stage in life, but there are also significant gender differences in mourning styles of which the caregiver needs to be aware. Anthropologically, across almost all societies women and men carry different expectations about acceptable expressions of grief. Jonker illustrates this difference in his study of Muslim funerals:

> Basically one can discern two classic reactions to loss, both backed up by a long history and many local variations. The first consists of extreme crying, accompanied by breast beating and scratching of the face, which is gradually moulded into a longwinded dirge, halfway between singing and crying. . . . The second response is one of constraint. It is a fierce attempt to "let go," to separate one's life

from that of the deceased, and strive towards the "point of no return," where the survivors face the fact that they will go on living and have to leave their dead behind. The attainment of this inner attitude is encouraged by Quran recitation. The latter reaction is generally considered a male preserve, while the first is considered a woman's duty. (154–55)

Jonker goes on to point out that the two styles are not always practiced on an amiable, equal level, where one party witnesses the performance of the other. Some men abhor the women's reaction to their loss, and try to suppress any overtly expressed emotion by keeping the women apart, or forbidding them to attend the funeral for fear of crying or tumultuous scenes. One cannot deny, however, that there is an inner coherence and link between the two attitudes. The first generally works as a catharsis for the men and women who are witnesses. And it allows for an attitude of serene stoicism to be built upon it.

From the tradition of American gender-role culture comes an autobiographical account by Ronald Grimes. Immediately after Grimes's young son Trevor died, his parents arrived to support him in his grief:

The day after they arrived I asked Dad to help me build a cross in the backyard. He said nothing as we stuck it into the mound where Trevor's red Buddha sat doing nothing. I knew Dad's Methodist sensibilities were probably being scraped by this pagan earthmound stuff, so I confessed, "I am not sure why I wanted to do this, but I don't expect much from the funeral tomorrow. I don't know who they design funerals for, but I am sure they are not designed for me."

"Me either," he replied, surprising me. "Must be for women. All those flowers."

I replied, "Probably not for women, but for some male funeral director's idea of women."

"Maybe so."

We dug in silence. Then Dad, obviously ruminating, said, "Making a cross is something I understand."

"Me too," I replied. "My religion is all in my hands." (109)

Culturally dictated gender roles are deeply ingrained in each person's sense of identity. The extended period of mourning and grief recovery is probably not the appropriate time for any caregiver to chastise a mourner for grieving "incorrectly." Rather, the caregiver should be alert to help men grieve *well* as men, and women as women, but more importantly to transcend even these cultural dictates to support each unique individual in traveling through the tasks of grief work toward relearning the world in the healthiest manner possible.

Pastoral Care of Those Who Are HIV-Positive

In Western societies the spectacular advances of medical science have given rise to the belief that death can be put off, postponed, held in check, or even conquered permanently. The belief in longevity allows one to distance oneself from one's own death and those of one's loved ones. It is not an event about which one needs to concern oneself unduly. Yet people die everyday, everywhere, and not all die of old age. No society has discovered the elixir of life (Laungani, "Conclusions I," 219). We particularly hide those who are dying too young—of cancer, of the new superviruses, and above all, those dying from AIDS.

In so many ways, those who are HIV-positive go through the phases and tasks of mourning already described in the same manner as any other human being. And yet at the same time, AIDS is its own unique disease, riddled with paradox. For many people a diagnosis of AIDS represents a physical and psychological challenge to survive and at the same time demands a spiritual and emotional preparation for death (Smith 1988, 164). Those diagnosed as HIV-positive can go through years of uncertainty and even of anticipatory grief. Slowly the anxiety of knowing that one is going to die, but not knowing when, whittles away even the strongest determination.

Ten years ago the vast majority of Americans with AIDS were gay men. Today, gay men account for approximately 55 percent of new cases (Hochstein, 77). In Western societies, more and more new cases are showing up among young heterosexual men and women. In almost all other countries of the world, AIDS has always been a heterosexually transmitted disease, not at all associated with homosexual sex. Perhaps this is why the church in many nonwhite countries has been so much quicker to respond with aggressive pastoral ministries to people who are HIV-positive; they do not need to deal with the additional fallacy that AIDS is God's curse upon "deviant" behavior.

In Western countries, however, much pastoral ministry is still being done among the HIV-positive gay population. For some pastors, this is problematic. Walter Smith explains:

> Involvement in the pastoral care of persons with HIV raises its own particular set of questions. To work effectively with persons with HIV disease, pastoral counselors must be open to understand the world of the gay community and the communities

of drug users and prostitutes, as well as the unique sociocultural features of the Black, Hispanic, and Native American communities. In addition, pastoral counselors must have special sensitivities to the mores of sexually active adolescents. (1993, 689)

Pastors who are unable to work nonjudgmentally with persons who are HIV-positive or have AIDS should refer this ministry to others who suffer less personal interference.

The societal stigma of AIDS, at least in Western countries, remains so intense that people who are HIV-positive must grieve losses that are unique to their condition. Sunderland and Shelp offer the following list (33):

- if married, relationships with spouse and family members
- the sense of well-being and security as a healthy individual
- the level of self-image and self-esteem that has been reached before knowing the result of the test or becoming ill
- identity as an active, productive member of the community
- the respect of peers
- the sense of acceptance as a worthwhile and acceptable person
- independence
- dreams, aspirations, goals around which life has been organized
- if parent, watching the family grow up and mature
- other particular personal losses.

With the acute stage of the disease, patients suffer increasingly severe physical, emotional, and mental losses, such as the following:

- loss of the ability to continue normal activities, including food preparation, basic personal hygiene, shopping for supplies, and even the ability to feed oneself

• acute health losses, such as vision, control of bowel and bladder, mental acuity, and massive deterioration of all physical and rational functions
• loss of life itself.

In addition to supporting people who are HIV-positive in their mourning, anticipatory or real, of these losses, the pastoral caregiver needs to be prepared to help plan funerals, write wills, and arrange health care proxies for men in their twenties, thirties, and forties. Finally, it means helping them to die well, and dealing with the complicated grief of the lovers and families who survive them. Pastoral care of persons with AIDS can be intensely personal on a one-to-one basis and yet require skillful support for an extended system of loved ones and families.

HIV-positive counselees and parishioners may bring complicated spiritual needs to the minister. The research team of Somlai et al. discovered that "HIV-positive participants with higher depression, loneliness, anxiety and thoughts of suicide were more likely to pray or pray to a God, Goddess, or divine being. Additionally, participants with higher scores on the emotional distress measures were more like to directly participate and experience a formal religion" (186). Other questions might include: Why does God allow this epidemic to happen? How can a good God permit this evil? Is this illness simply an indiscriminate virus or a punishment from God? Does God, then, punish children too? What is the meaning of this illness in my life, in the lives of my friends and family and community? Where is God in the midst of such pain? There are no easy answers to such questions, of course, but caregivers must be ready to stand alongside the questioners as the depths of the spiritual realm are explored.

In support of this courageous form of pastoral ministry, Walter Smith cites Jesus' ministry to the leper in Mark 1:40–45 (1988, 164–65). The leper approached Jesus and begged, "If you will, you can make me clean." The evangelist focuses on the reaction of Jesus. Many texts translate Jesus' emotional response as being "moved with pity." Some commentators note, however, that a more accurate rendition of Jesus' reaction is "moved with anger." The emotional response of Jesus, the sense of injustice he felt at the leper's social isolation, interpret his subsequent actions. The Gospel writer tells us that Jesus touched him, a most unlikely thing since it meant Jesus himself was defiled by that physical contact. Touch was—and is—a gesture of acceptance, support, of solidarity with the afflicted. Jesus' physical gesture of touch and his words helped restore the man to a rightful place in the community. Emphasis is not placed on the healing act itself, but on the indignation, understanding, compassion, and reconciliation of Jesus. Surely this is the correct model, blessed by Christ, for the pastoral care of people who are HIV-positive.

Mourning a Loss by Suicide

And finally, a brief note on suicide and mourning. One important issue here is the church's historical record of cruelty to the remains of those who took their own life and those who survived them. At times, the church refused Christian burial to the suicide's body; at other times it granted burial but only outside the graveyard fence. The church's record of support and pastoral care for the survivors is not much better. Oddly, suicide is not condemned in the Bible. Hewett provides a brief overview (86–88). The Hebrew Bible accounts include the suicide stories of Abimelech (Judg. 9:50-55), Samson (Judg. 16:23-31), Saul (1 Sam. 31:3-6; 2 Sam. 1:1-27; 1 Chron. 10:1-14), Ahithophel (2 Sam. 17:23), and Zimri (1 Kings 16:8-20). Most of these people were given honorable burials. No moral comment is made about the manner of their deaths. In fact, Saul is treated as a great servant of God (2 Samuel), and Samson is later hailed in the New Testament as one of the great heroes of faith "of whom the world was not worthy" (Heb. 11:38). The only recorded suicide in the New Testament is that of Judas Iscariot, and only one of three Christian traditions records it as such. While Judas is condemned by church tradition, it is for his betrayal of Jesus and not for his manner of death. More recent Protestant theological tradition has reversed the condemnation of suicide. In his *Church Dogmatics* (III/4, 405), Karl Barth wrote: "If there is forgiveness of sins at all, . . . there is surely forgiveness for suicide" (Hewett, 92). The pastoral caregiver has no justification for deepening the survivors' mourning by framing suicide as a sin. To do so is simply pastorally irresponsible.

Conclusion

Death—our own or that of one we love—finds us all at our most vulnerable, but indeed any significant loss makes us aware of our vulnerability, our frailty, and our need to be comforted. Perhaps for this reason we cherish the promise of Christ: "Blessed are those who mourn, for they will be comforted" (Matt. 5:4). The promise is the single sense of universality in the complicated field of grief and mourning. So much about the way we mark loss is culturally determined that the pastor's skills will be stretched to their fullest. And yet perhaps it is the pastoral care provided during times of loss and grief that makes the strongest lasting impression on those who turn to us for a tangible sign of God's love.

BIBLIOGRAPHY

Abrahams, Israel. *Hebrew Ethical Wills*. Philadelphia: Jewish Publication Society, 1926.

Amos, William. *When AIDS Comes to the Church*. Philadelphia: Westminster, 1988.

Anderson, Herbert, and Kenneth R. Mitchell. *Promising Again*. Louisville: Westminster/John Knox, 1993.

Atkins, Peter. "No Justice in Grief: The Pastoral Care of Families Whose Children Have Been Murdered." In *Pastoral Care in South Pacific Cultures*. Philip Culbertson, ed. 259–81. Auckland: Snedden & Cervin, 1997.

Attig, Thomas. *How We Grieve: Relearning the World*. New York: Oxford University Press, 1996.

Bolen, Jean Shinoda. *Close to the Bone: Life-Threatening Illness and the Search for Meaning*. New York: Scribner's, 1996.

Bowen, Murray. "Family Reaction to Death." In *Family Therapy in Clinical Practice*. 321–35. New York: Jason Aronson, 1978.

Bowlby, John. *A Secure Base: Parent-Child Attachments and Healthy Human Development*. New York: Basic, 1988.

Broom, Brian. *Somatic Illness and the Patient's Other Story*. New York: Free Association, 1997.

Burgess, Nancy. "Challenging the Myths: Pastoral Care of Pakeha Women Entering Retirement." In *Pastoral Care in South Pacific Cultures*. Philip Culbertson, ed. 283–301. Auckland: Snedden & Cervin, 1997.

Coffin, William Sloane. "My Son Beat Me to the Grave." *A.D.*, June 1982, 26.

Cooper-White, Pamela. *The Cry of Tamar: Violence against Women and the Church's Response*. Minneapolis: Fortress, 1995.

Creagh, Terry. *Give Sorrow Words*. Melbourne: Joint Board of Christian Education of Australia and New Zealand, 1982.

Crenshaw, David. *Bereavement: Counseling the Grieving throughout the Life Cycle*. New York: Continuum, 1990.

Culbertson, Philip. "Blessing Jacob's Sons, Inheriting Family Myths." *Sewanee Theological Review* 37:1 (Christmas 1993): 52–76.

Davidson, G. P. "A Community Affair: Grief, Death and Bereavement among New Zealand's Polynesian People." *New Zealand Nursing Journal* (July 1983): 12–15.

Gielen, Uwe. "A Death on the Roof of the World: The Perspective of Tibetan Buddhism." In Parkes, Laungani, and Young, eds. 73–97.

Grimes, Ronald. *Marrying and Burying: Rites of Passage in a Man's Life*. Boulder, Colo.: Westview, 1995.

Hewett, John. *After Suicide*. Philadelphia: Westminster, 1980.

Hochstein, Lorna. "What Pastoral Psychotherapists Need to Know about Lesbians and Gay Men in the 1990s." *Journal of Pastoral Care* 50:1 (spring 1996): 73–85.

Howe, Leroy. *The Image of God: A Theology for Pastoral Care and Counseling*. Nashville: Abingdon, 1995.

Ihimaera, Witi. *Tangi*. Auckland: Heinemann Reed, 1973.

Jonker, Gerdien. "The Many Facets of Islam: Death, Dying and Disposal between Orthodox Rule and Historical Convention." In Parkes, Laungani, and Young, eds. 147–65.

Kimble, Melvin. "Pastoral Care." In *Aging, Spirituality, and Religion*. Melvin Kimble, Susan McFadden, James Ellor, and James Seeber, eds. 131–47. Minneapolis: Fortress, 1995.

Kübler-Ross, Elisabeth. *On Death and Dying*. London: Tavistock, 1969.

Kushner, Harold. *When Bad Things Happen to Good People*. New York: Avon, 1981.

Laungani, Pittu. "Conclusions I: Implications for Practice and Policy." In Parkes, Laungani, and Young, eds. 218–32.

———. "Death in a Hindu Family." In Parkes, Laungani, and Young, eds. 52–72.

Lester, Andrew. *Hope in Pastoral Care and Counseling*. Louisville: Westminster/John Knox, 1995.

Levine, Ellen. "Jewish Views and Customs on Death." In Parkes, Laungani, and Young, eds. 98–130.

Lopez, Frederick. "Attachment Theory as an Integrative Framework for Family Counseling." *Family Journal* 3 (January 1995): 11–17.

McGoldrick, Monica. "Ethnicity and the Family Life Cycle." In *The Changing Family Life Cycle: A Framework for Family Therapy*. Betty Carter and Monica McGoldrick, eds. 2d ed. 69–90. Boston: Allyn and Bacon, 1989.

Meyer, Charles. *Surviving Death: A Practical Guide to Caring for the Dying and Bereaved*. Mystic, Conn.: Twenty-Third Publications, 1988.

Miller, William, and Kathleen Jackson. *Practical Psychology for Pastors*. Englewood Cliffs, N.J.: Prentice-Hall, 1985.

Miller-McLemore, Bonnie. "Doing Wrong, Getting Sick, and Dying." *The Christian Century* (February 24, 1988): 186–90.

Nerken, Ira. "Making It Safe to Grieve." *The Christian Century* (November 30, 1988): 1091–94.

Parkes, Colin Murray. "Conclusions II: Attachments and Losses in Cross-Cultural Perspective." In Parkes, Laungani, and Young, eds. 233–43.

———. "Help for the Dying and Bereaved." In Parkes, Laungani, and Young, eds. 206–17.

Parkes, Colin Murray, Pittu Laungani, and Bill Young. "Culture and Religion." In Parkes, Laungani, and Young, eds. 10–23.

———. "Introduction." In Parkes, Laungani, and Young, eds. 3–9.

———, eds. *Death and Bereavement across Cultures*. London: Routledge, 1997.

Pastan, Linda. *The Five Stages of Grief*. New York: W. W. Norton, 1978.

Rosenblatt, Paul. "Grief in Small-scale Societies." In Parkes, Laungani, and Young, eds. 27–51.

Rubenstein, Robert. *Singular Paths: Old Men Living Alone*. New York: Columbia University Press, 1986.

Russell, Bonnie, and Max Uhlemann. "Women Surviving an Abusive Relationship: Grief and the Process of Change." *Journal of Counseling and Development* 72:4 (1994): 362–67.

Silverman, William, and Kenneth Cinnamon. *When Mourning Comes: A Book of Comfort for the Grieving*. Northvale, N.J.: Jason Aronson, 1990.

Smith, Walter. *AIDS: Living and Dying with Hope*. New York: Paulist, 1988.

———. "Embracing Pastoral Ministry in the Age of AIDS." In *Clinical Handbook of Pastoral Counseling,* vol. 2. Robert Wicks and Richard Parsons, eds. 679–710. New York: Paulist, 1993.

Somlai, Anton, Jeffery Kelly, Seth Kalichman, Gregg Mulry, Kathleen Sikkema, Timothy McAuliffe, Ken Multhauf, and Bernadette Davantes. "An Empirical Investigation of the Relationship between Spirituality, Coping, and Emotional Distress in People Living with HIV Infection and AIDS." *The Journal of Pastoral Care* 50:2 (summer 1996): 181–91.

Sunderland, Ron. *Getting through Grief: Caregiving by Congregations*. Nashville: Abingdon, 1993.

Sunderland, Ronald, and Earl Shelp. *AIDS: A Manual for Pastoral Care*. Philadelphia: Westminster, 1987.

Ter Blanche, Harold, and Colin Murray Parkes. "Christianity." In Parkes, Laungani, and Young, eds. 131–46.

Viorst, Judith. *Necessary Losses: The Loves, Illusions, Dependencies and Impossible Expectations That All of Us Have to Give Up in Order to Grow*. New York: Simon & Schuster, 1986.

Walter, Tony. "Secularization." In Parkes, Laungani, and Young, eds. 166–87.

Westberg, Granger. *Good Grief*. Philadelphia: Fortress, 1971.

Worden, J. William. *Children and Grief: When a Parent Dies*. New York: Guilford, 1996.

Young, Bill, and Danai Papadatou. "Childhood, Death and Bereavement across Cultures." In Parkes, Laungani, and Young, eds. 191–205.

Part Three

~

Staying Safe in Ministry

9. THE PRAXIS OF PASTORAL COUNSELING

"The purpose of pastoral counseling is to offer something new, so that the persons within it will experience some freedom to change, to consider some new alternatives about their lives." (John Patton, 107)

Many books have been written on the subject of pastoral counseling, from a wide variety of therapeutic and theological positions. Due to the constraints of brevity, this chapter will reflect only one of the possible ways to describe and summarize the process of pastoral counseling and some of the professional issues it entails. For a more in-depth explanation, the reader is referred to the books listed at the end of this chapter, each of which is solidly based in counseling praxis. A number of books on the market are, however, not based in solid proven counseling praxis, or they describe the counseling praxis from such a narrow theological or scriptural point of view that they should be considered dangerous. If you already have experience as a counselor, you should be able to sort out for yourself which books make sense and which do not; if you are less experienced, you should consult with a more experienced counselor before reading church publications on counseling theory and praxis.

The Art of Counseling

In approximately 600 C.E., Gregory the Great wrote what became the most influential book on pastoral care in the history of the church, the *Liber Regulae Pastoralis* ("The Book of Pastoral Rule"). In the opening paragraph Gregory described pastoral care as "the art of arts." If pastoral care is the art of arts, then its subset, pastoral counseling, is even more so. The many skills involved in effective counseling can be taught and described, but in the end the application of these skills relies almost completely on the sensitivity and intuition of the practitioner.

Much more recently, and halfway around the world from Rome, New Zealand author Patricia Grace crafted a description of Maori wood carving that functions as a beautiful metaphor for the counseling process:

There was once a carver who spent a lifetime with wood, seeking out and exposing the figures that were hidden there. These eccentric or brave, dour, whimsical, crafty, beguiling, tormenting, tormented or loving figures developed first in the forests, in the tree wombs, but depended on the master with his karakia [prayers] and his tools, his mind and his heart, his breath and his strangeness to bring them to other birth.

The tree, after a lifetime of fruiting, has, after its first death, a further fruiting at the hands of the master.

This does not mean that the man is master of the tree. Nor is he master of what eventually comes from his hands. He is master only of the skills that bring forward what was already waiting in the womb of the tree—a tree that may have spent further time as a house or a classroom, or a bridge or pier. Or further time could have been spent floating on the sea or river, or sucked into a swamp, or stopping a bank, or sprawled on a beach bleaching among the sand, stones and sun.
. . .

The previous life, the life within the tree womb, was a time of eyelessness, of waiting, swelling, hardening. It was a time of existing, already browed, tongued, shoul-dered, fingered, sexed, footed, toed, and of waiting to be shown as such. But eyeless. The spinning, dancing eyes are the final gift from the carver, but the eyes are also a gift from the sea.

When all is finished the people have their ancestors. They sleep at their feet, lis-ten to their stories, call them by name, put them in songs and dances, joke with them, become their children, their slaves, their enemies, their friends. (8)

The carver is not master of the carving, any more than the counselor is the master of his or her counselees. The master and the carv-er simply draw forth new forms of beauty from the rich life experience already creat-ed by God, and finally give life to their sub-jects by letting them see—the carver by placing paua (abalone) shells in the eye sockets, the counselor by insightful reflec-tive therapeutic skills. And even these abalone shells and the therapeutic skills are gifts from God.

Pastoral Care or Cheap Therapy?

Pastoral counseling is a function practiced on occasion by virtually every lay and ordained member of the church. We are engaged in pastoral counseling in the aisles of the grocery store, while talking to others who wait with us outside the day-care center, riding in the car with friends or parishioners, taking a break at the office, or on a Saturday morning walk with our companions. We should be careful not to underestimate the power of those fleeting moments when someone reaches out to us for a kind word or a listening ear. But we who are engaged in the various ministries of the church will also find that we are approached regularly on a more formal basis by men and women who are hurting

inside and believe that we can help. For this reason, every minister of the church needs a sound grounding in counseling theory and praxis. People in pain are vulnerable and assume that we will practice healing skills well enough that they are safe opening up to us.

Pastoral counseling is sought by the faithful because they believe that we have something special to offer that they might not find with counselors and therapists out-side the church. It is a myth that people come to church caregivers because they are free or because their problems are too insignificant to need "real" therapy. People come to pastoral counselors because they wish to be understood in a holistic way that keeps their spiritual life integrated with their emotional and intellectual lives. They come because they perceive that pastoral counseling can offer them four specific gifts: an understanding of human nature rooted in the goodness of God, a relational humanity patterned after the humanity of Christ, a respect for the dignity and auton-omy of every human being, and a deep commitment to the health and ultimate good of each member of the church. Christian counseling should always be structured so that none of these expecta-tions is violated.

Pastoral counselors are not ordinarily trained in a specific school of therapeutic theory. They are more often generalists, practicing an eclectic blend of theories from a variety of sources. I would not claim that Jung's theories are more appropriate for Christians than Freud's, or that Carl Rogers's theories are more useful than Melanie Klein's. As Miller and Jackson point out, "the merit of an idea is to be judged on its helpfulness in the counseling process" (7). Specialization in a particular theory is best left to full-time professional counselors who have many more years' formal counseling training than most ministers do. There is, however, much of great importance to be learned from the classical theorists; ministers who do counseling should read widely and attend regular workshops to increase their skills and perceptions. As Martin Thornton comments in his book *The Rock and the River:*

> One calls in a plumber because he understands plumbing, not because of his wide experience in life, and one is coached by a golf professional *because* he is *not* a weekend amateur. One is suspicious of a doctor who has read no medical book for twenty years and knows nothing of modern drugs, and I suspect that intelligent modern Christians are getting suspicious of clergy who are ever engaged in something other than prayer, learning and such like professional occupations. . . . It is *because* a priest has time for prayer, for serious continuing education and frequent reading, and for reflection that his guidance of those in the world's hurly burly is likely to be worth having. (Thornton, 141)

The Physical Geography of Counseling

The physical space in which formal counseling takes place is actually part of the effective therapeutic process. It is the geography that surrounds counselor and counselee to allow the relationship to work. While many pastoral counselors inherit their counseling space as a part of the church offices, with a sharp eye and a little work most spaces can be adapted to function adequately.

If the counselor must have the counseling space in the same room as the pastor's desk, it should be at the opposite end of the room. A desk and computer area are for working with objects, and the counseling area is for working with people. The spheres of activity should never intrude into each other. The counseling area should include three comfortable and movable chairs, all of the same height and general description. Nothing like a coffee table should sit in the middle of the counseling area, though a small table beside each chair will be useful for notepads, coffee cups, or tissues. The chairs should be movable so that the counselees can choose for themselves how close they sit to the counselor or, in the case of a quarreling couple, how far they sit from each other. The counselor's chair should not sit directly in front of the counselee chairs, but off at a slight angle. To sit looking directly at a vulnerable counselee can easily be interpreted as a form of aggression; when working with people from nonwhite cultures, the counselor should remember that staring into someone's face is quite inappropriate. If the counselor's chair is at an angle, the counselee can then easily look away from the counselor at moments of deep emotion or even "look outward into the past." As well, the counselor should not sit between the counselee and the door, for some counselees will feel trapped. A counselor seated in the wrong geographical location can actually inhibit the counseling process.

The counseling room should be cleaned regularly and should be soundproof. This ethical requirement raises two problematic issues: protecting the identity of counselees, and counselor safety. Both are sources of controversy in the pastoral and counseling literature. Sadly, in our present climate, two people behind a tightly closed door may raise suspicion and even the threat of a lawsuit. Some counseling literature now advocates that a counseling room should have a window in order to minimize the possibility of inappropriate behavior in the counseling space. If the room is to have a window, it should preferably open onto an alley instead of the waiting room or secretary's office, and should be shielded with vertical blinds or gauze curtains. This protects the identity of the counselee to a large degree while still ensuring that the counselee is physically and sexually safe from the advances of an unethical counselor. But it is not only the counselee who needs protection. Counselors may be the victim of sexual advances or worse, of physical threat. Much of the recent counseling literature suggests that the door to the counseling space be left barely ajar, or that the counseling room be equipped with an emergency alarm. In certain instances, it may be appropriate to suggest that the counselee bring an advocate or support person along. The support person is generally expected to remain silent during the session, but even silent support can be particularly important for recovering victims of sexual abuse who fear being alone with the counselor. Under no circumstances should the counselor and counselee be alone together in a building. Someone else should be present in case help is required; this same person may also be charged with protecting the counseling time from phone interruptions or drop-in visits. In the same vein, a counselor should never see a counselee alone in a home, particularly someone of the opposite gender.

The counseling space should be decorated in a subdued taste but one that reflects the personality of the counselor. Art, furniture, and other decorations should be chosen so as not to intrude on the counseling relationship. A counselor's credentials are sometimes hung on the wall, but family photos should be kept to a minimum; the counselor's private life is not an appropriate subject of discussion in a counseling session. Most pastoral counselors believe that a cross should be easily visible in the room, to remind both counselor and counselee of the source of their health. If there is a clock in the room, the counselor should be able to see it, but the counselee should not, for it too is a distraction from the therapeutic process.

As a general rule, holding counseling sessions in the same space repeatedly is deemed to facilitate the counseling relationship. On occasion, however, it may be therapeutically appropriate to change the counseling location. A walk together, a time talking at the church altar, or a session in a public park on a sunny day might help a counselee get through to some new material. But the counselor should be aware that each time a space changes—whether the geography within the office or the location of the session—most counselees take time to readjust and so part of the limited counseling time is lost.

Intake Counseling

Intake counseling, usually the first formal counseling contact a minister has with a counselee, can take two forms: intake for the purposes of referral, or intake for the purposes of establishing a counseling contract with the minister him- or herself.

In the first instance, the minister is a trusted professional whose advice is sought about where the careseeker needs to turn next. Because little of use can be established in one session only, intake counseling should always entail two or three meetings. The purpose of intake counseling for referral is to establish the sort of help needed by what type of professional and, as closely as possible, the exact nature of the presenting problem. Referrals, including those for long-term counseling, will be discussed later in this chapter.

Even if the careseeker wishes to establish a counseling contract with the minister him- or herself, the first two to three sessions should be treated as intake, separate from the agreed-upon subsequent course of counseling. In the case of most ministers, these will be intake sessions for short-term counseling. The purpose of these sessions is to explain the process of short-term counseling, to determine and circumscribe the complaint that will be addressed, and to identify the desired outcomes.

Short-Term Counseling

Short-term counseling is usually defined as three to ten planned sessions, and is the type of counseling for which most pastoral counselors have been trained. It is sometimes also known as "brief pastoral counseling," "time-limited counseling," or "goal-oriented counseling." Much counseling offered by pastoral counselors is even briefer than I have just suggested: the norm seems to be one to three sessions. But whether three or ten, the principles of short-term counseling are very useful to pastoral counselors with limited time availability and minimal training. Short-term counseling is generally behavior- and intervention-oriented. In general, counseling theory holds that all human behavior is adaptive. The behavior may, over the long run, turn out to be maladaptive, but it is still designed to meet some conscious or unconscious need from the counselee's past. "Intervention" in such situations suggests

that the counselor actively intervenes, or "comes between," the present behavior of the counselee and its effects on other people, or the counselee's perception of reality, or the counselee's desired way of doing things, in order to allow the counselee to function in a more appropriate or rewarding manner. In other words, an intervention is a maneuver by the counselor to help bring about the desired changes identified by the counselee. The disadvantage of short-term counseling is that its effects may be only cosmetic; it may change behavior but usually cannot get to the root cause of the behavior.

Because short-term counseling is termination-oriented and not designed to deal with deeper therapeutic issues, it is not an appropriate method for everyone. Short-term counseling is not an appropriate modality for chronic depression, chemical addiction, psychoses, deep-seated neuroses, bipolar disorders, and most suicidal tendencies, to name but a few examples. (These terms are defined in the *Diagnostic and Statistical Manual of Mental Disorders* [*DSM-IV*], as listed in the bibliography.) In other words, short-term counseling is best suited to addressing the problems that generally healthy people face. Since it is always important to match the person in need and the presenting problem with the correct type of counseling, the following seven characteristics are the usual criteria for selecting appropriate counselees for short-term counseling (adapted from Sifneos, 27):

1. The counselee must be able to determine and circumscribe a specific chief complaint. Often this initial work is done in an intake session or two with the counselor; intake sessions do not count among the limited number of agreed-upon sessions.

2. There must be evidence of a give-and-take, or "meaningful relationship," with another person during early childhood. This criterion tests the counselee's relational literacy, for counselees who are relationship damaged cannot establish enough trust with the counselor in such a short time for this method to work. Further, the childhood experience allows for transference issues to surface during counseling and thus provide some possible insight into the motivations for the adaptive behavior.

3. The counselee must be emotionally literate—able to experience and express feelings freely. This capacity must be obvious even during the intake process.

4. The counselee must be of above-average intelligence and must be psychologically minded—that is, unafraid of psychological treatment.

5. The counselee must be motivated to change and not willing to settle simply for symptom relief.

6. The counselee must be inherently curious about what makes him or her "tick."

7. The counselee must be willing to make some sacrifice to cooperate in the counseling process and to accomplish the set goals.

During the intake session, the counselor and counselee work together to choose a specific outcome or goal for the agreed-upon number of meetings, and that goal must be realistically achievable. Short-term counseling will not solve all of any person's problems, and in fact, by definition must address only the problem that has been identified as the reason for the counseling relationship in the first place.

Bauer and Kobos define seven characteristics that distinguish short-term counseling from long-term counseling (6–9):

1. The counselor is active rather than passive in the counseling process.

2. The Focal Relational Problem (FRP) agreed upon by both the counselor and counselee is the exclusive material for each counseling session. Prior to the beginning of a course of time-limited counseling, an evaluation session or two is performed in which the counselor and the counselee have clearly described a circumscribed problem (FRP) and that is the focus for each counseling session.

3. The counseling is a process of two allies dealing with a particular problem, and this alliance is established early in the relationship.

4. The counselor persistently points out resistance in the counselee to solving the FRP when it arises. . . . The counselor must be resolute in confronting the counselee whenever the counselee resists doing something to change, particularly as it relates to the FRP.

5. The feelings that the counselee may have about the counselor, and the counselor's own feelings about the counselee, are important issues for the counseling process. . . . A major premise of short-term counseling is that the counselee's FRP will be enacted in three realms: in the counselee's past, in the counselee's daily life as reported to the counselor in the counseling session, and in the relationship with the counselor.

6. The purpose of counseling is to solve the presenting FRP.

7. Adherence to the time limitation of the counseling must be maintained.

Methodologically, short-term counseling requires careful strategization by the pastoral counselor to determine the correct intervention and its timing. The counselee must understand that once the agreed-upon number of sessions has been completed, the counselor will not engage that problem again. The counselee may choose to contract another series of sessions to deal with a different problem, or if the original problem has not been resolved, the counselor may refer the counselee to someone else. If the number of sessions originally agreed to is exceeded, the effectiveness of time-limited counseling is destroyed. In addition, each counseling session must begin with the counselor stating the specific goal for the entire series of three to ten sessions and end with the counselor stating how many sessions are left before the time limitation expires. Some pastors may find this hard-nosed approach uncomfortable; in that case, they should not even begin, but should refer immediately after the intake session.

Long-Term Counseling

Long-term counseling is not within the skill capacity of most ministers, nor is it easily available for many people due to the extended commitment and expense. But long-term counseling shapes our general expectations for what counseling involves and promises, and ministers need to understand its underlying theoretical base as well as its value. Unlike short-term counseling's emphasis on conscious goal setting and achievement, long-term counseling deals most often with the counselee's subconscious (that part of our minds not usually available to our conscious) or the unconscious (that part of our minds almost completely unavailable to the conscious). But like short-term counseling, long-term counseling relies heavily on the counselor's perceptive intuition. According to Eric Fromm, "psychoanalysis is a process of understanding man's mind, particularly that part which is not conscious. It is an *art* like the understanding of poetry" (192). In the United States, long-term counseling is usually provided by a psychiatrist (a licensed physician who specializes in the diagnosis, treatment, and prevention of mental and emotional disorders; his or her education includes college, medical school, and at least three years of psychiatric training) or a psychologist (someone with a Ph.D. in psychology and at least two years of supervised work in the treatment of mental disorders). In many parts of the world, the terms *psychotherapist, therapist,* and *counselor* are as yet not universally connected with specific training credentials, so the pastor should be cautious in suggesting referrals.

Certain types of long-term counseling are within the capacity of highly trained and experienced pastoral counselors, though the counselor should always be ready to interrupt the relationship at any time that it becomes obvious that she is in over her head. Fromm describes the qualities of a good long-term counselor:

• The basic rule for practicing this art is the complete concentration of the listener [counselor].
• Nothing of importance must be on his mind; he must be optimally free from anxiety as well as from greed.
• He must possess a freely-working imagination which is sufficiently concrete to be expressed in words.
• He must be endowed with a capacity for empathy with another person and strong enough to feel the experience of the other as if it were his own.
• The condition for such empathy is a crucial facet of the capacity for love. To understand another means to love him—not in the erotic sense, but in the sense of

reaching out to him and of overcoming the fear of losing oneself.

- Understanding and loving are inseparable. If they are separate, it is a cerebral process and the door to essential understanding remains closed. (192–93)

Fromm's description of a professional counselor could as easily describe the experienced pastoral counselor. This is one example of the many ways in which the foundational theory of long-term counseling informs the practice of short-term pastoral counseling. While the subject of counselor congruence will be discussed at greater length in chapter 11, we are here reminded that pastoral counselors need to be vigilant concerning the continuing nurture of their own intellectual, emotional, and relational health.

Dynamics of the Counseling Session

When Does a Counseling Relationship Begin?

Pastoral counselor Jack Hall points out that the decision to see a counselor is rarely impulsive, nor should it be likened to making a doctor's appointment for the flu:

> It may have been twelve years that the individual suffered before taking that step of making an appointment or should I say, reaching out to touch the hem of the garment [cf. Mark 5:24-34]. When it does happen, a healing does take place. The individual thinks: "All this time I have wanted to be in the presence of someone who will hear me and at last it has occurred. Already I feel better, a load has been lifted. Now I can begin to examine what has caused my pain." (123)

Hall's exegesis suggests that the process of healing may already have begun before the counselor has even been contacted. In the case of pastoral counselors, the counselee may be responding to signals we have been giving for months from the pulpit or in other pastoral contacts, or we may have been recommended by someone else in the parish with whom we did successful counseling work, or perhaps the counselee has seen us lead a workshop in a neighboring parish. All this reminds us to enter each counseling relationship cautiously, for we are entering a process in the middle, a process in a sense "begun without us," a process fraught with fantasies, expectations, and hopes. The counselee may have been rehearsing a projected therapeutic relationship and outcome for months.

While the counseling process may have already begun, the first formal structuring of the relationship with a counselor takes place with the initial phone call. Some pastoral counselors delegate their secretary to make the counseling appointments. To do so, however, both misses the beginning of the contractual structure implied in the counseling relationship and deprives the counselor of material that may be very important in the subsequent intake interviews. The first phone call to the counselor is the first request for help. As we wish God to hear our feeble requests for daily bread or forgiveness, so too we should hear the first "prayers" for help from our counselees. So we listen carefully during that first phone call—to the sense of urgency expressed, to the counselee's ability to express feelings and fears, to the tone of voice. In turn we should offer comfort, reassurance, and hospitality.

The "contract" for the intake sessions is made during this first phone call. The counselor should make clear the day and time of the appointment and how long the appointment will last. It should also be made clear that the intake process is designed to investigate whether a counseling relationship will even be possible, or whether the counselor will have to refer the counselee elsewhere for a different type of help. The counselee may be asked to bring along supportive materials, including medical records or family photos, depending on the nature of the presenting problem as it has been explained on the phone.

The Opening Moments of the Counseling Hour

Whether short- or long-term counseling, each session should have a similar rhythm. Just as regularity of time and location lends the necessary structure to the counseling process, so too does the shape of the counseling hour. Each hour can be divided into three parts: the opening process, the middle work, and the closing procedures.

Much of the tone during the opening process is set by the counselor. The counselor should have the office space readied and should always be on time. The counselor should not summon the counselee into the office, but rather go out into the waiting room to greet the counselee and extend an invitation to come in. The counselee either should be shown where to sit or should be given the choice of seats; if the counselor wishes to reserve his or her own seat, a notepad or sweater could be left on the chair. The counselor should then sit down, adopting an open and relaxed physical position. For the next hour, the counselee is the most important person in the counselor's life, and should be the subject of the same sense of hospitality that Abraham offered to the angels.

The counselor should unobtrusively be observing the counselee's appearance and body language. Physical grooming, body posture both standing and seated, the sparkle of the eyes, the color and condition of the skin, all give clues to the counselor as to the counselee's level of comfort or distress. Most theorists of communication agree that we communicate with each other much more in nonverbal ways than we do verbally.

The opening of a session may be awkward the first few times that counselor and counselee meet; thereafter, a comfortable rhythm is established that facilitates getting down to business. This opening process of meeting again is called "joining," and is an indispensable part of each session. The counselor might suggest that the session begin with prayer, perhaps asking if the counselee would like any special petition included in the prayer, or offering the counselee an opportunity freely to add spontaneous intercession. However, the pastoral counselor should not feel compelled to open with prayer (Hall, 139; Miller and Jackson, 29). In some instances it may feel inappropriate, but the counselee's preference should be ascertained (as in all other sessions, the counselor's values and preferences should not be allowed to interfere with the counselee's work). Some counselors then wait quietly for about fifteen seconds to see if the counselee wishes to begin. If nothing is forthcoming, the counselor should then begin with a question or an open-ended comment. The counselor might refer to material gleaned during the phone conversation, such as, "Charles, you mentioned that you were having problems in your marriage." If there is no previous information, the counselor might ask, "How can I help you, Susan?"

As the presenting problem unfolds, the counselor may wish to take some notes. These notes should be taken discreetly so as not to distract the counselee or interrupt the flow of conversation. In no circumstances should the counselor scribble madly each time the counselee says something particularly important; this will ultimately make the counselee quite suspicious. If the first session is an intake session, the counselor should record carefully what name the counselee prefers to be called, and all necessary statistical information such as phone numbers, address, and immediate family constellation. If notes are taken during the subsequent sessions, they should be encoded to some degree to minimize any breach of confidence should someone else stumble across them.

If the appointment is an intake session for short-term counseling, the counselor and counselee together should determine the specific goal of the time-limited counseling. This may require more than one intake session. If the appointment is an intake session for long-term counseling for relationship issues, the counselor may suggest additional intake sessions involving a "silent observer." In this model, a couple comes together for the first intake session, then two additional intake sessions are scheduled. In the first, one partner talks and the other listens silently. In the second, the other partner talks and the first listens silently. A final intake session may then be scheduled to work through the style and number of sessions over the long-term course.

Among other decisions the counselor needs to make is where to begin the counseling work. If the presenting problem is one of changing future behavior, short-term counseling may be the best choice. If the presenting problem is one involving deep unfinished business from the past,

long-term counseling will be the best choice. If the issue is very much in the present, the counselor will have to choose whether to suggest short-term or long-term counseling. This decision will be shaped by information gathered during the intake session.

The Main Body of the Counseling Hour
Once the opening processes have been completed, the session should pass smoothly into the middle work. The counselor has seven responsibilities during long-term counseling, to which an eighth must be added for short-term counseling.

1. To listen actively and reflectively.
2. To enter the world of the counselee, "to perceive the world as the client sees it, to perceive the client himself as he is seen by himself" (Carl Rogers in Patton, 149).
3. To attend carefully to "the music behind the words" (Hall, 60), to the level of communication that is behind and deeper than the words being said.
4. To guide the counselee constantly back to the affective or feeling level, avoiding the constant distraction of "getting the facts all out on the table." Focusing on facts avoids the counselee's pain, blames others, and prevents the counselor's entering the affective world of the counselee.
5. To respond to the counselee directly and honestly. The therapeutic process has no room for polite conversation, small talk, or lies.
6. To trust the process, all the while creating a climate of safety and of confidence so that the counselee can come to responsible adult insights and decisions.
7. To analyze the counselor's approach and the counselee's progress during and after each session.

8. In the case of short-term counseling, to keep the counselee focused on the reason for the therapy and the nonnegotiable time limitations.

Pastoral counselors who wish to explore the dynamics of long-term counseling could begin by reading a recent basic text-book in personality theory, developmental psychology, or psychodynamic therapy. This reading in turn should suggest to the counselor areas that he or she wishes to explore further. As I have already said, even those pastoral counselors who are limiting their work to short-term counseling will benefit from continuing education in the foundational theory behind long-term therapy. A counselor should have the largest repertoire of skills and insights possible, for no single approach will work with every client. What works in one situation will not necessarily work in another due to the unique needs and life experience of each counselee.

Certain methodological concepts are common to both short-term and long-term counseling, though they may be more obvious in long-term work. The following five terms are of particular importance in understanding the dynamic interpersonal relationship between counselor and counselee:

1. *Transference.* Fromm claimed that "transference is about the most significant problem in human life" (118). Transference is the displacement of reactions to and need from another person in one's past onto a person in one's present. According to John Patton, transference is therefore "an error in time" (171). Transference expresses the need of a person to have somebody who takes over the responsibility, who parents them, who gives a mother's unconditional love or a father's praise and punishment. Fromm continues:

And even if people had never had a father and a mother, even if people had never been children, they need that as long as they have not become fully human themselves, fully independent themselves. . . . It is a general human longing to have somebody whom you can choose as your idol, to whom you can say: "This is my god." This is the person who loves me, who guides me, who rewards me, because I cannot stand of myself. (119)

Transference is both promise and problem in the counseling relationship. Freud believed it should be encouraged in order to give the counselor access to the counselee's unconscious. Rogers believe it should be minimized for it interfered with the counselee's ability to address present reality. This would suggest that in short-term counseling, transference should be discouraged as much as possible.

Transference is unavoidable in the counseling relationship, even in short-term therapy, and for pastoral counselors it is even more severe. Because ministers work in an interpersonal environment where their several functions cannot be satisfactorily delimited either by themselves or by other parishioners, those bearing the authority of ministry are easily confused with all other forms of authority. The church counselor may be the object of the counselee's transference from an unsatisfactory relationship with God, with a parental figure, with supreme authority, with older or more powerful siblings, with a marital partner, with other church authorities. As Patton remarks, every minister "cannot avoid seeming to be more than they are" (172).

Because ministers are so frequently confused with people from other parishioners' pasts, ministers often find themselves the subject of displaced emotions, including anger and romantic love. Transference explains why parishioners may have outbursts of rage and then leave the parish, or why parishioners fall in love with unsuspecting ministers. The warmth, generosity, and hospitality that many ministers foster only encourage further transference. For some parishioners, the minister's caring may be the first time they have experienced the affirmation of unconditional human esteem. In any case, transference is involuntary and generally unconscious. Pastoral counselors should therefore treat displaced emotions, whether anger or romantic love, with kindness and a firm refusal to get involved.

Whether transference is encouraged or discouraged, it must always be controlled. Patton suggests three ways for a counselor to keep transference under control:

1. Set clear limits for yourself regarding what you will and will not do within counseling relationships. These include limits for demands on your time, for physical contact, etc. When such issues arise, communicate your limits clearly and stick by them. Often, firm boundaries will make the extent of the client's transference much more obvious. One of the easiest ways for a counselee to express transference, or hostility toward a parental or authority figure, is by being late to a counseling session, or even forgetting it altogether. Another common form of negative transference is resistance, as discussed below.

2. Become more comfortable in counseling people who have intense feelings. This may be difficult for ordained ministers, for studies of the psychology of clergy reveal that most ordained ministers have a fear of other people's anger.

3. Help careseekers to separate reality from fantasy. Where a transference issue is emerging, discuss it directly to separate yourself from the projected image. (184–85)

To these three may be added a fourth, that the counselee should be told information about the counselor's private life only when that information is appropriate and will further the counselee's therapeutic progress. While this at first may seem to increase the counselor's mystery and thereby encourage more transference, it actually serves to thwart the counselee's attempts to trade roles with the counselor.

Transference and its twin, countertransference, leave the pastoral counselor vulnerable to manipulating the counselee and to succumbing to sexual impropriety. In addition to its role within the counseling process, transference needs to be understood for ethical and legal reasons. In a recent study, many women reported that their sexual liaisons with their pastoral counselors began as a nonsexual relief that they had finally found someone who understood them.

2. *Countertransference.* According to Fromm, "the analyst has all sorts of irrational attitudes toward the patient. He is afraid of the patient, he wants to be praised by the patient, he wants to be loved by the patient" (120). For this reason, the counselor may mistakenly cooperate with the client's transference, a particular trap for ministers with a "fix-it" mentality, a desire to rescue, or a messiah complex. Since idealization is the most common form of transference by clients, the counselor may begin to internalize, or carry, the client's idealization, thereby losing objectivity, proportionality, and effectiveness.

"Abstinence" is the proper therapeutic term for "not gratifying the patient's infantile and neurotic wishes" (Greenson, 212). Countertransference is usually controllable if a counselor is in regular supervision. If countertransference becomes a problem, the counselee should quickly be referred to another counselor.

Countertransference is sometimes confused with counselor transference. Counselor transference is exactly like client transference, except working from counselor toward counselee. The counselor may confuse the counselee with someone from the counselor's past or displace onto the counselee emotions that belong elsewhere in the counselor's private life. In either instance—countertransference or counselor transference—the counselor is misusing the counselee to serve the counselor's personal ends.

A further distinction needs to be made between "therapeutic transference" and "affective projection." The counseling room is often full of emotion but the question remains: "Whose emotions is the counselor feeling? The client's or the counselor's own?" In therapeutic transference, the counselor is aware of emotional responses to the client that are displaced from the counselor's own past. In affective projection, the client hands feelings off to the counselor, leaving the counselor with the responsibility of "feeling the client's feelings for him" (Hopcke, 41). If the counselor becomes angry about something the counselee has said, and the anger response is clearly inappropriate to the counselor's professional involvement in the relationship, the counselor then needs to ask whether he or she is feeling displaced anger (therapeutic transference), or whether the counselor has accepted anger feelings that the client has given away because the client finds them too hard to deal with (affective pro-

jection). The confusion between the two can be clarified only if the counselor interrupts the flow of the session to inquire. The counselor might ask, "I'm feeling angry right now, and I need to check if it's anger I am picking up from you. Am I sensing correctly that you are angry?"

3. *Repetition Compulsion.* The concept is Freudian in origin and argues that a counselee will repeat dysfunctional patterns from the past. Having been deeply affected by an earlier event, the counselee will unconsciously return to it over and over, attempting to act it out in each new relationship in the hope that this time it will work out right. The Freudian concept is directly related to the Family Systems concept that successive generations within a family will repeat the same dysfunctional patterns unless there is an intervention to teach some family members new ways of being. Most repetition compulsions are severe enough that a counselee will also act them out in the midst of a transference relationship to the counselor and thus they can be analyzed and deconstructed.

4. *Resistance.* Both short-term and long-term counseling must deal with the problem of the counselee's resisting the therapeutic process. Karl Menninger suggests that resistance can be traced to five possible motivations:

1. The counselee is fearful of new things.

2. The resistance is a form of revenge, a power struggle because the counselor does not have the answers that the counselee anticipated.

3. The counselee wishes unconsciously to maintain the advantages of illness or the joys of getting so much attention.

4. The counselee cannot seem to let go of the status quo derived from past life patterns.

5. The counselee has an unconscious need for punishment. (104, 105–7)

As can be seen, it is not the counselor who is being resisted, but the therapeutic process itself. As perverse as it may seem for someone to remain in counseling and yet resist it, it is a very normal human reaction. Resistance may be heightened when the pastoral counselor offers more help or advice than the counselee wants. When resistance is encountered in the counseling process, it must be named and studied.

5. *Reframing.* The process of framing and reframing was described in more detail in the earlier chapter on narrativity. In brief, reframing is the process by which a counselee is brought to see things in a new way and thereby open up new possibilities of response and reaction. Skillful reframing is well within the means of a pastoral counselor, though it is usually more appropriate to long-term counseling than to short-term goal-oriented counseling. The confines of limited-term counseling do not easily provide the space for a story to be framed, dismantled, and reframed.

Ending a Session

The final ten minutes of each counseling hour should be reserved for closure and its attendant tasks. The counselor should summarize what has transpired during the session and give the counselee the opportunity to ask questions about the summary or about anything else of concern. The summary should leave the counselee with a sense of temporary closure and identify areas for further work in the future. The counselor should negotiate the next appointment or remind the counselee of the number of short-term appointments remaining. Homework such as journaling

or dream work or communication exercises may be assigned. The counselor should then stand up and escort the counselee to the door. Some theorists suggest that the counselor should shake the counselee's hand or offer some other form of touch. Many types of touch are, however, misinterpretable and even unwelcome, particularly by survivors of sexual abuse. I believe that the counselor's care and encouragement can just as effectively be conveyed by a warm smile and a few appropriate words.

Once the counselee has left the office, the counselor should rearrange the furniture to its original position, tidy up, and then may wish to return to the desk to jot down a few observations on the session that has just been completed. At the very least, the counselor should take a few minutes to reflect quietly on the progress of the pastoral relationship and the counselor's own methodology. If notes are taken, they should then be placed in a locked file or desk drawer; under no circumstances should anyone be able to stumble across these notes accidentally.

Terminating and Referring

Just as a counselor has carefully structured the intake sessions as well as each individual hour's appointment, so the termination of the counseling relationship needs to be carefully structured. The counselee should be given enough advance warning of the termination to be able to deal with its emotional impact—perhaps two or more sessions. Some counselors place some extra time between those final few sessions; instead of sessions being a week apart, the final two may be two weeks apart. Topics of conversation in the last sessions should recognize the client's success and look to the future in hope. It may be appropriate that some inexpensive symbolic gift be exchanged (a form of transitional object), or that the counseling course be terminated by a lunch or a walk together or a symbolic Eucharist.

Howard Stone points out that termination may be a difficult decision for a pastoral counselor to make:

> . . . The minister is trapped by sympathy— not empathy—and this endangers the counselee's well-being. A sure guide is to *believe what they do, not what they say.* Continuing to offer unlimited support as their minister may put the minister in the role of what Alcoholics Anonymous calls an "enabler." Enablers make it easy for people to cling to their old, destructive patterns of behavior and indefinitely put off "hitting bottom"—that is, experiencing the amount of pain they need to motivate them to action. (161)

It will help both pastoral counselor and counselee if the fear of abandonment is addressed directly. The counselor should make it clear that various types of contact will continue with the parishioner even though the counseling relationship is terminating. Counseling may be possible again in the future, but should not be promised too quickly. The counselor should inquire what not having counseling will feel like to the counselee, and how it will be to relate to the counselor in other ways.

Sometimes it is inappropriate for a counselor even to begin counseling with a certain counselee or there may be reason to interrupt an established relationship. This is called a referral. The professional counseling literature suggests twelve reasons for referring a counselee to some other counselor or form of treatment (adapted from Childs, 86):

1. the problem presented by the client is so complex or so far out of the experience or expertise of the pastor that adequate counseling would be difficult;

2. the pastor and the counselee have too much contact in other contexts that could compromise the counseling relationship;

3. there is not enough time in the pastor's schedule to allow for adequate counseling;

4. the counselee does not meet the usual criteria for time-limited counseling;

5. countertransference, that is, when the person is struggling with an issue that is too related to issues with which the counselor is also struggling;

6. the counselee seems not to want to change;

7. some other counselor would clearly be a better choice;

8. counseling is not what is needed, but rather the services of a lawyer or a physician;

9. group work would be more appropriate, as in the case of certain relationship issues;

10. when someone is suicidal;

11. when there is physical or domestic abuse involved in the case, whether toward the counselee's self or toward others;

12. when the counselee seems to be making no effort to improve.

The reasons for making the referral should be carefully explained to the counselee. By referring, the minister gives up his or her counseling relationship with the person, but all other forms of pastoral contact should be maintained. The counselor should facilitate the counselee's introduction to the new counselor but should leave the responsibility for making appointments with the counselee. When counseling is not voluntary, it is not effective. It is unethical to counsel someone who is already in counseling with another counselor, but it is pastorally responsible to check in with a former counselee who is a parishioner, from time to time, to make sure the parishioner is being cared for. For guidelines on the ethics of referral and other ethical issues in the therapeutic relationship, counselors should read the Ethical Guidelines of the American Association of Pastoral Counselors (found in Hall, 152–70).

Levels of Meaning in the Counseling Relationship

New Zealand therapist Joan Dalloway, drawing on the work of Petrouska Clarkson and Phil Lapworth, describes the therapeutic relationship as encompassing five levels of meaning within the overlapping spheres of counselor and counselee.

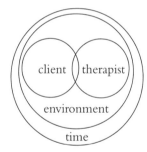

FIGURE: *domains of variation in psychotherapy*

The first level of meaning is what Martin Buber called the "I-Thou" relationship. Counselor and client meet each other in the richness of the fully empathic human encounter. Each sees the Divine in the other, greeting the other as both wholly different and a beloved friend. Both counselor and counselee are transformed by the encounter, for there is no true encounter unless both parties are equally vulnerable to each other. The second level of meaning is the working alliance: counselor and counselee are united in seeking the ultimate good of the counselee. Dalloway describes this relationship as being more like a grandparent and a grandchild than like a parent and a child. The counselor as loving grandparent inquires of the counselee, "Where are you?" "What do you want from me?" and "Will you be whole?"

The third level of relationship is the transferential. Through the counselor's controlled use of the counselee's transference, the counselee comes to understand his or her own uniqueness and dignity. The present is grasped in its fullness, offering new hope in place of compulsive repetition of past responses to hurt. The fourth level of meaning is the developmental reparative. Counseling offers the counselee the opportunity to revisit the past, perhaps to reframe it, perhaps to finish unfinished business, perhaps to lay it to rest. Once an earlier developmental stage has been revisited and set right, the counselee can move quickly through the subsequent ones in order to reenter the present as a more whole person.

The fifth level of meaning, and one to which pastoral counseling should be particularly suited, is the transpersonal, that part of human nature which transcends our particular physical, emotional, and intellectual capabilities. Some have called the transpersonal "the realm of personal blessing." In finding new spiritual health, integrated with our emotional, intellectual, and relational literacy—and indeed, every segment of the Wholeness Wheel—the counselee experiences the blessing of comprehensive healing (Culbertson). The old has not been erased or forgotten, but has been transformed to serve the present, thereby opening up a new future. When the counselee arrives at the transpersonal level, the depth work of counseling is completed.

The Principles of Active Listening

The method of counseling most widely used by pastoral counselors is often known as "active listening." It is not necessarily the best technique, but is probably the safest approach with the least possibility of a client's being damaged by a less experienced or less formally trained counselor.

Michael Basch describes the power of active listening:

When the patient first comes for therapy, he fully expects to have to continue his self-justification and to persuade the therapist of the inevitability and the correctness of his position. But the therapist's attitude undercuts such behavior. By taking it for granted that the patient must have good reason for behaving the way he does even though it gets him in trouble, the therapist implicitly and explicitly conveys to him that he, the therapist, is not condemning him out of hand. (174)

Active listening is the method that conveys the counselor's understanding of the counselee's behavior.

One of the most common sayings of Jesus in the Gospels is, "Let those who have ears hear!" But, as the Gospels make clear, hearing and understanding are not always synonymous. Often the disciples or the crowds hear Jesus but then have to ask him to explain what he meant. Active listening provides the means by which the counselor can let the counselee know that he or she has been understood.

The basic principle underlying active listening is that we each speak in encoded messages. All verbal messages are codes—language equivalents of our feelings, but not the feelings themselves. The simple question "What time is it?" may mean "I'm hungry" or "I want to go home" or "I'm bored." The speaker who asks the time may presume that he or she has communicated clearly, but the receiver of the question can only be sure what the speaker means by decoding the message and then reflecting it back to the speaker.

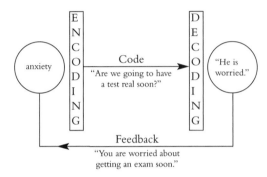

If the receiver of the message responds "three o'clock," it will be quite clear that the message was not understood. The speaker will be frustrated, feel unable to get his or her needs met, and may ultimately cease efforts to communicate because the situation seems hopeless.

Because a communication may mean a number of different things, as in the example above, the receiver cannot know whether he or she has understood unless the decoded message is reflected back to the speaker. The process of "feeding back" is what is meant by active listening. It is this final stage of reflecting that completes the effective communication process—communicating, decoding, reflecting.

A reflective statement signals an attempt to enter into the speaker's world in order to understand more fully. Chris Schlauch argues that this is the true meaning of the word *empathy*, "to search one's way into the experience of another" (4). A reflective statement always addresses feelings rather than facts, and is expressed as a statement rather than a question. Robert Brizee reminds us that active listening calls for a commitment to an unconditional acceptance of the other, a willingness to listen to the unattractive parts of another person (52). Active listening does not mean simply that "I'll be with you as long as you're nice to me." While we are often nice, we are not nice all the time. It is when we are not nice that we are in dire need of grace. Brizee thus understands active listening as a healing gift that Christians offer each other in God's name.

Active listening is not always easy. It requires a counselor's willingness to let go of personal values, to enter the world of another's values. Carl Rogers, who promoted active listening as "client-centered therapy," believed that listening was enough to bring people to new health. His interest was to find out what the speaker wanted, what was blocking the achievement of that want, and how the person might find ways to remove the block. The goal belonged to the speaker as did the steps to get there. As the speaker feels caringly understood, the process of healing begins. To empathize with another person requires four qualities from the counselor: extensive life experience, awareness of how responsive people are to a variety of internal and external stimuli, the ability to put thoughts and decoded messages into new words, and the wisdom to identify and name feelings—both one's own and those of another. The process of active listening then involves not only reflective communication but also waiting with caring. Before we can understand others we must wait patiently for them to speak to us. Through patience and careful reflective listening a counselor can sometimes love a person back to wholeness.

Expectations for a Cure

Will everyone we counsel find healing? Probably not. Counseling is in itself not a solution and does not depend upon advice, answers, or cures. The outcome of a series of sessions is ultimately in the hands of the counselee and well outside the assured control of the counselor. Erich Fromm lists seven variables that can determine whether a course of counseling will succeed or fail:

(a) Whether the time is right. Some people go for counseling before they have reached the bottom of their suffering. Others quit counseling before it has had time to take effect.
(b) Whether the patient acquires or has some idea of what his life ought to be, or could be—some vision of what he wants.
(c) Whether the patient is serious. Some narcissistic people go into counseling solely because they like to talk about themselves.
(d) Whether the patient has the capacity to differentiate between banality and reality. This capacity will determine how efficiently the counseling time is used.
(e) Whether the patient has successfully adapted the expression of his problems to a socially acceptable level so that there is little external pressure to change.
(f) Whether the counselee participates fully in the counseling process.
(g) Whether the counselor is congruent and has a therapeutic personality. (34–38)

Yet the final outcome of pastoral counseling is sometimes not immediately obvious. Counseling is a process that sets change in motion in the counselee. Sometimes we speak of the "internal therapist," the voice of transformation that gets turned on and continues to work, even while the counselee is not in a counseling session and often long afterwards. As Howard Stone observes, "The real work of counseling does not happen in the one hour of the counseling session—where a safe, friendly environment is established—but in the other 167 hours of the week" (35). Whether or not a cure has been effected may not be apparent for months or even years later.

Confidentiality and Counseling Supervision

All material that has been heard, stated, or alluded to in a counseling session should be considered bound by the strictest seal of confidentiality. It is unethical and unprofessional to reveal anything about a counselee to anyone, including the pastoral counselor's marital partner. It is also unethical to reveal the names of anyone you are counseling or even to mention in passing that you have a counseling relationship with so-and-so, even if asked. There are three standard exceptions: abuse is required by law to be reported to the police (if it is not reported, the pastoral counselor may be sued as an accomplice to a crime); a counselor may need to discuss a case with a supervisor (who is also bound to confidentiality by professional ethics); and on occasion, counselor records may be subpoenaed by a court. Many counselors deal with these possibilities by having their counselees sign a release form covering all three circumstances at the intake interview. Even when marital partners work as a ministry team, no information should be shared. All counseling material belongs to the counselee, and only the counselee has legal control over its use and dissemination. No counseling session should ever be taped or recorded with-

out permission, nor should counselees be referred to from the pulpit, no matter how thoroughly their identity seems to be disguised.

These and related issues ought to be obvious to anyone who is in professional supervision. However, ordained ministers and those lay ministers in a congregational leadership capacity should be aware of a distinction between ministry supervision—sometimes also referred to as "consultation"—and counseling supervision. Ministry supervision and counseling supervision are discussed in the next chapter. The reader is here reminded that "being" a counselor and "doing" counseling are simultaneous processes of growth and formation, requiring the constant oversight of a qualified professional who is specifically trained in the art of therapeutic supervision.

Counseling Cross-Culturally

The three great "isms" that divide, alienate, and oppress people are sexism, capitalism, and racism. All three are appropriate topics of address when counseling cross-culturally. Counselees who do not come from white Western cultures may have reached quite adaptive solutions within their native context, but look maladjusted by the sexist, capitalist, or racist values of a culture other than their own. Many counselees from other cultures will have acquired a split or negative sense of self-esteem from living among white people, reinforced by concepts of "shame" and "face" common to most nonwhite ethnic groups. The social context of pastoral counseling should be taken into account with any counselee, but particularly when counselor and counselee come from markedly different cultures. In most instances, the cultural gap will make it impossible for the counselor to enter the counselee's world to an effective degree without specialized training.

The two major psychiatric diagnoses of hospitalized nonwhite women are schizophrenia and paranoia, but often these are simply predictable reactions to a life of marginalization, discrimination, and sexism. Failing to take social factors into account therefore often produces only a more sophisticated form of "blaming the victim." Most behavioral schools of psychology are based on white Western norms of behavior and so are inappropriate for nonwhite counselees; most standard psychological tests are culturally biased in favor of whites. Since most societies are not as highly individualized as the Euro-American, group counseling provides a more comfortable ethos of communication and support than does one-to-one counseling.

Many nonwhites will have turned to community elders before coming to a counselor. Such practices at times offer very appropriate healing; at other times they delay appropriate intervention until it is nearly too late. Counselors who seek further training in cross-cultural issues should begin by reading Augsburger's book listed in the bibliography and then seeking specialized training courses.

Conclusion

"The eyes are the gift of the carver, but even they come from the sea," not from us. In this simple sentence we are cautioned about pastoral hubris, for what we pastors offer is never as much as the healing that God offers. In the end, pastoral counseling is a divinely inspired art. Like any artist, including the "carver who spent a lifetime with wood," we must first master the skills before our art can be of value

to anyone else. As we shall see in the following chapter, the source of fine pastoral care is God, and the artistic medium through which the pastor's skills are offered is the pastor's own cultivated Christian wholeness.

BIBLIOGRAPHY

American Psychiatric Association. *Diagnostic and Statistical Manual of Mental Disorders.* 4th ed. *(DSM-IV).* Washington, D. C.: American Psychiatric Association, 1994.

Augsburger, David. *Pastoral Counseling across Cultures.* Philadelphia: Westminster, 1986.

Basch, Michael. *Doing Psychotherapy.* New York: Basic, 1980.

Bauer, Gregory P., and Joseph C. Kobos. *Brief Therapy: Short-Term Psychodynamic Intervention.* Northvale, N.J.: Jason Aronson, 1987.

Brizee, Robert. *The Gift of Listening.* St. Louis: Chalice, 1993.

Childs, Brian H. *Short-Term Pastoral Counseling: A Guide.* Nashville: Abingdon, 1990.

Culbertson, Philip. "The Shadow of the Transcendent: Valuing Spirituality in Psychotherapy." *Forum: The Journal of the New Zealand Association of Psychotherapists* 4 (June 1998): 14–37.

Donnelly, Felix. *A Time to Talk: Counsellor and Counselled.* Auckland: George Allen & Unwin, 1981.

Fromm, Erich. *The Art of Listening.* New York: Continuum, 1994.

Grace, Patricia. *Potiki.* Auckland: Penguin Books, 1986.

Greenson, Ralph. *The Technique and Practice of Psychoanalysis.* New York: International Universities Press, 1967.

Hall, Jack. *Affective Competence in Counseling.* Lanham, Md.: University Press of America, 1995.

Hopcke, Robert. *Men's Dreams, Men's Healing: A Psychotherapist Explores a New View of Masculinity through Jungian Dreamwork.* Boston: Shambhala, 1990.

Menninger, Karl. *The Theory of Psychoanalytic Technique.* New York: Basic, 1958.

Miller, William, and Kathleen Jackson. *Practical Psychology for Pastors.* Englewood Cliffs, N.J.: Prentice-Hall, 1985.

Oden, Thomas C. *Care of Souls in the Classic Tradition.* Philadelphia: Fortress, 1984.

Patton, John. *Pastoral Counseling: A Ministry of the Church.* Nashville: Abingdon, 1983.

Schlauch, Chris R. "Empathy as the Essence of Pastoral Psychotherapy." *The Journal of Pastoral Care* 44:1 (spring 1990): 3–17.

Sifneos, Peter E. *Short-Term Dynamic Psychotherapy.* 2d ed. New York: Plenum Medical Book Co., 1987.

Stone, Howard W. *Brief Pastoral Counseling: Short-Term Approaches and Strategies.* Minneapolis: Fortress, 1994.

Taylor, Charles W. *The Skilled Pastor: Counseling as the Practice of Theology.* Minneapolis: Fortress, 1991.

Thornton, Martin. *The Rock and the River.* London: Hodder and Stoughton, 1965.

10. Pastoral Congruence and Ministry Supervision

"Lost in the rush toward technical innovation are the human dimensions of the relationships between people." (Jeffrey Kottler, 8)

One of the most famous approaches to pastoral identity is the paradigm of "The Wounded Healer," created by Henri Nouwen in his 1979 book by the same name. Nouwen argued that the personal wounds borne by every pastor, whether lay or ordained, create the sensitivity to pain and suffering that enable effective empathic ministry to occur. An integral part of the ministry of the Wounded Healer is revealing his or her own wounds to those among whom ministry is carried out. Nouwen writes:

> No minister can save anyone. He can only offer himself as a guide to fearful people. Yet, paradoxically, it is precisely in this guidance that the first signs of hope become visible. This is so because a shared pain is no longer paralyzing but mobilizing, when understood as a way to liberation. When we become aware that we do not have to escape our pains, but that we can mobilize them into a common search for life, those very pains are transformed from expressions of despair into signs of hope. (1979, 93)

Nouwen's words offered "signs of hope" to many in ministry who were painfully aware of their own loneliness, brokenness, woundedness, and pain, and who worried that these burdens might disqualify them from effective ministry. Instead, according to their reading of Nouwen, human community is built upon a shared pain and suffering and it is within this community bond that people can find the place to minister to one another.

What is often overlooked, unfortunately, is Nouwen's further claim that the woundedness itself is not the primary credential, but healing and recovery must be well under way before one can truly minister empathically. Only when one has found a way through suffering, or the road back from pain, can one describe that journey to another person. It is both the pain and suffering, and the continuing recovery from them, that enable effective ministry. Simply having been wounded is not enough to form ministerial character. The imitation of Christ does not stop with crucifixion but must continue through resurrection in order for a minister to have enough hope to offer another. Nouwen makes it clear that it is personal recovery, and not only personal woundedness, that is to be shared in ministry:

> When the imitation of Christ does not mean to live a life like Christ, but to live your life as authentically as Christ lived his, then there are many ways and forms in which a man can be a Christian. The minister is the one who can make this search for authenticity possible, not by standing on the side as a neutral screen or an impartial observer, but as an articulate witness of Christ, who puts his own search at the disposal of others. (1979, 99)

The search for authenticity is part and parcel of the personal recovery that engifts us for ministry.

Can One Be "Too Wounded" for Ministry?

In a sensitive but provocative article, Maxine Glaz argues that woundedness that is still raw and has not begun to be healed and put in some sort of perspective actually can destroy effective ministry. In answering the question "Can a Healer Be Too Wounded to Heal?" Glaz points out that those who have been wounded but have not yet begun to heal may be suffering from post-traumatic stress disorder:

> Whether induced by battle, disaster, crisis, or violence, the emotional state of the victim is similar in every trauma and carries a similar symptomology. The victim re-visualizes the traumatic event and repetitiously re-experiences the associated affected state. The trauma becomes a depressing and absorbing preoccupation that interferes with daily tasks. It intrudes into consciousness, whether wanted or not. (46)

Unless healing has begun, the victim of traumatic woundedness will involuntarily replay affective and behavioral scripts within the doing of ministry, thus destroying the potential for healing others. If anything, unrecovering victims of trauma create other victims. They may acknowledge their past helplessness to fend off violence but continue to live by fending off perceived threats of violence that are not even there. "Their psychological defensiveness, however understandable, is expressed either in extreme withdrawal and anxious self-preoccupation or in presumptuous counterattacks" (Glaz, 49).

The primary illustrations in Glaz's article are men and women in ministry training who have been sexually abused during their childhood. Citing supportive research from the Kempe Center in Denver, Colorado, Glaz argues that childhood victims who are able to conclude that the abuse they endured was not merited are better able to manage the aftermath of abuse. Those who have internalized the abuse as somehow having been their fault do not manage as well and continue to view themselves as victims who need to be constantly on the defensive. Men and women who are stuck in a victim mentality generally do not make good candidates for ministry or ministry training, argues Glaz, because their personalities tend to become disorganized under stress, they project their defensiveness upon their colleagues in a confusing manner, and they often present as too self-absorbed to be appropriately sensitive to the needs and messages of those around them. Such candidates are "too wounded to be healers" (Glaz, 57). On the other hand, victims of childhood sexual abuse who have intentionally diminished their attention to the past in order to attend to the present, who have been assisted toward "normalization" through counseling or psychotherapy, and who have a subsequent record of good, sustaining personal relationships, may be excellent candidates for the public ministry of caring, but will probably need some special attention in ministry training.

How Widespread Is Pastoral Woundedness?

Scientific studies of the personality profiles of ordained clergy have been conducted repeatedly over the past thirty years. Plante, Manuel, and Tandez, analyzing the results of the Minnesota Multiphasic Personality Inventory and the 16PF as administered to Roman Catholic clergy, found that these men ranked higher than average in social responsibility, traditionally feminine interests, trust, forthrightness, and self-assurance. But they also ranked higher than average in defensiveness (especially repression of needs and wishes) and in their inability to cope with negative emotions such as anger and hostility. Hands and Fehr trace clergy personality distortion to their families of origin. Their findings would be supported by the theories of Alice Miller, who argued that people in the "helping professions" developed a keen attunement to the needs of others often because they grew up in a family where they were given or assumed responsibility for meeting the needs of a narcissistically disturbed parent (1981). Along the way they learned to suppress their needs, wishes, and negative emotions to retain others' affections (Talbot, 347).

Hands and Fehr argue that this repression of personal need results in a "cognitive-affective" split, that is, the severing of connection between mind and emotions (8–9). "The 'facade' of such a person results from the attempt to present only a highly rational, intellectualized, and even morally superior front" to members of his or her congregation. The split is then acted out in one or the other of the two most common clergy roles: the hero or the clown/mascot. The hero's ego identity is distorted by the belief that her efforts are both supremely ordained and indispensable for others' health and salvation. The clown/mascot believes that he has special charisms to nurture and comfort people and to make them happy and whole. The gratification from exercising these charisms comes in people's devotion to his ministry and their cooperation in maintaining his "glittering image," as novelist Susan Howatch calls it. "Heroes," often fearing enmeshment, prefer to fix others. Taking on the dominant role of helper or spiritual director, they disappear into their ministry work, to the neglect of their families and their own spiritual life. "Clowns," fearing both conflict and aban-

donment, tend to be dependent people-pleasers, willing to placate others as "reconcilers" in order to keep relationships alive, despite the cost (Hands and Fehr, 22). Both roles, in their narcissism, can easily justify the violation of others' boundaries.

The three studies have in common the suggestion that ordained clergy are typically out of touch with their own emotions, needs, and wishes, and tend to repress their negative emotions such as anger and hostility rather than processing them within the practice of ministry. All three studies also suggest that these psychological patterns are the result of childhood experiences that taught the clergy to take care of others' needs and to deny their own. Is this, too, trauma? Probably not, at least in the sense that Glaz speaks of trauma. Each is a form of woundedness, however, and each holds out distinct possibilities that ministry facilitation will be impaired by the involuntary or unconscious acting out of aspects of the bearer's personality that have been carefully held apart from both public and self-scrutiny. In the case of both trauma and dysfunction, those who aspire to the caring ministry may discover they are their own worst enemies and, without careful attention to the formation of a pastoral ego, may not understand why.

Woundedness versus Congruence

Glaz's argument for normalization of the traumas of our past and the various studies of pastoral ego dysfunction both emphasize the necessity for significant healing prior to the public exercise of ministry. Of course there is probably no human being alive who is without need for healing. A claim can be made, however, that those who exercise the public ministry of pastoral care carry a variety of responsibilities that demand an ego strength and consistency above and beyond what is expected of those in many other vocations or professions. In ministry we are called to stand alongside not only the lovable but also the unlovable; to help bear not only the full range of human joy and gratitude, but also anger, despair, and ingratitude; to know how to respond not only to the simplest of faiths, but also to the most complex and contradictory; to discern not only the right answer to give at the right time, but also when it is most godly to admit that we have no answers. We are called to be self-assured and yet humble, self-aware without being self-centered, self-protective yet self-sacrificing, courageous yet meek, peacemakers yet zealous for the gospel—in short, as wise as serpents and as innocent as doves (Matt. 10:16). Above all, say the various schools of psychology, we are to be secure in our sense of self-worth, and theology would agree, by stating that we must begin our ministry in the belief that God loves us just as we have been created, in God's image, and calls us to a particular form of service.

How do we get from trauma and dysfunction to belief in our self-worth and the secure knowledge that we are loved by God? Through grace, of course, but not grace without our full cooperation. What Nouwen calls "the search for authenticity," what Glaz calls "attending to the present," what others call "the healing of memories," and yet others call "self-awareness," is called in the counseling field "congruence."

The etymology of the word *congruence* is unclear. A friend who is a Latin scholar advised me that it means "to fall together" (*ruo*) or "to flow together" (*gradior*), in either case implying integration, concord, and agreement. While not a biblical word, congruence is a biblical concept. Integration and agreement remind us of wholeness, particularly in the Hebrew sense of "shalom" and "shalem," that wonderful interchange of meaning between being at peace and being whole. Psychology claims that to know oneself leads to cure. The same claim is made in the Gospel of John 8:32, "The truth shall make you free." Meister Eckhart, the thirteenth-century German Dominican mystic and scholar, stated this principle even more baldly: "The only way of knowing God is to know oneself" (Fromm 1950, 45).

Pastoral congruence would include the integration of the psychological and the spiritual. Daniel Helminiak points out that "simply put, the specific focus of psychology is human psyche, and the specific focus of spirituality is human spirit. Of course, just as psyche cannot be treated apart from spirit, the functioning of spirit cannot be treated apart from psyche" (190). Psychology perforce includes spirituality, just as spirituality includes psychology. Human beings simply cannot be tidily compartmentalized.

The mandate for pastoral congruence is that the indispensable tool, the medium through which God's healing ministry of pastoral care is accomplished, is our very human individual self. We are all that God has to work with. In order that we be the best possible agents of God's love and care, we must present God with a "package" that is the combined result of our wisest introspection and best self-discipline. Rarely can we construct this ministry-appropriate agency on our own. The move toward congruence needs the help and challenge of others, for we human beings are masters of avoidance and self-deception.

Defining Pastoral Congruence

Many researchers, theoreticians, and practitioners have attempted to describe or even to quantify the dimensions of a congruent personality. Carl Rogers seems to have been the first to use the term *congruence;* his definition will be discussed in detail below. Robert Carkhuff specified empathic understanding and the ability to respond. Jerome Frank felt that confidence was the key to a counselor's persuasive power. Abraham Maslow believed that the more general striving for self-actualization was a crucial trait. While the term is a twentieth-century one, the concept of pastoral or therapeutic congruence is not. In the sixth century, Gregory the Great described the psychologically and spiritually healthy pastor in his *Book of Pastoral Rule* 2.1:

> It is necessary, therefore, that one should be pure in thought, exemplary in conduct, discreet in keeping silence, profitable in speech, in sympathy a near neighbor to everyone, in contemplation exalted above all others, a humble companion to those who lead good lives, erect in his zeal for righteousness against the vices of sinners. One must not be remiss in the care for the inner life by preoccupation with the external; nor must one, in solicitude for what is internal, fail to give attention to the external. (Culbertson and Shippee, 202–3)

Some fourteen centuries later, Carl Rogers's earliest definition of congruence was simple and straightforward:

> Though this concept of congruence is actually a complex one, I believe all of us recognize it in an intuitive and common-sense way in individuals with whom we deal. With one individual we recognize that he not only means exactly what he says, but that his deepest feelings also match what he is expressing. Thus whether he is angry or affectionate or ashamed or enthusiastic, we sense that he is the same at all levels—in what he is experiencing at an organismic level, in his awareness at the conscious level, and in his words and communications. We furthermore recognize that he is acceptant of his immediate feelings. We say of such a person that we know "exactly where he stands." We tend to feel comfortable and secure in such a relationship. (262–63)

Thus, speaking in the simplest manner, a pastor may be deemed "congruent" when his or her feelings and his or her words or behavior match. Rogers believed that only mature caregivers were able to achieve congruence.

The connection between "congruence" and "maturity" did not escape family therapist Virginia Satir. In fact, she preferred the latter term. In her classic *Conjoint Family Therapy*, she defines maturity (congruence) in a detailed but straightforward way:

> 1. The most important concept in therapy, because it is a touchstone for all the rest, is that of *maturation.*
>
> a. This is the state in which a given human being is fully in charge of himself.
>
> b. A mature person is one who, having attained his majority, is able to make choices and decisions based on accurate perceptions about himself, others, and the context in which he finds himself; who acknowledges these choices and decisions as being his; and who accepts responsibility for their outcomes.
>
> 2. The patterns of behaving that characterize a mature person we call functional because they enable him to deal in a relatively competent and precise way with the world in which he lives. Such a person will:

a. manifest himself clearly to others.

b. be in touch with signals from his internal self, thus letting himself know openly what he thinks and feels.

c. be able to see and hear what is outside himself as differentiated from himself and as different from anything else.

d. behave toward another person as someone separate from himself and unique.

e. treat the presence of different-ness as an opportunity to learn and explore rather than as a threat or a signal for conflict.

f. deal with persons and situations in their context, in terms of "how it is" rather than how he wishes it were or expects it to be.

g. accept responsibility for what he feels, thinks, hears and sees, rather than denying it or attributing it to others.

h. have techniques for openly negotiating the giving, receiving and checking of meaning between himself and others. (117–18)

For our purposes, having already used a Wholeness Wheel as a template for healthy Christian adulthood in earlier chapters, we can here define pastoral congruence as "that state of graced being in which a Christian pastor, lay or ordained, discovers each part of the wheel to be healthy and all parts to be in a state of integration with the others." Halstead equates pastoral formation with pastoral congruence in discussing the goals of theological education: "Intellectual and theological preparation, psycho-spiritual maturation and the acquisition of professional and pastoral skills are three distinct but related areas to which any man or woman preparing for public ministry must attend and in which the institutional churches have interest" (223). He goes on to point out that these three aspects of min-

istry roughly parallel the three conversions that Bernard Lonergan notes must be present in any mature Christian: intellectual, religious/spiritual, and moral/behavioral conversion. Because all three areas are related, pastoral congruence is marked by both consistency and integration. The pastoral gifts of congruence, then, would include literacy and competence: emotional literacy, intellectual literacy, relational literacy, personal theological literacy, and spiritual literacy; or affective competence, cognitive competence, interpersonal competence, volitional competence, and psychosynthetic competence.

Pastoral congruence is ultimately the responsibility of each person exercising God's public ministry. In *The Art of Listening*, Erich Fromm argued that intrapersonal consistency extends beyond the realm of speech and behavior, to the realm of motivation and desire. "A person is responsible not only for what he thinks but for his own unconscious" (Fromm 1994, 74). To know ourselves, and thus know God, is to know ourselves completely. Such knowledge demands skill and the intervention of trained and wise others, but it is ultimately an art. Yet as a pianist, I know that art necessitates practice. The great Artur Rubinstein used to say, "If I don't practice one day, I know it; if I don't practice two days, my family knows it; if I don't practice three days, the whole world knows it." To gain practice in the art of congruence, Fromm recommended that at least an hour a day be set aside for introspection and prayerful meditation (1994, 188). This discipline requires generous measures of both self-forgiveness and self-love. Fromm observed, "if I can form a helping relationship to myself—if I can be sensitively aware of and acceptant toward my own feelings—then the likelihood is great that I can form a helping relationship toward another" (1994, 51). Pastoral congruence begins with creating a trusting and safe environment within which we can hold our own selves. The qualities demanded by pastoral congruence include self-discovery and self-appreciation, healthy satisfying relationships with others, and an ever more intimate relationship with God (Hands and Fehr, 72).

Complete congruence, like permanent world peace, is impossible by human effort alone but, like peace, is worth ever striving toward. Each new experience, each new context, tests the limits of the personal congruence we have already achieved. Jeffrey Kottler remarks:

> We live with the pressure of trying to meet our own and others' expectations. Despite our best efforts to convince ourselves of our limitations, we feel responsible for clients' lives. We experience repetition and the boredom that comes from having an assembly line of people walk through our offices. We feel inadequate for not knowing enough, for not being able to help more. And as a result of these close encounters with people in pain, our own issues are constantly touched, our old wounds reopened. (2–3)

As old wounds and dysfunctional origins are repeatedly reopened, we must test our congruence to make sure it is up to the task of continuing to provide effective care for others. Hands and Fehr cite the ancient spiritual journey of the Via Purgativa, the Via Illuminativa, and the Via Unitiva—the purgative, the illuminative, and the unitive ways (15). They then reframe these disciplines in the language of the search for authenticity and congruence as "uncovery,

discovery, and recovery." Each encounter and each context presents new challenges. According to Carl Rogers, "different individuals differ in their degree of congruence, and the same individual differs at different moments in degree of congruence, depending on what he is experiencing and whether he can accept his experience in his awareness, or must defend himself against it" (342).

The search for authenticity can raise many questions along the way. Pastors should not be afraid of paradox and uncertainty as they seek to understand and integrate themselves, for paradox and uncertainty are part of life and part of pastoring. When we face our parishioners we do not always have all the answers. Roy Schafer reminds us that in counseling, "multiple and often contradictory meanings and consequences may be usefully ascribed to one phenomenon, and that common means and consequences may be ascribed to apparently diverse phenomena" (1983, 7). So too when we seek personal congruence. Stoltenberg points out that the rapid push toward diagnosis and certainty results in "black and white thinking," which automatically closes off options and leads us astray (59). Increasingly we learn in the church that those who think in such rigid oppositional terms do not make good candidates for ministry. Pastors must learn to sit comfortably with the "not yet" aspects of knowing themselves, for the achievement of pastoral congruence is a lifelong process. It may be that one's resistance is too high, or simply that the time to know is not yet ripe.

Rogers believes that congruence is the first prerequisite to building a pastoral alliance between caregiver and careseeker (61–62). The other two prerequisites are positive regard for those who seek our help, and empathic understanding. The combination of the three yields a therapeutic and pastoral environment that feels safe, trusting, and mutually respectful. Only in such a climate can our pastoring be ultimately effective. This alliance, this "holding" environment—in which we "hold" others safely and respectfully as in partially cupped hands—is necessary for others to trust us enough to open up, to grow, and ultimately to find healing. The pastoral task with this safe, trusting, and mutually respectful alliance is not to "do" anything. The pastoral task is simply to "be"—congruently. Kottler bemoans the constant temptation to "do" something:

> In the absence of certainty about what is best, in the presence of someone who is needy and vulnerable, there is a compelling urge to *do* something. It has become the zeitgeist of our times to embrace technical eclecticism, prescriptive treatments, strategic interventions, behavioral management, and other forms of helping that emphasize technique. In many ways, we have permission to adapt our style and methods according to the client's needs and clinical situation. Lost in the rush toward technical innovation are the human dimensions of the relationships between people. (8)

Addressing Peter on the Mount of Transfiguration, Jesus asked him, "Who do people say that I am?"—not "What do people say that I do?" It is pastoral identity, rather than pastoral technique, that offers others the opportunity to find healing.

A safe pastoral "holding environment" also demands a cognizance of personal boundaries. The pastor must know the difference between him- or herself and the careseeker. People who are in emotional pain often have fuzzy or easily permeable boundaries. The pastor, however unintentionally, may take advantage of weak boundaries to use the careseeker as a recipient for the pastor's own unresolved pain, mood, or issues, as Carrie Doehring has so clearly analyzed in her excellent book on power issues in the pastoral relationship. "Knowing ourselves, our motives and our needs, makes us more likely to be of real help. In that way we do not use others unawarely for our own ends, or make them carry bits of ourselves we cannot face" (Hawkins and Shohet, 14). The same projection, or interchange, can happen the other way: a pastor with poor emotional boundaries may discover that he or she is the unwitting repository for the careseeker's pain and is carrying the careseeker's problems as if they were his or her own. Donald Nathanson suggests that caregivers need to develop an "empathic wall" that functions dynamically, much in the manner of the living cell membrane, to protect and insulate us from the affect of the other, allowing us to remain ourselves in the face of the other person's mood (258). When boundaries are violated by either partner in the intimacy of a pastoral relationship, the environment no longer feels safe and the promise of growth and healing is destroyed.

Ultimately, congruence will look different from one person to the next. For example, relational health for a single woman in her late twenties will look different from relational health for a married man in his fifties. Spiritual health often looks different between men and women. Physical health includes many factors over which a person has little control, so that the definition must remain fluid. Some thirty years ago when I was in seminary, some of the faculty were quite concerned to shape our public personae. We were told how to dress for ministry success, how to speak, how to behave. But there was remarkably little concern shown by some faculty for what lay behind our personae, our egos, the site of true ministry formation. Pastoral congruence must be measured by standards of internal, not external, consistency and health. Effective ministry, then, is not performed by people who all look, think, and behave identically, but by a whole variety of congruent caregivers, each of whom reflects the wonderful variety with which God created humanity.

A Second Type of Congruence

Thus far I have spoken of congruence as applying to the internal qualities of the well-formed pastor, demanding self-awareness, consistency, and integration. This is the way Carl Rogers spoke of congruence, as applying only to the individual caregiver. But in the counseling literature, congruence has also come to describe the situation when two people—caregiver and careseeker—"fall together" or "flow together." Rogers preferred to call this state of harmony between two people in a counseling relationship "empathic understanding." Subsequently, other writers in the field have chosen to use the word *congruence* to describe when a counselor is in complete sync with a counselee.

Congruence between a counselor and a counselee offers both danger and opportunity. The primary danger, as described earlier, is a lack of proper boundaries between the two. Doehring explains the dangers of boundary violations in pastoral work:

> The word *merger* has legal origins, where it means "to sink or extinguish (a lesser estate, title, or such) in one which is greater or superior." . . . From this legal usage comes its more general usage: "to cause [something] to be absorbed into something else, so as to lose its own character or identity" and "to sink and disappear, to be swallowed up and lost to view."

Another word for merger is *fusion*. This word has its origins in the world of physics: heating something until it becomes fluid; blending together different things "as if by melting so as to form one whole." A fused relationship, unlike a merged relationship, does not involve a power imbalance. In a merged relationship, one person is subsumed in another. The boundaries of the dominant person remain intact, and the boundaries of the subordinate person dissolve as he or she is swallowed up. . . . In a fused relationship, both persons undergo a dissolution of boundaries. (91–92)

Merger and fusion are two of the most significant dangers in pastoral counseling and, indeed, in almost all pastoral work, just as they are in most marriages.

Healthy boundaries combined with a deep pastoral empathy allow for congruence between a pastoral counselor and a counselee. Congruence by definition should reduce the emotional and psychological abuse possible within the hierarchy of unequal power balance between an "expert" counselor and a "seeking" counselee. Congruence actually affirms the two roles of counselor and counselee, without setting up a power struggle or the possibility of manipulation.

This sort of congruence begins with hospitality. Henri Nouwen describes the characteristics of Christian hospitality:

> Hospitality means primarily the creation of a free space where the stranger can

enter and become a friend instead of an enemy. Hospitality is not to change people, but to offer them space where change can take place. It is to open a wide spectrum of options for choice and commitment. It is not an educated intimidation with good books, good stories, and good works, but the liberation of fearful hearts so that words can find roots and bear ample fruit. It is not a method of making our God and our way into the criteria of happiness, but the opening of an opportunity to others to find their God and their way. (1975, 51)

Because hospitality is so respectful of the other, seeking in no way to change the other but instead to offer new life, a sense of mutuality begins to emerge. As the safe pastoral holding environment grows, pastor and parishioner discover that both are changed when they speak to each other with their authentic selves. Paul Tillich argued that this mutuality is the true working out of Christian love. For him, caring and being cared for "is one act, not two, and only because it is one act is real care possible." Without mutuality, Tillich believed, we turn others into objects or cases and we breach "their self awareness as a person" (1959, 21–22). If caring and being cared for is one act, then caregiver and careseeker are in a pastoral relationship of Christian mutuality.

Mutuality, approached carefully and with all boundaries intact, creates empathy. Doehring explains that empathy "involves a capacity to look within (introspection) and to imagine what it would be like for the other to look within and become aware of what was happening to him or her (vicarious introspection)" (100). Robert Katz defines empathy as "imaginative role-playing" (54). Empathy means knowing our-

selves so well as pastors and persons that when we are asked to "help" another, we can look inside ourselves and find a place where we feel just as the other person feels. Only then can we understand enough of what the other is experiencing to be able truly to "stand alongside" him or her. This too is a part of the safe pastoral holding environment.

Empathy often takes a long time. It demands more listening than speaking, and it demands that one prize highly the other person's difference. Many pastors too quickly assume that they understand; we have already learned that this is most often simply a form of transference from the counselor onto the counselee. "If a student wants to learn about another's life, it takes time. He needs to immerse himself in his patient's most personal thoughts, fantasies, and feelings" (Jacobs, David, and Meyer, 9). We must not be too quick to judge, diagnose, or assume we understand another's situation and the attendant emotions. First of all, we must listen, for we only know of another person what he or she has told us.

"Nothing Is Foreign to Me"

Taking empathy to the extreme, most counseling theory assumes that a counselor is widely experienced in life and the nature of human beings. The search for congruence between two persons, therefore, presents a daunting challenge to pastors. How can we achieve that congruence if we have ghettoized ourselves within the faith or the church?

The second Lubavitcher Rebbe made the following confession regarding his own self-knowledge in relationship to counseling:

> The basis by which I can listen to people's problems, sins, and worries is that I can

always look into myself and find a disposition for the same problem within me. The last [pious congregant] I listened to told me such a heinous story that I could not find any similarity to his life within me. And upon that realization, I was mortified, because this not only meant that such a similarity did exist, but that it lay deeply repressed within me. (Katz, 75)

Erich Fromm argued the same point: "If I cannot experience in myself what it means to be schizophrenic or depressed or sadistic or narcissistic or frightened to death, even though I can experience that in smaller doses than the patients, then I just don't know what the patient is talking about" (1994, 38). Fromm, a Jewish psychoanalyst, social philosopher, and biblical scholar who died in 1980, even claimed to be able to find "the Adolph Eichmann" in himself (1994, 101).

As a lecturer in pastoral theology for nearly fifteen years now, I have known students who would not read a daily newspaper if it contained a horoscope, who would not watch television because it might corrupt them, and who would only associate with others who measured up to their definition of "Christian." Counseling theory from both secular and religious sources suggests that these people will have limited pastoral effectiveness, if any at all, for they will not be able to understand what the majority of the people in the world are talking about.

Ironically, it is the broadness of experience with "the world" that brings enough humility to a counselor that congruence will not be confused with perfection. However much we are called to strive as Christians for perfection (Matt. 5:48) and as ministers for congruence, we will never achieve either fully. In this lie our humility

and the seeds of our empathy with those who see our pastoral care. According to Harold Kushner:

> Dr. Rachel Naomi Remen, a California physician, describes how master psychologist Carl Rogers would approach a therapeutic encounter: "There is something I do before I start a session. I let myself know that I am enough. Not perfect. *Perfect wouldn't be enough.* But that I am human, and that is enough. There is nothing this man can say or do or feel that I can't feel in myself. I can be with him. I am enough."
>
> Dr. Remen adds, "I was stunned by this. It felt as if some old wound in me, some fear of not being good enough, had come to an end. I knew inside myself that what he said was absolutely true. I am not perfect, but I am enough. Knowing that . . . allows healing to happen." (7)

The Price of Incongruence

Neglect in striving for congruence opens up the possibility of failure, or worse, abuse between pastors and their parishioners and counselees. A pastor with unclear or easily permeable personal boundaries will be of inadequate assistance to those seeking help and support, for the relationship is likely to degenerate into merger or fusion. Pastors who cannot understand themselves can hardly be expected to understand others. Pastors whose counseling training has been limited to passages of Scripture and vocational "tricks of the trade" will rarely comprehend the life experience of others, and particularly those outside the narrowest definition of "Christian." The most predictable outcome of pastoral incongruence is failure, or at least irrelevance, in ministry.

Roy SteinhoffSmith has defined four types of abuse, all of which are present in

the church and all of which may go unrecognized by ministers whose own boundaries are unclear or who deal on an intimate
level with parishioners whose boundaries
are unclear:

> Abuse has four forms: physical, psycho-
> logical, social, and religious. Physical abuse
> occurs when one person or group of peo-
> ple physically injures another, when this
> injury is not done in the service of heal-
> ing, care, liberation, or love of the other.
> Physical abuse may occur through the use
> of force, as when a parent beats a child, or
> through the failure to use force, as when
> an adult with the power to do so fails to
> restrain a child from walking in front of a
> moving car.
>
> Psychological abuse occurs when one
> person or group of people injures another
> emotionally or cognitively. Such abuse
> often takes the form of the denial of the
> reality of the other's perceptions, insights,
> and experiences. Such a denial—whether
> it occurs emotionally or cognitively—
> destroys the basis for selfhood, the capacity
> to trust one's perceptions and understand-
> ing of the world.
>
> Social abuse occurs when a person or
> group of people exercise their superior
> power to bar another's participation in the
> construction of a shared social world. Reli-
> gious abuse occurs when a person or group
> of people denies another's capacity to par-
> ticipate in the construction of faith. (396)

Physical abuse can be present in the pastoral
relationship when a minister touches
another in an unwanted manner or when a
minister offers "the laying on of hands for
healing" accompanied by promises of its
absolute efficacy. Psychological abuse can
occur in any pastoral relationship wherein
the minister fails to take seriously and
respectfully the "perceptions, insights, and
experiences" of another. Social abuse can
occur when a minister takes advantage of

the power attributed to the pastoral office
to manipulate, deceive, or dominate another. Religious abuse can occur when a minister fails to take seriously the faith
perspective of another or uses shaming or
coercive methods of evangelism.

Sexual abuse can include any or all of
these other four forms of abuse, and in fact
is one of the most serious offenses a pastor
can commit against another person. Recent
studies have demonstrated repeatedly that
ordained clergy who are most likely to
abuse counselees sexually are those who are
narcissistic, emotionally shut-down, over-
stressed, and relationally dysfunctional—in
short, clergy who are incongruent. Incongruent clergy are less able to recognize
abuse of various kinds, or are more prone to
rationalize away its effects. Hoffman lists the
possible results of sexual abuse by a pastor or
counselor: "ambivalence; a sense of guilt;
feelings of emptiness and isolation; sexual
confusion; impaired ability to trust; identity,
boundary, and role confusion; emotional
lability (frequently involving severe depression and acute anxiety); suppressed rage;
increased suicidal risk; and cognitive dysfunction (especially in the areas of attention
and concentration, frequently involving
flashbacks, nightmares, intrusive thoughts,
and unbidden images)" (16). No amount of
rationalization can justify sexual harassment, exploitation, or abuse of a parishioner
by a minister. For the most part, church
adjudicatories continue to fail in their
responsibility to root out this form of violence that infects pastoral relationships.

To SteinhoffSmith's list of forms of abuse
we must also add "institutional abuse." Talbot observes that institutions often have a
rigidly delineated professional hierarchy,
with some positions or offices enjoying relatively more authority and more oppor-

tunity for professional and economic advancement (347–48). Ministers themselves may be the subject of such institutional abuse, finding themselves marginalized for viewpoints and pastoral methods that do not fit the rigid definitions of the local church or the national denomination. But more often, it is women, minorities, and gays and lesbians who find themselves disenfranchised and disempowered by a minister's or the church's refusal to recognize the validity of their life experience and insights.

The pastor's search for authenticity and congruence will mean that he or she must be particularly aware of attitudes, opinions, and ministry styles that are in any way abusive of others. The necessary consequence of the pastor's unexamined self is failure in ministry, or worse, abuse. The most significant ministry tool that pastors wield is a congruent self, particularly in a counseling relationship. As Jacobs, David, and Meyer point out, to do his work, a pastoral counselor must call upon his whole personality: "his intelligence, imagination, affective responses, fantasy life, areas of unresolved conflict, and so on. As a result, what is at stake in the learning situation is inherently more personal and risks exposure of fundamental aspects of oneself" (208). The medium through which the gospel message is mediated to others is the pastoral self. Therefore, authenticity and congruence are the basic tools of pastoral ministry. John Patton observes, "the message of God's care is inseparable from the messenger" (1993, 95).

Achieving Pastoral Congruence through Ministry Supervision

John Patton's two classic texts, *Pastoral Counseling: A Ministry of the Church* and *Pastoral Care in Context: An Introduction to Pastoral Care*, offer sound and effective explanations of the theory and practice of pastoral care. However, as much as I respect Patton as one of the most significant shapers of the field of pastoral theology, I disagree strongly with him on the definitions and purposes of ministry supervision. In the former of those two books, Patton insists that "in developing one's practice of Christian ministry, both supervision, where one is involved with a more experienced minister in the same situation of ministry, and consultation, where the use of the help of another is technically optional, are essential" (1983, 70). I believe, rather, that the following distinctions need to be made:

1. Practical Supervision for Ministry (Ministry Oversight)
2. Clinical Supervision for Ministry (Ministry Supervision)
3. Professional Consultation on Ministry Issues.

In addition to individual or group spiritual direction, I believe that everyone practicing the public ministry of pastoral care—whether lay or ordained—needs regular access to all three of these forms of supervision and consultancy.

Practical Supervision for Ministry (Ministry Oversight) has a long tradition in Christian history. Even in the early church, deacons and presbyters were responsible to their bishops, or overseers, for practical supervision. In more recent times, ordained clergy usually served a curacy or assistantship during which time their practice of ministry was closely supervised by a senior minister. Regrettably, with the declining financial security of the church today, such positions are increasingly rare. Still, it is preferable that everyone practicing the public ministry of pastoral care have someone to whom they are accountable for the daily conduct of pastoral work. The congregation cannot provide this service to its ministers, for often the subject matter that needs to be dealt with will include some members of the congregation, or even the congregation as a whole, as the subject matter of the specific confusion, complaint, or impasse. In the case of ordained pastors, Ministry Oversight can best be provided by an experienced older minister from a different congregation or denomination or by a peer group of pastors who meet regularly to supervise one another's ministry practice. In the case of lay pastors, Ministry Oversight can be provided by an experienced lay pastor, a senior clergyperson, or by a peer group of lay pastors, at least some of whom need to have several years of public lay ministry under their belts. In either case, such supervision is usually provided without charge.

Clinical Supervision for Ministry (Ministry Supervision) must *not* be conducted by the local church or a denominational representative, even though it should be a part of every member's compensation package. Clinical Ministry Supervision is designed to further liberate a pastor's personal gifts and address the pastor's dysfunction and ministry blockages. As Patton points out, "The classical pastoral paradigm insists that pastoral carers know not only the story but themselves and their relationships" (1993, 95). This type of supervision is critical for any minister who engages in more than two to three hours of contact per week with others, whether chairing meetings or in formal counseling, though the frequency of such supervision may vary. Optimally, Ministry Supervision is fee-based and takes place on a one-to-one level with a skilled and certified psychotherapeutic clinician. This form of Ministry Supervision will be the focus of the rest of this chapter.

Professional Consultation on Ministry Issues describes the sort of occasional consultation that any responsible caregiver must undertake. Brian Childs observes that many pastors have a variety of consultants from within their larger community: psychiatrist, medical doctor, social worker, learning disabilities specialist, alcohol counselor, and so forth (83–84). Such consultants are usually happy to speak with the individual pastor from time to time about a diagnosis, a referral, or locating a supportive network, and usually will do so without charge as a professional courtesy.

A further distinction needs to be made among Ministry Oversight, Ministry Supervision, and Consultancy. Ministry Oversight and Ministry Supervision create responsibility for the overseer and supervisor, who by virtue of the professional relationship become responsible for the safety of the recipients of the pastor's ministry. In some countries, this responsibility even extends to legal liability for the pastor's work and the recipients' well-being. This is true for both Ministry Overseers and Ministry Supervisors: in the United States, for example, a senior minister may be held legally responsible for the professional misconduct of her assisting ministers, and a bishop for the clergy under his charge. In countries in which this oversight or supervisory relationship does not create a legal liability, an ethical responsibility is still presumed. For these reasons, Ministry Oversight and, even more so, Ministry Supervision are being conducted only within the terms of a legal contract that spells out the specific responsibilities of both supervisor and supervisee. Consultancy, on the other hand, as an occasional and informal arrangement, is not usually presumed to create a legal responsibility, for the minister is not presumed to be obliged to follow the consultant's advice.

Ministry Oversight and Ministry Supervision both create networks of accountability. Far too many ministers, particularly in nondenominational churches, conduct their ministries without any formal accountability, except perhaps to a church executive board who often know little of the specific details of their pastor's works of ministry. Patton points out that this accountability cannot be created by a local parish, particularly in the area of Ministry Supervision:

> The individual congregation cannot provide this for the pastor. It can accept his or her inexperience and incompetence in a general way, offering support and care. It cannot, however, deal with the specific instances in which the pastor's immaturity and sin have been revealed in the concrete reality of pastoral work or with the expected or unexpected sin of one of its members. The pastor needs a different community to which that kind of clinical accountability can be expressed. . . . Pastors who work in depth with persons—whatever the type of pastoral relationship— need a non-parochial structure for supervision and/or consultation. (1983, 69)

As the discussion of the content of supervision proceeds below, it will be increasingly obvious why a congregation not only cannot provide this sort of accountability, but why it would be completely inappropriate.

Ordained ministers who function as overseers for lay ministers within their own congregations should understand that they are ultimately responsible for the safety of all those among whom ministry work is performed. Even ordained pastors who serve as consultants to the lay ministry of others in their parish should weigh seriously their personal responsibility, for in this case their liability will be greater than that of external professional consultants such as psychiatrists and social workers. Ordained ministers who oversee lay ministers should themselves be in regular Clinical Ministry Supervision.

What Clinical Ministry Supervision Is Not

A clear distinction must be made between Clinical Ministry Supervision and personal psychotherapy. The purpose of psychotherapy is to provide the individual with the opportunity for a deep and probing self-knowledge, and for healing from various psychological dysfunctions such as neurosis, personality disorders, addictive behaviors, relationship difficulties, and so forth. The purpose of clinical Ministry Supervision is to analyze the "fit" between an individual's personality, memories, fears, hopes, gifts, and inhibitions, and his or her conduct of ministry, including all interactions with others and the reactions to those interactions. Material may emerge during the course of supervision that should appropriately be dealt with through a course of psychotherapy. The supervisor will suggest that dealing with the material is the personal responsibility of the supervisee, but will not incorporate extensive psychotherapy into the supervisory relationship unless it can be shown to have direct bearing on the supervisee's professional performance. For example, if a young priest has transferred "fatherly" feelings onto his bishop and then has been disappointed in the bishop to the extent that it interferes with the young priest's ministry performance, the supervisor may deal with this issue as a part of clinical Ministry Supervision. The larger subject of the young priest's relationship with his birth father, however, and the unfinished business surrounding that which enabled the transference to occur, will probably be referred for psychotherapeutic treatment.

The style of clinical supervision that has proved to be most effective is didactic and evocative, insight-oriented, and feeling-oriented. It should not be authoritarian, confrontive, or laissez-faire. In an extensive survey of clinical supervisees, Michael Carifio and Allen Hess pinpointed the four styles of supervision that supervisees found particularly objectionable:

> (a) *constrictive* (overly restrictive in that a student's use of certain techniques in psychotherapy is dogmatically limited); (b) *amorphous* (students are not provided with sufficient levels of guidance or direction); (c) *unsupportive* (observed when the supervisor is seen as cold, aloof, uncaring, or generally hostile); and (d) *therapeutic* (most objectionable to supervisees; the focus is on the student as the patient and on his or her personality structure during supervisory interactions). (248)

Nor should the supervisor attempt to make the supervisee a clone or copy. The supervisee can always be expected to model the supervisor, to a greater or lesser extent, through idealization and "twinning." But the point of supervision is to help the supervisee develop his or her own unique gifts and talents, not to copy the supervisor's style and affect.

The above comments are most true for those who are in individual one-to-one Clinical Ministry Supervision. There are actually four different types of supervision appropriate for use with pastors who wish to gain greater congruence and increase their ministry effectiveness: self-supervision, individual clinical supervision, group supervision, and peer supervision. Each of these types will be discussed individually,

with particular reference to their usefulness in specific situations and to whom they are most applicable.

Self-Supervision

Every minister should be engaged in a regular routine of self-examination, particularly as it pertains to the dialogic relationship between the pastor and his or her pastoral work. As mentioned earlier, Erich Fromm recommended that at least an hour a day be set aside for introspection and prayerful meditation (1994, 188). According to Jacobs, David, and Meyer, self-reflection or self-supervision involves using the mind to observe its own workings (115–20). The minister should contemplate at depth the nature of his or her own ministry activities and his or her characteristic modes of thought or response. One may work intuitively, relying mainly on associative thinking and a capacity to grasp imaginatively the underlying meaning of others' words and needs. Others may work in a more methodical, incremental, data-gathering, inductive mode. Hawkins and Shohet, citing the work of Borders and Leddick, provide some very useful questions for the reflection process (27):

Self-Observation (linking the pastor's thoughts, feelings, actions with another's behavior)

(a) What was I hearing my parishioner say and/or seeing my parishioner do?
(b) What was I thinking and feeling about my observations?
(c) What were my alternatives to say or do at this point?
(d) How did I choose from among the alternatives?
(e) How did I intend to proceed with my selected response(s)?
(f) What did I actually do?

Self-Assessment (evaluating pastoral performance by observing another's response)

(a) What effects did my response have on my parishioner?

(b) How, then, would I evaluate the effectiveness of my response?

For Fromm and others, this sort of self-supervision was best done in a quiet reflective mode, perhaps combined with some form of centering mediation. For others, the most effective medium for self-supervision is journaling. Journal keeping involves a systematic written reflection on one's ministry activities, styles, affective reactions, and the responses received. Journaling is generally ineffective if it is conducted sporadically or simply becomes an activity record devoid of reflection. As well, in certain countries journaling raises legal issues of confidentiality. The caregiver should ascertain whether written records of pastoral work can be subpoenaed in a court of law in his or her geographic location. In any case, all written records of pastoral work should be encoded in such a way that only the caregiver can access the information, and should be kept in a secure location at all times.

While self-reflection is an essential ingredient in expanding ministry effectiveness, the pastor should also be aware that any deepening of self-awareness may be destablizing to the pastor's established sense of self. Therefore, self-supervision is best done in conjunction with at least occasional access to one of the other three forms of supervision discussed here, which may function as an appropriate sounding board for the questions and doubts that may arise through intensive self-reflection.

Self-supervision is particularly well suited for those who conduct their ministry work in geographically isolated areas. While a great deal can be learned through self-reflection and journaling, the isolated minister should speak with a clinical supervisor over the phone at least twice a month (with a contractual relationship), or the more experienced might participate once or twice a month in a peer supervision group. In this way, excellent supervision is available even for those who are far removed from larger urban centers where clinical supervisors are readily available.

Individual Clinical Supervision

Clinical Supervision for Ministry, or Ministry Supervision, is perhaps the most neglected tool for effective ministry in the history of pastoral care. Many jurisdictions give lip service to the need for Ministry Supervision, but few have built a convincing case for it or defined it well, and even fewer actually enforce their own recommendations.

Reasons for Ministry Supervision

Why should pastors be in Ministry Supervision? Five reasons justify the investment:

1. Supervision frees the pastor to address more effectively certain contextual and role expectations as part of formation for Christian ministry. According to Jeffrey Means, formation "also begins with an emphasis on the student's motivation to enter the formation process and be transformed by it. Formation cannot be made to happen. It is up to the person in the formation process to make use of the experiences and environments provided" (202–3). In supervision, the pastor understands that formation is something to which he or she commits actively, rather than something spoon-fed from the outside.

2. Supervision equips the pastor to deal with the stresses of ministry in a healthier

manner. Ministry stress proceeds from a variety of sources, each of which must be addressed intentionally (adapted from Kottler, 82):

Parishioner-Induced Stress—
- angry outbursts from parishioners
- accusations of incompetence
- power play by member of the congregation
- suicide, sudden death, or other crisis
- triangulation into others' family systems
- premature departure from congregation
- major deterioration of a counselee

Work Environment Stress—
- time-management pressures
- denominational or parish politics
- rules and restrictions on pastoral method
- nonsupportive ministry peers
- supervisory incompetence
- excessive paperwork
- torn allegiances

Self-Induced Stress—
- feelings of perfectionism
- ruminating about ministry effectiveness
- need for approval
- self-doubt
- physical exhaustion
- unhealthy lifestyle
- emotional depletion
- excessive responsibility for parish's welfare

Event-Related Stress—
- personal financial pressures
- major life transition (divorce, relocation, etc.)
- change in pastoral responsibilities
- cutbacks in church budget
- disapproval or censure from church hierarchy
- involvement in legal action

3. Supervision teaches a pastor to steward his or her God-given gifts. In this sense it is both a form of self-care and a prophylactic against ministry burnout. Supervision can be an important way of remaining open to new learning and an indispensable part of a pastor's ongoing self-development and self-awareness. Lack of supervision can contribute to the feelings of staleness, rigidity, and defensiveness that can very easily occur in a vocation that requires us to give so much of ourselves. In extremes, staleness and defensiveness contribute to the syndrome known as "ministry burnout." "Supervision can help stop this process by breaking the cycle of feeling drained which leads to a drop in work standards which produces guilt and inadequacy which lead to a further drop in standards" (Hawkins and Shohet, 5).

4. Supervision enables a pastor to do ministry that proceeds out of his or her authentic self instead of the cultivated public image or persona. Ministry not only brings powerful expectations from others; we also bring unrealistic expectations to our ministries and then attempt to live up to standards and modes of behavior that proceed from without rather than from within. Supervision creates an environment in which we can explore styles of ministry that are more true to the way we were each created by God and that more authentically model the values of our personal faith.

5. Supervision reminds the pastor that ministry is never done alone. The pastor learns the value of working as a team and of asking for help. As John Patton observes, "Learning to ask for help is a key element in the process of discovering myself, in staying in touch with the being which I attempt to bring into dialogue with my

action" (1983, 76). By affirming the importance of asking for help, supervision confirms that ministry belongs to the whole Christian community rather than being an Oscar-nominated solo performance.

As well, Clinical Supervision for Ministry has important theological outcomes:

1. Supervision offers a rich environment for healing and for the mediation of the Holy Spirit. In a famous 1952 essay, Paul Tillich discussed the difference between psychiatry and theology. Applying the esteem with which Tillich holds both disciplines, we may conclude with him that clinical supervision provides "a rich environment for the generation and transformation of spiritual experience, a potential medium of the Spiritual Presence, and a powerful resource in the process of sanctification" (Rutland–Wallis, 260).

2. Supervision models incarnational theology by attending intensively to the needs of one of God's children. Erich Fromm, tracing the origins of clinical supervision to the early work of Sigmund Freud, identified therapeutic work as an act of spiritual care and love: "I believe that there is perhaps no greater evidence of Freud's genius than his counsel to take the time even if it should require many years to help one person to achieve freedom and happiness" (98).

3. Supervision births "The New Being" in and through experiences of accepting that one is accepted (the New Being as paradox). Frequently such experiences of acceptance invite deeper awareness of unacceptable features of the personality, which in turn enables greater freedom and relatedness. "Thus even the daily grind of psychotherapeutic process occurs under the impact of the Spiritual Presence" (Rutland–Wallis, 262).

4. Supervision provides an experience of grace. In supervision we learn not to perceive ourselves only as knowledgeable technicians who make healing happen. Rather, we experience ourselves as servants or representational ministers of the Divine Healer. "We are channels of the healing grace and love of God" (Haight 1995, 158).

Role of the Supervisor

The correct choice of a supervisor is critical to the success of supervision. A clinical supervisor is trained as such and is certified in supervision and/or psychotherapy. You may want to ask others who are in supervision how they feel about their own supervisors and if they are willing to give you a referral. The pastor should ask about the supervisor's credentials before entering into a supervision relationship, particularly in countries in which the supervisor assumes some legal responsibility for the pastor's work and the safety of others.

A Clinical Ministry Supervisor should be nonjudgmental, open, and supportive; vibrant, inspirational, charismatic; sincere, loving, and nurturing; wise, confident, and self-disciplined. A supervisor will have a dramatic impact through the sheer force and power of her essence, regardless of her theoretical or theological allegiances. Supervisors should be supportive, noncritical, confident, enthusiastic, and open to a supervisee's questions and input. Jacobs, David, and Meyer provide an excellent summary definition of a good supervisor's character:

> A basic objective for the supervisor is to promote a safe learning atmosphere. Supervision ought to be an enterprise in which the [trainee] feels able to think openly, express half-formed ideas, raise

questions (no matter how basic) and discuss inner experiences that arise, . . . to the extent that he feels motivated to do so, without undue fear of criticism, humiliation, or intimidation. To learn optimally, the student must have the opportunity to express instinctive reactions to [others], to talk about countertransference, to wonder aloud and to offer incomplete associations and hunches in a spirit of open inquiry. The supervisor, who spends much of her professional life looking below the surface of manifest content, must maintain a respect for the educational context of supervision, as distinct from a treatment context, and respond to self-revelation with this in mind. (232)

It should be obvious, therefore, that not every certified supervisor is necessarily a good supervisor, since these qualities are relatively rare. The pastor should choose a supervisor carefully, and may wish to interview two or three before making a final decision.

Once a supervisor has been chosen, a specific contract needs to be discussed. Again, this is more critical in countries in which the supervisor assumes some legal responsibility for the pastor's work and the safety of others. Supervision contracts will be dealt with in greater detail at the end of this chapter.

Frequency of supervision will vary according to the pastor's level of experience in ministry, his or her specific pastoral responsibilities, other types of complementary support to which the pastor is committed, and the level of financial support that the parish is willing to provide. Sigmund Freud believed that even the most expert psychotherapist needed to undertake a full course of supervision every five years (Kottler, 74). The American Association of Pastoral Counselors stipulates that counselors should be in "regular" supervision, though it does not define exactly how frequently. Highly expert pastors, with a long background of Clinical Ministry Supervision, will need less frequent supervision than inexperienced pastors or pastors who carry an unusually heavy ministry load. Every pastor, lay or ordained, should see a supervisor at least once a month for an hour. Those who are lucky enough to receive weekly supervision will discover that the investment pays off with a deepened and more effective ministry to others.

As mentioned earlier, the effectiveness of supervision is very much dependent upon the pastor's personal commitment to making it work. "Formation cannot be made to happen. It is up to the person in the formation process to make use of the experiences and environments provided" (Means, 202–3). This is the most important quality any minister brings to the supervision process. Karen Horney remarked wistfully that she wished everyone who entered supervision would begin with the attitude: "I want to know who I am, how I am, what I am doing, and how I can change whatever is not desirable" (70). Erich Fromm listed other qualities with which one should enter supervision as: (a) some idea of what his life ought to be, some vision of what he wants; (b) seriousness about the task; and (c) the capacity to differentiate between banality and reality, by which he meant what is worth talking about in supervision and what is a waste of time (1994, 34–38).

Pastors also bring their limitations to supervision, which is, after all, the point of being there in the first place. Ekstein and Wallerstein refer to these as our *blind spots*, *deaf spots*, and *dumb spots*, though their terminology is lamentable. "Dumb spots" refer to areas where lack of knowledge and pastoral experience prevent us from understanding the values and worldview of those whom we pastor. "Blind spots" are where the pastor's own patterns of thought and behavior get in the way of seeing clearly the type of ministry needed in each situation. "Deaf spots" are those where the pastor can hear clearly neither the careseekers he or she encounters nor the supervisor. These are likely to involve particularly defensive reactions based on guilt, anxiety, or otherwise unpleasant and disruptive feelings, or on hostility to authority figures (Hawkins and Shohet, 48).

While one then wishes to select the most skilled supervisor possible, in the end the success or failure of supervision depends on the investment the pastor makes in it and his or her willingness to address courageously the need for personal change.

The complex process of being supervised justifies both its frequency and its extended duration. Jacobs, David, and Meyer identify the six most common forms of activity during supervision as modeling, didactic instruction, Socratic questioning, encouragement and permission, clarification, and interpretation (204). These tasks divide, then, between the rational (didactic and educational) and the emotional (affective and sensory/intuitive). The educational and didactic tasks expand the supervisee's learning base, functioning as a form of continuing education, and increase pastoral skills of human interaction and healing intervention. Pointing out that the word *Paraclete* can mean "counselor," "advocate," or "teacher," Emily Haight understands this rational component of being supervised as a

significant way of fulfilling the promise of John 14: "But the Counselor, the Holy Spirit, whom the Father will send in my name, he will teach you all things" (1994, 86).

Transference and Countertransference

The primary affective content of being supervised is the addressing of transference and countertransference reactions. Pastors transfer and countertransfer, and are transferred onto.

We transfer and are transferred onto. According to Erich Fromm, Harry Stack Sullivan used as an example of transference a person whom he analyzed for a week. After a week this person remarked while saying goodbye: "But doctor, you don't have a beard" (1994, 118). Sullivan had a little mustache but was otherwise clean shaven. For a week the analysand had believed Sullivan had a beard, because indeed he was so much the father for her that the whole image of her father (who had a beard) was literally transferred to him. How often are we pastors confused with people from others' pasts, and then they react to us in a manner that hardly conforms to the relationship we thought we were providing! Jeffery Kottler describes transference even more poignantly:

> Clients bring us their nightmares, drop them in our laps, and then leave us to sort them out for ourselves. They have been enduring sleepless nights for years. Now the challenge for us is to keep away their demons. Especially at night, when we are relaxed and our defenses are down, images creep into our dreams, or if we are lying awake, they invade our peace. (78)

Transference places other people's burdens, memories, and reactions on us and asks us to carry them. When we agree to do so, it is called countertransference. Pastoral countertransference includes those times when we respond to parishioners by promising what we do not have the power to promise: "remedies, cures, complete mental health, philosophies of life, rescue, emergency-room intervention, emotional Band-Aids, or self-sacrificing or self-aggrandizing heroics" (Schafer 1983, 11). Superhuman efforts to effect these countertransferential promises can burn us out or kill our spirit. God alone has the power to heal, and we cannot promise what God alone is in charge of delivering. Thus, to keep ourselves healthy, we must deal directly with transference (others' onto us and our own onto others) and countertransference. If we do not, Kottler reminds us, it is like trying to keep from drowning while treading water with someone on our back (80).

The focus of both supervisor and supervisee must remain on the supervisee's professional skills, opportunities, and relationships. Such focus does not mean that the pastor's personal issues are avoided, but in supervision they are addressed only insofar as they connect directly to pastoral responsibilities. The pastor has chosen the supervisor to provide supervision and not psychotherapy. While the two are not easily separable, both supervisor and pastor should remain aware that the pastor might have chosen someone else for psychotherapy. Therefore, on some occasions the supervisor will suggest that material that has arisen in the session needs to be dealt with outside by supervisory relationship, through recourse to psychotherapy or some other form of counseling. On other occasions the personal material is relevant enough that it needs to be drawn into the supervisory relationship. But, as Hawkins and Shohet point out, "The basic boundary in this area is that supervision sessions should always start from exploring issues from work and should end with looking at where the supervisee goes next with the work that has been explored" (45). Confirming this boundary, Jay Haley has drafted a "supervisee's bill of rights":

> No teacher may inquire into the personal life of a therapy student, no matter how benevolently, unless, (1) he/she can justify how this information is relevant to the immediate therapy task in a case, and (2) he/she can state specifically how this inquiry will change the therapist's behavior in the way desired. (176–77)

Importance of Feedback

No matter how successful a safe holding environment the supervisor creates, the pastor will still receive regular feedback on the way he or she is performing those pastoral tasks brought into the supervisory relationship for examination. Receiving feedback is not easy for most people, and particularly not easy for pastors, who, as we have seen earlier, are highly defensive (Plante, 39). Hawkins and Shohet explain that feedback should not be received passively by the pastor, but should be an integral part of the active engagement with the supervisor (84). What is done with the feedback is nearly entirely the responsibility of the receiver. They suggest:

• If the feedback is not given in the way you can understand or hear, you can ask for it to be more clear, balanced, owned, regular, and/or specific.

• Listen to the feedback all the way through without judging it. Jumping to a defensive response can mean that the feedback is actually misunderstood.

• Try not to explain compulsively why you did something or even explain away the positive feedback. Try and hear others' feedback as their experiences of you. Often it is enough just to hear the feedback and say "Thank you."

• Ask for feedback you are not given but would like to hear.

Carl Rogers adds that feedback should be (a) *systematic* (objective, accurate, consistent, and reliable feedback that is less influenced by subjective variables); (b) *timely* (feedback is delivered soon after an important event); (c) *clearly understood* (both positive and negative feedback are based on explicit and specific performance criteria); and (d) *reciprocal* (feedback is provided in two-way interactions in which suggestions are made, not as the only way to approach a problem, but as only one of a number of potentially useful alternatives) (247). Feedback, given and received in a caring dialogic manner, gives us a window into the truth of our selves as persons and our work as pastors. We must not fear or avoid such feedback from supervisors, but must remember, in keeping with John 8:32, that "The truth shall make you free."

In 1968, Alfred Kadushin published a landmark article entitled "Games People Play in Supervision." The article begins by addressing why pastors and other supervisees might be tempted to play games with their supervisor. Kadushin lists seven possible reasons (23–24):

1. supervision is often directed toward change, and change creates anxiety;

2. change suggests disloyalty to and rejection of models with whom we have previously identified, including parents, mentors, and those who formed our faith and ministry style;

3. supervision may feel like a threat to the pastor's independence and autonomy;

4. the pastor's adequacy in ministry may feel threatened;

5. the pastor may feel that he or she is inadequate as a self;

6. supervision may at times feel like a parent-child relationship, thereby bringing out anxieties and rebellion associated with the pastor's family of origin;

7. the supervisor may be in a position to provide formal evaluation of the pastor to a powerful church hierarchy.

A desire to keep losses to a minimum and to maximize the rewards that might derive from a "successful" supervisory relationship explain why the pastor may feel the need to manipulate the situation to his or her advantage.

Kadushin then goes on to list fourteen games that pastors may be tempted to play in supervision. (He also lists some games the supervisors play, but the focus of this chapter is on being supervised rather than on being a supervisor.) While there is not room here to list and explain all fourteen, the article is a critical resource for anyone entering supervision to read. Five of Kadushin's games serve to illustrate his point (25–30):

• "Be Nice to Me Because I Am Nice to You," in which the pastor attempts to subvert any criticism that might be offered by the supervisor.

• "If You Knew Dostoyevsky Like I Know Dostoyevsky," in which the pastor attempts to convince the "ignorant" supervisor that if she had only read more pastoral theory, she would agree with the pastor's actions or approach.

• "Heading Them Off at the Pass," in which the pastor attempts to avoid any critical analysis by using the session as a dumping ground for all his or her ministry mistakes.

• "I Did Like You Told Me," in which a pastor slavishly applies the supervisor's earlier suggestions without regard to whether the context or timing is right.

• "What You Don't Know Won't Hurt Me," in which the pastor intentionally withholds from the supervisor any information that might reflect badly on the pastor's work or transference and countertransference.

To Kadushin's list we might add another game, perhaps called "Trouble in the Trinity," in which the pastor attempts to play off the Ministry Supervisor against the Ministry Overseer. In such a situation one of the three parties involved can easily become negatively triangulated, so that two of them discuss how "wrong" the third one is. Or the pastor may attempt to split the two responsible parties, creating a "good overseer" and a "bad supervisor." In this kind of situation it may be helpful for all three parties to meet together from time to time for a three-way assessment and evaluation (Hawkins and Shohet, 88).

Kadushin suggests that games are most easily defused by naming them, focusing on the disadvantages in playing games: "These games have decided drawbacks for the supervisee in that they deny him the possibility of effectively fulfilling one of the essential, principal purposes of supervision—helping him to grow professionally" (32).

Inevitably, the progress of growth in supervision is slow and takes time. It is significantly facilitated by the pastor's having come to each session with material prepared for presentation, perhaps in the form of notes, a case study, dreams, or a tape. In her final set of lectures, Karen Horney reminded her students to go slow: "If you need to know and understand quickly, you may not see anything" (23). Brigid Proctor has drawn up an additional list of responsibilities for supervisees (in Hawkins and Shohet, 29–30):

• identify practice issues with which you need help and ask for help;
• become increasingly able to share freely;
• identify what responses you want;
• become more aware of the organizational contracts that affect supervisor, client, and supervisee;
• be open to feedback;
• monitor tendencies to justify, explain, or defend;
• develop the ability to discriminate what feedback is useful.

One of the most significant sources retarding the process of being supervised will be the pastor's resistance, a technical term describing what the individual is unwilling or not yet ready to learn or to see in him- or herself. Fromm traced the source of this resistance to the pastor's tendency to maintain the status quo (73). Later on, he enlarged that definition to include not only the maintenance of the status quo, but also the pastor's wish to improve the functioning of his or her neurosis by hanging on to it but getting rid of the difficulties and disturbances arising from it. In other words, we have a tendency to want to hang on to our psychological and emotional dysfunctions because we have become so comfortable with them and incorporated them into our self-definition. We want simply to divest ourselves of their negative fallout! It is the job of supervision to break through the resistance of these dysfunctions, so that our true self and our pastoral identity can emerge more fully.

The Process of Counselor Development

A skilled supervisor will adapt the level and intensity of supervision to match the professional experience of the pastor. This is generally referred to as the "developmental" approach to supervision. While over twenty-five different models of counselor development exist, the most famous is Cal Stoltenberg's "Counselor Complexity Model." Drawing on the work of Hogan and Hurt, Stoltenberg proposed that counselors move through four levels as they develop from beginning to "master" counselors. Level 1 counselors are seen as highly motivated, yet dependent, uninsightful, and insecure, and they require supervision that emphasizes structure, teaching, and support. Level 2 counselors are characterized as striving for independence and experiencing fluctuating motivation, and as needing supervision that is low in normative structure yet high in support. In Level 3, counselors are seen as experiencing increased insight and an early person-counselor identity, while requiring a supervisory environment that encourages autonomy, sharing, and confrontation. Level 4 counselors are described as "master," capable of independent practice and requiring collegial supervision on an as-needed basis (Chagnon and Russell, 556; Stoltenberg and Delworth, 49–51). As pastors move across developmental levels in both their counseling work and their general pastoral experience, the supervisory environment should adapt to meet the changing needs of the supervisee.

As the supervisor proceeds through a series of changing strategies designed to meet the pastor's needs, so the pastor will also undergo a developmental process in his or her relation to the supervisor. Emily Haight describes three stages of supervisee development as the pastor grows in confidence and skill (1994, 90–92). In Stage 1, "Imitation/Idealization," the pastor feels safe and calm in the supervisory environment

and can "borrow" confidence from the supervisor, safe in the assurance that should there be trouble, expert assistance is near. Stage 2 is marked by the supervisee's growing confidence and willingness to experiment and explore; Haight calls it "Internalization/Self-Expansion." Stage 3 is "Claiming Colleagueship/Mature Narcissism," in which the supervision takes on the feel of consultation, focusing in particular on the clues that pastoral countertransference gives for increasing ministry effectiveness.

Haight's three stages coordinate nicely with the three types of learning within supervision hypothesized by Fleming and Benedek: (1) learning by *imitation*, based on identification with the supervisor without an awareness of the rationale; (2) *corrective* learning, in which different possible approaches to understanding and doing ministry can be discussed in relation to the pastoral theory and technique; and (3) *creative* learning, in which the pastor's accumulated knowledge of the dynamics of intrapsychic conflict and interpersonal relationships adds a new and deeper awareness to his or her insight and pastoral confidence (adapted from Jacobs, David, and Meyer, 53). In any case, the supervisory relationship should always be understood as a dynamic one in which both supervisor and pastor are constantly changing and growing. Freud cautioned against taking anything for granted about the possibility of change, the direction in which change will take place, and the extent to which change will be effected.

There is no "correct" methodology of supervision, particularly for pastors, since the field is relatively new. Supervisors should take into account the developmental processes just discussed, as well as the pastor's individual type inventory. Johnson-Laird has described a typology of thought from which Haber has selected four as most relevant to the tasks of supervision: (1) inductive thinking, (2) associative thinking, (3) creative thinking, and (4) self-reflective thinking (59). The reader will be reminded of the Myers-Briggs Type Inventory, and indeed, such test results may be helpful in tailoring supervision to the pastor's unique needs and abilities.

Whatever methodology is adopted by the supervisor, material covered during supervision must always also include the wider context within which the pastor works. Conversation should include the pastor's reactions to developments in his or her denomination on a regional and national level, cultural and cross-cultural issues in ministry, the pastor's prophetic voice, arts and literature, and even the role and purpose of the pastor's personal hobbies. Family-of-origin work, when tied to the supervisory task rather than to psychotherapy, must be included, for the family is but a paradigm of the larger system in which the minister lives and works. And Haight reminds us that the pastor's spirituality must also be addressed directly, even when the pastor has another spiritual director: "Supervision that does not fully explore, deepen, and facilitate the expression of the spiritual motivation behind the desire for training may be technically helpful but will be experienced as useless in quenching the thirst that brought the person to training in the first place" (1995, 157). Pastoral development cannot be separated from spiritual development in Ministry Supervision, for the two are inextricably intertwined. "The specific focus of psychology is human psyche, and the specific focus

of spirituality is human spirit. Of course, just as psyche cannot be treated apart from spirit, the functioning of spirit cannot be treated apart from psyche" (Helminiak, 190). Spirituality perforce includes psychology, just as psychology includes spirituality.

Ministry Supervision and the Health of the Larger Church

At a rate of up to U.S.$100 per hour or more, Clinical Ministry Supervision can seem expensive. With shrinking budgets, many parishes would be tempted to argue this as an expense to be cut from the budget. But, as I believe I have made clear, the long-range effects of supervision are increased ministry skills and effectiveness, better assurance that members of the congregation are safe from pastoral manipulation and malpractice, a greater sense of corporate accountability, the reduced possibility of divisiveness and bitterness within the body of Christ, and the liberation of creative pastoral resources as an evangelization strategy. Ultimately, then, Clinical Ministry Supervision must be seen as an issue of stewardship—not only of those who exercise public pastoral ministry, but also of the psychological health and spiritual welfare of whole congregations. In this sense, Ministry Supervision is a form of "preventative" pastoral care, of closing the barn door before the horses get out, if you will.

Pastors who function without clinical supervision potentially jeopardize the welfare of the entire church. This should be obvious from the plague of scandals that have affected pastoral ministry in this decade, including embezzlement, sexual harassment and abuse, and clergy adultery. Hawkins and Shohet speak of the contagion of dysfunction and psychological ill-health, pointing out how poor ministry performance by one individual can affect the entire church. Supervision serves to contain individual malpractice, create a holding environment in which ideas and impulses can be tested before being applied to others, and, by providing greater insight into the workings of individual minds and larger systems, offer the opportunity to nip trouble in the bud before it infects whole groups of people. This containment process is necessary because the church is, by its very nature, an organization to which people bring their problems, disappointments, anger, exaggerated expectations, and deepest wishes.

> We sometimes describe the containment process in a way that one organization called "the bucket theory." All helping organizations are, by their very nature, importing distress, disturbance, fragmentation and need. This is usually met by individual workers, who, if they are empathically relating to the client's distress, will experience parallel distress and sometimes disturbance and fragmentation within themselves. How much of this they will be able to contain and work through will depend on the size of their emotional container (or bucket), will relate to their personality, their emotional maturity and professional development, the amount of pressure and stress they are currently under at work and at home and, most important, the quality and regularity of the supervision they receive.
>
> What the organization does not contain, process, and understand, can then spill over the boundaries of the whole organization and get played out between professions and organizations. This is not only enormously costly to all the helping professions, but very hard to supervise. (Hawkins and Shohet, 121–22)

Hawkins and Shohet further argue that every organization needs a clear statement of policy on supervision (132). This would certainly be true of church organizations and judicatories. Such a statement needs to state clearly:

- why supervision is important
- who should receive supervision from whom
- when and with what frequency supervision should happen
- how supervision should be carried out— what sort of style and approach
- what supervision should focus on
- what priority supervision should be given in relation to other tasks.

To this we should add the need for the ecclesiastical policy to stipulate that the cost of supervision will be borne by either the local or regional church budget, without its being subtracted from the ordained pastor's compensation package, or without cost to the lay pastor. In this sense, clinical supervision may be understood as a form of health insurance, assuring the health of all involved in pastoral ministry.

Group and Peer Supervision

Two other forms of supervision also have the potential to provide pastors with insight, growth, and increased effectiveness. As long as it is recognized that neither of these other forms is as effective as individual clinical supervision, they may be used to offer alternative assistance in the face of financial problems ("We can't afford to pay for our pastors' supervision") or geographical isolation. Perhaps those in geographical or emotional isolation are in the most need for these types of supervision. As Hands and Fehr point out, arguing that intimacy with God is impossible without a deep self-knowledge, "What is crucial . . . is that clergy have someone (or some group) with whom they can speak candidly about their own condition and needs. To be emotionally isolated and utterly private makes it all too easy to stay a stranger to one's actual state" (58). The church has always understood itself as a community, and those who pastor need a community involvement outside their local jurisdiction where they be an equal, and not, even for a while, a pastor.

Group supervision describes the situation in which several pastors meet regularly, as a group, with one clinical supervisor. The group should be limited in number from four to six persons, but may be mixed in composition between lay and ordained persons. Members of the group should be at approximately the same level of experience, whether generally inexperienced or highly experienced. Members should have had some history of individual clinical supervision, though it need not be extensive, and should share the same general concerns and issues within pastoral ministry. A supervisor should be employed by the group as a whole, preferably one already experienced in group supervision since it is a specialized subfield.

Peer supervision describes a group of pastors who meet regularly without a clinical supervisor being present. These groups, too, should be limited in number, from four to six persons, and each should have extensive experience in individual clinical supervision. Both types of groups would benefit from some basic contractual arrangement, even if only verbal, covering mandatory attendance, confidentiality, respect for individual and group boundaries, equality of participation, and general subject matter and methodology.

Gender Issues in Supervision

Richard Meth and Robert Pasick write that men and women are "socialized to be incongruent since only certain feelings are appropriate for each gender" (136). We can claim that the same socialization is true for behavior and values as well. While, as Elizabeth Ridgely points out, "the formula of man as 'provider' and woman as 'caretaker' died externally for some men and women" (Haber, 72), distinct gender roles and gender assumptions continue to survive in the subconscious layers of our identity. Because this is true, gender becomes an important issue in the supervisory relationship. Just as gender organizes families, so too it organizes supervision. When a female supervisor and a female pastor are working together, the supervision must recognize the absence of the male voice, and similarly when a male supervisor and a male pastor are working together. Ridgely argues that such recognition must be frank and direct; she suggests making statements during family-of-origin work such as:

- We are two men and have no female brain here to help our work with the mother of the family.
- We are two women with no male brain to work with the father of the family.

Describing "gender dialogue" as a form of cross-cultural communication, Ridgely employs the metaphor of travel in a foreign land:

> Men and women do not know the world view of the other. In therapy and in supervision, it is essential to research this as one would when traveling in a foreign country. Curiosity about the other, without assumptions, is helpful in the therapeutic process. In spite of the popular literature on this topic, naïeveté about the

opposite gender has prevailed in therapy. For a male therapist to be taught by a woman client about her experiences as a woman—and to restrain himself from wanting to correct these experiences—is a challenge not unlike gender clarification in marriages. Add working with the female on her presenting dilemma to this context and the process becomes more challenging. Similarly, women must work with men from their frame of reference and forego female logic that defines problems and solutions in ways that are not understandable to men. (Haber, 71)

The choice of a supervisor, therefore, must take into account whether that supervisor is capable of thinking and speaking in the "genderlect" of the supervisee. In the case of supervising the other sex, the supervisor needs to become like a tourist who asks for directions about gender assumptions, experiences, and worldview. What was it like to be a man or woman in this family? How did you feel about discussing the issues of puberty and sexual development? How did you handle your value differences? How was this man socialized as a boy to assume the mantle of manhood? How does this affect his view of other men and of women? How can I help you develop more empathy for the client's experience?

Ridgely is not alone in arguing that each gender must move out of its familiar patterns in order to make supervision and pastoring more effective. In a provocative article, Denise Haines claims that female pastors need to be supervised in a manner that moves them away from the comfortable women's roles of nurturing and networking: "The problem is that female gender roles are designed for the private, personal sphere of family and home, and not designed for public leadership" (192).

Haines argues that the skills into which women have been socialized may be adequate for private ministry in small congregations that seek a "family" identity, but even in these, women's traditional role is not adequate to leadership because women have not been equipped to deal easily with the hard-nosed side of administration, prophetic righteous anger, and community organization. When "family" congregations ignore these critical elements of public ministry, they live out only half the gospel. The other half of the gospel will not be available to them as long as women pastors rely on the nurturing skills intended for private family life to attend to public roles of leadership.

Therefore, argues Haines, issues that need to be explored in order that pastoral supervision will prepare women for public as well as private ministry include:

1. Conflict resolution and decision making. A willingness to tolerate disagreement and to use conflict as a potential catalyst for change means that women leaders must refrain from moving too quickly into peacemaking and accommodation. While there are times to defer to others or to avoid unproductive conflict, accommodation as a habitual style results in an abdication of leadership to others, sometimes misnamed as a "facilitating" style of leadership. An inability to be competitive means that a woman will have difficulty making independent decisions that affect others. A woman who cannot stand alone will be inclined to negotiate or collaborate over much. Such a leadership style uses process at the expense of action.

2. Being a mentor; training assistants. A public role as an authority person calls a leader to be a mentor and guide for future

leaders. In this way, the woman leader can develop assistants as well as serve the future. To do so, she must be comfortable in the unequal power position that these relationships require and will have to be able to set boundaries around the relationships.

3. Developing a public role with a public agenda. Justice issues point toward advocacy and social change which require women to shift out of their nurturing parent role and into the prophetic realm. (198)

The American Psychological Association has also addressed the negative consequences of women's traditional roles. In its *Guidelines for Therapy with Women* (1978), the APA argues that supervisors and therapists must not affirm traditionally female roles for women who wish to move beyond them. Supervision "should be free of constrictions based on gender defined rules, and the options explored between client and practitioner should be free of sex-role stereotypes" (Haber, 110). This challenges women pastors to use supervision to move beyond the sorts of gendered skills that Haines describes as inadequate for public ministry and thereby to claim new strengths and gifts.

One cautionary note: married pastors who through supervision have begun to claim more strengths and gifts may feel new tensions develop in their home life. This will be particularly true for women in more traditional marriages, which assume that women's power must remain subservient to men's.

Men in supervision also have their gender-role work to do. The first will be to bring their affective literacy into better balance with their rationality literacy. Men have a long tradition of relying on women to meet their emotional needs, and this is no different for male pastors. Such reliance is fertile ground for the development of the harassment and abuse of women by certain male pastors. Hands and Fehr argue that men will benefit from working with male supervisors, or even more so from an all-male peer supervision group, because it will break the cycle of reliance upon women:

> The argument is made convincingly that when men learn to have certain fathering and mentoring needs met by other men, there is reduced likelihood of men turning to women in hopes that they will satisfy these needs. Such men's group work, outside the parish, can help those clergy who tend to turn to female parishioners for "mothering," which leads to further boundary confusions as genital sexuality enters. (68)

Once male pastors have nurtured their affective literacy in supervision, they will be ready to move on to other tasks for the improvement of ministry effectiveness. Rigazio-Digilio, Anderson, and Kunkler name some of these as (a) promoting collaborative versus hierarchical relationships, (b) attending more to the proper expression of their newfound affective literacy, and (c) reallocating power more equitably among adult members of their own family (and members of their congregation) (349–50). Further supervision will equip male pastors to listen more carefully to the voices of those who are not white, male, heterosexual, and powerful. Whatever gender issues emerge during supervision, they must be addressed as part of the formation process between supervisor and pastor.

Narrative Theory and Supervision
Both Narrative Theory and Object Relations Theory have been discussed in earlier

chapters, but their relationship to supervision suggests that they both be discussed briefly here. To describe a relationship during the supervision process—any relationship, whether family of origin, one's present family, or a relationship with a parishioner or colleague—is to tell a story. As with all stories, the component parts may be implied, or overtly present: a cast of characters, a plot, a catharsis, and a denouement. The pastor in supervision should attempt to describe such relationships accurately. The supervisor may ask further questions, such as:

• What is the history of the relationship?
• How did you meet?
• What did you first notice about this person?
• How and why did this parishioner choose you for pastoral support?
• What systems and networks affect this person's behavior and thinking?
• Can you tell the story of the past history of your relationship up until now? (adapted from Hawkins and Shohet, 63)

The supervisor may also zero in on specific details of the person being described, including their physical appearance; how they move and hold themselves; how they breathe, speak, look, or gesture; their language, metaphors, and images; and the story of their own life as they would tell it.

What is being ascertained by the supervisor's investigation is not a factual description of the person, parishioner, relationship, or incident, but the pastor's *perception* of the person, parishioner, relationship, or incident as filtered through the pastor's own "ideological editor." This is the way the pastor views the person or incident through his or her own belief-and-value system. This includes conscious prejudice, racism, sex-

ism, and other assumptions that color the way we mis-see, mis-hear, or mis-relate to the client (Hawkins and Shohet, 67). This will be all the information that the supervisor has to work with; the supervisor will probably never hear the other person's side of the story. Therefore the supervisor will be expected to act similarly to a marital counselor, insofar as the supervisor must keep the interests of both parties in balance, taking neither the side of the pastor nor that of the parishioner against the other. At times the pastor may find this approach frustrating. The more emotionally he is invested in the incident, the more he will want to convince the supervisor that his version is "the only true" way to tell the story. However, as Jacobs, David, and Meyer comment, "The patient supervisor and supervisee speak about is not the real and complicated person existing somewhere beyond the supervisor's consulting room, but rather the person constructed through the sensibilities (observations, emotions, and conflicts) of the therapist" (10).

Because of the functioning of the ideological editor, the pastor's story will be full of transference and countertransference, and this is the raw material with which the supervisor should begin to work. The pastor's story, therefore, is necessarily colored by wishes, fears, fantasies, magic, and unconscious conflicts. Because the story is not technically "factual," it must be malleable, which is turn provides the supervisor with the opportunity to help the pastor reframe the story to draw out other meanings or possible reactions. The pastor's story will also be shaped by his or her transference and countertransference onto the supervisor. "What will most please my supervisor to hear?" "How can I avoid being shamed when telling this story to my supervisor?" These and similar questions are directly related to Kadushin's "Games People Play in Supervision," as described earlier, but at the same time they also provide raw material for the supervisor to work with.

In this sense, the parishioner or person described by the pastor is what Heinz Kohut called a "self-object." Kohut theorized that an infant is actively involved with its mother from birth, but that when the infant looks at the mother she or he does not see that mother as you and I would see her, but as a reflection of the infant, the infant's nascent self mirrored on the face of the mother. The mother is a "self-object," rather than an object because it is this *empathic quality of responsiveness*, rather than her own unique personal qualities, that define her for the infant. The infant's only picture of the mother is as "the responder" to the infant's self. The term *self-object,* then, refers to the *function* that another fulfills for a "self," rather than to a person. The person or parishioner being described by the pastor in supervision serves a specific function for the pastor, perhaps as a result of immature relationship patterns or unresolved emotional needs, not unlike an empty stage. The supervisor will then question the pastor not so much about the person or incident narrated, but about the pastor's feelings and reactions to what was going on and how they connect to the pastor's past.

Building on this understanding of the role of self-object in supervision, Emily Haight diagrammed the supervisory relationship in the following manner:

Supervision has often conjured the image of the supervisor overseeing the work the supervisee does with a client, through direct observation or through the use of *audio or videotape, verbatims, or session notes. One might draw the interaction like a triangle:*

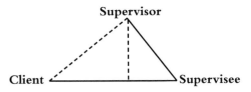

Paravision, however, provides a quite different model. From a position alongside the supervisee, together they engage, not the client, but the supervisee's self-object experience of being in relationship to the client.

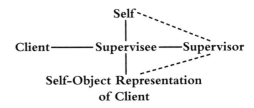

Haight defines the supervisor's role as "standing alongside" the pastor, attempting to see the pastor's self-object in relation to the pastor's self and through the pastor's eyes. For this reason she prefers the term *paravision* (to see alongside) rather than *supervision* (to see from above). "From a position alongside the supervisee, together they engage, not the client, but the supervisee's self-object experience of being in relationship to the client" (Haight 1994, 87). In "paravision," the role distinctions between supervisor and pastor remain, but because the two are "standing alongside," an atmosphere of mutuality and safety is created that would not be there in a more hierarchical relationship.

With the supervisor's help, the pastor can come to realize that his or her reaction to and interaction with the parishioner are in fact reactions to and interactions with a self-object. The pastor can then learn to look first to him- or herself in order to understand a difficult relationship, rather than resorting to blaming and scapegoating.

Toxic and Benign Shame during Supervision

Blaming and scapegoating create shame, and shaming another person is rarely if ever a useful pastoral tool. But a pastor's shame is also a powerful affect within the supervisory relationship and therefore needs to be understood carefully.

Shame must first be differentiated from guilt. According to Leon Wurmser, "Shame refers to some sort of failure, weakness, flaw of the *self*, while guilt refers to some violation or attack upon the *other*" (85–86). Shame, then is intrapersonal, while guilt is interpersonal. Nancy Talbot distinguishes between shame generated externally and shame generated internally. "Interpersonally, shame is the emotion associated with the humiliating revelation of personal failure to another. Intrapsychically, shame is felt when the individual painfully experiences a discrepancy between the actual self and the ideal self" (339).

Either of these two types of shame, externally sourced or internally sourced, can be benign or toxic. Benign shame is normal: we all feel shame from time to time, but if we have a way of processing it so that it becomes somehow "enhancing" to our sense of self, then we grow from the experience in positive ways. Toxic shame, on the other hand—shame that is internalized as an integral part of one's self-conception rather than being processed in an enhancing manner—is pathological and detracting, and will ultimately spill over into the pastor's ministry and other personal relationships. For most people, toxic shame originates in the background experience of

their lives, but other individuals seem to have shame-prone personalities. While both types of shame reveal the same flaw, toxic shame in particular reveals a significant vulnerability in one's narcissistic development. Andrew Morrison explains: "No one is completely immune to contempt or scorn; but, in the language of self-psychology, shame wounds to the extent that one is the bearer of a defective self" (272). In benign shame, the narcissistic wound that is uncovered is quickly healed when exposed to fresh air and careful treatment. In toxic shame, the narcissistic wound festers and remains raw, usually infecting the whole system with its poison.

While almost everyone feels some element of shame about something in their lives, that shame is not always an appropriate subject for discussion in supervision. Citing the principles in Haley's "supervisee's bill of rights" mentioned above, it should be clear that personal shame, particularly the toxic kind, should be dealt with in supervision *only* when it is interfering with the pastor's ministry. Otherwise, it is an issue for psychotherapeutic treatment and not for treatment by the supervisor. Talbot, however, identifies three types of shame that are appropriate in supervision because they are directly generated by the relationship between the supervisor and the pastor:

1. Shame that evolves from the relationship between therapist and patient. Countertransference shame is likely to be manifested in a "parallel process" in the supervision: the pastor who feels degraded and dismissed by a parishioner may, by his behavior in supervision, engender similar feelings in the supervisor.

2. Shame that arises from the minister's fears of or actual experience of not being

approved by or admired by an idealized supervisor.

3. Shame inherent in revealing personal material in a supervisory relationship. The supervisee reveals personal and professional vulnerabilities to an idealized other, the supervisor. The supervisee's affective response to the power differential [between supervisor and pastor] is intensified by personal associations to earlier relationships with authority figures. (343–44)

If the lay or ordained minister recognizes that self-exposure in supervision is part of the quest to become the best pastor possible, then even if shameful self-revelation is temporarily anxiety-provoking and narcissistically destabilizing, it will be worth it.

In addition to the three types of shame that Talbot suggests are appropriate to supervision, we might add three other sources of shame specific to the practice of public ministry that can interfere enough with ministry that they deserve discussion in supervision:

1. Shame that comes from identifying the church as a "bad family." Many of us have a tendency to split families into "good families" and "bad families." Our values suggest that "bad" families shame their members, often unfairly and mercilessly. Negative or unjust feedback from parishioners or the church hierarchy can cause us to identify the church as a "shame-based" family, particularly if we came from one ourselves. This transference is further complicated by the many shame-based theologies that are presently flourishing.

2. Shame that results from realizing that we cannot live up to people's expectations, particularly when those expectations have been incorporated into our "ideal self." Jeffrey Kottler remarks, "Therapists in our society are, after all, treated *as if* we have special powers that allow us to see inside people's hearts and souls, predict the future, and heal suffering" (94). Pastors are treated in the same manner.

3. Shame that accompanies the suspicion that we are inadequate to God's call to ministry. Such suspicions are normal from time to time (and in fact are praised as a qualification for ordination by Origen; see Culbertson and Shippee, 37–39). But if such feelings persist with any regularity, the pastor may wish to raise this "vocational crisis" with the supervisor.

Bringing shame to light suggests the potential for exploring its meaning and resolving it to yield new fruits of pastoral ministry.

Conclusion

Robert Duffet, citing the work of Young and Griffith, articulates the differences among religious counseling, pastoral mental health work, and pastoral psychotherapy (256). *Religious counseling* is the day-to-day individual interaction many pastors have with those in their parish. Such counseling is short-term, viewed as part of the pastoral role, done in church settings, and is not on a fee-for-service basis. The goal is spiritual guidance, and ministers who perform it have little or no formal training in psychotherapy. *Pastoral mental health work* attempts to integrate theology with some understanding of mental health, counseling, personality dynamics, and psychotherapy for the purpose of individual psychological and religious growth. Clergy of this type have some formal training in counseling and psychotherapy and attempt to link faith with mental health. *Pastoral psychotherapy* retains the theological nature of pastoral work but unites it with psychotherapy. Its practitioners have formal supervised training and experience in psychotherapy.

Duffet continues:

> There is a significant opportunity in mental health for pastoral counseling. Through its intellectual foundation with some religious perspective at the core, coupled with learnings, techniques, and treatment developed from clinical psychology and psychiatry, pastoral counseling offers to society a wholistic view of mental health. It does not remove or trivialize religious belief and practice but can utilize it for healing and wholeness. Further, it will not engage in biological reductionism of many emotional and mental health problems. (256)

Yet, pastoral care is rarely clean of the pastor's personal issues, as I have demonstrated. Object Relations theorist Moshe Spero reminds us how often the images of God that we bring into pastoral ministry are rarely free from the caregiver's transferences. He calls these images "transference gods" (similar to what I have termed "The Object God" in chapter 3), and speaks of how both the caregiver and the parishioner can benefit from the caregiver's psychotherapeutic sophistication:

> There is required a tremendous step in psychological growth and courage before transference gods can be surrendered, involving a large degree of self-knowledge and experience. This step enables the individual to understand when and where he has been stamping the universe with his own design and in his own image and how truly limited is this image and how false this endeavor. In that moment the religious patient is able to recognize that one knows very little about God, other than that He is not what we would like to make Him out to be. As with the resolution of interpersonal transference, the patient now begins the work of rediscovering the true characteristics and identity of the object originally perceived only through transference, and in this process rediscovers new senses of self as well. (13)

Christian wholeness is impossible without an ever new sense of self. However well intentioned our pastoral ministry may be, it is only through self-examination, self-criticism, and clinical supervision that we can arrive at a point of congruence where our ministry is maximally effective. This journey toward wholeness means strengthening our knowledge of our self at the same time that we let go of our defenses and illusions. Only when we are on our way to wholeness are we ready to undertake ministries that envision and support others' journeys toward wholeness. As we have been taught repeatedly to help others surrender transference hates and loves for realistic emotions, and to rediscover the true nature of those among whom and to whom we minister, so must we aid persons to surrender their transference gods along the path toward realistic relationships with God (Spero, 23).

BIBLIOGRAPHY

Anderson, Herbert. "Forming a Pastoral Habitus: A Rich Tapestry with Many Threads." *Journal of Supervision and Training in Ministry* 15 (1994): 231–42.

Anderson, Herbert, David Hogue, and Marie McCarthy. *Promising Again.* Louisville: Westminster/John Knox, 1995.

Carifio, Michael, and Allen Hess. "Who Is the Ideal Supervisor?" *Professional Psychology: Research and Practice* 18:3 (1987): 244–50.

Chagnon, Jean, and Richard Russell. "Assessment of Supervisee Development Level and Supervision Environment across Supervisor Experience." *Journal of Counseling and Development* 73 (1995): 553ff.

Childs, Brian. *Short-Term Pastoral Counseling: A Guide*. Nashville: Abingdon, 1990.

Culbertson, Philip, and Arthur Bradford Shippee, eds. *The Pastor: Readings from the Patristic Period*. Minneapolis: Fortress, 1990.

Doehring, Carrie. *Taking Care: Monitoring Power Dynamics and Relational Boundaries in Pastoral Care and Counseling*. Nashville: Abingdon, 1995.

Doehrman, Margery Jean Gross. "Parallel Processes in Supervision and Psychotherapy." *Bulletin of the Menninger Clinic* 40:1 (January 1976): 3–104.

Duffett, Robert. "The Intellectual Foundation of Pastoral Counseling: A Perspective on the Future of the Profession." *The Journal of Pastoral Care* 49:3 (fall 1995): 255-263.

Fromm, Erich. *Psychoanalysis and Religion*. New Haven: Yale University Press, 1950.

———. *The Art of Listening*. New York: Continuum, 1994.

Glaz, Maxine. "Can a Healer Be Too Wounded to Heal?" *Second Opinion* 20:3 (January 1995): 45–57.

Haber, Russell. *Dimensions of Psychotherapy Supervision: Maps and Means*. New York: W. W. Norton, 1996.

Haight, Emily S. Demme. "Paravision: A Model for Pastoral Supervision." *Journal of Supervision and Training in Ministry* 15 (1994): 86–95.

———. "What Is Pastoral about Pastoral Supervision?" *Journal of Supervision and Training in Ministry* 16 (1995): 155–59.

Haines, Denise. "The Power to Lead: Forming Women for Public Ministry." *Journal of Supervision and Training in Ministry* 15 (1994): 190–99.

Haley, Jay. *Problem-Solving Therapy*. San Francisco: Jossey-Bass, 1976.

Hall, Jack. *Affective Competence in Counseling*. Lanham, Md.: University Press of American, 1995.

Halstead, James. "Boundary Issues in Formation and Supervision: Objectives, Roles, and Responsibilities." *Journal of Supervision and Training in Ministry* 15 (1994): 223–30.

Hands, Donald, and Wayne Fehr. *Spiritual Wholeness for Clergy: A New Psychology of Intimacy with God, Self and Others*. Washington, D.C.: Alban Institute, 1993.

Hawkins, Peter, and Robin Shohet. *Supervision in the Helping Professions*. Philadelphia: Open University Press, 1989.

Helminiak, Daniel. *The Human Core of Spirituality: Mind as Psyche and Spirit*. Albany: SUNY Press, 1996.

Hoffman, Rose Marie. "Sexual Dual Relationships in Counseling: Confronting the Issues." *Counseling and Values* 40:1 (October 1995): 15–23.

Horney, Karen. *Final Lectures*. Douglas Ingram, ed. New York: W. W. Norton, 1987.

Jacobs, Daniel, Paul David, and Donald Jay Meyer. *The Supervisory Encounter: A Guide for Teachers of Psychodynamic Psychotherapy and Psychoanalysis*. New Haven: Yale University Press, 1995.

Kadushin, Alfred. "Games People Play in Supervision." *Social Work* 13:3 (July 1968): 23–32.

Karl, John C. "Forming the Inner Cup: The Ministry of Supervision with Pastoral Counselors." *Journal of Supervision and Training in Ministry* 7 (1984–85): 15–35.

Katz, Robert. *Pastoral Care in the Jewish Tradition: Empathic Process and Religious Counseling*. Philadelphia: Fortress, 1985.

Kottler, Jeffrey. *On Being a Therapist.* Rev. ed. San Francisco: Jossey-Bass, 1993.

Kushner, Harold S. *How Good Do We Have to Be? A New Understanding of Guilt and Forgiveness.* Boston: Little, Brown, 1996.

Maloney, H. Newton, and Richard Hunt. *The Psychology of Clergy.* Harrisburg: Morehouse, 1991.

Means, J. Jeffrey. "The Professional Formation of Pastoral Counselors." *Journal of Supervision and Training in Ministry* 15 (1994): 200–208.

Meth, Richard, and Robert Pasick, et al. *Men in Therapy: The Challenge of Change.* New York: Guilford, 1990.

Miller, Alice. *Prisoners of Childhood: The Drama of the Gifted Child and the Search for the True Self.* R. Ward, trans. New York: Basic, 1981.

Morrison, Andrew. "The Eye Turned Inward: Shame and the Self." In Nathanson, ed., 271–91.

Nathanson, Donald. "Shaming Systems in Couples, Families, and Institutions." In Nathanson, ed., 246–70.

———, ed. *The Many Faces of Shame.* New York: Guilford, 1987.

Nouwen, Henri J. M. *Reaching Out.* New York: Doubleday & Co., 1975.

———. *The Wounded Healer.* Garden City, N.Y.: Image, 1979.

Okun, Barbara. *Effective Helping: Interviewing and Counseling Techniques.* 5th ed. Pacific Grove: Brooks/Cole, 1997.

Patton, John. *Pastoral Counseling: A Ministry of the Church.* Nashville: Abingdon, 1983.

———. *Pastoral Care in Context: An Introduction to Pastoral Care.* Louisville: Westminster/John Knox, 1993.

Plante, Thomas, Gerdenio Manuel, and Jeannette Tandez. "Personality Characteristics of Successful Applicants to the Priesthood." *Pastoral Psychology* 45:1 (September 1996): 29–40.

Rigazio-Digilio, Sandra, Stephen Anderson, and Kara Kunkler. "Gender-Aware Supervision in Marriage and Family Counseling: How Far Have We Actually Come?" *Counselor Education and Supervision* 34 (1995): 344–55.

Rogers, Carl. *On Becoming a Person: A Therapist's View of Psychotherapy.* London: Constable, 1961.

Rutland-Wallis, John. "A Theology of Psychotherapy." *The Journal of Pastoral Care* 50:3 (fall 1996): 257–67.

Satir, Virginia. *Conjoint Family Therapy.* 3d ed. Palo Alto, Calif.: Science and Behavior Books, 1983.

Schafer, Roy. *The Analytic Attitude.* Basic, 1983.

———. *Retelling a Life: Narration and Dialogue in Psychoanalysis.* New York: Basic, 1992.

Spero, Moshe HaLevi. "Transference as a Religious Phenomenon in Psychotherapy." *Journal of Religion and Health* 24:1 (spring 1985): 8–25.

SteinhoffSmith, Roy. "Dreaming of Spiders: Abuse, Economics, and Theological Insecurity in Pastoral Counseling." *Pastoral Psychology* 44:6 (July 1996): 395–406.

Stoltenberg, Cal D. "Developmental Considerations in Supervisory Ministry." *Journal of Supervision and Training in Ministry* 16 (1995): 57–62.

Stoltenberg, Cal D., and Ursula Delworth. *Supervising Counselors and Therapists: A Developmental Approach.* San Francisco: Jossey-Bass, 1987.

Talbot, Nancy. "Unearthing Shame in the Supervisory Experience." *American Journal of Psychotherapy* 49 (1995): 338–49.

Tillich, Paul. "Anxiety, Religion, and Medicine." In *The Courage To Be.* 70–78. New Haven: Yale University Press, 1952.

———. "The Theology of Pastoral Care." *Pastoral Psychology* 10 (October 1959): 21–26.

Wilmot, Joan, and Robin Shohet. "Parallel-
ing in the Supervision Process." *Self and
Society: European Journal of Humanistic Psychology* 13:2 (1985): 86–92.

Wurmser, Leon. "Shame: The Veiled Companion of Narcissism." In Nathanson, ed.,
64–92.

Appendix to Chapter 10: The Supervisory Contract

Virtually all the literature on supervision argues that a contractual relationship is critical. Various authors disagree over whether the contract should be written or verbal. In countries where the supervisor assumes some legal responsibility for the functioning of the pastor and the safety of those to whom the pastor ministers, a written contract is strongly recommended. Russell Haber believes that a contract must address the following items: time of supervision meetings; delimitation of supervisory responsibilities, including whether written evaluations of the pastor must be prepared for church authorities; whether the supervisor is available outside hours to consult over pastoral emergencies; referrals (whether a minister can refer someone from her own parish to the same supervisor); confidentiality; the pastor's responsibility to prepare for supervision; knowledge of and willingness to abide by the applicable codes of ethics; content of supervision; modalities of supervision; occasional mutual review of progress and nature of the supervisor-pastor relationship, particularly as part of the termination process; and grievance procedures (130–31).

Here is a contract that I have found adequate in acting as a supervisor for pastors. It will need to be adapted to meet the various requirements of the particular supervisor-pastor relationship.

A Joint Contract for a Supervisory Relationship

_____, (Supervisor)

_____, (Supervisee)

Sessions and Finances

a. We shall meet once every _____. The length of each appointment will be 50 minutes.

b. The cost of each session will be $_____, payable at the beginning or end of each session unless some other arrangement has been made. Checks should be made payable to Philip Culbertson.

c. In the event that you have to cancel or miss a session, I will need one week's notice. Sessions canceled on shorter notice will be billed.

d. The initial period of this contract is ____ months, from __/__/__ to __/__/__. The contract can be renewed by mutual agreement of both parties.

Confidentiality

a. I will maintain professional confidentiality in respect to the contents of each session, and the arrangements pertaining thereto, with one exception: I will need regularly to share material about our work together with my own supervisor, in order to ensure the objectivity and skills required for quality supervision.

b. Depending on my own arrangements with my supervisor, some sessions may need to be tape-recorded, or I may need actively to take notes on what is being said. These tapes or notes will be kept under lock and key for no more than one month, and after that will be destroyed.

Professional Boundaries

a. Professional ethics require that we both observe our boundaries carefully. Normally, this will preclude most personal friendship or frequency of contact outside the office while our relationship is under contract.

b. In case you need to phone me for any reason, I can be reached through my office phone at _____. I am generally not available for out-of-hours consultation.

Expectations

a. In some instances, homework outside the regularly scheduled sessions will be expected in order to sharpen the supervisory experience. This may take the form of mutual reading and discussion, verbatims, tape recordings, case studies, or summations. The nature and extent of this homework will be mutually agreed upon between us.

b. Feelings of shame and inadequacy are part of the supervisory process, as are regression, transference, and parallel process. The more courageous the supervisee can be in revealing her/his professional conduct, diagnoses, judgment, interventions, and affective or intuitive responses, the more effective the supervision will be.

Focus and Style

a. Supervision will include four areas of focus over the long run: data and content concerning the supervisee's contact with others, the supervisee's professional relationship with others, the supervisee's interpersonal systems (exclusive of the treatment relationships), and patterns of transference and countertransference.

b. We will agree together whether it is more effective to concentrate for an extended period of time on one relationship or incident, or whether we should select a series of relationships and incidents to discuss. Any such agreement can be renegotiated at any time.

c. I prefer a working style which feels safe to both of us, and which makes us feel mutually empowered. This is in keeping with the suggestion of Jacobs, David, and Meyer: "We favor a more interactive, mutually responsive model in which the talents and personal style of the supervisee are given center stage and the supervisor helps expand on them, strengthening available talents, identifying weaker areas, and rounding out the supervisee's repertoire with additional approaches" (205). My goal is to facilitate a mutually interactive collaboration which evolves toward collegiality, within appropriate professional boundaries.

d. I understand the purpose of supervision to be the training of the supervisee, not to do therapy directly with the supervisee, though in many instances the line of demarcation between the two may seem fuzzy. Of course therapeutic issues will enter into our conversations. The operational principle is that they must proceed directly out of the supervisory material and then reconnect directly with it again. It is your responsibility to maintain your own psychological safety, just as it is my responsibility to respect that, except when I believe it is decreasing your effectiveness as a pastor or counselor.

Goals

a. Within three months after we begin our supervisory relationship, I would like you to present me with a written statement of goals for your own supervision. We will then discuss these in detail to be sure that we are both working toward the same goals.

Termination

a. When you plan to terminate this supervisory relationship, you should notify me four sessions in advance of the date which you intend to be your final session.

b. At least two of those four final sessions will be spent in a joint evaluation of our experience together as supervisor and supervisee.

Dated: _____

11. CONCLUSION

"Going into ministry without understanding how people work and how they relate to each other is like going into the dense forest with a blindfold on: you're bound to get hurt." (my lecture notes)

Some months ago I was asked to write a short piece on what Pastoral Ministry will look like in the year 2025. I here reproduce in its entirety what I wrote:

> In the parts of the world with which I am familiar—the U.S., Europe, and the South Pacific—we must be paying attention to new social realities which dictate that pastoral care in the coming millennium will need to be markedly different from its historical forms. Three factors mandate change in the manners and situations in which we exercise pastoral ministry.
>
> The model of pastoring presently in effect licenses lay and ordained ministers to geographic localities. Yet increased electronic communications, unstable employment patterns and increased mobility, and the growing disconnection from traditional family structures means that people have less and less sense of loyalty to local parish structures. In the new millennium, the call will be for ministry to go "global"—moving outside of parochialism to create new opportunities for ministry in unexpected places, unbounded by geographic definitions.
>
> The democratization of church polity means that more and more of the laity are demanding opportunities to exercise ministries which are publicly honored by the church. Various forms of team ministry are emerging in which the best-educated clergy are serving less as absolute authorities and more as facilitators *primus inter pares* [the first among equals], coordinating the ministry of a trained and responsible laity. The thrust of the future is away from defining the ordained as pastoral experts and ritual specialists, toward defining the ministry of all baptized Christians as agents for social change.
>
> Governments intrude increasingly into areas of teaching, care, and healing which have traditionally been reserved to local ministries. Yet, rapidly increasing populations mean there are fewer resources to go around, and so secular institutions and agencies are resorting to managed care policies, severely curtailing the amount and quality of care and support available to those who most need them. Rather than retreat, the church of the new millennium is called to advance aggressively into areas of care and support for the needy—including the facilitation of people's hierarchy of physical needs in addition to their spiritual hunger. (In Atkins, 170)

In the context of this book's emphasis on people skills for better pastoral ministry, and the changing face of the church in a new millennium, lay and ordained caregivers must be prepared to serve the needs of people traditionally outside the boundaries of the church as well as within it. Michael Mayne, dean of Westminster Cathedral, has set forth a theological manifesto that challenges each Christian to take up the mantle of responsibility to care for those in need, wherever they may be:

> Truly incarnational theology believes that all people are made in God's image, that we should be constantly hopeful about human nature and the image of God to be found in it, undying optimists about the power of God's grace. Truly incarnational theology knows that ours is a God-haunted world in

which God is to be known and loved in and through all God has made; that God is as active outside the Church as within it; that it was the world and its life for which God gave Jesus and with which God's Kingdom is concerned. "Our main job," writes John Austin Baker, "is to make the secular Christlike, not necessarily Christian"; and, I would add, to celebrate the Christlike in the secular.

Good pastoral practice does not just happen. Without doubt, some people are more naturally skilled at it than others. But everyone involved in pastoral ministry of any kind needs five assets to ensure that the highest quality pastoral ministry is provided to careseekers in a God-haunted world:

1. a solid base in psychological theory that is regularly renewed and employed to empower others toward new wholeness;
2. experience, with a sensitivity to all sorts and types of people;
3. self-critical skills, compelled by courage;
4. quality, professional, clinical supervision;
5. a deep, adult faith that God is present, even in the least expected places.

This book has attempted to provide the first of that list; the other four are up to the readers.

Jozef Denys argues that empowerment and faith are identical processes. After surveying a number of technical definitions of "empowerment" in the psychological literature, Denys concludes:

What a thorough examination of these delineations of empowerment brings to light is that it is a process whereby people intervene in their lives and relationships to sort out, apportion and implement what is perceived to be possibly helpful in bringing about an increased sense of well-being. All of these elements are similar to and can be subsumed under the overarch-ing religious process whereby people audaciously attempt to find a place for everything in their life's experience and everything in its appropriate place. (173–74)

When we are working with people through the modalities of Family Systems Theory, Narrative Counseling Theory, or Object Relations Theory, we are offering them the chance to become a New Being, as Paul Tillich envisaged. The cornerstone of empowerment rests on the participation of people wherever and however they can in the creation of their own well-being. Sometimes the New Being is brought into effect through the sorting out of our family-of-origin issues, the reframing of our coherent personal narrative so that it becomes life-giving, or personal growth in object constancy. At other times the New Being is brought into effect as we mirror health in others and, particularly in the social context of our pastoral work, strive for the redistribution of power among stakeholders to bring about a more proportionate social justice. Denys's definition affirms that pastoral care is that liminal area where Christian faith, psychotherapeutic theory, ecclesiology, missiology, and issues of justice all intersect.

Many people have spoken about the basic needs in life. Pioneering psychologist Abraham Maslow popularized the phrase with his ranking of a "hierarchy of needs," the most basic of which are the physiological needs (oxygen, food and drink, housing, sleep, and sex) and the safety needs (stability, predictability, and freedom from anxiety and chaos). All human beings need these, and our address to social justice is only begun once we have assured that everyone has equitable access to meeting these needs.

Beyond Maslow's definition, Craig Ellison nominates four others that are the next logical development in our hierarchy of needs, once Maslow's basic ones have been met:

- *The need for having.* This refers to the acquisition of material necessities and related impersonal resources in life. We might expand this, through the eyes of Object Relations Theory, as the need for transitional objects. But Ellison also points to the extensive research over the past two decades that indicates the destructive hollowness of Western consumerism. An abundance of material goods does not lead to wholeness; it more frequently destroys it.
- *The need for relating.* This refers to patterns of social relationships. The need to belong, to experience intimacy, to be needed, are central to human life. Many studies point out that this need is met at least as often through a network of intimate friendships as through marriage.
- *The need for being.* This refers to a general sense of satisfaction with one's self. Self-fulfillment seems to be related to feelings of competence, direction over one's life, and self-worth, or what the Wholeness Wheel calls "volition."
- *The need for transcendence.* This refers to the sense of well-being that we experience when we find purposes to commit ourselves to that involve ultimate meaning for life. Christians usually refer to this as faith, though as more and more people find spiritual satisfaction outside the church, we Christians must be ready to recognize God at work in many nontraditional locations. Indeed, I find my nonchurched psychotherapy clients as eager to talk about spirituality as are my Christian seminary students. (330)

Experience is the great teacher in life, yet too often those in pastoral ministry have little firsthand knowledge of how those outside the traditional boundaries of the church view the world. I certainly am not arguing, as do many committees who select candidates for ordination, that several years of employment in the "secular" world are a necessary prerequisite to ordination. My generation is perhaps the last that has actually "grown up" in ministry. We were ordained when we were twenty-five years old or less, and very few of us had much experience in secular employment. Yet, this pattern produced generations of great pastoral leadership, with vision and international influence, in a way that present generations seem unable to do. The difference perhaps is that instead of being taught to disappear into church buildings to meditate on our Christian identity, as Hauerwas and Willimon seem to suggest in their book *Resident Aliens*, we were taught to work out our faith in the "mean streets," among people in need who asked us to salve their pain first, well before we began a conversation about doctrine. Experience, with a sensitivity to all sorts and types of people, comes over time when we are not afraid to minister outside the boundaries of parish life.

In chapter 10, I quoted Meister Eckhart on self-knowledge as the path to God. Thomas Merton held the same point of view: "In order to find God whom we can only find in and through the depths of our own soul, we must first find ourselves" (44). Yet, we human beings are so extraordinarily self-deceptive that finding ourselves can be very hard work. As Teresa of Avila observes: "There are few dwelling places in this interior castle [of the inner self] in which the devils do not wage battle" (I.ii.15; in

Kavanaugh and Rodriguez, 46). Pastors who live in fear, who read Scripture literally instead of hearing the many voices at work in the narrative text, or who bind themselves by rigid moral codes, will find it nearly impossible to discover the God Beyond the subject-God and the object-God.

Also in chapter 10, I argued strongly that every pastor, lay or ordained, has the obligation to be in professional clinical supervision. Pastors who function without clinical supervision potentially jeopardize the welfare of the entire church, because the church is, by its very nature, an organization to which people bring their problems, disappointments, anger, exaggerated expectations, and deepest wishes. Sometimes the students in my Pastoral Theology classes ask why I teach them so much psychology instead of just concentrating on the basic "tricks" of pastoral care. My answer is that going into ministry without understanding how people work and how they relate to one another is like going into the dense forest with a blindfold on: you're bound to get hurt. The role of the clinical supervisor is to protect careseekers from our human dysfunctions, and our pastoral ministry from ourselves.

And what of faith? Without the Christian pastor's faith, none of the other four assets add up to ministry. In fact, as I remind students, unless you can see Christ standing before you in everyone you meet, you might as well be in secular employment somewhere. But the faith whose eyes see Christ in every person is an adult faith. John Shea defines the deep adult faith that fuels all pastoral ministry and is ultimately the single most indispensable aspect of Christian wholeness:

> Adult faith is comprised of two distinct yet directly related realities, the second presupposing the first. The first and foundational reality is simply adulthood itself, what is usually understood as human, psychological adulthood or as the realization of personal maturity. The second reality is an adult relationship with God, maturity in the religious dimension of one's life. There are, I believe, people who are psychological adults who are not at all religiously inclined (and who would, in fact, be offended if you suggested that they were). There are also people who are psychological adults, and who are religious, but who do not seem to have an adult relationship with God. There are people who are not psychological adults and who do not have an adult relationship with God. There are not, however, people who are not yet psychological adults who still somehow have an adult relationship with God.
>
> For adult faith, it seems, two things are needed: human, psychological adulthood and an adult relationship with God. (259)

Shea connects adulthood and maturity, just as Virginia Satir, as discussed in chapter 10, connects maturity and congruence. So we may claim, then, that the characteristics of a deep faith in God that feeds and compels pastoral ministry are adulthood, maturity, and congruence. Perhaps it is for this reason that the early church was so careful about whom it approved for pastoral ministry. Ultimately it was to be reserved to those who had the greatest strength of character, the clearest sense of insight, the most eager willingness to serve wherever they were needed, and the deepest proven commitment to the God Beyond.

In the fourteen centuries since Gregory the Great wrote the first and still one of the wisest instructional manuals in the practice of pastoral care, few have improved on his opening words. To Gregory, then, in honor of his profound vision, goes the right to close this book:

> No one ventures to teach any art without having learned it after deep thought. With what rashness, then, would the pastoral office be undertaken by the unfit, seeing that the government of souls is the art of arts! (Culbertson and Shippee, 197)

BIBLIOGRAPHY

Atkins, Peter. *Worship 2000! Resources to Celebrate the New Millennium.* London: HarperCollins, 1999.

Culbertson, Philip, and Arthur Bradford Shippee, eds. *The Pastor: Readings from the Patristic Period.* Minneapolis: Fortress, 1990.

Denys, Jozef. "The Religiosity Variable and Personal Empowerment in Pastoral Counseling." *The Journal of Pastoral Care* 51:2 (summer 1997): 165–76.

Ellison, Craig. "Spiritual Well-Being: Conceptualization and Measurement." *Journal of Psychology and Theology* 11:4 (1983): 330–40.

Hauerwas, Stanley, and William Willimon. *Resident Aliens: Life in the Christian Colony.* Nashville: Abingdon, 1989.

Maslow, Abraham. *Motivation and Personality.* 3d ed. New York: HarperCollins, 1987.

Mayne, Michael. Sermon preached at Friends and Former Members Day, Westminster Cathedral, June 8, 1995.

Merton, Thomas. *The New Man.* New York: Farrar, Straus and Giroux, 1961.

Shea, John. "Adult Faith, Pastoral Counseling, and Spiritual Direction." *The Journal of Pastoral Care* 51:3 (fall 1997): 259–70.

Teresa of Avila. *The Interior Castle.* Kieran Kavanaugh and Otilio Rodriguez, trans. New York: Paulist, 1979.

Worthington, Everett. "Religious Faith across the Life Span: Implications for Counseling and Research." *The Counseling Psychologist* 17:4 (October 1989): 555–612.

INDEX